THE RIGHTS OF WAR AND PE

BOOK I

NATURAL LAW AND
ENLIGHTENMENT CLASSICS

Knud Haakonssen
General Editor

Hugo Grotius

INTRODUCTION

In the famous dedication of his *Discourse on the Origin of Inequality* to
the Republic of Geneva, Jean-Jacques Rousseau drew a vivid picture of
his father sitting at his watchmaker's bench. "I see him still, living by
the work of his hands, and feeding his soul on the sublimest truths. I
see the works of Tacitus, Plutarch, and Grotius, lying before him in the
midst of the tools of his trade. At his side stands his dear son, receiving,
alas with too little profit, the tender instruction of the best of fathers. . . ." Rousseau's reminiscence is testimony to the authority which
Grotius's *De Iure Belli ac Pacis* had come to possess in the century since
it was first published in 1625; in the eyes of both father and son, the book
had the same standing as the great works of classical antiquity. Rousseau
was to devote much of his life to a complicated and subtle repudiation
of Grotius, but he never lost his sense of the book's importance, describing Grotius in *Emile* as "the master of all the savants" in political
theory (though he added that, nevertheless, he "is but a child, and, what
is worse, a dishonest child," and that "true political theory is yet to appear, and it is to be presumed that it never will").[1] The same sense of
Grotius's importance, without any of Rousseau's reservations, had led
the Elector Palatine in 1661 to endow a chair in the University of Heidelberg for the express purpose of providing a commentary on the *De
Iure Belli ac Pacis*, a fact which is noted in the *Life* prefaced to this edition;
as the *Life* also notes, the book was issued as a full edition with notes by

---

1. For the dedication, see *The Social Contract and Discourses,* trans. G. D. H. Cole,
revised ed. J. H. Brumfitt and John C. Hall (Everyman 1973), 34; for *Emile,* see Rousseau, *Political Writings,* ed. C. E. Vaughan (Oxford: Oxford University Press, 1915),
2:147.

various commentators,[2] "by which means *our Author*, within 50 Years after his Death, obtained an Honour, which was not bestowed upon the *Ancients* till after *many* Ages." The idea that the book represented something new and important for the modern age was repeatedly voiced in the "histories of morality," which began to appear in the late seventeenth century; Grotius was described as "breaking the ice" after the long winter of ancient and medieval ethics.[3] By the end of the seventeenth century there had been twenty-six editions of the Latin text, and it had been translated into Dutch (1626, reissued three times in the century), English (1654, reissued twice), and French (1687, reissued once). Its popularity scarcely slackened in the eighteenth century: there were twenty Latin editions, six French, five German, two Dutch, two English, and one Italian (and one Russian, circulated in manuscript).[4]

However, for many eighteenth-century readers the definitive version of the book had appeared in Latin in 1720, when Jean Barbeyrac issued a new edition, followed by a French translation in 1724 with elaborate notes.[5] Barbeyrac was a leading figure in the French Protestant diaspora, the network of scholars whose families had been driven out of France following the revocation of the Edict of Nantes by Louis XIV in 1685. He worked tirelessly to put his own version of modern natural law before the European public, and his editions of Grotius built on the success of a similarly elaborate edition which he had produced of Samuel Pufendorf's *De Iure Naturae et Gentium* in 1706. The notes to these editions

2. This was the edition that appeared in 1691 from a press at Frankfurt-on-Oder, with commentary by Gronovius, Boecler, Henniges, Osiander, and Ziegler, names that will become familiar from Barbeyrac's notes in this edition.

3. See Barbeyrac's remark in his *An Historical and Critical Account of the Science of Morality*, prefaced to his edition of Pufendorf, *The Law of Nature and Nations* (London, 1749), 67.

4. This information is from J. ter Meulen and P. J. J. Diermanse, *Bibliographie des écrits imprimés de Grotius* (The Hague, 1950). For an exemplary modern edition of the Latin text, see B. J. A. De Kanter–van Hettinga Tromp's 1939 edition, reprinted with extensive additional material by R. Feenstra and C. E. Persenaire (Aalen: Scientia Verlag, 1993).

5. Both the Barbeyrac Latin and French editions were from Amsterdam; the French version was dedicated to George I of England.

keyed their texts into all the relevant discussions of natural law from antiquity down to the 1720s, and the two works together quickly became the equivalent of an encyclopedia of moral and political thought for Enlightenment Europe. The French version of *De Iure Belli ac Pacis* was reprinted steadily through the middle years of the century, and it found an audience beyond the French-speaking polite world in an English translation of 1738, which is reprinted in this edition, and which seems to have been produced in a large print run.[6] Copies of it are very common, and are found in most academic and private libraries of the period—for example, General Washington, like most well-educated English gentlemen, possessed a copy, which is now in the Houghton Library at Harvard. An Italian translation appeared in 1777.

As this publishing history in itself illustrates, it would be hard to imagine any work more central to the intellectual world of the Enlightenment. But from the late eighteenth century onward, the stream of new editions dried up, and the book came to be treated not as the formative work of modern moral and political theory but as an important contribution to a different genre, "international law" (a term coined by Jeremy Bentham in 1780). Many intellectual developments of the period contributed to this shift, including the criticisms of Grotius found (alongside his admiration) in Rousseau, and the contempt expressed by Kant for the "sorry comforters" such as Grotius and Pufendorf, whose works "are still dutifully quoted in *justification* of military aggression, although their philosophically or diplomatically formulated codes do not and cannot have the slightest *legal* force, since states as such are not subject to a common external constraint."[7] William Whewell, professor of international law at Cambridge and translator of Grotius, tried in the mid-nineteenth century to restore Grotius as a major moral thinker, but with limited success; by the time of the post–First World War settlement, Grotius was regarded almost exclusively as the founder of modern civilized interstate relations, and as a suitable tutelary presence for the new

---

6. For full details, see "A Note on the Text" at the end of the introduction.

7. Immanuel Kant, *Political Writings,* ed. Hans Reiss, trans. H. B. Nisbet, 2d ed. (New York: Cambridge University Press, 1991), 103.

such as the sultan of Johore and offering them military protection and beneficial trading arrangements. The Indian Ocean and the China Sea were an arena in which actors had to deal with one another without the overarching frameworks of common laws, customs, or religions; it was a proving ground for modern politics in general, as the states of Western Europe themselves came to terms with religious and cultural diversity. The principles that were to govern dealings of this kind had to be appropriately stripped down: there was no point in asserting to a king in Sumatra that Aristotelian moral philosophy was universally true, and not much more point in telling the admiral of the Dutch East India Company's fleet that he had to wait for some judicial pronouncement by an appropriate sovereign before making war on a threatening naval force. The minimalist character of the principles that emerged from this setting caught the imagination of modern Europe, for they seemed to offer the prospect of an understanding of political and moral life to which all men—the poor and dispossessed and religiously heterodox of Europe as well as the exotic peoples of the Far East or the New World—could give their assent.

Grotius boldly stated his central argument as follows:

> God created man αὐτεξούσιον, "free and *sui iuris*," so that the actions of each individual and the use of his possessions were made subject not to another's will but to his own. Moreover, this view is sanctioned by the common consent of all nations. For what is that well-known concept, "natural liberty," other than the power of the individual to act in accordance with his own will? And liberty in regard to actions is equivalent to ownership in regard to property. Hence the saying: "every man is the governor and arbiter of affairs relative to his own property."[19]

Grotius remained committed to this view in *De Iure Belli ac Pacis*, remarking in one of its most striking passages that "there are several Ways of living, some better than others, and every one may chuse what he

---

19. *De Iure Praedae Commentarius,* trans. Gwladys L. Williams and Walter H. Zeydel (Carnegie Endowment for International Peace, Oxford University Press, 1950), 1:18.

pleases of all those Sorts."[20] He thus presupposed the naturally autonomous agents familiar to us from later seventeenth- and eighteenth-
century political theory, who constructed their political arrangements
through voluntary agreements. Though he did not have precisely the
concept of the "state of nature," which was so central to Hobbes and his
successors, and which they always contrasted with "civil Society" (the
product of agreement among naturally free men), he did use the terms
in somewhat similar ways;[21] and of course the domain of foreign trade
and war was in itself the best example of such a state, and was always
used as such by later writers.

The principles governing these autonomous natural individuals were
also stated very plainly in *De Iure Praedae*. The Prolegomena to the work
began with two fundamental laws of nature:

> first, that It shall be permissible to defend [one's own] life and to shun
> that which threatens to prove injurious; secondly, that It shall be per-
> missible to acquire for oneself, and to retain, those things which are
> useful for life. The latter precept, indeed, we shall interpret with Cicero
> as an admission that each individual may, without violating the precepts
> of nature, prefer to see acquired for himself rather than for another, that
> which is important for the conduct of life. Moreover, no member of
> any sect of philosophers, when embarking upon a discussion of the ends
> [of good and evil], has ever failed to lay down these two laws first of all
> as indisputable axioms. For on this point the Stoics, the Epicureans,

---

20. I.III.8. As its context illustrates, of course, this stress on fundamental moral
liberty is compatible with a voluntary renunciation of *civil* liberty—I.III.8 is the famous defense of absolutism. The term αὐτεξούσιον also occurs three times in *De Iure
Belli ac Pacis*, with the same meaning as in *De Iure Praedae*. See, for example, his
description of a child who has grown up and left home as "altogether αὐτεξούσιος,
at his own Disposal" (II.V.6), and also II.XX.48.2 n. 6 and II.XXI.12.

21. See in particular II.VII.27.1, which contrasts "the State of Nature" with civil
"Jurisdiction." II.VI.5, which in the English translation also refers to "a meer State
of Nature" in opposition to civil society, in the original Latin refers to *ius naturae*.
Other references to the state of nature, in the Latin as well as the English texts, occur
at II.V.9.2 and II.V.15.2, though they contrast nature with grace, in a more traditional
fashion. Grotius uses the term *civil society*: see, for example, I.IV.2.

of natural justice, the laws obliging us to abstain from injuring our fellow men. But in his discussion of this part he always insisted on its subordinate status to the right of self-preservation and on its minimal character—mutual aid and distributive (as distinct from corrective) justice were not part of this natural "*cognatio*"[29] but appeared with cities and civil society.

In the Prolegomena to *De Iure Belli ac Pacis,* Grotius set out a very similar theory, though its similarities to the earlier work were appreciably clearer in the first edition than in the edition he produced while attempting to return to the United Provinces. Just as in *De Iure Praedae* he had restricted the derivation of natural law to what all men agreed on as the basic physical principles governing all beings, so in the Prolegomena to *De Iure Belli ac Pacis* he asserted that it "necessarily derives from intrinsic principles of a human being."[30] He was now even more blunt about the exiguous role of God, declaring in the most famous remark of the book that "what I have just said would be relevant even if we were to suppose (what we cannot suppose without the greatest wickedness) that there is no God, or that human affairs are of no concern to him."[31] As in *De Iure Praedae,* Grotius accepted that God had indeed created the world and peopled it with beings constituted along these lines; but one did not need to think about the divine character of the creation to apprehend what the constitution of the physical world was, and all peoples at all periods of history, irrespective of their religious commitments, had agreed on the principles of natural law. Self-preservation was still the first of these principles: "nature drives each animal to seek its own interests [*utilitates*]," and this was true "of man before he came to the use of that which is special to man [*antequam ad usum eius quod homini proprium est, pervenerit*]." But this was balanced by the same ideas as in

---

29. That is, "relationship" or "similarity." *De Iure Praedae Commentarius,* ed. Hanaker, 13.

30. See my translation of the Prolegomena in the appendix to Book III.

31. This is the notorious *etiamsi daremus* clause, so called from the Latin for "even if we were to suppose."

the earlier work, that what is *proprium* or special to man is a desire for a much richer social life than is possessed by any other animals, and in particular for a social life governed by rational principles. This desire is the basis for our respect for one another's rights, and is "the source of *ius*, properly so called, to which belong abstaining from another's possessions, restoring anything which belongs to another (or the profit from it), being obliged to keep promises, giving compensation for culpable damage, and incurring human punishment." Anything further, involving distributive justice and the recognition of merited distinctions between people, might arise from this natural justice but was not, strictly speaking, part of it. Grotius now denied that Horace had been right in saying that *utilitas* was the mother of justice, but since he had qualified his endorsement of the remark in *De Iure Praedae*, his new comment on the passage did not represent a major repudiation of his old view.

It is clear that both Grotius's derogation of the role of God and the priority he gave to self-interest were alarming to many of his contemporaries, particularly among the Calvinists who surrounded the Prince of Orange. In order to accommodate the book more to their views when he produced the second edition, Grotius toned down his argument. Thus he cut out the claim that man was driven purely by self-interest "before he came to the use of that which is special to man" and replaced it with the emphatic assertion that "*the Saying, that every Creature is led by Nature to seek its own private Advantage, expressed thus universally, must not be granted.*" Similarly, he contrived to widen the scope of God's authority. For example, in 1625 the very first sentence of the Prolegomena included the claim that "few people have tackled the law that mediates between different countries or their rulers, whether that law stems from nature itself or from custom and tacit agreement, and so far no one at all has dealt with it comprehensively and methodically." In 1631, this read "*that Law, which is common to many Nations or Rulers of Nations, whether derived from Nature, or instituted by Divine Commands, or introduced by Custom and tacit Consent, few have touched upon, and none hitherto treated of universally and methodically*"—Grotius now allowed that the law of nature might be "instituted by Divine Commands." Similarly, he dropped the word "necessarily" from the sentence where he had said that the natural law "necessarily derives from intrinsic principles of a human being" and added to his discussion at that point the thought that

> *God by the Laws which he has given, has made these very Principles more clear and evident, even to those who are less capable of strict Reasoning, and has forbid us to give way to those impetuous Passions, which,* contrary *to our own Interest, and that of others, divert us from following the Rules of Reason and Nature;*[32] *for as they are exceeding unruly, it was necessary to keep a strict Hand over them, and to confine them within certain narrow Bounds.* (*Preliminary Discourse,* XIII)

So he now conceded that the natural law might properly be deduced not from the necessary constitution of the physical world, but from the records of God's pronouncements about the law directly to mankind.

Almost all these changes are found in the Prolegomena; the remainder of the book continued to lay out the same case that Grotius had advanced in the first edition. The result of this was to throw many of his later readers, including Barbeyrac, into some confusion; Barbeyrac consistently sought to emphasize the wider character of Grotian sociability and to bring him in line with Pufendorf (whose main aim was to attack the account of man's narrow and self-interested natural life found in Hobbes).[33] But anyone who read the first edition (as Hobbes himself

---

32. This is a translation of the sentence "& in diversa trahentes impetus, qui nobis ipsis, quique aliis consulunt, vagari vetuit," which appears in all the editions seen through the press by Grotius. Barbeyrac supposed that *aliis consulunt* should read *male consulunt,* but that seems to me to be a misrepresentation of what Grotius was saying. Grotius's point was that our self-interested and benevolent impulses did in principle keep us on the right road, though they might (as he claimed in 1631) need some sort of control by God to make sure that they did so. A better translation would read, "God has made these same principles more conspicuous by giving laws, even to those whose powers of reasoning are feeble: and he has forbidden those powerful impulses which attend to the interests of both ourselves and others from straying into the wrong courses, by strictly restraining the more vehement of them and by coercing them in both their ends and their means."

33. See for example what he did to Grotius's remark at I.I.10, that *ius naturale* is "a dictate of right reason, indicating of any act whether it possesses moral turpitude or moral necessity, from its congruity or incongruity with rational nature itself, and consequently whether it was forbidden or permitted by God the author of nature"

probably did), or who could see through the confusion artfully introduced by Grotius (as Rousseau seems to have done), would be aware that
Grotius's theory of the law of nature was more like Hobbes's than Pufendorf and Barbeyrac were ever prepared to acknowledge. When Rousseau said of Grotius and Hobbes (in the passage I quoted earlier) that
"their principles are exactly the same," he may well have been surpris-
ingly close to the mark.

I now want to turn to the practical implications of Grotius's ideas.
The first and most obvious implication was that private war was legitimate. The East India Company, though legally a private individual,
could indeed make war as if it were a state when it encountered any
people with whom it did not already have some kind of civil association.
Grotius was still an adviser to the company when he wrote *De Iure Belli
ac Pacis,* and he continued to assert its right to engage in this kind of
activity. The second implication, though less obvious, was even more
far-reaching: the kind of war that private individuals could make included acts of *punishment*—that is, it encompassed much more than the
limited violence which almost all moralists (other than the radically
Christian ones) had allowed individuals to use in their own immediate
self-defense. Grotius permitted the company, and anyone else dealing
with the complicated power struggles and internecine violence of the
world in which the European traders found themselves, to make judgments about the morality of the various parties and to punish those who
seemed to be violating other people's rights, even if there was no immediate threat to the Europeans themselves. Grotius was quite clear in
De Iure Belli ac Pacis about the interventionary character of his theory,
arguing in his great chapter on punishment (Book II, Chapter XX) that

> We make no Doubt, but War may be justly undertaken against those
> who are inhuman to their Parents, as were the *Sogdians,* before *Alex-
> ander* persuaded them to renounce their Brutality; against those who
> eat human Flesh, . . . and against those who practise Piracy. . . . And

---

(my translation). Barbeyrac inserted at his own initiative the words "and social" (*ac
sociali*) after the word "rational" in this passage—a revealing attempt to make Grotius
more of a theorist of sociability than in fact he was.

having badly when they tried to resist the settlements, and who could be punished for their conduct.[35]

However, one practice that could *not* be used as justification for the conquest of primitive peoples was their religion. It had occasionally been argued that "infidels" could rightly be conquered by Christians, but Grotius was always adamant that war could never be made against any theists on the grounds that their religion was false. As he said in II.XX.46, "That there is a Deity, (one or more I shall not now consider) and that this Deity has the Care of human Affairs, are Notions universally received, and are absolutely necessary to the Essence of any Religion, whether true or false," and "those who first attempt to destroy these Notions, ought, on the Account of human Society in general, which they thus, without any just Grounds, injure, to be restrained, as in all well-governed Communities has been usual." So atheism was a moral crime, as it was to be for Locke (though not for Hobbes). But any religion that corresponded to this minimal definition should be tolerated, and Christianity could not be forced on its adherents (II.XX.48), though Christianity itself had to be tolerated by nonbelievers on pain of international punishment (II.XX.49).

A third and equally surprising practical implication of Grotius's minimalist political principles was that he sanctioned certain kinds of slavery. As he said in his discussion of the issue in chapter V of Book II,

> perfect and utter Slavery, is that which obliges a Man to serve his Master all his Life long, for Diet and other common Necessaries; which indeed, if it be thus understood, and confined within the Bounds of Nature, has nothing too hard and severe in it; for that perpetual Obligation to Service, is recompensed by the Certainty of being always provided for; which those who let themselves out to daily Labour, are often far from being assured of. . . . (II.V.27)

---

35. See II.II.17. Grotius there and elsewhere distinguished between "Property" and "Jurisdiction": Just as a fleet at sea can claim the right to regulate the use of the sea in its neighborhood (always allowing for the moral rights of other people to use surplus resources), so an aboriginal nation could regulate the use of its territory. But if it failed to allow settlement under its aegis, the land could be taken from it as punishment for its breach of the law of nature.

The fundamental right to preserve oneself naturally (on Grotius's view) led to the legitimacy of voluntary slavery, if one's circumstances were such that only such a course of action would keep one alive. Similarly, parents could reasonably sell their children into slavery (II.V.29). But of course, the master of a slave could have no right to kill the slave, since such a right would defeat the object of the relationship from the point of view of the slave (II.V.28). This—to our eyes—disconcerting consequence of Grotius's minimalist liberalism was a common feature of the rights theories of the seventeenth and eighteenth centuries, and it was of course one of the primary reasons why Rousseau was to turn in disgust from the Grotian tradition.

These implications of Grotius's theory, all in various ways, relate to his defense of individual rights, including the private right to make war. But *De Iure Belli ac Pacis* also contains an influential account of the nature of a state. As we have seen, Grotius believed that all its rights "come to the state from private individuals; . . . the power of the state is the result of collective agreement."[36] Individuals agree to pool their rights of self-preservation, and in addition to help their fellow citizens in ways that they would not think of doing in a state of nature. As he said in *De Iure Belli ac Pacis* I.I.14, "The State[37] is a compleat Body of free Persons, associated together to enjoy peaceably their Rights, and for their common Benefit" (the last phrase expressing what is added by civil association) (I.III.7). As long as this "body of free persons" was independent of any other such body, it was itself free and sovereign: "we . . . exclude the Nations, who are brought under the Power of another People, as were the *Roman* Provinces; for those Nations are no longer a State, as we now use the Word, but the less considerable Members of a great State, as Slaves are the Members of a Family."

But Grotius had to tread very carefully over the question of how such

36. *De Iure Praedae Commentarius,* trans. Williams and Zeydel, 1:91.

37. In the Latin original, he used the word *civitas* or "city," the word which continued to be used by, for example, Hobbes and Pufendorf in their Latin writings to mean "state."

The publishers of this edition (D. Brown, T. Ward, and W. Meares) included one of the publishers of the 1738 edition (Brown); the publishers of the various English translations of Pufendorf also included some of the publishers of both the 1715 and the 1738 Grotius, and the two projects were clearly regarded as similar.[4] The quality of the translation of Grotius's text varies, with most of the more egregious errors being toward the end (see, for example, my notes at III.VII.9 and III.XIX.14), and it is likely that these passages were translated by Spavan or Littlehales. Elsewhere, Morrice remembered that at the presentation to the prince "he was promised Great Things," though nothing materialized until 1724, when he was appointed chaplain to the prince. In the meantime he made money acting as minister of the chapel in the New Way, Westminster, translating, and writing anonymously for the *Tatler* and the *Spectator*. The prince succeeded to the throne as George II in 1727, and Morrice continued to hope for great things, from a monarch who clearly had a rather vague memory of him:

> Thursday, Dec[r]. 17th 1730. at Half Hour past One a-Clock, Mr. Brigman, Closet-Keeper to the King, plac'd me at the Door between the Bed-Chamber & Closet, to deliver a Memorial to His Majesty, about Grotius, and my having been Chaplain, w[ch] was very graciously rec[d]: Ld. Pagett [son of the Earl of Uxbridge] was Ld of the Bed-Chamber in waiting. . . .[5]

It is unclear whether Morrice envisaged some new edition of Grotius as a way of winning the favor of the king (not unreasonably, given that Barbeyrac had dedicated his edition to the king's father), nor is it clear whether he in fact had any hand in the 1738 edition. (The longer autobiography goes down to 1740, but it is very sketchy about the last few years of Morrice's life.) The notes were translated by someone with views of his own about some of the material (see, for example, II.V.14.1 n. 2), which may suggest Morrice; he died in 1740, without having received

---

4. Ward also published, in 1718, a Latin edition of *De Iure Belli*, which is extremely rare.

5. Ibid., 31 (no folio numbering).

any sign of royal favor. It is likely that the 1738 edition was largely a project driven by its publishers (this is implied by the absence of a dedication, other than the translation of Grotius's own dedication to Louis XIII), and the publishers may have recruited someone other than Morrice to translate the notes.

My own editorial remarks in the text or notes of the edition are contained within double square brackets, thus: [[. . .]]. This is because both Barbeyrac and his translator use ordinary parentheses and square brackets; the latter usually signify alterations or comments added to Grotius's own text, though they can also function in the same way as ordinary parentheses. Where I have introduced a footnote of my own, it is marked in the text with the symbol †. Again, this is because Barbeyrac and Grotius themselves used numbers, letters, and asterisks (*) to label their footnotes and marginal notes. Page breaks in the 1738 edition are indicated here by the use of angle brackets. For example, page 112 begins after <112>.

ACKNOWLEDGMENTS

I would like to acknowledge the constant help and support in this project of the General Editor, Knud Haakonssen, and the scholarly assistance of Tim Hochstrasser, Istvan Hont, and Noah Dauber. I would also like to thank the editor at Liberty Fund, Diana Francoeur, for her patience and helpfulness.

R. T.

THE RIGHTS OF WAR AND PEACE

BOOK I

THE
RIGHTS OF
WAR AND PEACE,

IN THREE BOOKS.

Wherein are explained,
The LAW of NATURE and NATIONS,
AND
The Principal POINTS relating to GOVERNMENT.
Written in *LATIN* by the Learned

HUGO GROTIUS,

And Translated into *ENGLISH*.
To which are added,
All the large NOTES of Mr. *J. BARBEYRAC,*
PROFESSOR of LAW at *Groningen,*
And MEMBER of the ROYAL ACADEMY of SCIENCES
at *Berlin.*

LONDON:

Printed for W. INNYS and R. MANBY, J. and P. KNAPTON,
D. BROWN, T. OSBORN, and E. WICKSTEED.

MDCCXXXVIII.

THE CONTENTS

Book I

CHAPTER I

What War *is, and what* Right *is.*

---

1. Omitted in original table of contents.

CHAPTER II

Whether it is ever lawful *to make* War.

CHAPTER III

The Division of War *into* publick *and* private; *together with an Explication of the* Supreme Power.

CHAPTER IV

Of a War *made by* Subjects *against their* Sovereigns.

CHAPTER V

Who may lawfully *make* War.

Book II

CHAPTER I

Of the Causes of War; *and* first *of the* Defence *of* Persons *and* Goods.

CHAPTER II

Of Things which belong in common to all Men.

CHAPTER III

Of the original Acquisition *of Things; where also is*
treated of the Sea *and* Rivers.

CHAPTER IV

Of a Thing presumed to be quitted, *and of the Right of*
Possession *that follows; and how such* Possession *differs
from* Usucaption *and* Prescription.

CHAPTER V

Of the original Acquisition of a Right over Persons; where also is treated of the Right of Parents: Of Marriages: Of Societies: Of the Right over Subjects; and over Slaves.

CHAPTER VI

Of an Acquisition (Possession *or* Purchase) *derived from a Man's* own *Deed; where also of the* Alienation *of a* Government, *and of the* Things *and* Revenues *that belong to* that *Government.*

CHAPTER VII

Of an Acquisition *derived to one by Vertue of some* Law; *where also of* succeeding *to the* Effects *and* Estate *of a* Man *who* dies *without a* Will.

CHAPTER VIII

Of such Properties *as are commonly called* Acquisitions by the Right of Nations.

CHAPTER IX

When Jurisdiction *and* Property *cease.*

CHAPTER X

Of the Obligation that arises from Property.

CHAPTER XIII

Of an Oath.

CHAPTER XVI

Of Interpretation, *or the Way of explaining the* Sense *of a* Promise *or* Convention.

CHAPTER XXII

Of the unjust Causes *of* War.

CHAPTER XXIII

Of the dubious Causes *of* War.

CHAPTER XXIV

Exhortations *not rashly to engage in a* War, *tho' for* just *Reasons.*

CHAPTER XXV

Of the Causes *for which* War *is to be undertaken on the* Account *of* others.

CHAPTER XXVI

Of the Reasons *that* justify *those who, under* another's
Command, *engage in* War.

Book III

CHAPTER II

How Subjects *Goods are by the* Law of Nations *obliged*
for their Princes *Debts; where also of* Reprisals.

CHAPTER V

Of Wasting *and* Plundering.

CHAPTER VI

Of the Right to Things taken *in* War.

CHAPTER VII

Of the Right over Prisoners.

CHAPTER X

Some Advices *concerning what is done in an* unjust War.

CHAPTER XI

The Right of Killing *in a just War,* qualified.

CHAPTER XII

The Right of Wasting, *and such other* Violences, *qualified.*

CHAPTER XIII

The Right over Things taken in War, qualified.

CHAPTER XIV

Moderation in Regard to Prisoners.

CHAPTER XX

Of the publick Faith *by which* War *is* concluded; *where also of* Treaties of Peace, *of* Lots, *of* Set Combats, *of* Arbitration, *of* Surrenders, *of* Hostages, *and of* Pawns.

CHAPTER XXII

Of the Faith *of* Generals *and* Officers.

CHAPTER XXIII

Of the Faith *or* Promises *of* private *Persons during the* War.

To look into the Manners of *Antiquity,* and recover the Memory of *preceding* Ages, is an Entertainment of the highest Pleasure and Advantage to the Mind, it establishes very lasting Impressions of *Virtue* in us, *enlarges* the Soul, and moves our Emulation to follow and excel the *leading* Characters before us; when we are tracing the Exploits of some *Worthy* of *Old,* with what *Delight* do we pursue him in every Circumstance of Action, we admire the *Example,* and transmit the *Beauties* of his Life into our own Conduct by *Practice* and *Imitation;* for the *Mind* of Man is of a *searching* Nature, very *wide* and *extensive* in her Speculations; and as she is *blind* to the Transactions of *Futurity,* so she receives a greater Lustre from the *Reflection* of Instances that are *past,* than from the *Rules* of *Wisdom,* or the *Determination* of the *Schools:* φιλοσοφία ἐκ παραδειγμάτων, *Philosophy* from *Example,* in the Opinion of the *Historian,* advances human Life beyond the Power of *Precept,* or the *Distinctions* of *Morality,* it opens a large Scene for *Observation,* it displays all the *Occurrences* and *Revolutions of Providence,* how far *Application* and *Industry* improve the *Abilities* of the Soul, and offer us to the *Notice* of *Mankind,* and the *Wonder* of *Posterity.*   Thucydides.

    This LIFE of *GROTIUS* is not writ with a Design to enlarge upon his *Merit,* or to *adorn* his Character, who has left such *Illustrious* Testimonies of his *Learning, Zeal,* and *Piety,* that the Letter'd World submits to his *Authority,* and *reveres* his *Judgment* so much, <ii> that his *Name* will be venerable to *latest* Ages: Our present Aim is only to reduce the *Circumstances* of his *Life* into such a Method as will shew us by what *Steps* and *Degrees* he attained to so *high* an Esteem, as to derive an *Honour* upon the *Century* he lived in, and to recommend him as a *Pattern* to succeeding Ages.

HUGO GROTIUS, in *Dutch, de Groot,* one of the greatest Men in *Europe,* was born at *Delft* the 10th of *April,* 1583; where his *Family* had been *Illustrious* between *Four and Five Hundred* Years. He made so early a Progress in his *Studies,* that he writ some *Verses* before he was *nine* Years of Age; and at *Fifteen* he had a great Understanding in *Philosophy, Divinity* and the *Civil Law;* but he was still better skill'd in *Philology,* as he made it appear by the Commentary he writ at *that* Age upon *Martianus Capella,* a very difficult Author. So prodigious was his *Memory,* that being present at the *Muster* of some Regiments, he remembered the Names of every Soldier there. In the Year 1598 he accompanied the *Dutch* Embassador, the famous *Barnevelt,* into *France,* where *Henry* IV gave him several Marks of his *Esteem;* he took there his Degree of *Doctor of Law,* and being returned into his Country, he applied himself to the *Bar,* and *pleaded* before he was *Seventeen* Years of Age; he was not *Twenty four* Years old when he was made *Advocate-General;* he settled at *Rotterdam* in 1613, and was *Pensionary* of that Town; he would not accept of that Employment, but upon Condition that he should not be deprived of it; for he foresaw that the Quarrels of *Divines* about the Doctrine of *Grace,* which formed already a thousand *Factions* in the *State,* would occasion many *Revolutions* in the chief Towns; he was sent into *England* in the same Year, by reason of the Misunderstanding between the *Merchants* of both Nations; he wrote a Treatise upon that Subject, and called it *Mare Liberum,* or a Treatise shewing the Right the *Dutch* have to the *Indian* Trade. He found himself so far engaged in the Affairs which undid *Barnevelt,* that he was arrested in *August* 1618, and condemned to *perpetual Imprisonment* the 18th Day of *May* 1619, and to *forfeit* his *Estate;* he was confined to the Castle of *Louvestein* the 6th of *June* in the same Year, where he was severely used for above 18 Months; from whence, by the Contrivance of *Mary de Regelsberg* his *Wife,* he made his Escape, who having observed that the *Guards,* being weary of searching a large *Trunk* full of Books and Linnen to be washed at *Gorcum,* a neighbouring Town, let it go without opening it as they used to do, advised her Husband to put himself into it, having made some Holes with a Wimble in the Place where the fore-part of his *Head* was, that he might not be stifled. He followed her Advice, and was in that manner carried to a *Friend* of his at *Gorcum;* from whence he went to *Antwerp* in the usual Waggon, after he had crossed the publick Place in the Disguise of a *Joyner,* with a Ruler in his Hand. That *good Woman* pretended all the while that her *Husband* was <iii> very *Sick,* to give him time to make his Escape into a *Foreign* Country: But when she thought he was safe, she told the *Guards,* laughing at them, that the *Birds were fled.* At first there was a Design to *Prosecute* her, and some *Judges* were of Opinion she should be kept in Prison instead of her *Husband;* but by a Majority of Votes she was released, and praised by every Body, for having by her Wit procured her Husband's *Liberty.* Such a Wife deserved not only to have a *Statue* erected to her in the *Commonwealth of Learning,* but also to be *canoniz'd;* for we are indebted to her for so many excellent Works published by her Husband, which had never come out of the Darkness of *Louvestein,* if he had remained there all his Life-time, as some *Judges* appointed by his Enemies designed it.

He retir'd into *France,* where he met with a kind Reception at *Court,* and had a *Pension* assigned him; the *Dutch* Embassadors endeavoured to prepossess the *King* against him, but that Prince did not regard their *Artifices,* and gave a glorious Testimony to the Virtue of that *Illustrious Refugee,* and *admired the Virtue of the Man, who being so ill used in his Country, never omitted an Opportunity to advance its Interest, and encrease its Grandeur.* He applied himself very closely to *Study,* and to compose *Books.* The *first* he published after he settled in *France,* was *An Apology for the Magistrates of Holland,* who had been turned out of their Places. The *contrary* Party was very much displeased with this *Treatise,* they thought *GROTIUS* made it appear that they had acted against the Laws, and therefore they endeavoured again to ruin and defame him, but the Protection of the *French* Court secured him against their Attempts.

He left *France* after he had been there *Eleven Years,* and returned into *Holland* full of Hopes, by reason of a kind Letter he received from Prince *Frederick Henry,* who succeeded his Brother in that *Republick;* but his Enemies prevented the good Effects of that Letter, and therefore he was forced once more to leave his Country; he resolved to go to *Hamburg,* where he stayed till he accepted the Offers he received from the Crown of *Sweden,* in the Year 1634. Queen *Christina* made him one of her *Coun-*

sellors, and sent him *Embassador* to *Lewis* XIII. Having discharged the
Duties of that Employment about *Eleven Years,* he set out from *France*
to give an Account of his Embassy to the Queen of *Sweden;* he went
through *Holland,* and received many Honours at *Amsterdam;* he saw
Queen *Christina* at *Stockholm,* and after he had discoursed with her
about the Affairs he had been entrusted with, he most humbly begged
of her, that she would grant him his Dismission. The *Queen* gave him
no positive Answer when he asked leave to retire, which displeased some
great Men, who were afraid that she would keep him in her *Council:* He
perceived their Discontent, and was so pressing to obtain his Dismission,
that it <iv> was granted him at last. The *Queen,* upon his Departure,
gave him several Marks of her great Esteem for him. The *Ship* on Board
which he embarked was violently tost by a Storm on the Coasts of *Pom-
erania; GROTIUS* being sick, and uneasy in Mind, continued to travel
by Land, but his Illness forced him to stop at *Rostock,* where he *died* in
a few Days, on the 28th of *August* 1645. His Body was carried to *Delft*
to be buried among his Ancestors; he left behind him three *Sons,* and
one *Daughter.* The *Daughter* was married to a *French* Gentleman called
Mombas, who was very much talk'd of, on Occasion of a Trouble he was
brought into soon after the *French* had passed the *Rhine* in the Year 1672.
The *eldest Son* and the *youngest* pitched upon a *Military* Life, and died
without being *married.* The *second,* whose Name was *Peter de Groot,*
made himself *illustrious* by his *Embassies.* The Elector *Palatine* being
restored to his Dominions by the Treaty of *Munster,* appointed him his
Resident in *Holland:* He was made *Pensionary* of the City of *Amsterdam*
in 1660, and discharged the Duties of that Place with great Ability for
the Space of *Seven Years.* He was sent *Embassador* to the *Northern*
Crowns in the Year 1668. At a Year's End he went into *France* with the
same Character, and acquitted himself in that Employment with great
Dexterity and *Wisdom.* When the *War* was kindled 1672, he returned
into his Country, and was deprived of his Office of *Pensionary* at *Rotterdam,* which he had enjoyed ever since his Return from his Embassy
into *Sweden:* He was deprived of it during the *Popular* Tumults, which
occasioned so many Alterations in the Towns of *Holland.* He retired to
Antwerp, and then to *Cologne,* whilst the Peace was treating there, and

acted for the *Good* of his *Country* as much as ever he could; and yet when he returned into *Holland* he was accused of a *State Crime;* the Cause was tried and he was acquitted: He retired into a *Country-House,* where he died at 70 Years of Age.

The Calumnies, maliciously dispersed by the *Enemies* of GROTIUS, about his *Death,* are irrefragably confuted by the Relation of the *Minister* who attended upon him when he was *dying.* The *Minister,* called *John Quistorpius,* was *Professor of Divinity* at *Rostock.* His Relation imports, "That he went to *GROTIUS* who had sent for him, and found him almost dying; that he exhorted him to prepare for *Death,* in order to enjoy a more happy *Life,* to *acknowledge* his *Sins,* and to *repent* of them; that having mentioned to him the *Publican,* who confessed himself a *Sinner,* and begged *God's* Mercy, the sick Man answered, *I am that Publican;* that he went on and told him he should have Recourse to *Jesus Christ,* without whom there is no Salvation, and that *GROTIUS* replied, *I place all my Hopes in Jesus Christ alone;* that he repeated in a *loud* Voice a *Prayer* in *High-Dutch,* and that the sick Man said it softly after him with his Hands joined; that having ended, he asked him whether he understood <v> him, and his Answer was, *I understood you very well;* that he continued to repeat to him some Passages of the *Word* of *God,* which *dying* People are usually put in Mind of, and to ask him, *Do you understand me?* and that *GROTIUS* answered, *I hear your Voice, but I do not understand every thing that you say;* that with this Answer the sick Man lost his *Speech,* and *expired* soon after." It were an absurd thing to call in Question the *Sincerity* of *Quistorpius,* nothing could move him to be false in his Account, and it is certain that the *Lutheran* Ministers were no less displeased than the *Calvinists* with the particular Opinions of *GROTIUS,* and therefore the Testimony of the Professor of *Rostock* is an authentick Proof; and if such Evidence is not sufficient in Matters of Fact, we make way for *Scepticism,* and it will be difficult to *prove* any thing. It is therefore an *undeniable* Case that *GROTIUS* being a dying, was affected like the Publican mentioned in the *Gospel,* he *confess'd* his Faults, he was *sorry* for them, and *implor'd* the Mercy of his *heavenly Father;* that he placed all his *Hopes* in *Jesus Christ* alone; that his *last* Thoughts were those that are contained in the *Prayer* of *dying* People, according to the *Liturgy* of the *Lutheran* Churches. The Result of which is, that those who say *he died a Socinian,* would be too gently used if they were only told, that they are guilty of a rash Judgment; they are Persons *prejudiced* against the Character of this *Great Man,* and therefore very unworthy of our Belief. Several People have wondered that his *Grand-Children* did not ask Satisfaction for this *Injury* done to his *Memory,* and that they appeared less sensible in this Point, than *Jansenius's* Relations upon slighter Calumnies; but some Persons highly approve their waving all *Juridical* Proceedings. There is a solid Answer to that *Reflection* upon our Author made by a Book entitled *l'Esprit de Mr. Arnauld;* and since the *Accuser* made no *Reply* to it, it is a plain Sign he has been convicted of Calumny. The *Apologist* for the Character of *GROTIUS* begins thus, "*But,* Sir, *what that* Author *and Father* Simon *say of* GROTIUS, *is nothing, if compared to what the* nameless Author *of the* scandalous *Libel intitled* l'Esprit de Mr. Arnauld *says of him; it is true, he slanders every Body in that Book, and the manifest Lies that are in it, ought to make one disbelieve every thing else; but because some are so weak, as to be imposed upon by his bold way of speaking, because some of those to whom you shew my Letters, entertain an ill Opinion of* GROTIUS *upon that Account, you will give me leave to undeceive them. Perhaps they will not be displeased to find an Author, for whom they have so great an Esteem, guilty of the most horrid Calumny that ever was; this will teach them, that one ought to suspect those who appear so zealous for Truth, and that sometimes a prodigious Malice and Detraction are concealed under the zealous Pretence of defending the Church of God. Afterwards the Apologist examines the* four *Accusations one after another; I shall not dwell on what* <vi> *he says upon the first Head,* viz. That *GROTIUS* was a violent *Arminian.* GROTIUS, *says our Author, in the second Place, was a* Socinian, *as appears from his enervating the Proofs of Christ's Divinity. Sir, desire your Friends to read* GROTIUS's *Annotations upon the Passages of St.* Mark *and St.* John *which I have mentioned to you, and if they do not say that it is an abominable* Calumny, *I am willing to be accounted a most wicked* Calumniator. *See also the* DXLVIIIth *Letter among the* Literae Ecclesiasticae & Theologicae." *I should be too long should I mention what he says upon the* third *Head, I shall only set down this Passage out of it,* "When Mr. *Arnauld* says something that is *injurious* to the *Reformed,* the *Author* of the Libel ex-claims violently against him, and Mr. *Arnauld* is then an *unsincere* Man, an *unfair Accuser,* an *Infamous Calumniator;* but when he says something that may serve this *Satyrical* Writer to *inveigh* against those whom he *hates,* every thing is then *right,* it serves him to fill up his *Page,* and to prevent his being placed among the *little Authors.*"

I must not forget that Mr. *Arnauld* blames the *Lutheran* Minister for not asking *GROTIUS in what Communion he would die,* this is a material Thing, says Mr. *Arnauld,* "with respect to a *Man who was known to have had no* Communion *a long time with any* Protestant *Church, and to have* confuted *in his* last Books *most of the* Doctrines *that are* common *to them.* Whereupon the *Apologist* says, that Mr. *Arnauld* and the *Author* of the *Libel* do wrongly fancy, that a Man has *no Religion* when he joins with none of the *Factions* that condemn *Mankind,* and each of which pre-tends to be the *only Church* of *Christ. GROTIUS* abstained from com-municating with the *Protestants,* as well as with the *Papists,* because the *Communion,* which was appointed by *Christ* as a *Symbol* of *Peace* and *Concord* among his *Disciples,* is accounted in those Societies a *Sign* of *Discord* and *Division.*"—Quistorpius acted the Part of a wise Man in not asking him what Communion he would die in, since he saw him dying in the Communion of *Jesus Christ,* by Virtue of which we are saved, and not by Virtue of that of the Bishop of *Rome,* or of the several *Protestant* Societies.

Without enquiring whether *Quistorpius* was in the *Right* or the *Wrong* for not asking such a Question, we observe, that a Man who believes the *Fundamental* Doctrines of *Christianity,* but forbears receiving the *Com-munion,* because he looks upon that Action as a Sign that one *damns* the other *Christian* Sects, cannot be accounted an *Atheist,* but by one who has forgot the *Notions* of *Things* or *Definitions* of *Words;* nay, we go farther, and maintain it cannot be denied that such a Man is a *Chris-tian;* we allow you to say, that his believing *all the Sects* that receive the *Gospel* to be in the *way to Salvation* is an *Heresy;* we allow you to assert, that it is a *pernicious* and *dangerous* Doctrine; notwithstanding which, can it be said that <vii> those who believe that *Jesus Christ is the Eternal Son of God, coessential* and *consubstantial with the Father,* that *he died for us,* that *he sits at the right Hand of God his Father;* that *Men are saved by Faith in his Death and Intercession;* that *one ought to obey his Precepts, and repent of one's Sins,* &c. we say, can it be affirmed that *such* People are not *Christians?* No Man of Sense can affirm it; but none would be more unreasonable in affecting such a thing than the Author of *l' Esprit de Mr. Arnauld,* since he published another Book, wherein he shews that *all those who believe the Fundamental Points, belong to the true Church, whatever Sect they may be of.* We omit several other *Maxims* advanced by him, whereby it appears, that *one may be saved in all Religions;* we only mention such Doctrines as he cannot deny, and according to which he ought to acknowledge, that *GROTIUS,* who believed the *Fundamental* Doctrines, without approving *Calvinism* or *Popery,* &c. in every thing, was *a Member of the true Church.*

We suppose that what has been delivered may be of sufficient Force to overthrow the *Calumnies* that have been raised against our *Author,* in respect to his *Principles* in *Religion;* we shall now take a short Survey of the most eminent *Books* that were *published* from him.

During his Stay at *Paris,* before he was Embassador of *Sweden,* "he translated into *Latin* Prose his Book *concerning the Truth of the Christian Religion,* which he had writ in *Dutch* Verse, for the Use of the *Seamen* who travelled into the *Indies,* that they might have some Diversion in singing such a pious Poem." Thus *du Maurier* speaks of it; but he is very much to blame for giving such a *mean* Notion of the *Author's* Design, for *GROTIUS* aimed at a *nobler* End; he had a Mind to enable the *Dutch,* who travel to the *Indies,* to promote the *Conversion* of the *Infidels;* this is the Character he gives of it himself, *My Resolution was to do something of Advantage to all my Countrymen, but especially for Seamen, that in all their Leisure they have Aboard, they may use their Time with Profit to themselves, and not loiter away their Hours as some do. And therefore beginning with a Panegyrick upon my own Nation, which infinitely excels all others in this Art; I encouraged them, that they would improve their Art, not only for their Benefit and Gain, but that they would regard it as the Mercy of Heaven, and use it for the propagating of the Christian Religion.* It is an Excellent Work, and the Notes upon it are very learned. It was translated into *English, French, Dutch, German, Greek, Persian,* and

Arabick; but we do not know whether all those Translations have been published; the *Greek* was not printed in the Year 1637. In the Year following *GROTIUS* mentions the *Persian* Translation only, as a Book which the *Pope's* Missionaries had a Mind to publish. *My Book,* says he, *concerning the Truth of the Christian Religion, that is accounted* Socinian *by some, is so far from having that Character here, that it is to be turned by the Pope's Missionaries into the* Persian <viii> *Tongue, to convert, by the Favour of God, the* Mahometans *who are in that Kingdom.* In the Year 1641, an *Englishman,* who had translated that Book into *Arabick,* was desirous his Translation should be printed in *England.* There came a very learned *Englishman* to me within these few Days, says he, who lived a long time in the *Turkish* Dominions, and translated my Book *of the Truth of the Christian Religion* into *Arabick,* and will endeavour, if he can, to have it published in *England:* He thinks no Book more profitable, either to instruct the *Christians* of those Parts, or to convert the *Mahometans* that are in the *Turkish, Persian, Tartarian, Punic,* or *Indian* Empire. That Translation made by the famous Dr. *Edward Pocock,* was printed at *London* in the Year 1660. There are three *German* Translations of that Work, two in Prose, and one in Verse, and two *French* Translations in Prose.

GROTIUS writ an *History* of the *Low-Countries;* it contains an Account of what happened in the *Netherlands* from the Departure of *Philip* II. It is divided into *Annals* and *History,* the *Annals* comprehend *five* Books; the *History* contains *eighteen,* and begins in the Year 1588. *Casaubon,* who had read something of it in the Year 1613, speaks well of it in a Letter written from *London* to *Thuanus.* The Judgment of the Author of the *Parrhasiana* runs thus, " *We may add to* Polybius, *a famous Historian among the* Moderns, *who though he had been a Sufferer by the Injustice of a* great Prince, *relates his noble Actions as carefully as any other Historian, and speaks of him according to his Merit, without saying any thing, whereby it may appear that he had Reason to complain of him; I mean the incomparable* HUGO GROTIUS, *who speaks in his History of the* Netherlands *of Prince* Maurice de Nassau, *as if he had never been ill treated by him; this is a remarkable Instance of* Impartiality, *which shews that it is not impossible to overcome one's Passion, and speak well of one's* Enemies, *as several People fancy, who judge of others by themselves.*" The

Author who observes this fine Passage in *GROTIUS*'s History, did it not out of Flattery, for he blames him afterwards for a thing that deserves to be blamed; he does not approve *GROTIUS*'s Style, and shews thereby that he is a Man of a good Taste. "None," says he, "of those who spoke well at *Athens,* and at *Rome,* expressed himself so obscurely in Conversation, as *Thucydides* and *Tacitus* did in their Histories; doubtless they had a Mind to raise themselves above common Use, and thereby they fell into that Obscurity for which they are justly reproved. It cannot be denied they have an affected Style, and that they hoped to recommend their Histories as it were by a manly Eloquence, whereby it seems that many things are expressed in few Words, and raised above the Capacity of the Vulgar; I cannot apprehend why some learned Men undertook to imitate them, as *HUGO GROTIUS,* and *Dionysius Vossius* in his Translation of *Rheide*'s History, and <ix> how they could relish such a Style; for certainly good Thoughts need not be obscure to be approved by good Judges; and when a Reader is obliged to stop continually, in order to look for the Sense, he does not think himself in the least obliged to an Historian who gives him the Trouble; this is the Reason why some Histories, though excellent as to the Matter, are read by few People; whereas if those Historians designed to write for the Instruction of those who have a sufficient Knowledge of the *Latin* Tongue to read a History with Pleasure, they should endeavour to make themselves easily understood, and useful to as many People as ever they could. The more a History deserves to be read by reason of the Events contained in it, the more it deserves to be of a general Use; the Authority of the Ancients who neglected the Clearness of the Style, cannot justify the Moderns, who have imitated them contrary to the Reasons I have mentioned, or rather contrary to good Sense. There is nothing in *Tacitus* that less deserves to be imitated, than his too concise, and consequently obscure Style; I am sorry *GROTIUS* was one of those who did not avoid it, it makes the Translation of his Writings more difficult, and his Thoughts more obscure."

But his Book *Of the Rights of War and Peace* was the *Master-piece* of his Works, and therefore deserves a more particular Account; it was printed at *Paris* in 1625, and dedicated to *Lewis* XIII. "King *Gustavus* of

Sweden having read and admired it, resolved to make use of the Author, whom he took to be a great *Politician* by reason of that Work; but that Prince having been killed at the Battle of *Lutzen* in the Year 1632, Chancellor *Oxenstern,* according to his own Inclination, and the Design of the late King *Gustavus,* nominated him to be sent Embassador into *France."* *Colomies says,* "It is believed that *GROTIUS* exhausted his Parts upon that Book, and that he might have said of it what *Casaubon* said of his Commentary upon *Perseus,* in a Letter to Mr. *Perillan* his Kinsman, which is not printed, *in Perseo omnem ingenii conatum effudimus;* and indeed that Work of *GROTIUS* is an excellent Piece, and I do not wonder that it has been explained in some *German* Universities."—Here follows the Judgment which M. *Bignon,* that unblamable Magistrate, makes of that Book in a Letter to *GROTIUS,* dated the 5th of *March,* 1633. "I had almost forgot," says he, "to thank you for your Treatise *De Jure Belli,* which is as well printed as the Subject deserves it; I have been told that a great King had it always in his Hands, and I believe it is true, because a very great Advantage must accrue from it, since that Book shews, that there is Reason and Justice in a Subject, which is thought to consist only in Confusion and Injustice; those who read it will learn the true Maxims of the *Christian* Policy, which are the solid Foundations of all Governments; I have read it again with a wonderful Pleasure." They did not make the <x> same Judgment of it at *Rome,* where it was placed among prohibited Books the 4th of *February* 1672. M. *Chauvin*'s Memorial concerning the Fate and Importance of that Work is so curious, that we cannot forbear transcribing some things out of it. It informs us that *GROTIUS* undertook to write that Book at the Solicitation of the famous *Peireskius. He himself says so, in a Letter he writ to him, when he presented him with the Copy of that Work.* "The Subject of it was thought to be so important and useful, that it gave Occasion to make a particular Science of it; for the Explication of which, some Professors have been appointed on purpose in the Universities. *Charles Lewis,* Elector *Palatine,* did so highly value that Book, that he thought fit it should serve as a Text to the Doctrine concerning the Right of Nature, and the Law of Nations, and in order to teach it he appointed *M. de Puffendorf* in the University of *Heidelberg;* and in Imitation of that Prince, the like Settlements have been made in other Universities. It does not appear that any Body criticized upon this Work of *GROTIUS* during his Life-time"; but when he was dead it occasioned many Disputes, and was published over all the World of Letters, and commented upon by the most *learned* of all Nations. It came out at last, *cum Notis Variorum,* by which means *our Author,* within 50 Years after his Death, obtained an Honour, which was not bestowed upon the *Ancients* till after *many* Ages.

Thus have we given the *History* of this *great Man,* taken from the best Accounts that have contributed to derive his Memory to our Times; but as an *Improvement* of his Character receive the Testimony of *Salmasius,* one of his Enemies, in a Letter to him, *You have laid but a small Obligation upon the Cardinals, and upon myself likewise, by bestowing a Title upon me, which is peculiar to the most eminent* GROTIUS; *for why should I not call him so, whom I had rather resemble, than enjoy the Wealth, the Purple, and Grandeur of the Sacred College?* <xi>

H. GROTIUS

TO

His Most CHRISTIAN MAJESTY
LEWIS XIII.
King of FRANCE and NAVARRE.

This Book presumes, most illustrious Prince, to intitle itself to Your great Name, from a Confidence, not of itself, or its Author, but of the Subject Matter of it, which is JUSTICE; a Virtue in so distinguishing a Manner Yours, that by it, both from Your own Merits, and the general Consent of Mankind, You have acquired a Title worthy so great a King, and are now every where known by the Name of JUST, no less than that of *LEWIS*. It was the Height of Glory to the *Roman* Generals, to be sirnamed from some of their conquered Countries, as *Crete, Numidia, Africa, Asia,* and the like. But how much more glorious Your Sirname, by which you are declared the irreconcileable Enemy, and perpetual Conqueror, not of any Nation or Man, but of Injustice? It was esteemed a great thing among the *Egyptian* Kings, for one of them to be stiled, the Lover of his Father, another the Lover of his Mother, another of his Brother. But how far short these of Your Name, which comprehends not only those, but every thing else that can be conceived beautiful and virtuous? You are JUST, as you honour the Memory of the great King your Father by imitating him: JUST, as You instruct your Brother by all imaginable Methods, but none more than that of Your own Example: JUST, as You procure the greatest Matches for Your Sisters: JUST, as You revive the Laws almost dead, and, to the utmost of Your Power, oppose the growing Wickedness of the Age: JUST, but at the same time Merciful too, as You deprive Your Subjects, whom the Ignorance of Your Goodness had caused to transgress the Bounds of their Duty, of nothing but

THE PRELIMINARY DISCOURSE

Concerning the Certainty of Right in general;
and the Design of this Work
in particular.

I. *The Civil Law, whether that of the* Romans, *or of any other People, many* I. The LAW of
have undertaken, either to explain by Commentaries, or to draw up into Nations.
short Abridgments: But that Law, which is common to many Nations or
Rulers of Nations, whether derived from Nature, or instituted by Divine
Commands, or introduced [1] *by Custom and tacit Consent, few have touched*
upon, and none hitherto treated of universally and methodically; tho' it is
the Interest of Mankind that it should be done.

II. Cicero [1] *rightly commended the Excellence of this Science, in the Business* Of War and
of Alliances, Treaties, Conventions between States, Princes, and foreign Na- Peace.
tions, and in short, in all Affairs that regard the Rights of War and Peace.

I. (1) The Author here means what he calls *the Law of Nations,* which he distinguishes from the *the Law of Nature* as making a separate Class. But in this he is
mistaken; as is acknowledged by most, who have pursued this Study. *See Note* 3. on
B. I. *Chap.* I. § 14.

II. (1) This is not Cicero's Sense. The Words here quoted only signify that
Pompey, of whom he is speaking, was very well versed in Alliances, Treaties, and Conventions made, concluded, and formed, between States, Princes, and foreign Nations,
*&c. Equidem contrà existimo, Judices, quum in omni genere ac varietate Artium, etiam
illarum, quae sine summo otio non facilè discuntur,* Cn. Pompeius *excellat,* SINGU-
LAREM QUAMDAM LAUDEM EJUS ET PRAESTABILE MESSE SCIENTIAM *in foederibus,
pactionibus, conditionibus Populorum, Regum, exterarum Nationum: in omni denique
Belli Jure ac Pacis.* Orat. pro L. Corn. Balbo, Cap. VI.

And Euripides *prefers this Science before the Knowledge of all other Things, whether Divine or Human, when he makes* Helen *say thus to* Theonoe:

[2] 'Twould be a base Reproach
To you, who know th' Affairs present and future
Of Men and Gods, not to know what Justice is.

Some think Interest alone the Rule of Justice. III. *And indeed this Work is the more necessary, since we find some, both in this and in former Ages, so far despising this Sort of Right, as if it were nothing but an empty Name. The Saying of* Euphemus *in* Thucydides *is almost in every ones Mouth,* [1] *To a King or Sovereign City, no-<xiv>thing is unjust that is profitable. Not unlike to which is this,* [2] *That amongst the*

2. Ἀισχρὸν τὰ μέν σε θεῖα πάντ' ἐξειδέναι,
Τά τ' ὄντα, καὶ μὴ, τὰ δὲ δίκαια μὴ εἰδέναι.
HELEN. Ver. 928, 929.

This *Theonoe* was an *Egyptian* Priestess, who dealt in Divination. HELEN does not here design to prefer the Knowledge of what is just and unjust, to that of all things human and divine, as our Author pretends. The Poet only intimates, that we ought to join the Study of Morality with the Study of Religion. In this Sense the Verses here quoted may very justly be understood as addressed to all employed in the publick Ministry of Religion, either to remind them of their Duty, or reprove them for the Faults committed in the Discharge of it, which has been but too often the Case at all Times. See what I have said on this Subject in my Preface to PUFENDORF, § 7, &c.

III. (1) These Words occur in the sixth Book of that Historian. (*Chap.* LXXXV. *Edit. Oxon.*) We find the same Maxim in the fifth, where the *Athenians,* whose Power was then very considerable, speak thus to the *Melians. For you cannot but know that, according to the common Notions of Mankind, Justice is regulated by the equal Necessities of the Parties; and that those who are invested with a superior Power, do all they find possible, while the Weak are obliged to submit.* (Chap. LXXXIX.) GROTIUS.

The former of these Passages is not properly applied. It may be observed that the Word here used is ἄλογον, which signifies *unreasonable,* not *unjust.* Besides, it appears from the Sequel of the Discourse that the Question does not here turn on what is just, or unjust. *Hermocrates,* the *Syracusan* Embassador, had remonstrated to the *Camarinians,* that there was not the least Probability, that the *Athenians* would, after the Reduction of *Chalcis,* grant the *Leontines* their Liberty, who were Inhabitants of the same Country. *Chap.* LXXIX. To which *Euphemus* replies, that the *Athenians* had an Interest in making that Distinction, and shews how they would find their Account in it. So that ἄλογον in this Place signifies, *what is not conformable to the Rules of good Policy,* and is the same as οὐκ εὔλογον in *Chap.* LXXVI.

2. The Words here used by the Author, are taken from TACITUS. *Id in summâ fortunâ, aequius, quod validius.* Annal. Lib. XV. Cap. I.

Great the stronger is the juster Side; and, That no State can be governed [3] *without Injustice. Besides, the Disputes that happen between Nations or Princes, are commonly decided at the Point of the Sword. Now, it is not only the Opinion of the Vulgar, that War is a Stranger to all Justice, but many Sayings uttered by Men of Wisdom and Learning, give Strength to such an Opinion. And indeed, nothing is more frequent than the mentioning of Right and Arms, as opposite to one another. Thus* Ennius, [4]

> They have recourse to Force of Arms, not Law.

And Horace [5] *thus describes the Fierceness of* Achilles:

> Laws as not made for him he proudly scorns,
> And every Thing demands by Force of Arms.

Another Latin *Poet* [6] *introduces another Conqueror, who entering upon War, speaks in this Manner,*

> Now, Peace and Law, I bid you both farewell.

Antigonus, [7] *though old, laughed at the Man, who presented him with a Treatise concerning Justice, at the very Time he was besieging his Enemies*

---

3. The Author alludes to a Fragment of the second Book of CICERO's Treatise *De Republicâ,* preserved by St. AUGUSTIN; where *Scipio,* on the contrary, maintains, that it is impossible to govern a State well, without observing the Rules of Justice with the utmost Exactness. *De Civit. Dei. Lib.* II. *Cap.* XXI.

4. This Fragment, which may be seen in CICERO's Oration for *Muraena,* Cap. XIV. is more entire in AULUS GELLIUS, *Lib.* XX. *Cap.* X.

> *Non ex jure manu consertum, sed mage ferro*
> *Rem repetunt, regnumque petunt, vadunt solidâ vi.*

But the Poet speaks only of Civil Laws; and sets violent Measures, the distinguishing Characteristicks of War, in Opposition to the legal Proceedings, used for composing Differences in Times of Peace. The same is to be observed of some of the following Passages.

5. *Art. Poet.* Ver. 122.

6. LUCAN puts this Speech into the Mouth of *Julius Caesar* on his passing the *Rubicon.*

7. PLUTARCH *De fortuna Alexand. Mag.* p. 330. Tom. II. Edit. *Wech.*

Cities. And Marius *said* [8] *he could not hear the Voice of the Laws for the* [9] *clashing of Arms. Even the* [10] *modest bashful* Pompey [11] *could have the Face to say,* Can I think of Laws, who am in Arms?

IV. *Among Christian Writers we find many Sayings of the same kind; let that of* Tertullian *suffice for all;* [1] Fraud, Cruelty, Injustice, are the proper Business of War. *Now they that are of this Opinion, will undoubtedly object against me that of the Comedian,*

> [2] You that attempt to fix by certain Rules
> Things so uncertain, may with like Success
> Strive to run mad, and yet preserve your Reason.

8. He spoke of the Civil Laws. The Words here referred to are that General's Answer on Occasion of his being blamed for conferring the Freedom of *Rome* on a thousand valiant Soldiers, who had signalized themselves in the War against the *Cimbri,* without the Authority of any Law. See the Passage at Length in PLUTARCH's *Apophthegms,* p. 202. Tom. II. See likewise the Life of *Marius* by the same Author; and VALERIUS MAXIMUS, *Lib.* V. *Cap.* II. *Num.* 8.

9. The Inhabitants of *Argos* being ingaged in a Dispute with the *Lacedemonians* about some Lands, and the former having supported their Claim with the best Reasons, *Lysander* drew his Sword, saying: *He, who is Master of this, reasons best about the Boundaries of Lands.* PLUTARCH's *Apophthegms,* p. 190. The same Author, in the Life of *Caesar,* p. 725. Tom. I. relates that *Metellus,* Tribune of the People, opposing that General for taking Money out of the publick Treasury, and alledging some Laws against that Practice, *Caesar* replied, that *the Laws must give Place to the Exigencies of War.*

SENECA in his fourth Book *De Beneficiis,* Cap. XXXVII. observes, that *Princes make many Grants, without enquiring into the Reasonableness of the Demand, especially during a War, when a just and equitable Man is not able to gratify so many Passions supported by Force.* He adds, that *it is not possible to be at the same Time an honest Man, and a good General.* GROTIUS.

10. He was very apt to blush, especially when he was obliged to appear in the Assembly of the People. See SENECA's eleventh Epistle, and GRONOVIUS's Note on it.

11. PLUTARCH, in the Life of *Pompey,* relates the Matter thus, The *Mamertines* pretending to be independent on *Pompey,* by Virtue of an old *Roman* Law, that General broke out into the following Expression: *Will you still continue to alledge the Laws against us, while we have our Swords by our Sides?* QUINTUS CURTIUS observes that *War inverts even the Laws of Nature.* Lib. IX. (Cap. IV. Num. 7.) GROTIUS.

IV. (1) This Passage is taken from the ninth Book of his Treatise against the *Jews.*
2. TERENCE in his *Eunuch,* Act I, Scene I, Ver. 16, *&c.*

V. But since it would be a vain Undertaking to treat of Right, if there is
really no such thing; it will be necessary, in order to shew the Usefulness of
our Work, and to establish it on solid Foundations, to confute here in a few
Words so dangerous an Error. And that we may not engage with a Multitude
at once, let us assign them an Advocate. And who more proper for this Purpose
than Carneades, *who arrived to such a Degree of Perfection, (the utmost*
his Sect aimed at,) that he could argue for or against Truth, with the same
Force of Eloquence? This Man having undertaken to dispute against Justice,
that kind of it, especially, which is the Subject of this Treatise, found no
Argument stronger than this. [1] *Laws (says he) were instituted by Men* <xv>
for the sake of Interest; and hence it is that they are different, not only in
different Countries, according to the Diversity of their Manners, but often
in the same Country, according to the Times. As to that which is called
Natural Right, *it is a mere Chimera. Nature prompts all Men, and in*
general all Animals, to seek their own particular Advantage: So that either
there is no Justice at all, or if there is any, it is extreme Folly, because it engages
us to procure the Good of others, to our own Prejudice.

VI. But what is here said by the Philosopher, and by the Poet after him,

[1] By naked Nature ne'er was understood   1. Natural.
    What's Just and Right.   Creech.

must by no Means be admitted. For Man is indeed an Animal, but one of
a very high Order, and that excells all the other Species of Animals much
more than they differ from one another; as the many Actions proper only to
Mankind sufficiently demonstrate. Now amongst the Things peculiar to
Man, is his Desire of [2] *Society, that is, a certain Inclination to live with*

V. (1) In Lactantius, *Instit. Divin.* Lib. V. Cap. XVI. Num. 3. *Edit. Cellar.*
VI. (1) Horace, *Lib.* I. *Sat.* III. *Ver.* 113.
2. The natural Inclination of Mankind to live in Society is a Principle which has
been admitted by the Wise and Learned of all Ages. Aristotle advances it in all his
Books of Morality and Politics. *Man,* says he, *is a sociable Animal in regard to those,*
to whom he is related by Nature. There is therefore such a Thing as Society, and somewhat
that is just, even independently of what we call Civil Society. Eadem. *Lib.* VII. *Cap.* X.
p. 280. *Edit. Paris.* The same Philosopher observes elsewhere, that Man is by Nature
more strongly inclined to Society than Bees, or any other Animals, which are observed

Understanding, [2] *is the Fountain of Right, properly so called; to which belongs the Abstaining* [3] *from that which is another's, and* <xviii> *the Restitution of what we have of another's, or of the Profit we have made by it, the Obligation of fulfilling Promises, the Reparation of a Damage done through our own Default, and the Merit of Punishment among Men.*

---

but refer the Reader to the Explication and Defence of the general Principle of *Sociability,* in my Notes on PUFENDORF's *Law of Nature and Nations,* Book II. Chap. III. So that, on the whole, a Man must be very wrong headed, who will hereafter expose himself by starting and multiplying frivolous Difficulties against a Truth, which when well understood, leaves no room for any plausible Objection.

2. SENECA makes an excellent Application of this Principle. "That a Sentiment of Gratitude," says he, "is a Thing valuable in its own Nature, appears from the odious Character which Ingratitude bears in the World, there being nothing so destructive of Concord and the Union of Mankind, as this shameful Vice. In reality, on what does our Security depend, but on the mutual Exchange of good Offices? Certainly nothing but this Commerce of Benefits can make Life commodious, and put us in a Condition of guarding against unforeseen Insults and Invasions. How miserable would Mankind be, if every one lived apart, and had no Resource, but in himself? So many Men, so many Persons exposed every Moment to be the Prey and Victims of other Animals: Blood continually ready to be spilt, in a Word, Weakness itself. Other Animals are strong enough to defend themselves. All such as are designed for a wandering Life, and whose natural Ferocity doth not allow them to go in Bodies, come into the World armed, as I may say. Whereas Man is defenceless on all Sides, having neither Claws nor Teeth to make him formidable. But in Society with his like he finds the wanted Succours. Nature to make him amends, has furnished him with two Things, which from weak and miserable as he would have been, render him very strong and powerful; I mean, Reason and a Disposition to Society. So that he, who when alone was not able to resist any other, by this Union becomes Master of all. The Disposition to Society gives him the Dominion over all the Animals, not even excepting those bred in the Sea, which live in another Element. It is Society also that furnishes him with Remedies against Distempers, Assistance in his old Age, Relief and Comfort in the midst of Sorrows and Afflictions. This is what puts him in a Condition of defying Fortune, if I may use the Expression. Take away the Disposition to Society, and you will at the same Time destroy the Union of Mankind, on which the Preservation and Happiness of Life depend. Now to maintain that Ingratitude is not a detestable Vice and what ought to be avoided for its own Sake, but only on the Account of its pernicious Consequences, is no better than destroying the Disposition to Society." *De Benefic.* Lib. IV. Cap. XVIII. GROTIUS.

3. PORPHYRY, *Of Abstinence from Animals,* Book III. Justice consists in this, the Abstaining from what is another's, and the doing no Injury to those that do none to us. GROTIUS.

IX. *From this Signification of Right arose another of larger Extent. For by reason that Man above all other Creatures is endued not only with this Social Faculty of which we have spoken, but likewise with Judgment to discern Things* [1] *pleasant or hurtful, and those not only present but future, and such as may prove to be so in their Consequences; it must therefore be agreeable to human Nature, that according to the Measure of our Understanding we should in these Things follow the Dictates of a right and sound Judgment, and not be corrupted either by Fear, or the Allurements of present Pleasure, nor be carried away violently by blind Passion. And whatsoever is contrary to such a Judgment* [2] *is likewise understood to be contrary to Natural Right, that is, the Laws of our Nature.*

X. *And to this belongs a* [1] *prudent Management in the gratuitous Distribution of Things that properly belong to each particular Person or* [2] *Society,*   Improperly and more loosely.

IX. (1) *Indicium ad aestimanda quae delectant aut nocent—& quae in utrumvis possunt ducere.* These Words Mr. BARBEYRAC renders—*choses agréables & desagréables,* &c. On which Occasion he professes to follow the Author's Sense, rather than his Expression. The Word *delectant,* says he, is not directly opposed to *nocent;* and I suspect some Omission in the Text; though the Passage appears the same in all Editions of this Work. It is probable, continues our learned Commentator, that GROTIUS wrote, or designed to write, *Quae delectant* AUT DOLOREM CREANT, *quae juvant, aut nocent,* &c. and that the Words here given in the *Roman* Character being left out, he did not observe the Omission in reading over this Place.

2. It is evident that this includes those Duties of Man in regard to himself, which are enjoined him even by the Frame of his Nature, and which may be seen at large in PUFENDORF's *Law of Nature and Nations,* Book II. Chap. IV.

X. (1) St. AMBROSE treats of this in his first Book *Of Offices.* GROTIUS.

Our Author probably had his Eye upon Chap. XXX, where that Father treats of *Beneficence,* and speaks, as usual, in a loose and confused manner of the Rules to be followed in the prudent Management of the Good we do to others.

2. [[The footnote is wrongly included as part of the previous one in the original.]] Our Author speaks here of such Rewards as are given by the State, or those who represent it, to Persons distinguished by their Merit; as also of the Collation of publick Offices. For they who receive the former, or are placed in the latter, had no full Right to demand them, nor to claim considerable ones as their due, how great soever their Merit may be, or how glorious soever the Actions are, which recommended them. See *Book* II. *Chap.* XVII. § 2.

without Exception, especially since he has so many Ways shewn his infinite Goodness and Almighty Power; whence we have Room to conclude that he is able to bestow, upon those that obey him, the greatest Rewards, and those eternal too, since he himself is eternal; and that he is willing so to do ought even to be believed, especially if he has in express Words promised it; as we Christians, convinced by undoubted Testimonies, believe he has.

2. Voluntary.   XII. *And this now is another Original of Right, besides that of Nature,*
  1. Divine.   *being that which proceeds from the free Will* ¹ *of God, to which our Under-*

XII. (1) For this Reason, according to the Sentiment of MARCUS ANTONINUS, every Man, who commits an Act of Injustice, renders himself guilty of Impiety. Ὁ ἀδικῶν ἀσεβεῖ. *Lib.* IX. § 1. GROTIUS.

This Passage is beautiful, but ill applied. The Author ought to have placed it among those quoted in the following Note. In Reality, he is here talking of *Voluntary Divine Law,* as he himself calls it, *Book* I. *Chap.* I. § 15. or of that, which, being in its own Nature indifferent, becomes just or unjust, because GOD hath commanded or forbidden it. This is evident from the very Terms he employs, and the Sequel of the Discourse; for he calls the Will, which is the Source of this Right, a free or arbitrary *Will;* and afterwards observes, as it were occasionally, that the *Law of Nature,* of which he has been laying the Foundation, may be also considered as flowing from the Divine Will, *because it was his Pleasure to establish such interior Principles in Men;* or that his Nature should be framed in the Manner it is. Our Author's Meaning therefore in this Place is, that even though there were no *Natural Right,* or though the Frame of our Nature did not of itself engage us to act in such or such a manner, yet upon the Acknowledgment of a Deity, of whose Existence we cannot reasonably be ignorant or doubtful, we must likewise own ourselves obliged to obey him, whatever he commands, even though his Laws had no other Foundation but his absolute and arbitrary Will. Thus we should always find a Source of Right there; for that GOD, who has so clearly revealed himself to Men in the Books, which we call the HOLY SCRIPTURES, has there prescribed them a Set of Laws entirely like those, which we say were imposed on them by the Frame of their own Nature. But it may be farther said that the Law of Nature, though sufficiently founded in itself, does likewise derive its Origin from GOD, independently of Revelation, *as it was his Pleasure,* &c. This I take to be the Meaning of our Author, and the Connexion of his Discourse, which does not appear at first Sight. The Impropriety of this Quotation will appear still more from the Words immediately following, which it is not amiss to produce. The Emperor gives a Reason for what he had advanced, *viz.* that every Injustice is a real Impiety. *For,* says he, *universal Nature having made reasonable Creatures for one another, that they may assist one another, according to the Merits of each Individual, and do no Hurt to others; he who disobeys her Will, is manifestly guilty of Impiety against the most antient Divinity.* Many Pagan Authors have also acknowledged that the Law of Nature is a divine Law. See some Passages alledged in my Remark on PUFENDORF, *Book* II. *Chap.* IV. § 3. *Num.* 4.

standing infallibly assures us, we ought to be subject: And even the Law of Nature itself, whether it be that which consists in the Maintenance of Society, or that which in a looser Sense is so called, though it flows from the internal Principles of Man, may notwithstanding be justly ascribed [2] *to God, because it was his Pleasure that these Principles should be in us. And in this Sense* Chrysippus [3] *and the* Stoicks *said, that the Original of Right is to be derived from no other than* Jupiter *himself; from which Word* Jupiter *it is probable* [4] *the* Latins *gave it the Name* Jus.

XIII. *There is yet this farther Reason for ascribing it to God, that God by the Laws which he has given, has made these very Principles more clear and evident, even to those who are less capable of strict Reasoning, and has forbid us to give way to those impetuous* [1] *Passions, which, <xx> contrary* [2] *to our own Interest, and that of others, divert us from following the Rules of Reason*

2. "When I speak of Nature," says St. CHRYSOSTOM, on 1 *Cor.* xi. 3. "I mean God; for he is the Author of Nature." And CHRYSIPPUS expresses himself thus. "For it is not possible to find any other Principle or Origin of Justice, than *Jupiter* and universal Nature; for there we must always begin, whenever we design to treat of Good and Evil." Book III. *Of the Gods.* GROTIUS.

This last Passage cited from a Stoick, whose Works are not extant, though he published a great Number, is preserved by PLUTARCH, in his Treatise *De Stoicorum repugnantiis,* p. 1035. Tom. II. *Edit. Wechel.*

3. See the preceding Note. CICERO also maintains, that the wisest and most learned Men have been of Opinion that the Source of all Law and Justice is to be sought for in the Divinity. See his Treatise *de Legibus,* Lib. II. Cap. IV. and Lib. I. Cap. V, VII, X.

4. Perhaps, it might be rather said that as *Ossum* has been converted into *Os,* so *Jussum* has been changed into *Jus,* Gen. *Jusis,* which was afterwards made *Juris,* as *Papisii* was turned into *Papirii.* See CICERO *Ep. ad Fam.* Lib. IX. Ep. XXI. GROTIUS.

XIII. (1) Disorderly Passions are condemned through the whole SCRIPTURE, especially in the New Testament, which forbids us, under very severe Penalties, to allow ourselves to be hurried away by those blind Motions. The Apostle St. JOHN includes them all under three Heads, *the Lust of the Flesh, the Lust of the Eyes, and the Pride of Life,* 1 Ep. Chap. II. Ver. 16. that is, in the Language of the Philosophers, sensual *Pleasure, Covetousness, and Ambition.*

2. In the Original it is quite the reverse: *Quae nobis ipsis, quique aliis consulunt.* But though all the Editions I have seen, and even that of 1632 read it so, it is evidently faulty. It should be read *malè consulunt,* as I have corrected it in my Edition of the Original, where the Reader may see the Reason why the Word supplied is here absolutely necessary. [[But see my introduction, p. xxiv n. 30, in support of the original reading.]]

and Nature; for as they are exceeding unruly, it was necessary to keep a strict Hand over them, and to confine them within certain narrow Bounds.

XIV. *Add to this, that sacred History, besides the Precepts it contains to this Purpose, affords no inconsiderable Motive to social Affection, since it teaches us that all Men are descended from the same first Parents. So that in this Respect also may be truly affirmed, what* Florentinus *said in another Sense, That* [1] *Nature has made us all akin: Whence it follows, that it is a Crime for one Man to act to the Prejudice of another.*

XV. *Amongst Men, Parents* [1] *are as so many Gods* [2] *in regard to their Children: Therefore the latter owe them an Obedience, not indeed unlimited,*

XIV. (1) *Digest.* Lib. I. Tit. I. *De Justitiâ & Jure.* Leg. III. The Ideas of the Stoicks, and such was this Lawyer, concerning the Origin of Mankind, were very confused; and though they introduced the Divinity, it was in a very different Manner from what Moses uses in his History of the Creation. See Justus Lipsius's *Physiolog. Stoic.* Lib. III. Dissert. IV. The *Kindred,* which they conceived as subsisting among Men, did not consist in their considering all Mankind as descended from the same Father and the same Mother; but only in the Conformity of their Nature, and the Principles or Materials of which they thought them composed. See Marcus Antoninus, *Book II.* § 1. and Gataker's learned Notes on that Place.

XV. (1) The Author here passes almost imperceptibly to another Species of *Voluntary Law,* which however is founded in Nature; it is what a Father and a Mother prescribe to their Children; for Children are obliged to obey their Parents, because they gave them Birth; in which Action, though the Husband and Wife are no more than blind Instruments, they in some Measure imitate God.

2. Hierocles, in his Comment on Pythagoras's Golden Verses, says that a Father and a Mother are *terrestrial Gods.* Philo, on the Decalogue, calls them *visible Gods, who imitate the unoriginated God, in producing living Creatures.* Pag. 761. *Edit. Paris.* St. Jerom (Ep. XLVII. Tom. 1. p. 224. *Edit. Basil,*) says that the Relation between Parents and their Children is next to that between God and Men; *secunda post Deum foederatio.* Plato calls Fathers and Mothers *Images of the Divinity.* De Legib. Lib. XI. (p. 930, 931. Tom. II. *Edit. H. Steph.*) Parents are to be honoured like the Gods, according to Aristotle. *Ethic. Nicomach.* Lib. IX. Cap. II. Grotius.

The Passage here quoted out of Hierocles, is not in his Commentary on the *Golden Verses.* They occur in Stobaeus, *Serm.* LXXVII. where he says *a Man would not commit a Mistake, who should call them* (Parents) *Gods of a second Class, and terrestrial Deities.* Pag. 461. *Edit. Wechel.*

*but as extensive [3] as that Relation requires, and as great as the Dependence
of both upon a common Superior permits.*

XVI. *Again, since the fulfilling of Covenants belongs to the Law of Nature,* 2 Human.
*(for it was necessary there should be some Means of obliging Men among
themselves, and we cannot conceive any other more conformable to Nature)
from this very Foundation [1] Civil Laws were derived. For those who had* Civil of every
incorporated themselves into any Society, or subjected themselves to any one State.
*Man, or Number of Men, had either expresly, or from the Nature of the
Thing must be understood to have tacitly promised, that they would submit
to whatever either the greater part of the Society, or those on whom the Sovereign Power had been conferred, had ordained.*

XVII. *Therefore the Saying, not of* Carneades *only, but of others,*

> [1] Interest, that Spring of Just and Right.   CREECH.

*if we speak accurately, is not true; for the Mother of Natural Law is human
Nature itself, which, though even the Necessity of our Circumstances should
not require it, would of itself create in us a mutual Desire of Society: And
the Mother of Civil Law is that very Obligation which arises from Consent,
which deriving its Force from the Law of Nature, Nature may be called as
it were, the Great Grandmother of this Law also. But to the Law of Nature
Profit is annexed: For the Author of Nature was pleased, that every Man in*

---

3. See below *Book* 1. *Chap.* IV. § 6. *Num.* 2.

XVI. (1) So that the *Civil Law,* though no kind of Law is in itself more arbitrary,
is at the Bottom no more than an Extension of Natural Law, a Consequence of that
inviolable Law of Nature, *that every one is obliged to a religious Performance of his
Promise.*

XVII. (1)

> *Atque ipsa Utilitas Justi propè mater, & Aequi.*
> HORAT. Lib. I. Sat. III. Ver. 98.

Upon which Place, an ancient Commentator on HORACE, whether ACRON or any
other Grammarian, makes the following Remark. "The Poet here opposes the Tenets
of the Stoicks; for his Design is to prove that Justice is not Natural, but derived from
Interest." See what St. AUGUSTIN says against this Opinion, *De Doctrina Christiana,*
Lib. III. Cap. XIV. GROTIUS.

particular ² should be weak of himself, and in Want of many Things necessary for living commodiously, to the End we might more eagerly affect Society: Whereas of the Civil Law Profit was the Occasion; for that entering into Society, or that Subjection which we spoke of, began first for the Sake of some Advantage. And besides, those who prescribe Laws to others, usually have, or ought ³ to have, Regard to some Profit therein.

XVIII. *But as the Laws of each State respect the Benefit of that State; so amongst all or most States there might be, and in Fact there are, some Laws agreed on by common Consent, which respect the Advantage not of one Body in particular, but of all in general. And this is what is called the Law of* Nations, ¹ *when used in Distinction to the ² Law of Nature. This <xxi> Part of Law Carneades omitted, in the Division he made of all Law into Natural and Civil of each People or State; when notwithstanding, since he was to treat of the Law which is between Nations (for he added a Discourse concerning Wars and Things got by War) he ought by all means to have mentioned this Law.*

Of Nations; of all or most States.

XIX. *But it is absurd in him to traduce Justice with the Name of Folly.* ¹ *For as, according to his own Confession, that Citizen is no Fool, who obeys the Law of his Country, though out of Reverence to that Law he must and ought to pass by some Things that might be advantageous to himself in particular: So neither is that People or Nation foolish, who for the Sake of their own particular Advantage, will not break in upon the Laws common to all Nations; for the same Reason holds good in both. For ² as he that violates*

II. Objections confuted: Justice not Folly.

2. *Ibid.* § 8. *Note* 2.
3. See PUFENDORF, *Book* VII. *Chap.* IX. § 5.
XVIII. (1) See *Book* I. *Chap.* I. § 14.
2. For these two Names are sometimes confounded. See what I have said on PUFENDORF, *Book* II. *Chap.* III. § 23. *Note* 3.
XIX. (1) Add to all this what PUFENDORF says *Book* II. *Chap.* III. § 10.
2. The Emperor MARCUS ANTONINUS makes a judicious Use of this Comparison. *Every Action of yours, which has not a near or remote Relation to the Publick Good, as its End, destroys the Harmony and Uniformity of Life: It is seditious, like that of a Citizen, who by forming Cabals, breaks the Union of the State.* Book IX. § 23. And in another Place he says, *He who divides himself from another, cuts himself off from all human*

*the Laws of his Country for the Sake of some present Advantage to himself,
thereby saps the Foundation of his own perpetual Interest, and at the same
Time that of his Posterity: So that People which violate the Laws of Nature
and Nations, break down the Bulwarks of their future Happiness and Tranquillity. But besides, though there were no Profit to be expected from the
Observation of Right, yet it would be a Point of Wisdom, not of Folly, to
obey the Impulse and Direction of our own Nature.*

XX. *Therefore neither is this Saying universally true,*

    [1] 'Twas Fear of Wrong that made us make our Laws.   CREECH.

which one in Plato *expresses thus,* [2] *The Fear of receiving Injury occasioned
the Invention of Laws, and it was Force that obliged Men to practice Justice.
For this Saying is applicable only to those Constitutions and Laws which
were made for the better Execution of Justice: Thus many, finding themselves
weak when taken singly and apart, did, for fear of being oppressed by those
that were stronger, unite together to establish, and with their joint Forces to
defend Courts of Judicature, to the End they might be an Overmatch for
those whom singly they were unable to deal with. And now in this Sense only
may be fitly taken what is said, That Law is that which the stronger pleases*

Society. Book XI. § 8. In Reality, as the same Emperor elsewhere observes, what is
useful to the whole Swarm, is useful to each particular Bee. GROTIUS.

    The Author, who probably trusted his Memory on this Occasion, has misquoted
the second of these Passages; for instead of ὅλης τῆς κοινωνίας ἀποπέπτωκε, he writes
οὐ δύναται μὴ καὶ ὅλου φύλου ἀποκεκόφθαι, i.e. *must necessarily be cut off from the
whole Body* of Mankind. The Mistake was occasioned by the last Words immediately
preceding the former Sentence, and making part of a Comparison; which the Author
forgetting, and confounding with what follows, has changed φυτοῦ, the Word in the
Original, into φύλου. The whole Passage runs thus: *A Branch broken off from the
Branch to which it grew, must necessarily be broken off from the whole Tree; so likewise
a Man,* &c. The last Passage is in *Book* VI. § 54. and stands thus: *What is not good
for the Swarm, is not good for the Bee.*
    XX. (1)

Jura inventa metu injusti fateare necesse est.
       HORAT. Sat. III. Ver. III.

    2. Book II. *Of the Common-Wealth,* Tom. II. p. 359. *Edit. H. Steph.* See likewise
GORGIAS, *Tom.* I. *p.* 483, and PUFENDORF, *Book* I. *Chap.* VI. § 10.

certainly, to render Wars just, they are to be waged with no less Care and Integrity, than judicial Proceedings are usually carried on.

XXVII. *Let it be granted then, that* [1] *Laws must be silent in the midst of Arms, provided they are only those Laws that are Civil and Judicial, and proper for Times of Peace; but not* <xxiv> *those that are of perpetual Obligation, and are equally suited to all Times.* For it was very well said of Dion Prusaeensis, [2] *That between Enemies, Written, that is, Civil Laws, are of no Force, but Unwritten* [3] *are, that is, those which Nature dictates, or the Consent of Nations has instituted. This we are taught by that ancient Form of the* Romans, [4] These Things I think must be recovered by a pure and just War. *The same ancient* Romans, *as* Varro *observed,* [5] *were very slow and far from all Licentiousness in entring upon War, because they thought that no War but such as is lawful and accompanied with Moderation, ought to be carried on. It was the Saying of* Camillus, [6] *That Wars ought to be managed with as much Justice as Valour: And of* Scipio Afri-

XXVII. (1) See the Commentators on these Words of CICERO, in his Oration for *Milo; silent enim Leges inter Arma.* Cap. IV.

2. *No written Law is of Force in Regard to Enemies; but there are certain Rules and Customs, which are observed by all, even when the Enmity is carried to the greatest Length.* Orat. περὶ ἔθους. This Passage is quoted by PETER DU FAUR, *Semestr.* Lib. II. Cap. I. p. 8. *Edit. Genev.* The Orator instances in the Permission of burying the Dead, the Security of Embassadors, &c.

3. Upon this Principle it was, that King *Alphonsus,* being asked which of the two he had been most obliged to, Books or Arms; answered, that he had learned by Books, both the Art of War, and the Rights of War. PLUTARCH says, that *amongst good Men there are Laws of War; and that we ought not to push the Desire of conquering so far, as to make an Advantage of wicked and impious Actions.* GROTIUS.

PLUTARCH has put these Words into the Mouth of *Camillus,* when he generously declined making an Advantage of the Schoolmaster's Treachery, who betrayed the Children of the *Falisci* into his Hands. *Life of Camillus,* Tom. 1. p. 134.

4. This Formulary is found in LIVY, Book I. Chap. XXXII.

5. This occurs in a Fragment of that learned Author, preserved by *Nonius,* and was taken from his second Book *De Vitâ Populi Romani.* See what is said on this Passage, *Book* III. *Chap.* III. § 11. *Note* 2.

6. These are the Words of that great General, as related by LIVY, on the Occasion of the perfidious School-Master; whence PLUTARCH has taken Occasion to ascribe to him a Speech very like this, which we have related above, *Note* 3. *There are Laws of War as well as of Peace; and we have learnt how to carry on a War with as much Justice as Bravery.* Book V. Chap. XXVII.

canus, [7] *That the* Romans *both begin and finish their Wars with Justice. An Author* [8] *maintains,* There are Laws of War, as there are of Peace. *Another* [9] *admires* Fabricius *for a very great Man, and remarkable for a Virtue which is extremely difficult, Innocence in War, and who believed that there are some Things, which it would be unlawful to practise even against an Enemy.*

XXVIII. *Of how great Force in Wars is the Consciousness of the Justice of* [1] *the Cause, Historians every where shew, who often ascribe the Victory*

7. LIVY makes him speak thus, in his Answer to the Embassadors from *Carthage,* who came to sue for a Peace, *that, though he was almost secure of Victory, he does not refuse to make a Peace, that the whole World may know the* Roman *People have a strict Regard to Justice both in engaging in and finishing their Wars.* Book XXX. Chap. XVI. The thing itself, however, is far from being indisputable. On the contrary, if we look into the Conduct of the *Romans,* we shall find Injustice practised in several of their Wars, either in regard to the Subject, the Manner, or Conclusion of them; though ALBERIC GENTILIS has taken upon him to justify that People in his Treatise *De Armis Romanis.* See Mr. BUDDEUS's Dissertation, intitled, *Juris prudentiae Historicae Specimen,* § 82, &c. among his *Selecta Juris Naturae & Gentium;* and what GROTIUS himself says in his Book *De Verit. Rel. Christ.* Lib. II. § 12. I remember a Passage in CICERO, where that celebrated Orator and Philosopher says, that *Equity and Fidelity are most commonly observed in entering on, pursuing, and ending a War.* De Legib. *Lib.* II. *Cap.* XIV.

8. LIVY, whose Words have been quoted *Note 6.*

9. SENECA, *Ep.* CXX. *We admired that great Man, persevering in his Resolution of giving a good Example, and unmoved by all the King's Offers, or the Promises made him on the other Side; preserving his Innocence in War, which is extremely difficult, being persuaded that some Things were not allowable even in an Enemy,* P. 595. *Edit. Gronov.* 1672.

XXVIII. (1) APPIAN makes *Pompey* speak thus to his Army: "We ought to rely upon the Gods and the Goodness of our Cause, since we are engaged in this War out of an honest and just Desire of maintaining the Government and Liberty of our Country." *De Bell. Civil.* Lib. II. p. 460. *Edit. H. Steph.* (p. 755. *Edit. Amstel.*) The same Historian introduces *Cassius* saying, that in War nothing gives so great Hopes as the Justice of the Cause (*De Bell. Civil.* Lib. IV. p. 645. *H. Steph.* 1034. *Edit. Amst.*) JOSEPHUS says that King *Herod* made use of this Consideration to animate his Soldiers, that God is with those, who have Justice on their Side. *Antiq. Jud.* Lib. XV. We find in PROCOPIUS many Thoughts to the same Purpose; as for Instance, what *Belisarius* says in the Speech he made, when he went into *Africa.* "Valour will not render us victorious, unless it be regulated and conducted by Justice." (*Vandalic.* Lib. I. Cap. XII.) See also another Speech of the same General's before an Engagement, near *Carthage* (*Ibid.* Cap. XIX.) In the Discourse of the *Lombards* to the *Herculi,* we have the following Passage, which I have a little corrected. "We call God to witness, whose

chiefly to this Reason. Hence the <xxv> Proverbial Sayings, [2] *A Soldier's Courage rises or falls according to the Merit of his Cause;* [3] *seldom does he return safely, who took up Arms unjustly; Hope is the* [4] *Companion of a good*

Power is so great, that the least Particle of it infinitely surpasses all human Force. There is Reason to believe, that having a Regard to the Causes of the War, he will give to it an End answerable to the Deserts of both." (*Gothic.* Lib. II. Cap. XIV.) And it is remarkable, that this Prediction was soon accomplished by a wonderful Event, which the Historian afterwards recites. *Totilas,* in the same Author, says to the *Goths:* "It is not possible, no, it is not possible, that those who commit Acts of Injustice and Violence, should acquire Glory by Arms; but every one is fortunate or unfortunate, as he behaves himself well or ill." (*Ibid.* Lib. III. Cap. VIII.) After the taking of *Rome,* *Totilas* makes another Speech, tending to the same Purpose. (*Ibid.* Cap. XXI.) AGA-THIAS, another Historian of those Times, tells us, *Book* II. *Chap.* I. that Injustice and Irreligion ought always to be guarded against, and are very prejudicial, but especially when we are obliged to make War, and to come to an Engagement with the Enemy. He proves it elsewhere (*Cap.* V.) by the Examples of *Darius, Xerxes,* and the *Athenians* in their Expedition against *Sicily.* See also what *Crispinus* says to the Inhabitants of *Aquileia* in HERODIAN, *Lib.* VIII. (*Cap.* VI. *Edit. Oxon.* 1678.) THUCYDIDES observes, that the *Lacedemonians* believed they had brought upon themselves, by their own Fault, the Disasters they met with at *Pylos* and other Places, because they had refused to submit to the Decision of Arbitrators, though summoned thereto by the *Athenians,* according to their Treaty. But the *Athenians* having afterwards refused in their turn to give the same Satisfaction, after several Infringements and unjust Enterprizes, the *Lacedemonians* from thence conceived good Hope of success in their Affairs for the future. *Lib.* VII. GROTIUS.

The Passage of THUCYDIDES, which our Author means, is in § 18. *p.* 421. of the *Oxford* Edition. Several States of *Peloponnesus* making Preparations for War against the *Athenians,* the *Lacedemonians* joined them with so much the more Resolution and Confidence, as they believed the Event would not be the same as in the preceding War; which, they themselves acknowledged, had been occasioned rather through their own Fault, than that of the *Athenians.* For, having sided with the *Thebans,* when the latter came to attack *Plataeae,* during a Truce (*Lib.* II. § 1. *& seq.*); and having more-over refused, contrary to an express Clause of their Treaty, (*Lib.* V. § 18. p. 302.) to terminate some Difference in a judicial Way, though they had been summoned to it by the *Athenians;* they were fully persuaded they had been unsuccessful on that Ac-count, and ingenuously ascribed to their Breach of Faith the Calamities that befel them at *Pylos,* and upon other Occasions. But after the *Athenians,* having equipped a Fleet, were gone to ravage the Lands of *Epidaurus, Prasia,* and other Places, and from *Pylos* made Incursions into their Country; after they refused, in their turn, to submit to a Decision in an amicable Manner, when any Dispute arose in relation to their Treaties: I say, after that time, the *Lacedemonians* believing they had made the Injustice to pass over to the other Side, eagerly sought an Opportunity of declaring War against them.

2. The Author here makes use of the very Terms of PROPERTIUS, and not of OVID, as GRONOVIUS pretends. His Memory failed him on this Occasion, which was also

Cause; and others to the same Purpose. Nor ought any one to be moved at the prosperous Successes of unjust Attempts; for it is sufficient that the Equity of the Cause has of itself a certain, and that very great Force towards Action, though that Force, as it happens in all human Affairs, is often hindered of its Effect, by the Opposition of other [5] Causes. The Opinion that a War is not rashly and unjustly begun, nor dishonourably carried on, is likewise very prevalent towards procuring Friendships; which Nations, as well as private Persons, stand in need of upon many Occasions. For no Man readily asso-

---

the Case of the learned Mr. MENAGE. This Mistake has been corrected by the last Commentator on the Poet last mentioned.

Frangit & adtollit vires in milite causa:
Quae nisi justa subest, excutit arma pudor.
      Lib. IV. Eleg. VI. Ver. 51, 52.
            Edit. Brockhuis.

3. This Thought is contained in the following Verse of EURIPIDES, taken from one of his Tragedies, not now extant.

'Ουδεὶς στρατεύσας ἄδικα, σῶς ἦλθεν πάλιν.
      Erechtei Fragm. Ver. 44. *Edit. Barnes.*

4. LUCAN introduces *Pompey* employing this Reason for encouraging his Soldiers before the Battle of *Pharsalia.*

Causa jubet melior superos sperare secundos.

Our better Cause bids us hope for the Favour of the Gods.
      Lib. VII. Ver. 349.

But long before that Poet's Time, *Menander* had said in general:

Ὅταν τι πράττεις ὅσιον, ἀγαθὴν ἐλπίδα
Πρόβαλλε σαυτῷ, τοῦτο γινώσκων, ὅτι
Τόλμῃ δικαίᾳ καὶ Θεὸς συλλαμβάνει.

When you engage in any good Action, entertain Hopes of Success; being assured that God favours a just Enterprize.
      Fragm. è Vulcanalib. p. 190. *Edit. Cleric.*

See also some Passages cited by our Author, *Book* II. *Chap.* I. § 1.

5. TACITUS makes *Otho* say that *good and lawful Undertakings are frequently attended with very bad Success, for want of a judicious Manner of proceeding,* Hist. Book I. Chap. LXXXIII.

ciates with those, who, he thinks, have Justice, Equity and Fidelity in Contempt.

III. The Author's Reasons for writing this Book.

XXIX. *Now for my Part, being fully assured, by the Reasons I have already given, that there is some Right common to all Nations, which takes Place both in the Preparations and in the Course of War, I had many and weighty Reasons inducing me to write a Treatise upon it. I observed throughout the*

Restraining the Licentiousness in making War.

Christian World a Licentiousness in regard to War, which even barbarous Nations ought to be ashamed of: a Running to Arms upon very frivolous or rather no Occasions; which being once taken up, there remained no longer any Reverence for Right, either Divine or Human, just as if from that Time Men were authorized and firmly resolved to commit all manner of Crimes without Restraint.

XXX. *The Spectacle of which monstrous Barbarity worked many, and those in no wise bad Men, up into an Opinion, that a Christian, whose Duty consists principally in loving all Men without Exception, ought not at all [1] to bear Arms; with whom seem to agree sometimes* Johannes Ferus [2] *and our Countryman* [3] Erasmus, *Men that were great Lovers of Peace both Ecclesiastical and Civil; but, I suppose, they had the same View, as those have who in order to make Things that are crooked straight, usually* [4] *bend them as much the other Way. But this very Endeavour of inclining too much to the opposite Extreme, is so far from doing Good, that it often does Hurt,*

XXX. (1) *Gladius bené de Bello cruentus, & melior homicida.* TERTUL. *De Resurr. Carnis.* Cap. XVI. GROTIUS.

See below, *Book* I. *Chap.* II. § 8. and my *Preface* to PUFENDORF, § 9; where I have inserted other Passages from the Fathers of the Church, who have condemned War as absolutely unlawful.

2. He was a *Franciscan* Preacher at *Mentz,* who lived in the Reign of *Charles* V. ZIEGLER on this Place quotes *Sixtus* of *Sienna,* Biblioth. Lib. VI. Annot. 115, 156; where the Author produces and criticizes the Passages of those two Writers on this Subject.

3. This great Author has a long Digression on the Proverb, *Dulce Bellum inexpertis.*

4. This has very often been the Practice of several Moralists, in all Ages. See a beautiful Passage of SENECA on this Subject, which I have given at Length, with a Translation in my Treatise *On Gaming,* Book I. Chap. III. § 12.

because Men readily discovering Things that are urged too far by them, are apt to slight their Authority in other Matters, which perhaps are more reasonable. A Cure therefore was to be applied to both these, as well to prevent believing that Nothing, as that all Things are lawful.

XXXI. *At the same Time I was likewise willing to promote, by my private Studies, the Profession of Law, which I formerly practised in publick [1] Employments with all possible Integrity; this being the only Thing that was left for me to do, being unworthily [2] banished my Native Country, which I have honoured with so many of my Labours. Many have before this designed* <xxvi> *to reduce it into a System; but none has accomplished it; nor indeed can it be done, unless those things (which has not been yet sufficiently taken Care of,) that are established [3] by the Will of Men, be duly distinguished from those which are founded on Nature. For the Laws of Nature being always the same, may be easily collected into an Art; but those which proceed from Human Institution being often changed, and different in different Places, are no more susceptible of a methodical System, than other Ideas of particular Things are.*

> An endeavour to promote the Knowledge of Law, by giving an Example of a Method for it.

XXXII. *But if the Professors of true Justice would undertake to treat of the several Parts of that Law which is perpetual and natural, setting aside every Thing which owes its Rise to Voluntary Institution, so that one for Instance would treat of Laws, another of Tributes, another of the Office of Judges, another of the Conjecture of Wills, another of the Evidence in Matters of Fact, there might at last from all the Parts collected together be a Body of Law composed.*

XXXIII. *What Method we thought fit to use, we have shewn in Deed rather than in Words in this Treatise, which contains that Part of Law, which is by far the noblest.*

> IV. The Contents and Order of the Work.

XXXI. (1) The Author had been Advocate-General, and Pensionary of *Rotterdam.*
2. He wrote this at *Paris* in 1625.
3. Laws merely positive.

XXXIX. *What was most wanting in all those,* viz. *Illustrations from History, the most Learned* [1] Faber *has undertaken to supply in some Chapters of his* Semestria, *but no farther than* <xxvii> *served his Purpose, and only by alledging some Authorities. The same has been done more largely, and that by applying a Multitude of Examples to some general Maxims laid down, by* Balthazar [2] Ayala, *and still more largely by* Albericus [3] Gentilis, *whose Labour, as I know it may be serviceable to others, and confess it has been to me, so what may be faulty in his Stile, in Method, in distinguishing of Questions, and the several Kinds of Right, I leave to the Reader's Judgment. I shall only say this, that in the Decision of Controversies, he is often wont to follow either a few Examples that are not always to be approved of, or even the Authority of modern Lawyers in their Answers, not a few of which are* [4] *accommodated to the Interest of those that consult them, and not formed by the invariable Rules of Equity and Justice. The Causes, from whence a War is denominated just or unjust,* Ayala *has not so much as touched upon:* Gentilis *has indeed described after his Manner some of the general Heads; but neither has he touched upon many famous Questions, which turn upon Cases that are very common.*

I. The Author's Case,

XL. *We have been careful that nothing of this Kind be passed over in Silence, having likewise shewn the very Foundations upon which we build our Decisions, so that it might be easy to determine any Question that may happen to be omitted by us. It remains now, that I briefly declare with what Assistance, and with what Care I undertook this Work. My first Care was, to refer the Proofs of those Things that belong to the Law of Nature to some*

1. In proving the Law of Nature.

XXXIX. (1) PETER DU FAUR of *St. Jori,* Counsellor in the Grand Council, afterwards Master of Requests, and at last First President of the Parliament of *Toulouse.* He was Scholar to CUJAS. His Work intitled *Semestrium Libri tres,* is full of Erudition. It has born several Impressions at *Paris, Lyons,* and *Geneva.*

2. He was a Native of *Antwerp* of *Spanish* Extraction. His Treatise, *De Jure & Officiis Bellicis,* was printed in that City in 1597, in 8vo. The Edition I make use of is that of *Louvain,* 1648.

3. This Author has written *De Jure Belli:* My Edition is printed at *Hanau,* 1612.

4. This Reproach does not fall on the modern Lawyers alone; Mr. NOODT has plainly proved that the antient Professors of that Science have sometimes been guilty of the same Fault. See his *Probabilia Juris,* Lib. II. Cap. II.

such certain Notions, as none can deny, without doing Violence to his Judgment. For the Principles of that Law, if you rightly consider, are manifest and self-evident, almost after the same Manner as those Things are that we perceive with our outward Senses, which do not deceive us, if the Organs are rightly disposed, and if other Things necessary are not wanting. Therefore Euripides *in his* Phoenissae *makes* Polynices, *whose Cause he would have to be represented manifestly just, deliver himself thus:*

> [1] I speak not Things hard to be understood,
> But such as, founded on the Rules of Good
> And Just, [2] are known alike to Learn'd and Rude.

And he immediately adds the Judgment of the Chorus, (*which consisted of* Women and those too Barbarians) *approving what he said.*

XLI. *I have likewise, towards the Proof of this Law, made Use of the Testimonies of* [1] *Philosophers, Historians, Poets, and in the last Place, Orators;*

XL. (1)

Ταῦτ' ἀνθέκαστα, μᾶτερ, οὐχὶ περιπλοκὰς
Λόγων ἀθροίσας ἔιπον, ἀλλὰ καὶ σοφοῖς
Καὶ τοῖσι φαύλοις ἔνδιχ', ὡς ἐμοὶ δοκεῖ.
                    Ver. 497, &c.

See my *Preface* to PUFENDORF, § 1, &c. *Cassiodorus* observes, that *to teach Men the Duties of Justice is indeed a Work of some Difficulty, but not impossible; because the Divinity has been so indulgent to all, that even they, who are unacquainted with the Principles of Law, are yet sensible of the consequential Truths derived from them.* Var. VII. 26.

2. The same Poet introduces *Hermione* speaking thus to *Andromache.*

ὐ βαρβάρων νόμοισιν οἰκοῦμεν πόλιν.

"We do not govern our State by the Laws of Barbarians." To which *Andromache* replies:

Κἀκεῖ τά γ' αἰσχρὰ κἀνθάδ' αἰσχύνην φέρει.

"What is dishonourable or dishonest among them, bears the same Character also among us."   *Androm.* Ver. 242, 243. GROTIUS.

XLI. (1) Why should they not be thus employed? The Emperor *Alexander Severus* read every Day CICERO's Books *De Republicâ*, and his Treatise *Of Offices.* GROTIUS. This Account is taken from the Life of that Prince, written by AELIUS LAMPRIDIUS,

not as if they were to be implicitly believed; for it is usual with them to accommodate themselves to the [2] Prejudices of their Sect, the Nature of their [3] Subject, and [4] the Interest of their Cause: But that when many Men of different Times and Places unanimously affirm the same Thing for Truth, this ought to be ascribed to a general Cause; which in the Questions treated of by us, can be no other than either a just <xxviii> Inference drawn from Of Nations. *the Principles of Nature, or an universal Consent. The former shews the Law of Nature, the other the [5] Law of Nations. The Difference between which is not to be understood from the Testimonies themselves (for the Law* 2. In distin- *of Nature and of Nations are Words used every where [6] promiscuously by* guishing both *Writers) but from the Quality of the Subject. For that which cannot be de-* of them, and *duced from certain Principles by just Consequences, and yet appears to be every where observed, must owe its rise to a free and arbitrary Will.*

---

who says, *when he read* Latin *Books, he preferred none to* CICERO's *Pieces* Of Offices, *and* On the Commonwealth, *Cap.* XXX.

2. The Philosophers, in Consequence of certain false Principles, with which they were infatuated, frequently advanced very false Maxims, and sometimes contradicted themselves. The *Academists* were particularly remarkable on this Account, valuing themselves on the Art of maintaining both Sides of all manner of Subjects. See BUD-DEUS's Dissertations *Of Moral Scepticism,* and the *Errors of the Stoicks,* among his *Analecta Historiae Philosophicae,* and the Morality of the antient Philosophers, abridged in my *Preface* to PUFENDORF's great Work.

3. The Historians, as well as the Poets, with a View of keeping up the Character of the Persons introduced, often put Maxims into their Mouths, which are false and contrary to Natural Law. The Writers of both Classes entertained likewise some Ideas which were far from being just, and sometimes very gross, on several Subjects; but the Poets exceeded the Historians in this Particular. In regard to the former, see my *Preface* to PUFENDORF, § 16; and as to what concerns the latter, Mr. LE CLERC's *Parrhasiana,* Tom. I. p. 200, &c. Our Author, in the Course of this Work, produces a great Number of Passages, which may serve to prove beyond Dispute what he here advances. We have already seen some of them, at the Entrance of this *Preliminary Discourse,* § III. *Notes* 1, 2. which are taken from THUCYDIDES and TACITUS, two of the greatest and most judicious Historians of Antiquity, the one *Greek,* and the other *Latin.*

4. This relates to the Orators. See PUFENDORF's *Law of Nature and Nations,* Book IV. Chap. I. § 21. *Note* 1.

5. See what I say on *Book* I. *Chap.* I. § 14.

6. See on PUFENDORF, *Book* III. *Chap.* III. § 23. *Note* 3.

THE PRELIMINARY DISCOURSE

XLII. *Therefore these two I have very carefully endeavoured always to distinguish no less from one another, than from the Civil Law: And even in the Law of Nations, I have made a Distinction between that which is truly and in every Respect lawful, and that which only produces a certain external Effect after the Manner of that primitive Law; so that, for Instance, it may be lawful to resist it, or that it even ought to be every where defended with the publick Force, for the Sake of some Advantage that attends it, or that some great Inconveniences may be avoided. Which Observation, how necessary it is in many Respects, will appear in the following* [1] *Treatise. We have been no less careful in distinguishing Things belonging to Right properly and strictly so called, whence arises the Obligation of making Restitution, from those which are only said to belong to it, because that the acting otherwise is repugnant to some other Dictate of right Reason: Which Distinction we have already touched upon.*

the Civil Law.

The Species of each.

XLIII. *Among Philosophers* Aristotle *deservedly holds the chief Place, whether you consider his Method of treating Subjects, or the Acuteness of his Distinctions, or the Weight of his Reasons. I could only wish that the Authority of this great Man had not for some Ages past degenerated into Tyranny, so that Truth, for the Discovery of which* Aristotle *took so great Pains, is now oppressed by nothing more than the very Name of* Aristotle. *I, for my Part, both in this and in all my other Writings, take to myself the Liberty of the ancient Christians, who espoused no Sect of Philosophers; not that they held with those who asserted that nothing can be known, than which there is nothing more foolish; but were of Opinion, that there was no one Sect that had discovered all Truth, nor any but what held something that was true. Therefore to collect into a Body the Truths that were dispersed in the Writings of each Philosopher and each Sect, they conceived to be nothing else, but* [1] *to deliver the true Christian Doctrine.*

II. Assistance in the Work.

1. Philosophers. *Aristotle,* his Praise.

XLII. (1) See, for Example, *Book* III. *Chap.* VII. § 6, 7.

XLIII. (1) This is what LACTANTIUS says, *Would any one but collect what Truths are scattered through the Writings of each of them, and diffused through the several Sects, and reduce them into one Body, he would not differ from us.* Instit. Divin. *Lib.* VII. *Cap.* VII. (*Num. 4. Edit. Cellar.*) JUSTIN MARTYR speaks to the same Purpose in his first Apology: *Not,* says he, *because the Doctrines of* PLATO *are entirely different from*

His Faults. XLIV. *Among other Things, (that I may mention this by the by, as not being foreign to our Purpose,) it is not without Reason, that some of the* Platonists *and ancient* [1] *Christians seem to dissent from* Aristotle *in this, that he placed the very Nature of Virtue* [2] *in a Mediocrity of Passions and Actions; which being once laid down, drove him to this, that of Virtues of a different Kind, as for Instance,* [3] *Liberality and Frugality, he made but one; and* <xxix>

---

those of CHRIST; *but because they are not conformable to them in every Particular. Which is also the Case in regard to the Tenets of the other Philosophers, as of the Stoicks, and of the Poets and Historians; for each of them, being directed by a Ray of the Light of innate Divine Reason, discovered something conformable to it, and spoke well so far* (p. 34. Edit. Oxon.) TERTULLIAN frequently calls SENECA, *our Seneca;* but then he observes that, *none but* CHRIST *could give us a complete Body of Spiritual Virtues,* (Adv. Jud. Cap. IX.) St. AUGUSTINE lays it down as a Fact that *those Rules of Morality, which are so highly commended by* CICERO, *are taught and learnt in the Christian Churches, diffused through the whole World,* Ep. CCII. See what the same Father says in regard to the *Platonists,* whom he maintains to be almost Christians, *Ep.* LVI, in his Treatise *De Verâ Religione,* Cap. III. and *Confess.* Book VII. Chap. IX. and Book VIII. Chap. II. GROTIUS.

To these Authorities we may add that of CLEMENT of *Alexandria,* who talks in the same manner, *Strom.* Lib. I. p. 338, 349. *Edit. Oxon.* See the Life of that Father, written by Mr. LE CLERC, in his *Bibliotheque Universelle,* Tom. X. p. 187, &c. and the Dissertation of the late Mr. OLEARIUS, *De Philosophiâ Eclecticâ,* p. 1216, in the *Latin* Version of Mr. STANLEY's *Philosophical History,* printed at *Leipsick* in 1712.

XLIV. (1) LACTANTIUS treats on this Point at large in his *Divine Institutes,* Books VI. Chap. XV, XVI, XVII. Let us add this Passage of CASSIODORE: *Non adfectibus moveri, sed secundum eos moveri, utile vel noxium.* GROTIUS.

2. *Ethic. Nicom* Lib. II. Cap. VI.

3. Whatever the learned GRONOVIUS may say on the Subject, these are really two different Virtues. ARISTOTLE might give the *Greek* Word Ἐλευθεριόστης a compound Idea, including both that Disposition, by which a Man is inclined to give freely, and that which directs him to a prudent Regulation of his Expences; but they are in Reality two different Dispositions, and two distinct Ideas. It is true, the more saving we are, the more we have to give away; but it does not therefore follow that *Frugality,* or a commendable Savingness, is only Part of *Liberality.* It is a very different Modification of the Soul, which indeed puts us in a Condition of performing more numerous and more considerable Acts of Liberality, on certain Occasions; but which is not therefore more a Part of Liberality itself, than Sobriety and a Love of Work are Parts of Chastity, because they are good Preservatives against Temptations to Impurity, and because those three Virtues, like most others, mutually assist one the other. Whoever takes a Delight in relieving the Indigent with his Substance, and actually does it on proper Occasions in a judicious manner, and as far as his present Circumstances permit, is so far truly liberal, even though for want of that Oeconomy, and Care of his Affairs, which compose the Character of a good Manager, he should be reduced to a Station, in which he is no longer able to give as much as would otherwise

*assigned*⁴ *to Veracity two Opposites between which there is not an equal Contrariety,* viz. *Boasting and false Modesty; and imposed the Name of Vice upon some Things, which either are not in Nature, or in themselves are not*

---

have been in his Power. We shall sometimes see Persons, who, in spite of all their Negligence, and after their superfluous Expences, have still something to give, and bestow it freely on all, whom they have an Opportunity of assisting; will any one deny such Men the Character of Liberality? In a Word, *Liberality,* and *Frugality,* are two different Virtues; but they are both to be equally acquired and cultivated, but the Want of the latter should hinder the Practice of the former, or at least confine the Exercise of it to too narrow a Compass. The Philosopher himself owns that *Liberality,* according to his Definition, consists more in giving and spending judiciously than in getting Debts in, and keeping one's Money. *The Use of Money seems to consist in Expences and Gifts; for receiving and keeping it are rather to be called Possession; so that it is the Business of a liberal Man rather to give to whom he ought to give, than to receive from those who are indebted to him, and not receive where it is not due.* Ethic. Nicomach. *Lib.* IV. *Cap.* I. Thus our Author rightly observes that ARISTOTLE was obliged to reduce the two Virtues under Consideration to one, in order to find two opposite Vices, one by Defect, the other by Excess; for *Avarice* is indeed opposite to *Liberality,* according to the common Ideas; but *Prodigality* is so far from being in itself contrary to Liberality, that it bears some Resemblance to that Virtue, and may have some Tendency toward promoting the Practice of it, which at least is not incompatible with it. If some prodigal Persons become niggardly, when the Necessitous are to be relieved, there are others, who give freely, and take a Pleasure in doing good, though they often do it without much Judgment, or a sufficient Regard to all Circumstances.

4. There are several Faults in this Distinction. I. The Philosopher does not distinguish the Virtue in question by any particular Name, but only calls the Person endowed with it ἀληθέντικος and φιλαλήθης; and understands by it that Disposition which directs a Man to love Truth, and commit no violence on it by his Actions, in Things indifferent, *i.e.* in regard to which we were otherwise under no Obligation to speak and act sincerely from the Laws of Fidelity and Justice; *for,* says he, *Sincerity in Dealings, and every thing that regards Justice and Injustice, relates to another Virtue.* Ethic. Nicom. *Lab.* IV. *Cap.* XIII. Thus he makes a faulty Distinction of two Sorts of *Sincerity,* and *Veracity,* one relating to Things indifferent, the other to those, which are obligatory; as if the Diversity of the Objects on which one and the same Virtue is employed, would privilege the Multiplication of that Virtue into as many different Species. 2. He no where treats of that other Sort of *Veracity* and *Sincerity,* which is only occasionally mentioned in this Place; and that which he here treats of is entirely reduced to indifferent Things; which relate only to the Person of him, who speaks or acts. But is it not possible for a Man to lie, feign, or dissemble in a thousand other indifferent things, on a Point of History, for Example, a Phaenomenon of Nature, an Event, on some Action or Quality of another Man, which does neither good nor harm to any one?: Strictly speaking, Boasting and Dissimulation, which ARISTOTLE gives us for the two opposite Extremities, are both of them contrary to *Truth* and *Sincerity* by Defect, and not by Excess. Both he who attributes to himself Qualities,

All Virtue has
not Vice in
Excess.

XLV. But that this Principle of Mediocrity, taken universally, is not rightly laid, appears from the Instance of Justice itself, whose Opposites, too much and too little, when he could not find in the Affections and their subsequent Actions, [1] *he sought for* Both *in the Things themselves* <xxxi> *about which*

Persons, Times, and Things require, are chargeable with Folly. They seem miserable, incapable of being affected, or revenging an Injury. To which he adds that *to suffer patiently in such Cases, and neglect the Defence of our Friends, is a Mark of a mean and servile Mind.* Ethic. Nicom. *Lib.* IV. *Cap.* XI. Hence it appears that ARISTOTLE considers the Disposition of all those in general, who command their Passion, when they have just Reason to be angry, as a Vice opposite to *Lenity* by Defect; and that he does not, as GRONOVIUS pretends, confine that Censure to the stupid and mean Patience of Buffoons and Parasites, who tamely submit to the greatest Affronts and Indignities, in Consideration of some paultry Advantage. But if we consider the Matter in itself, the Tranquillity of a Mind, free from Anger, is not a moral Defect. For supposing, what is very seldom to be found, a Man either naturally or by the Force of long Custom so hard to be moved, that he is seldom or never angry, he is thus very happy, as being secured from the Excesses of a blind Passion; nor will such a Man be less disposed, or less able to maintain his just Rights, and that of his Friends. On the contrary, by being Master of his Passions, and of a peaceable Disposition, he will be able to take more just Measures, and manage his Interest better than those, who are actuated by a Passion so hard to govern as Anger. Though Anger is not evil in its own Nature, and may be allowed to a certain Point, it is never absolutely necessary. We always may, and that with more Security, support our Dignity and maintain our Right, without being in a Passion. But it is evident that our Philosopher makes a Virtue of a moderate Degree of Anger, and a Desire of Revenge, the natural Effect of that Passion; which being in itself vitious, never allows Anger to be kept within due Bounds.

XLV. (1) He speaks in the following Manner of *Justice,* properly so called, which he terms *particular* or *private,* to distinguish it from *universal* or *general Justice,* including the Practice of all the Virtues which relate to our Neighbour. *This Distinction being made, it is evident that a just Action consists in observing a Medium between doing an Injury and receiving one. He that does an Injury, has more, and he who is injured, less than his due. Justice is a Mediocrity; not in the same manner as the Virtues already spoken of; but as the Medium is its Object, and Injustice includes the two Extremes. Justice therefore is a Disposition to act what is right with Choice and Deliberation, and to render every one his Due, both in our Dealings with others, and those which others have with one another; so that we do not take to ourselves more of what is agreeable and advantageous, or less of what is disagreeable and prejudicial than is our Due, leaving others too small a Share of the former, and too much of the latter, but observe a just Proportion here, as well as in the Distribution to be made among others. Injustice, on the contrary, is a Disposition of doing Wrong designedly, that is of giving each Person too much or too little of what is advantageous or prejudicial, without any regard to exact Proportion. Thus there is both Excess and Defect in Injustice, because it consists in giving too much and too little, that is, in appropriating to ones self too large a Share of what is simply advantageous, and taking too little of what is prejudicial; and observing the same unequal Distribution in regard to other Men, deviating from the Rule of Proportion sometimes on one Side, and sometimes on the other. The Extreme in unjust Actions, by way of Defect, is to receive an Injury; that by way of Excess, to do one.* Ethic. Nicom. *Book* V. *Chap.* IX. GRONOVIUS thinks ARISTOTLE sufficiently defended against our Author's Criticism, by saying, that whereas in other Virtues there is but one *Medium,* fixed by Geometrical Proportion, *Justice* observes sometimes the Medium of this *Geometrical Proportion,* and sometimes that of *Arithmetical Proportion;* so that here is only an Explication and Distinction of Terms, not a Transition from one kind of Thing to another. But the present Question does not turn on the Nature of the Medium, or the Proportion to be observed for determining it. The Subject, in which this Medium is placed, must be specified, so as to be found between two opposite Extremes of the same Thing, whatever Proportion is observed for determining it. According to ARISTOTLE, the Medium, in which the Essence of Moral Virtue consists, is planted, as one may say, in certain Sorts of *Passions* and *Actions,* not vicious in themselves, but which become such, by deviating from that Medium, and thus form two opposite Vices, one by Excess, the other by Defect. *Fear,* for Example, is a Passion not evil in its own Nature; too much Fear is *Timidity,* or *Cowardice;* too little is *Audacity,* or a rash Boldness: The just Medium is *Fortitude,* or rational Courage. Speaking, laughing, a regular Composure of the Face and exterior walking, standing still, in short all we say or do in Conversation are in themselves indifferent. Behaving ourselves in these Particulars so as to endeavour at pleasing every one, or certain Persons on all Occasions, is *Flattery:* on the contrary, to act as if we had no Concern for pleasing any one, is *Clownishness* or *Incivility;* the just Medium is *Civility,* or a *reasonable Complaisance.* See *Ethic. Nicom.* Book II. Chap. VI, VII. To return to *Justice,* the Virtue under Consideration, according to our Philosopher, its Medium consists in a certain *Equality,* an equal Distribution of Advantages and Disadvantages; for this is what he means by that *Equality* to which the Actions, whereby we practice Justice, relate. An exact Observation of this Equality, is the proper Employment of Justice, and what constitutes its Nature. A Disregard of this Equality, whether we take or give more or less than it requires, is a Vice opposite by Defect; the *more* or the *less* is not then in *Matter* of Justice, but in the Things about which it is employed: We do not observe this Equity too much or too little, we do not exceed the just Equality, but always fall short of it, even when we take or give too much, this is no more than a different manner of Inequality. Where then is the other opposite Extreme, which ought to consist in an excessive Concern for maintaining the Equality in question? It will not be the *Jus summum,* that rigorous Justice, which is called the Height of Injustice. (*Summum Jus, Summa Injuria,* CICERO *De Offic.* Lib. I. Cap. X. TERENCE *Heautont.* Act. IV. Scene V. Ver. 48.) For when a Man pushes his Demands as far as he may according to the Rigor of the Law, or presses the Terms of the Law too severely in pronouncing Sentence, it is a Defect of Equity: He offends against the Spirit of the Law, against that very Equality which the Law designs to establish, and introduces a real Inequality contrary to Equity, as ARISTOTLE himself makes appear, *Book* V. *Chap.* XIV. In a

Justice is conversant. Which very thing is in the first Place to leap from one kind of Thing to another, which he deservedly blames in others; and in the next Place, to receive less [2] *than one's Due may indeed happen to be a Vice, when the Circumstances of himself or his Family cannot allow of any Abatement; but certainly it cannot be repugnant to Justice, since it consists wholly in abstaining from that which is another Man's. Like to which Mistake is that of his not allowing* [3] *Adultery proceeding from Lust, and Murder from*

Word, our Philosopher was very sensible of the Lameness of his Principle of *Mediocrity,* when applied to this Virtue, and shews it plainly enough in the Words already quoted. He owns that Justice is a Mediocrity, not in the same manner as other Virtues are, but as a Medium is its Object, and Injustice only is its opposite Vice, which alone includes the two Extremes. This abundantly shews the Uselessness and Insufficiency of ARISTOTLE's Principle. Besides, it will appear, on a careful Examination of the Matter, that the Nature of all the Virtues may be accurately explained without having recourse to that Principle. See a Passage from Mr. GREW, an ingenious *Englishman,* quoted in my *Preface* to PUFENDORF, *p.* xciv, xcv. of the second Edition.

2. The learned GRONOVIUS calls this Chicanry; because, says he, this *less,* according to ARISTOTLE, relates to Hardships and Disadvantages, and not Profits and Advantages. But he is himself guilty of the Fault with which he charges our Author. GROTIUS has his Eye on the Definition of an Unjust Action, which occurs in the Close of the Passage quoted in the foregoing Note; according to which *receiving an Injury,* or *having less than one's due* is comprehended in the Idea of *Injustice,* as well *doing an Injury,* or *taking more than one's Due.* The Philosopher explains himself clearly in another Place, where he says, *It is evident that both receiving and doing an Injury are evil; for by the former a Man has less, and by the latter more than the Medium requires—But doing an Injury is the more culpable of the two, because done maliciously; whereas a Man receives an Injury without Malice, or an Inclination to Injustice.—So that receiving an Injury is in itself the less evil, though it may by Accident become a greater.* Ethic. Nicom. *Lib.* V. *Cap.* XV. *p.* 73. On reading this last Sentence, we immediately perceive the tacit Allusion which GROTIUS makes to it, while he explains it, and refutes the Philosopher's Opinion.

3. *Supposing one Man commits Adultery for Lucre's Sake, and receives his Reward; another is guilty of the same Crime out of a Motive of Lust, and pays for it. The latter seems rather sensual than covetous; whereas the former is unjust, but not sensual, because he acted with a View of Gain. Besides, every other unjust Action has always a Relation to some View. Thus Adultery relates to Intemperance; abandoning one's Comrade in an Engagement, to Cowardice: striking, to Anger. But when a Man gains by his Crime, it relates only to Injustice.* Ethic. Nicom. *Lib.* V. *Cap.* 4. We see here that the Philosopher does not sufficiently distinguish between the Principle or Motive, which induces a Man to commit an Injustice, and the unjust Action itself; for he pretends that one and the same Action, by which we invade another's Property, relates either to *universal Justice,* or to *particular Justice,* which is Justice properly so called, as the Agent is influenced

Anger, to belong properly to Injustice: Whereas the very Nature of Injustice
consists in nothing, else, but in the Violation of another's Rights; nor does it
signify, whether it proceeds from Avarice, or Lust, or Anger, or imprudent
Pity, or Ambition, which are usually the Sources of the greatest Injuries. For
to resist all Temptations of what Kind soever, and that for this only Reason,
viz. the preserving of Human Society inviolable, is indeed the proper Busi-
ness of Justice.

XLVI. *To return from this Digression, true indeed it is, that to some Virtues*
it happens, that they moderate the Affections, yet not for the Reason, that it

---

by a Motion of Sensuality, Cowardice, Anger, or by a formal Design of seizing on
what belongs to another, and taking more than one's Due. Now besides that this
formal Design is seldom found in Injustice, few Men doing an Injury merely for the
Sake of doing it, and without being actuated by some Passion, without which they
would rather choose to leave their Neighbour's Right untouched; besides this Consideration, I say, the Diversity of Principle may indeed make us offend at the same
Time both against Justice, properly so called, and against some other Virtue, relating
either to ourselves or others; but, this notwithstanding, every Action tending to the
Prejudice of another's Right, such as Adultery and Murder, will always be a real Injustice in itself; and all that GRONOVIUS has advanced in Defence of ARISTOTLE, is
nothing to the Purpose. He may, if he pleases, alledge the Example of *Mnester* the
Comedian, who was proof against all the Solicitations of *Messalina,* till the Emperor
Claudius, her Husband, commanded him to do whatever she should require of him.
This Comedian, according to our Commentator, did indeed commit an unjust Action, and an Act of Intemperance; but if we judge of his Conduct in a moral Manner,
he was neither chargeable with Injustice nor Intemperance. I own he was not so culpable, as if he had solicited *Messalina;* but even granting that a Husband can yield to
another Man his Right to his Wife's Body, this was by no means the Emperor's Intention, whose general Order to obey the Empress did not extend to this Action. So
that the Comedian ought still to have persisted in his Refusal, and by his Compliance
he certainly became even more guilty of Injustice than Intemperance; though this
single Action did not denominate him habitually unjust or intemperate, which is not
the present Question. As to Murder committed by a Motion of Anger, it is sufficiently
specified in the Passage here quoted, *striking,* relates *to Anger.* So that GRONOVIUS
had no Reason to say he knew not whence this was taken, and that it could only be
from *Eth. Nicom.* Lib. V. Cap. X. p. 68, in which he pretends our Author contradicts
himself; for he himself quotes and commends this very Passage, *Book* III. *Chap.* XI.
§ 4. But the Question there turns on a different Thing, *viz.* the Distinction between
unjust Actions committed maliciously, and such as are done without any premeditated Design.

is the proper and perpetual Office of all Virtue to do so; but because right

Consists often in the utmost we are capable of.

Reason, which Virtue always follows, [1] *prescribes a Measure to be followed in some Things; in others it excites us to the utmost we are capable of. We cannot, for instance,* [2] *serve God with too much Ardour; for the Crime of*

XLVI. (1) AGATHIAS makes a famous General speak thus: *Those Motions of the Soul, which by Nature prompt us to what is pure, good, eligible and our Duty, are to be indulged without Restraint. Those, which have a contrary Tendency, are not to be followed on all Occasions, but only so far as is consistent. Thus Prudence is in the Opinion of all Mankind a pure Good, without the least Mixture of Evil; and Anger, so far as animates us to Action, is commendable; but an Excess of that Passion is to be avoided as prejudicial.* In *Belisarius*'s Speech, *Book* V. (*Chap.* VII.) GROTIUS.

2. Here GRONOVIUS makes two Replies in Favour of ARISTOTLE. *First,* that the Philosopher is to be excused for not ranking *Piety, Faith, Hope* and *Charity* among the Moral Virtues, as they are known only by Revelation delivered to *Christians;* for ARISTOTLE, says he, as all the ancient Pagan Philosophers did, included the Worship of the Deity under *Magnificence. Ethic. Nicom.* Lib. IV. Cap. V. This Idea is followed by SALLUST, *Bell. Catilin.* Cap. IX. *In suppliciis Deorum magnifici,* &c. and by JUSTIN, *Book* XXIV. *Chap.* VI. speaking of the Presents offered in the Temple of *Delphos.* Now Excess in this Case is possible, as appears from that ancient Law: *Pietatem adhibento: opes amovento.* CICERO de Legib. Lib. II. Cap. VIII. and from the Reason assigned by LYCURGUS for a Law he had made for regulating the Expence of the Sacrifices. PLUT. *Apophthegm. Lacon. p.* 229. *Tom.* II. *Edit. Wech.* The other Answer is, that solid Piety indeed cannot be carried too far, and the same is to be said of all other Virtues, which, as such, are always found in the just Medium, to what Length soever they are carried; but that there may be Excess in exterior Actions, by which alone one Man can form a judgment of another's Sentiments. For how do we make it appear that we serve God? Is it not by frequenting Places of Worship; by praying on our Knees, bear-headed, and with our Hands joined and raised up to Heaven: By giving Alms, by contributing to the necessary Expences of the publick Worship; by observing Festivals; by reading and meditating on the Holy Scriptures; by abstaining from every thing, which we think contains any Impiety, and hindering the Commission of it, as much as in us lies, &c? Now who does not know that in each of these Particulars we may do more than God requires, and sound Reason allows? Thus, conformably to ARISTOTLE's Principle, *Piety* will certainly hold the middle Way between *Superstition,* which makes its Excess, and *Impiety* or *Atheism,* which is its Defect. This is our learned Commentator's Reasoning; on which I have two observations to make. First, it is no very easy Matter entirely to justify ARISTOTLE's Omission of so considerable a Virtue as *Piety;* and several judicious Authors have with good Reason blamed him for allowing Religion no Place in his System of Morality, as I have shown in my *Preface* to PUFENDORF, § 24. In Reality, as soon as we acknowledge a Deity, as he did, if we reason with ever so little Exactness, we must necessarily discover certain Duties in which we stand engaged to that Being. Thus we see several of the Pagan Philosophers have spoken very finely on that Subject. In vain does GRONOVIUS pretend that according to the Ideas of all the ancient Heathen Writers, the Worship of the Divinity

Superstition consists <xxxii> *not in serving God with too much Ardour, but in serving him perversely. Neither can we too much desire eternal Happiness, nor too much dread eternal Misery, nor too much hate Sin. It is therefore truly said of* Gellius, [3] *there are some Things whose Extent has no Bounds, and which are so much more commendable as they are carried to a higher Pitch.* Lactantius, [4] *after having discoursed largely on the Passions, says,* Wisdom does not consist in moderating them, but in regulating the Impressions of the Causes that produce them, for they are excited by external Objects. Neither ought a Restraint to be put principally upon them, because it is possible for them to be very weak in those who commit the greatest Crime, and to be very violent without leading to any Crime at all. *Our Purpose is to set always a high Value upon* Aristotle, *but so as to reserve to ourselves the same Liberty which he himself took with his Masters, for the Sake of finding Truth.*

XLVII. *Histories have a double Use with respect to the Subject we are upon,*   Histories. *for they supply us both with Examples* [1] *and Judgments. Examples, the better*

---

is included in that Virtue, which ARISTOTLE calls *Magnificence.* He had forgot that beautiful Passage of CICERO. *The best, the purest, most holy and most pious Worship of the Gods is always to honour them with Purity, Sincerity, and Integrity both of Mind and Words. For the Philosophers are not the only Persons, who have distinguished Piety from Superstition; our Ancestors have done the same.* De Nat. Deor. Lib. II. Cap. XXVIII. See also his Oration *Pro domo suâ, ad Pontifices,* Cap. XLI. with GRAEVIUS's Notes, and the Passages quoted from SENECA and EPICTETUS in my first Note on PUFENDORF, *Book* II. *Chap.* IV. § 3. It is evident from those and several other Authorities, which might easily be produced, that many of the wise Pagans made *Piety,* and the Worship of the Divinity consist principally in the interior Sentiments, and not in the exterior Acts of Devotion. Secondly, we must then find out two vicious Extremes in the interior Sentiments: It must be possible for a Man to entertain too exalted an Idea of God, respect and love him too much, be too submissive to his Will, *&c.* in all which there never can be any Excess. So that whatever they may say who are resolved to reconcile ARISTOTLE with Reason and good Sense at any Rate, it will still be certain that here, as in several other Virtues, there is no Medium, equally or almost equally removed from two opposite Extremes, in the same Kind of Things, which are the proper Object of Virtue.

3. *Noct. Attic.* Lib. IV. Cap. IX. at the End.

4. *Instit. Div.* Lib. VI. Cap. XVI. *Num. 7. Edit. Cellar.*

XLVII. (1) Which are to be used with much Caution. See the Author's Reflection on that Subject. *Book* I. *Chap.* III. § 5. *Num.* 6.

2. The *New* Testament.

LI. *The* New Testament *I use for this Purpose, that I may shew, what cannot be elsewhere learned, what is lawful for Christians to do; which Thing itself, I have notwithstanding, contrary to what most do, distinguished from the Law of Nature; as being fully assured, that in that most holy Law a greater Sanctity is enjoined us, than the meer Law of Nature in itself requires. Nor have I for all that omitted observing, what Things in it are rather* [1] *recommended to us than commanded, to the Intent we may know, that as to transgress the Commands is a Crime that renders us liable to be punished; so to aim at the highest Perfection, in what is but barely recommended, is the Part of a generous Mind, and that will not fail of a proportionable Reward.*

3. The Canons of Councils.

LII. *The Canons of Councils,* [1] *when they are just and reasonable, are Consequences drawn from the general Maxims of the Divine Law, fitted to particular Cases that happen: These likewise either shew what the Divine Law commands, or exhort us to what God recommends. And this is the Office of*

Preface to PUFENDORF, § 7. BOECLER accuses GROTIUS of not reading the Books of the Rabbies with sufficient Care and Attention, and confining himself almost wholly to *Moses* the Son of *Maimon.* But others, perhaps, will think he allows them too much Weight, and lost too much of his Time in perusing them, though the Strength of his Judgment preserved him from the Contagion.

LI. (1) See my nineteenth Note on *Book* I. *Chap.* II. § 9.

LII. (1) These Canons can be of no great Use to our Author's Design. First, because we have very little remaining of the Councils of the two or three first Centuries, when, according to him, the Doctrine of the Church must have been in its greatest Purity; and several of those that have come to our Hands, are either suppositious, falsified, or corrupted in several Places. Secondly, because, generally speaking, the Decisions of Councils commonly run either on speculative Points, or on Ecclesiastical Discipline. Thirdly, because the Councils not only were subject to Error, but have very often actually erred, even in such Things as were very easy. Our Author gives us to understand as much, when he says, *Synodici Canones, qui recti sunt;* i.e. *Those Synodical Canons which are just and reasonable.* So that, after all, Recourse must be had to the Scripture, which, when well interpreted, is the Touchstone for examining the Decisions of the Councils, in order to see whether they are just and reasonable. Lastly, it is well known that the Proceedings of most of the Councils were very irregular, and they were generally only so many Cabals of Men devoted to the Emperors, or some other prevailing Party; so that the least Concern on those Occasions was to furnish the Mind with necessary Knowledge, or bring an upright and Christian Heart to such Assemblies.

the true Christian Church, to deliver to us those Things that are delivered to her of God, and in the same Manner as they are delivered. But even the Customs [2] *likewise that <xxxiv> were received or commended amongst those antient Christians, who maintained the Dignity of so high a Title, have deservedly the Force of Canons. The next in Authority to these, are the Decisions of those who* [3] *were famous in their Times for their Christian Piety and Learning, and were not charged with any gross Error: For even what these assert with great Positiveness, as if they were certain of it, ought to have no little Weight in interpreting the Places that seem obscure in Holy Scripture, and that the more, by how much the more there are that consent in the same Thing, and the nearer they are to the Times in which the Church was*

4. The Manners and Customs of the first Christians.

5. Both the Writings and the Consent of the Fathers.

2. It is a great Mistake to imagine the Generality of the primitive Christians Men of a Piety and Probity exactly conformable to the Rules of the Gospel. See Mr. LE CLERC's *Ecclesiastical History,* Saec. I. Anno LVII. § 6, &c. But how good soever they might have been, their Judgment and Conduct cannot be here admitted as a Rule, in Matters not otherwise clearly and expresly decided in Scripture. The Extent of their Knowledge, and the Justness of their Judgment were not always equal to the Warmth of their Zeal, and the Integrity of their Heart. Every one knows that several of them entertained too high a Notion of the Necessity of Martyrdom, and thus prepossessed run to it with some Rashness. The Generality of them seemed to think it unlawful to engage in a War, to go to Law, to bear publick Offices, to take an Oath, to carry on Trade, to marry a second Time, or receive Interest for Money; all which it is impossible to prove evil in themselves, either from Reason or Scripture. Thus too great a Veneration for the uninlightened Simplicity of those first Ages seems to have induced our Author to give into the Distinction of *Evangelical Councils,* and *Precepts;* as appears from *Book* I. *Chap.* II. § 9. where my Remarks on that Subject may be seen at Length.

3. I have been pretty large in shewing, in my *Preface* on PUFENDORF, § 9, and 10, that the Fathers of the Church, of whom our Author speaks in this Place, are but indifferent Masters, and even bad Guides in Law and Morality. I have not changed my Opinion since Father CELLIER, a *Benedictin* Monk opposed me on that Head in a Book in 4*to,* entitled, *An Apology for the Morality of the Fathers of the Church,* published at *Paris* in 1718. I could easily make it appear that I have been so far from dealing in false Accusations, that I have advanced nothing on the Subject in Question, but what may be demonstrated either by the Confession of my Antagonist himself, or the Weakness of the Reasons he offers in Favour of these antient Doctors of the Church, whom he undertakes to justify at any Rate. Their Cause is not in very good Hands, since their Apologist, on one Side, does not understand the State of the Question; and on the other, distrusting the Force of his Proofs, calls in Invectives and abusive Language to his Assistance; not to mention an Infinity of trifling Things, nothing to the Purpose.

that not by a sort of tacit Agreement, but by Imitation of one another, or even by a casual Consent. But again, *those Things which really belong to the Law of Nations, they often handle promiscuously and indiscriminately with those that belong to the* Roman *Law, as appears from the* [6] *Title concerning* Captives *and* Postliminy. *Therefore we took Pains to have these distinguished.*

2. Those of the middle Age.   LV. *The second Class, being regardless of the Divine Law and ancient Histories, studied to determine all Controversies between Kings and Nations from the* Roman *Laws, to which they sometimes joined the Canon Law. But these were likewise hindered, by the Infelicity of their Times, from discovering the true Sense of those Laws, though otherwise sagacious enough in searching into the Nature of Equity: From whence it comes, that they often make very good Overtures for new Laws, at the same Time that they are but bad Interpreters of Laws already made. But they are then chiefly to be attended to, when they give Testimony to such a Custom, as now in our Time passes for a Law of Nations.*

3. Modern.   LVI. *The Professors of the third Class, confining themselves within the Limits of the* Roman *Law, and either never, or but lightly, meddling with this Law common to Princes and Nations, are scarce of any Use to us in our Subject.*
Spaniards.   *Amongst these,* Covarruvias [1] *and* Vasquez, [2] *two* Spaniards, *have joined Scholastick Subtilty with the Knowledge of Laws and Canons; so that they could not forbear treating of the Controversies between Nations and Kings; the one with a great deal of Freedom, the other more modestly, and not without some Exactness of Judgment. The* French *have with most Care at-*

6. See *Book* III. *Chap.* IX.
LVI. (1) DIEGO COVARRUVIAS was born at *Toledo,* and was the first Professor of Canon Law at *Salamanca.* He enjoyed several publick Employments, and died Bishop of *Segovia* in 1577. His Works have been printed several Times, in two Volumes in *Folio.*
2. FERNANDO VASQUEZ, was Scholar to COVARRUVIAS. His *Controversiae Illustres* is the chief Piece used in this Work. It is divided into six Books, and has born more than one Impression. Our Author has some Quotations from his Book *De Successionibus & ultimis voluntatibus,* which makes three Volumes in *Folio.*

tempted to introduce History into the Study of Law, amongst whom Bodin, [3] *and* Hottoman [4] *are in great Esteem, the one for a continued Treatise, the other for some scattered Questions. Their Decisions and Reasons will often furnish us with Matter for the Search of Truth.*

LVII. *In this whole Work there were three Things that I chiefly proposed to myself; to render the Reasons of my Decisions as evident as possible, to dispose the Matters to be treated of into a regular Method, and to distinguish clearly those Things which might appear to be the same, but were not.*

VII. The Design and Order observed through the whole Work explained.

LVIII. *I have forborn meddling with those Things that are of a quite different Subject, as the giving Rules about what it may be profitable or advantageous for us to do: For they properly belong to the Art of Politicks,* [1] *which* Aristotle *rightly so handled by itself, that he mixed nothing foreign with it:* Bodin *on the contrary has confounded it with that which is the Subject of this Treatise. Yet in some Places I have made mention of the useful, but by the by, and to distinguish it more clearly from a Question of the just.*

LIX. *He will do me wrong whoever shall think that I had Regard to any Controversies of the present Age, either already risen, or that can be foreseen*

---

3. JOHN BODIN, a Lawyer of *Anjou,* died in 1585. The Work here meant by our Author, is his famous Treatise *of the Commonwealth,* which is extant both in *Latin* and *French;* but the *Latin* Edition is the better and more compleat. That which I make use of is printed at *Francfort* in 1622.

4. FRANCIS HOTMAN, a Native of *Paris,* and descended from a *Silesian* Family, died at *Basil* in 1590, after having written a great Number of Books. His *Quaestiones Illustres,* the Treatise here meant, appeared in 1573.

LVIII. (1) Good Policy ought to authorize nothing against the invariable Rules of Justice; and that of the *Machiavellians,* which makes the Advantage of the State, or of those who rule it, the only Principle, is false and abominable. However, the *Just* and the *Useful* are really two different Things, even in Politicks; as will be easily comprehended by one single Example taken from the Matter of the Work before us. Before engaging in a War, it is above all Things necessary, that a just Cause should appear for so doing. But how good soever the Reasons for such a Step may be, if Circumstances do not allow of taking Arms, without acting to the Prejudice of the Publick Good, if there is Danger of losing as much as, or even more than will be gained, it would then be contrary to good Policy.

to arise. For I profess truly, that as Mathematicians consider Figures ab-stracted from Bodies, so I, in treating of Right, have withdrawn my Mind from all particular Facts.

A concise way of speaking.

LX. *As to the Style, I was not willing, by joining a Multitude of Words with a Multitude of Things to be treated of, to create a Distaste in the Reader, whose Advantage I consulted. I have therefore followed, as much as I could, a concise way of speaking, as convenient for such as undertake to instruct; that so, they who are employed in publick Affairs, may, as at one View, see, both what Kinds of Controversies usually arise, and also the Principles by which they may be* <xxxvi> *decided; which being known, it will be easy to suit the Discourse to the Subject Matter, and enlarge upon it as much as they please.*

The very Words of Authors quoted.

LXI. *I have sometimes quoted the very Words of the ancient Writers, when they were such as seemed to be expressed, either with a singular Force or Elegancy; which I have done sometimes in regard to* Greek *Authors, espe-cially when either the Sentence was short, or the Beauty of it such as I could not hope to equal in a Translation; which notwithstanding I have always subjoined, for the Use of those who have not learned the* Greek *Language.*

The Liberty of judging left to the Reader.

LXII. *And now, whatever Liberty I have taken in judging of the Opinions and Writings of others, I desire and beseech all those, into whose Hands this Treatise shall come, to take the same with me. They shall no sooner admonish me of my Mistakes, than I shall follow their Admonitions. And moreover, if I have said any thing contrary either to Piety, or to good Manners, or to Holy Scripture, or to the Consent of the Christian Church, or to any Kind of Truth, let it be unsaid again.* <1>

Book I

What War is, and what Right is.

I. All [1] the Differences of those who do not acknowledge one common Civil Right, whereby they may and ought to be decided; such as are a multitude of People [2] that form no Community, or those that are Members of different Nations, whether [3] private Persons, or Kings, or other Powers invested with an Authority equal to that of Kings, as the Nobles of a State, or the Body of the People, in Republican Governments: All such Differences, I say, relate either to the Affairs of War, or Peace. But because War is undertaken for the Sake of Peace, and there is no Con-

I. *The Order of the Treatise.*

I. See PUFENDORF, *Law of Nature and Nations.* B. I. Chap. I. § 8. *Note* I.

2. Such were the antient *Patriarchs,* who lived in Tents, and travelled from Place to Place, without forming a Community or depending on any Government; though there were civil Societies already established in the World at that Time. The learned GRONOVIUS on this Place, alledges the Example of the *Aborigines,* the first Inhabitants of *Italy,* and of several People in *Africa; The* Aborigines, *a savage People, free and independent, without Laws or Government.* SALUST. Bell. Catil. Cap. VI. The Getulians *and* Libyans, *a rough and uncivilized Set of Men, were the first Inhabitants of* Africa . . . *they lived without any Government or Laws, or the least Measures of Discipline among them.* Idem Bell. Jugurth. Cap. XXI. Edit. Wass. *They* (the remote Inhabitants of *Cyrenaica*) *being scattered about the Country in Families, and living under the Direction of no Law, had no common Regulations.* POMPONIUS MELA, Lib. I. Cap. VIII. Num. II. Edit. Voss. We find even at this Day amongst the *Arabians,* and *Africans* several Nations of *Savages,* and *Vagrants,* without Laws, Magistrates or any Form of Government.

3. See *B.* II. *Chap.* XI. § I. *Num.* 5.

troversy from whence War may not arise, all such Quarrels, as commonly happen, will properly be treated under the Head of the Right of War; and then War itself will lead us to Peace, as to its End and Purpose.

II. The Defini-
tion of War,
and the Origi-
nal of the
Word (bellum).

II. 1. Being then to treat of the RIGHT OF WAR, we must consider what that *War* is which we are to treat of, and what the *Right* is which we search for. *Cicero* [4] defines WAR *a Dispute by force.* But Custom has so prevailed, that [5] not the <2> Act of Hostility, but the State and Situation of the contending Parties, now goes by that Name; so that War is the State or Situation of those (considered [6] in that Respect) who dispute by Force of Arms. Which general Acceptation of the Word comprehends

4. II. *For since there are two Ways of disputing Things, one by Debate, the other by Force,* &c. De Offic. Lib. I. Cap. XI. See PUFENDORF. *B.* V. *Chap.* XIII. where he treats of other Ways of deciding Differences in the independent State of Nature.

5. PHILO the Jew considers as Enemies *not only such as actually attack us by Sea or by Land, but also those who make Preparations for either, those who erect Batteries against our Ports, or Walls, though no Battle is given.* De Specialib. *Lib.* II. *p.* 790. *Edit. Paris.* SERVIUS, on Verse 545, of the first Book of the *Eneid.*

——— *Quo justior alter*
Nec pietate fuit, nec BELLO *major & armis.*

Makes this Remark. *This is not an idle Repetition; for the Word* Bellum, (War) *includes Counsels, and Measures, taken against the Enemy; that is a Skill in Military Affairs. Whereas the Word* Arma, (Arms) *is used only to express the very Act of employing Forces: thus the former relates to the Mind, the latter to the Body.* The same Commentator, on Verse 547. of B. VIII. says: Bellum *is the whole Time employ'd in making the necessary Preparations for fighting or in Acts of Hostility: and* Praelium *denotes an actual Engagement.* GROTIUS.

6. For not only those who are at War, stand in several different Relations to other Persons, who observe a Neutrality, by Vertue of which they do many Things that by no Means relate to a State of Hostility: but they also may and frequently do act towards each other, as if they were not Enemies; so that in such Cases the Use of Force, and the Laws of War are suspended. This takes Place when two Enemies enter into an Agreement, or Treaty; as the Author shews at large in the proper Place. GRONOVIUS, in a Note on this Place, and HUBER *De jure Civitatis,* Lib. III. Sect. IV. Cap. IV. §. 2. allow of no Difference in the Main between CICERO's Definition, and that given by our Author. It is sufficient however, if the latter is more clear and extensive than the former. OBRECHT, in his Dissertation *De ratione Belli* (which is the eighth in the Collection published in 1704.) has defended our Author's Definition against the mistaken Criticisms of some Commentators.

all the kinds of War of which we shall hereafter treat, not even excluding single Combats, which being really ancienter than Publick Wars, and undoubtedly of the same Nature, may therefore well have one and the same Name. This agrees very well with the Etymology of the Word; for the *Latin* Word *Bellum* (*War*) comes from the old Word *Duellum* (*a Duel*) as *Bonus* from *Duonus,* and *Bis* from *Duis.* Now *Duellum* was derived from *Duo,* and thereby implied a Difference between *two* Persons, in the same Sense as we term Peace *Unity* (from *Unitas*) for a contrary Reason. So the [7] *Greek* Word Πόλεμος, commonly used to signify *War,* expresses in its Original an Idea of Multitude. The ancient *Greeks* likewise called it Λύη, which imports a *Disunion* of Minds; just as by the Term Δύη, they meant the *Dissolution* of the Parts of the Body.

2. Neither [8] does the Use of the Word (*War*) contradict this larger Acceptation. For tho' sometimes we only apply it to signify a Publick

7. Our Author, giving the Etymology of πόλεμος, derives it from πολυς; while others search elsewhere for the Origin of that Word; nor are we to be surprised at this. The Country of Etymologies is of a very large Extent, and affords great Numbers of different Roads, where each Man may walk at his Ease. However, in Complaisance to those who delight in such Enquiries, and for the Sake of clearing up our Author's Meaning, we must say something on the last Words of this Paragraph, which stand thus in the Original: *Veteribus etiam* λύη *dissolutione, quomodo & corporis dissolutio* δύη. Here the Commentators are silent, not excepting GRONOVIUS, a Critic by Profession; who only explains δύη by other *Greek* Words, signifying *any Sort of Unhappiness.* But this neither shews the Reason of our Author's Etymology, nor his Application of it. At first sight it might be imagined that the Text is faulty; and I know some have been of Opinion, that λύη ought to be repeated in this Place; but we find δύη in all the Editions of this Work; and I firmly believe I have found out what our Author Means, and what induced him to propose the Etymology of this Word, which he tacitly derives from δύω. He took δύη in the Sense which some Lexicographers give to λύπη, *dolor;* and at the same Time was thinking of PLATO's Etymology of λύπη, *Pain,* which he derives from λύω, *to dissolve; because,* says he, *when we suffer Pain, the Body suffers a Dissolution;* in Cratylo, p. 419. Vol. I. *Edit. H. Steph.* Our Author in Imitation of that ancient Philosopher, derives δύη from δύω for the same Reason; for on a Separation of the Parts of the Body, it follows that those which before appear'd only as one continued whole, by their Union, become *more than one.* The Principles of the old Philosophy, in which our Author was educated, helped him moreover to form this Etymology; for we know that according to those Principles, *Pain* is caused by a *Dissolution* of Continuity.

8. See, for Example, HORACE *B.* I. *Sat.* III. v. 107. and TERENCE *Eunuch.* Act. I. Scen. I. v. 16.

Quarrel, this is no Objection at all, since 'tis certain, that the more eminent [9] *Species* does often peculiarly assume the Name of its *Genus*. We do not include *Justice* in the Definition of War, because it is the Design of this Treatise to examine, whether any War be just, and what War may be so called. But we must distinguish that which is in Question, from that *concerning* which the Question is proposed.

III. *Right, as it is attributed to Action, described, and divided into that of Governors and governed, and that of Equals.* III. 1. Since we intitle this Treatise *Of the Rights of War,* we design first to enquire (as I said before) whether any War be just; and then what is just in that War? For *Right* in this Place signifies meerly *that which is just,* and that too rather in a negative than a positive Sense. So that *the Right of War* is properly *that which may be done without Injustice* with Regard to an *Enemy.* Now that is unjust which is repugnant to the Nature of a Society of reasonable Creatures. So *Cicero* says, it is unnatural to take from another to enrich one's self; which he proves thus, because, [10] if *every one were to do so, all Human Society and* Intercourse *must necessarily be dis-<3>solved. Florentinus* [11] declares, that *it is a villainous Act for one Man to lay an Ambush for another, because Nature has founded a kind* of Relation between us. And *Seneca* [12] observes, *As all the Members of the Human Body agree among themselves, because on the Preservation of each depends the Welfare of the Whole, so should Men favour one another, since they are born for Society, which* [13] *cannot subsist but by a mutual Love and Defence of the Parts.*

2. But as in Societies, some are equal, as those of *Brothers, Citizens, Friends and Allies.* And others unequal, καθ' ὑπεροχὴν, [14] *by Preemi-*

---

9. The Author gives Instances of this *B.* II. *Chap.* XVI. § 9.

10. III. *De Officiis. Lib.* III. *Cap.* V.

11. I have quoted this Law in my first Note on § 14. of the Preliminary Discourse.

12. *De Ira. Lib.* II. *Cap.* XXXI.

13. In *Ep.* XLVIII. he says thus: *We ought to observe carefully and religiously the Laws of this Society, which unite us all together, and teach us that there is a Law common to all Mankind.* The Reader may likewise see what S. CHRYSOSTOM says on this Subject on 1 *Cor.* Chap. XI. v. I. GROTIUS.

14. Καθ' ὑπεροχὴν. But the Philosopher makes this Distinction with Regard to Friendship, which is the Bond of Societies. *The Friendships already mention'd therefore, are founded on Equality. . . . But there is another Sort of Friendship, established on Pre-*

nence, as *Aristotle* terms it; as that of *Parents* and *Children, Masters* and *Servants, King* and *Subject,* [15] God and Man: So that which is *just* takes Place either among Equals, or amongst People whereof some are Governors and others governed, considered [16] as such. The latter, in my Opinion, may be called the [a] *Right of Superiority,* and the former the [b] *Right of Equality.*

[a] *Jus Rectorium.*
[b] *Jus Equatorium.*

---

eminence, such as that between Father and Son, the Elder and the Younger, Husband and Wife, and between every Prince and his Subjects. Ethic. Nicom. B. VIII. Chap. VI. VII.

15. Concerning this Society, see PHILO the Jew, on these Words ἐξένηψε Νῶε *Noah awaked (from his Wine)* p. 281, 282. *Edit. Paris.* PLUTARCH also has something on the same Subject in his Life of *Numa.* p. 62. *Edit. Wech.* Vol. I. GROTIUS.

I am surprised that our Author has not quoted the following remarkable Passage of CICERO, which is much more express, and more to his Purpose than those, to which he refers us. *Since therefore nothing is more excellent than Reason, which is common to God and Man, the first rational Society is between God and Man. For where there is a Participation of Reason, there is also a mutual Participation of right Reason. Now this being a Law, we are to conclude a Society between the Gods and Men founded on Law. Farther, where there is one common Law, there is likewise a common Right; and those who hold these in common, are to be esteem'd, as it were, fellow-citizens.* De Legib. *Lib.* I. *Cap.* VII. But, properly speaking, there is no *Law,* or *Right* common to God and Man. See PUFENDORF *B.* II. § 3. and *Chap.* III. § 5, 6. As also Mr. THOMASIUS's Dissertation call'd, *Philosophia Juris, de Obligat. & Action.* which is the third in the Collection printed at *Leipsic.* Cap. I. § 8, &c.

16. This Restriction is to be carefully observed. For, as ZIEGLER very well remarks on this Place, in all Dealings between a Superior and an Inferior, independently of the Relation of Superiority, the *Right of Equality* takes Place, as amongst Equals; thus, for Example, Contracts between a Prince and one of his Subjects require no other Rules than those which ought to be observed between two private Persons. When a Merchant has sold his Goods to his King, the King is as much obliged to pay for them, on the Terms, and at the Time agreed on, as the meanest Purchaser. To which I add, that there are some Cases, wherein a Superior becomes in certain Respects the Inferior; and that then the Right of Superiority is changed in Regard to the same Persons, according to the Nature of the Things. Thus a Magistrate is bound to honour his Parents, and consequently to submit to their Will to a certain Degree, whenever the Administration of publick Affairs is not concern'd; but, in the Character of Magistrate, he is to have no Regard for the Will of his Parents, but may even command them. See *B.* II. *Chap.* V. § 6. *Note* I.

IV. *Right taken for Quality divided into Faculty, and Aptitude or Fitness.* IV. There is another Signification of the Word *Right* different from this, but yet arising from it, which relates directly to the *Person:* In which Sense *Right* is [17] a *moral Quality* annexed to the Person, *enabling him to have, or do, something justly.* I say, *annexed to the Person,* tho' this Quality sometimes follows the things, as [18] *Services of Lands,* which are called *real Rights, in Opposition to Rights,* [19] *meerly personal,* not because the first are not annexed to the Person, as well as the last, but because they are annexed only to him [20] who possesses such or such a Thing. This moral Quality when [21] perfect, is called by us a *Faculty;* when imperfect, *an Aptitude:* The former answers to the *Act,* and the latter to the *Power,* when we speak of natural Things.

V. *Faculty strictly taken divided into Power, Property, and Credit.* V. Civilians call a *Faculty* that Right which a Man has to his [22] *own;* but we shall hereafter call it a *Right properly, and strictly taken.* Under which are contain-<4>ed, 1. A Power either over our selves, which is term'd [23] *Liberty;* or over others, such as that of a *Father over his Children,* or a

17. IV. See Pufendorf, *B.* I. *Chap.* I. § 19, 20.

18. See the same Author, *B.* IV. *Chap.* VIII.

19. Such, for Example, is the Power of a Father over his Child, the Right of a Husband over his Wife, the *Usufructuary* Right and the Right of demanding the Performance of a Promise, by which a Man has personally engaged himself, &c.

20. Thus the Right of *Passage,* belonging to the Proprietor of a Country House in the Neighbourhood, is inherent only in the Possessor of the said House, and is transmitted to all, who shall possess the same, till that Right is extinct.

21. *Perfect Right,* is that which we may assert by Force, and the Violation of which is a *Wrong* properly so called. Whence it is easy to judge what is *Imperfect Right.* See Pufendorf, *B.* I. *Chap.* I. § 7. and our Author, *B.* II. *Chap.* XXII. § 16.

22. V. As when we say, *Suum cuique tribuendum est,* we must give every Man his own.

23. Hence the *Roman* Lawyers very well called this Liberty *Facultas.* Grotius. This Definition occurs twice in the Body of the Law: *Libertas est naturalis Facultas ejus, quod cuique facere libet, nisi quid Vi, aut Jure, prohibetur.* Digest. *Lib.* I. *Tit.* V. *De statu Hominum.* Leg. V. and Instit. *Lib.* I. *Tit.* III. *De Jure Personarum,* § 1. In order to understand it thoroughly, it will be proper to read Mr. Noodt's excellent Commentary on the first Part of the *Pandects,* p. 29. See Pufendorf's Remark on the Manner, how this natural Power of Man over himself is to be understood. *B.* I. *Chap.* I. § 19.

Lord over his Slave. 2. [24] Property, which is either *compleat,* [25] or *imperfect.* The last obtains in the Case [26] *of Farms,* for Instance, or *Pledges.* 3. The *Faculty of demanding what is due,* and to this [27] *answers the Obligation of rendering what is owing.*

24. The Scholiast on HORACE says the Word *Jus* is taken for *Property* or a *Right* to a Thing. *Jus pro Dominio.* GROTIUS.

Our Author probably had the following Passage in View:

Permutet Dominos, & cedat in altera Jura.
Lib. II. Ep. II. v. 174.

On which the Scholiast says: *In altera Jura,* id est, *in alterius Dominium.*

25. See PUFENDORF. B. IV. Ch. IV. § 2.

26. *Ut Ususfructus, Jus Pignoris,* says our Author. As these Words stand, they insinuate that the *Usufructuary,* and the *Creditor* have a Sort of Right of Property, though imperfect, the former to the Goods in his Possession by vertue of his Tenure, the latter to the Thing pledged in his Hands for Security of the Debt. But, if we reason conformably to the Ideas of the Law of Nature, neither of them has any such Right, of Property, properly so call'd. The whole Matter is, that the Enjoyment of the Goods by the *Usufructuary,* till the Time of the Tenure is expired; and the Detention of the Pledge by the Creditor till he is pay'd, renders the Property imperfect, of which the Master of the said Things, who remains solely such, has not all the Profits, or full Exercise, during that Time. But our Author had the Niceties of the *Roman* Law in View, which allows an *Usufructuary* Creditor, *&c.* a real Action for recovering the Possession of another Man's Goods, in the same Manner as if they were the real Proprietors of them; and thus they are often considered as such, and the Right to them near to that of Property: *Jus dominio proximum,* say the Interpreters.

27. *Creditum: Debitum.* Short, and very proper Expressions, taken from the *Roman* Law. See what I have said on PUFENDORF *B.* I. *Chap.* I. § 20. *Note* 3. of the second Edition: and *B.* V. *Chap.* XI. § I. *Note* 5. The learned GRONOVIUS, without Reason, restrains the Terms in Question to Contracts of Loan, properly so called. It is surprising, that he did not observe, that our Author here imitates the Language of the *Roman* Lawyers; and the more so, because some other Commentators, much less skill'd in Criticism, have perceived this Allusion. In my Opinion it may be affirm'd, without the least Hesitation, that by the Word *Creditum,* we are here to understand, not only the Right a Man hath to demand what is due to him by Vertue of some Contract, Bargain, Promise, or Law; but also the Right we have to require Satisfaction for any Damage or Injury received; all which is included in the Idea affix'd to that Word by the *Roman* Lawyers. CREDITORUM *Appellatione non hi tantum accipiuntur, qui pecuniam crediderunt, sed omnes, quibus ex qualibet causâ debetur, ut si cui ex empto, vel ex locato, vel ex alio ullo debetur: Sed etsi ex delicto debeatur, mihi videtur Creditoris loco accipi.* DIGEST. *Lib.* I. *Tit.* XVI. *De verborum, & rerum signif.* Leg. XI, XII. See *B.* II. *Chap.* I. § 2. and *Chap.* XVII. § I. I believe our Author goes still farther, and

VI. *Another*
Division of
Faculty into
private and
eminent.

VI. *Right strictly taken* is again of two Sorts, either *private* and *inferior,* [28] which tends to the particular Advantage of each Individual: Or *eminent* and *superior,* such as a Community has over the Persons and Estates of all its Members for the common Benefit, and therefore it [29] excells the former. Thus a regal Power is above [30] that of a *Father* and *Master;* a King has a [31] greater Right in the Goods of his Subjects for the publick

---

extends the Word *Creditum* to the Right of punishing, and that of *Debitum* to the Obligation of submitting to condign Punishment. I am induced to think so, because first the *Perfect Right,* to which the *Debitum & Creditum* in Question relate, answers to the *Law of Nature,* or *Natural Right,* properly so called, of which the Author has spoken in his preliminary Discourse, § 8. Now one of the general Rules of that Law is, that *those who violate its Maxims, deserve to be punished.* See what I have said on § 10, *Note 7.* It is very probable therefore, that our Author, while he was enumerating the several Things which may be required in Rigour, would not forget the Punishment of Criminals. *Secondly,* because he elsewhere actually ranks *Debitum ex poena,* or *poenale* among those things, which we may demand of another in Rigour. *B.* III. *Chap.* XIII. § 1, 2. and makes a Right to punish belong to *Justitia expletrix,* which is the Matter of *Perfect Right.* B. II. Chap. XX. § 12.

28. VI. This takes in all those Rights, natural or acquired, with which each Man is invested, independently of the Relation of a Citizen, or Member of the State. The Author produces Examples of this kind which are sufficient for making the Matter clear and intelligible. See what he says concerning Promises, *B.* II. *Chap.* XI. § 8. and *Chap.* XIII. § 20.

29. Because the Design and Good of civil Society necessarily require, that the natural and acquired Rights of each Member should admit of Limitation several Ways and to a certain Degree by the Authority of him or them, in whose Hands the sovereign Authority is lodged.

30. So that a Subject ought to obey his Prince preferably to his Father and his Master. And the Prince may allow a Father and a Master more or less Power over their Children, and Slaves, as he shall judge most conducive to the Public Good. See *B.* II. *Chap.* V. § 7, and 28.

31. This is the Observation of PHILO the *Jew,* who says: *Certainly Silver, Gold, and all other valuable Things, which Subjects treasure up, belong more to those who govern, than to those in Possession of them,* περὶ φυτουργίας (of *Noah's* Planting.) p. 222. *Edit. Paris.* PLINY the younger declares, that a Prince, *to whom the Possessions of every one of his Subjects belong, is as rich as all of them together.* Paneg. Cap. XVII. And a little after: *What does* CESAR see, that is not *his own?* See JOHN OF SALISBURY in his *Polycrat.* Lib. IV. Cap. I. p. 335. *Edit. Lugd.* 1639. GROTIUS.

The latter Passage of PLINY is not rightly quoted or applied, for the Panegyrist says the direct contrary, in commendation of *Trajan,* Est quod *Caesar* non suum videat, &c. *That Caesar sees something which is not his own; and that the Prince's Empire is now larger than his Patrimony.* Cap L. *Num.* 3. *Edit. Cellar.* Besides, there is some-

Advantage, than the Proprietors themselves. And when <5> the Exigencies of the State require a Supply, every Man is more obliged to contribute towards it, than [32] to satisfy his Creditors.

VII. *Aristotle* calls *Aptitude* or *Capacity,* [1] ἀξίαν [2] *Worth,* or Merit: And *Michael* of *Ephesus* terms that which is called Equal or Right, according to that Merit, τὸ προσάρμοζον καὶ τὸ πρέπον, *Fit and Decent.*

VII. *What Aptitude is.*

---

what extravagant, or at least too figurative, in the Expressions of the antient Writers, quoted by our Author, as well as in those of the Moderns, who imitate them. For, strictly speaking, the Goods of each Subject belong no more to his own Sovereign than to a foreign Prince. The whole Truth of the Matter is, that in case of a pressing Necessity, the Sovereign may, for the publick Advantage, dispose of the Goods of his Subjects, even against their Will, in the same Manner as if they were his own. But he then acts, not as Proprietor of such Goods, but as Head of the Society, in favour of which every one of its Members is engaged, either expressly or tacitly, to make such a Sacrifice. See what is said, *B. I. Chap.* III. § 6. *Num.* 4. *B.* II. *Chap.* XIV. § 7 and *B.* III. *Chap.* XX. § 7.

32. And consequently, the Sovereign may discharge a Debtor from the Obligation of paying, either for a certain Time, or forever, if the publick Good requires it. We have an Example of this in LIVY, *Lib.* XXIII. *Cap.* XIV. *Num.* 3. which is here produced by GRONOVIUS. After the fatal Battle of *Cannae; Marcus Junius Pera,* the Dictator ordered publick Notice to be given, that *he would pardon all who had been guilty of capital Crimes, and exempt from Payment all such as were in Chains for Debt, if they would list under him.*

VII. (1) Ἀξία. The Philosopher uses this Word when he treats of *Distributive Justice,* by Vertue of which we are to give every one what is due to him, according to his Merit. *Ethic. Nicom. B.* V. *Chap.* VI. But I find that CICERO uses the *Latin* Word *Dignitas,* which answers to the *Greek* Ἀξία, in a large Sense, including both *perfect* and *imperfect Right:* His Words are, *Justitia est habitus animi, communi utilitate conservata,* SUAM *cuique tribuens* DIGNITATEM. De Invent. *Lib.* II. *Cap.* LIII. And the Author of a Treatise on Rhetorick, ascribed to that great Orator and Philosopher, makes Justice consist in rendering to every one his *due,* (*Jus*) according to his *Merit,* (*pro* DIGNITATE *cujusque*) Ad Heren. *Lib.* III. *Cap.* II. HUBER, in his Treatise *De Jure Civitatis,* and his *Praelect. in Institut. & in Pandect.* quotes these two Passages wrong, as if he had read *quae cuique* jus *suum &* dignitatem *tribuit;* and on the sole Authority of this false Quotation, he pretends that CICERO expresses *perfect Right* by the Term *Jus,* and *imperfect Right* by *Dignitas.*

2. CICERO has given us an Example of several Degrees of *Merit* and *Fitness,* which confer more or less of this *imperfect Right;* which I shall here set down, translated from the Author's Note on this Place.

But if there be any Dispute or Enquiry, to whom we are obliged to render most Service, let our Country and our Parents, to whom we stand most indebted, hold the first Rank.

VIII. 1. 'Tis expletive Justice, Justice properly and strictly taken, which respects the *Faculty,* or *perfect Right,* and is called by *Aristotle* συναλλακτικὴ, *Justice of Contracts,* but this does not give us an adequate Idea of that Sort of Justice. For, if I have a Right to demand Restitution of my Goods, which are in the Possession of another, it is not by vertue of any *Contract,* [1] and yet it is the Justice in question that gives me such a

---

Next to these are our Children, and our whole Family, who depend on us alone, and can have no other Refuge. In the next Place we must think of our Relations, with whom we live in a good Understanding, and whose Fortune is most commonly united with our own. The necessary Supports of Life are therefore principally due to those whom I have already mentioned. But living in Society, giving Advice, Conversation, Exhortations, Consolations, and sometimes even Reproofs, take Place chiefly in Friendship. De Offic. *Lib.* I. *Cap.* XVIII. See *B.* II. *Chap.* VII. § 9, 10. of this Treatise. SENECA, speaking of *Wills,* says, *We look out for Persons of the greatest Worth,* (or *Merit,* dignissimos) *to whom we may leave our Estates.* De Benef. *Lib.* IV. *Cap.* XI. See St. AUGUSTIN, *De Doctr. Christ.* Lib. I. Cap. XXVIII. and XXIX. GROTIUS.

VIII. (1) Our Author's Criticism in this Place, has been justly censured, for the Word συνάλλαγμα, according to ARISTOTLE's Sense of it, expresses all Dealings Men may have one with another, and in which any Inequality appears that ought to be redressed by the Exercise of the Species of Justice in question. The Philosopher, (*Ethic. Nicom.* Lib. V. Cap. V.) distinguishes these συναλλάγματα into *voluntary,* by which he understands *Contracts* properly so called, as those of *Sale, Loans, Bail, Trusts, Hiring, &c.* and *Involuntary,* under which he comprehends all Sorts of Damage and Injuries done to another; either clandestinely, or by open Violence; in short, what the *Roman* Lawyers call *Delictum,* and which the learned GRONOVIUS improperly compares to *Quasi contractus,* which, according to them, *Non ex maleficio substantiam capiunt* INSTITUT. *Lib.* III. *Tit.* XXVIII. The same Commentator (in order to shew, that the Example of a Person in possession of another Man's Goods may relate to ARISTOTLE's *Permutative Justice*) observes, that ever since the Establishment of Property, there has been a tacit Agreement among all Men, by which each of them is obliged to restore the Goods of another. This is a false Principle, laid down by our Author himself, *B.* II. *Chap.* X. § I. in which he has been followed by PUFENDORF, *B.* IV. *Chap.* XIII. § 3. I have confuted them both, in my Note on the Passage of the latter, here referred to. I am not therefore surprised that GRONOVIUS grounds his Argument on it; for besides that he had a better Talent at commenting on the Thoughts and Expressions of others, than at examining and considering Subjects of this Nature, he thus found an Argument *ad hominem,* against GROTIUS, in favour of his dear ARISTOTLE. But it is very strange that he has not added a Remark, very proper for supporting his Criticism, and the more so, as it depends on a grammatical Nicety, *viz.* that the Word συνάλλαγμα does not signify the Foundation of the Obligation arising from the Justice under Consideration, but only the Object or Matter on which this Sort of Justice is employed, which ARISTOTLE therefore calls, Δικαιοσύνη, or

Right. Wherefore he also calls it more properly ἐπανορ-<6>θωτικὴν, [2] *corrective* Justice. *Attributive Justice,* stiled by *Aristotle* διανεμητικὴ [3] *Distributive,* respects Aptitude or *imperfect Right,* the attendant of those Virtues [4] that are beneficial to others, as Liberality, Mercy, and prudent Administration of [5] Government. But whereas the same Philosopher

versant about Things common nor that about Things private.

Δίκαιον, τὸ ἐν τοῖς συναλλάγμασι διορθώτικον, *Lib.* V. *Cap.* V. and τὸ διορθώτικον, ὅ γίνεται ἐν τοῖς συναλλάγμασι καὶ τοῖς ἑκουσίοις καὶ τοῖς ἀκουσίοις *Cap.* VII. that is, *corrective Justice in Mans Dealings one with another,* or barely *corrective Justice,* a Term which Interpreters would have done well to preserve, as much more expressive of the Philosopher's Sense than that of *commutative Justice,* which conveys a very different Idea. Thus when our Author says, it is not by Vertue of a *Contract,* (ἐκ συναλλάγματος) that the Possessor of another Man's Goods is obliged to restore them, it makes nothing against ARISTOTLE, according to whose Principles, συνάλλαγμα is here a Detention of what belongs to another; but the Obligation of restoring, is founded on an Inequality subsisting to the Prejudice of the Proprietor, an Inequality which the Justice under Consideration requires to be redressed. To which it may be added, that ARISTOTLE's *Corrective* or *Permutative Justice,* does no more answer exactly to our Author's *Expletive Justice,* than the *Distributive Justice* of the former does to the *Attributive Justice* of the latter, and that there is a wide Difference between those two Distinctions, both in regard to their Foundation, and the Extent of each particular Member. But all this is of little Consequence in the Main, and it would be better to leave the Philosopher with his Division, which besides that it is very defective, is useless at present, as several Authors have observed. See PUFENDORF, *B.* I. *Chap.* VII. § 12. Mr. THOMASIUS's *Institutiones Juris Divini,* Lib. I. Cap. I. § 106: As also the *Principia Juris, secundum ordinem digestorum;* by Mr. WESTENBERG, Professor at *Franeker,* Lib. I. Tit. I. § 15, &c.

2. Ἐπανορθωτική *Ethic. Nicom.* Lib. V. Cap. VII. p. 65. *Edit. Paris.* Vol. II. Or, as ARISTOTLE more frequently calls it, Διορθωτική.

3. It is not the same Thing. See *Note* 1. on this Paragraph.

4. For the Justice in question regulates the Exercise of those Virtues, which consist in doing such Things in favour of others, as cannot in Rigour be demanded, and directs a proper Application of the Acts of those Virtues, by a prudent choice of Persons the most worthy, to feel the Effects of them. See the second *Note* on *Paragraph* 7th, and what has been said in the *Preliminary Discourse,* § 10, and the Notes of that Place; as also our Author, *B.* II. *Chap.* I. § 9. *Num.* 1.

5. The Author has here in view, chiefly the Distribution of Rewards and publick Employments; for tho' the Prince on such Occasions ought to prefer Persons of most Merit, and greatest Abilities, no private Person can in Rigour demand this Preference. See PUFENDORF, *B.* I. *Chap.* VII. § 11. So that *Catiline* made use of a very frivolous Pretence, in Justification of his Conspiracy, when he said, *Deprived of the Fruits of my Labour and Industry, I was not raised to a Post equal to my Merit. . . . I saw Men of no Worth promoted to Honours, and myself repulsed upon groundless Surmises.* SALLUST, *Bell. Catilin.* Cap. XXXVI. *Edit. Wass.*

2. Neither is that more true which some maintain, that *Attributive Justice* is exercised about Things belonging to the whole Community; and *Expletive* about Things belonging to private Persons. For on the contrary, if a Man would bequeath his Estate by Will, he does it commonly *by Attributive Justice;* and when the State repays out of the [11] publick Funds what some of the Citizens had advanced for the Service of the Publick, it only performs an Act of *Expletive Justice.* This Distinction *Cyrus* learnt of his Tutor: For when *Cyrus* had adjudged the lesser Coat to the lesser Boy, tho' it belonged to another Boy of a bigger size; and so on the other side gave his Coat, being the bigger, to that bigger Boy. His Tutor told him, ὅτι ὁπότε μὲν κατασταθείν τοῦ ἁρμόττοντος

---

it with the other, as he has rectified it; for they are still very different at the bottom, as will easily appear on a careful perusal of that great Philosopher's Moral Treatises.

11. I am inclined to think the Author here had in view a Passage of ARISTOTLE, where he says, that *Distributive Justice always follows Geometrical Proportion. For,* continues the Philosopher, *upon a Distribution of the Publick Money, it must be made in Proportion to what each has contributed.* Ethic. Nicom. *Lib.* V. *Cap.* VII. p. 62. I suppose the Philosopher designed to speak of the following Case. Several private Persons have furnished the State with Money for the Demands of the Publick, and that in different Sums; the proper Officers are inclined to reimburse them, but the Sum destined for that End, is not sufficient for the Payment of all the Creditors; so each receives in Proportion to what he lent. But this very Example may serve to shew, how little Justness there is in ARISTOTLE's Ideas. For, properly speaking, there is no Comparison between the Degree of the Merit of the Persons, and the Quantity of the Things, but only between what is advanced, and what is restored. If it be said that each Person deserves more or less to be reimbursed, as he had lent more or less, it may be easily shewn, that this Circumstance is but a very ambiguous Proof of more or less Merit; for it may, and often will happen, that those, who have furnished the largest Sums, have not lent so much in Proportion, as Persons of smaller Fortunes, who perhaps have very much streightened themselves to assist the Publick, whilst the former have suffered little or no Inconvenience, by depriving themselves for some Time of a Sum, very inconsiderable in comparison of what remained in their Hands. Now can it be doubted, that on this Supposition, they, who have expressed most Zeal for the publick Good, and have suffered most by promoting it, deserve to receive in Proportion to a larger Share of the Sum, which is not sufficient to discharge the whole Debt, than they whose Debt is in itself the most considerable? I reason here on the Principle established by our Lord JESUS CHRIST, in regard to Alms, in the Judgment he pronounces of a poor Widow's Charity, who gave only two small Pieces of Money for the Use of the Poor. MARK xii. 42, &c.

κριτὴς, &c. That [12] *had he been appointed Judge of what fitted each of them best, he ought to have done as he did: But since he was to determine whose Coat it was, his Business was to have considered* [13] *which had a just Title to it, whether he who took it away by Force, or he who made it, or bought it.* <8>

IX. There is also a third Sense of the Word *Right,* according to which it signifies the same Thing [1] as *Law,* when taken in its largest Extent, as

IX. *Right taken for a Rule or*

---

12. *Cyropaed.* Lib. I. Cap. III. § 14. *Edit. Oxon.*

13. See the same Writer, *Lib.* II. of the *Cyropaedia.* To the same Purpose God forbids the Judges of his People to *countenance a poor Man in his Cause, or respect the Person of the Poor,* in giving Judgment, EXOD. xxiii. 3. LEVIT. xix. 15. In truth, as PHILO the *Jew* observes, *the Merits of the Cause are to be considered in themselves, and abstractedly from any Regard to the contending Parties.* Lib. *De Judice,* p. 720. *Edit. Paris.* GROTIUS.

I do not find in the second Book of XENOPHON's *Cyropaedia,* to which our Author refers his Readers, any one Passage, that can relate to the Matter before us, but the following Reflection of *Cyrus.* One of that Prince's Favourites proposed to him, that all his Soldiers should not equally share the Booty taken from the Enemy, but that it should be divided according to each Man's respective Merit, and Behaviour in the Time of Action. *Cyrus* thought the Proposal reasonable, but was of Opinion, that the Consent of the whole Army should be first asked. "Where is the Necessity of such a Condescention? said *Chrysanthes.* "Is it not enough that you declare such is your Pleasure, and that the Distribution shall be made on that Foot? When you established Combats for the Prize, did not you at the same Time regulate each Person's Reward?" To which *Cyrus* replied, *The Case is not parallel; for I imagine the Soldiers will look on all the Plunder that shall be made, as their own Property; whereas they are persuaded that the general Command of the Army belongs to me, and perhaps is even my Birth-Right. So that I believe they think I commit no Injustice, to any one, when I dispose of the Charges in the Army.* Cap. II. §10, 11. *Edit. Oxon.*

IX. (1) In this Sense HORACE says,

JURA *inventa metu injusti fateare necesse est.*
     Lib. I. Sat. III. v. 3.

and

JURA *neget sibi nata.*
     Art. Poet. v. 122.

On which Words the Scholiast says, *Legum sit contemptor.* GROTIUS.

Law defined and divided into Natural and Voluntary. being *a Rule of* [2] *Moral Actions, obliging* [3] *us to that which is good and commendable.* I say, *obliging:* for [4] Counsels, and such other Precepts, which, however honest and reasonable they be, lay us under no Obligation, come not under this Notion of *Law,* or *Right.* As to *Permission,* it is not [5] properly speaking an Action of the Law, but a meer In-<9>

2. See PUFENDORF, *B.* I. *Chap.* V. Where he explains the Nature and Foundation of moral Actions.

3. The Author's Expression in this Place seems to insinuate, that the Law *obliges* by its self, and merely as it is a Rule; whereas, all Laws derive their Power of obliging from a *Superior,* who makes them; that is, from some Intelligent Being, who has a Right of imposing an indispensible Necessity of submitting to his Direction, on those whose Liberty he restrains. To which may be added, that the Author reduces the whole Effect of the Law to the *Obligation;* whereas *Permission* ought to be joined to it, which he without Reason excludes.

4. See PUFENDORF, *B.* I. *Chap.* VI. § 1.

5. I cannot be of our Author's Opinion in this Point. *Permission* is as real an Effect of the Law, taken in its utmost Extent, as the strongest and most indispensible *Obligation.* The Superior, who gives Being to the Law, has a Right of positively directing either all the Actions of those who depend on him, or at least, all those of a certain kind: In regard of all those Actions, he has a Power of imposing a Necessity of acting or not acting in a certain manner. But no Superior exercises his Authority so extensively; there is always a considerable Number of Things subject to his Direction, in which he leaves every one the Liberty of doing as he pleases. This is not a mere Inaction, or *Negation of Action,* as our Author pretends, but a real positive Act, though commonly tacit, by which the Superior or Legislator makes an Abatement of his Right. So that, as the Actions commanded or prohibited, are regulated positively by the Law, so far as it imposes an indispensible Necessity of doing the former, and forbearing the latter, the Actions permitted, are likewise positively regulated by the Law in their own Way, and according to their own Nature, so far as the Law either originally gives a Power of doing or not doing them at Pleasure, or confirms and leaves Men in Possession of a Liberty, which it might have taken away either entirely, or in Part. There is no manner of Necessity of an express Permission, which seldom takes place in Divine or Human Laws: The Silence of the Legislator sufficiently infers a positive Permission of whatever is neither enjoined nor prohibited. Thus when GOD, who alone can regulate all the Actions of Men, of what Nature soever they be, forbad the *Jews* the Use of certain Animals for Food, as he might, if he had pleased, [[have]] extended the Prohibition to several other Kinds, by his only forbidding some Particulars, he actually and positively allowed them the Liberty of eating or not eating all others. As to human Laws, either they turn on Things already commanded or prohibited in some manner by Divine Law, natural or revealed; and in that Case, they give as much as in them lies, a Permission of doing several other Things of that Kind, where they are silent; which is a necessary Consequence of Impunity: Or they relate

action, unless as it obliges every other Person not to hinder the doing of that, which the Law permits any one to do. I add moreover, that the Law obliges us *to that which is good and commendable,* not barely to that which is *just:* Because Right in this Sense does not belong to the Matter of Justice alone (such as I have before explained it) but also to that [6] of other

---

to Things otherwise indifferent in themselves; and then they of course permit whatever they do not forbid; there being an Infinity of Actions of such a Nature, that a Man invested with Authority may lay a Restraint on the Liberty of others, which the Law of Nature allows only so far as a lawful Superior does not think proper to bound it. In one Word, whoever fixes certain Limits, and declares no one shall be allowed to exceed them, does by that very Action express how far he grants Men Liberty to go, if they please. This Way of Reasoning is the more just, because, as our Author owns, the Permission which a Law gives to any one, lays an Obligation on others not to form any Obstacle to his acting, when he is disposed to do what the Law permits. Now this Obligation arises, and ought necessarily to arise from a Right inherent in him, to whom the Law gives a Liberty of acting as he pleases; for in all Obligations in which we stand engaged to others, there is some correspondent Right; and we have not a Right to require a Thing, because another is obliged to do it, but on the contrary, he is obliged to do it, because we have a Right to require it. Whence then arises this Right? It can certainly arise only from the Permission granted by the Law, a Permission, by vertue of which we are also empowered to resist those, who disturb us in the Enjoyment of this Right, and employ either the common Means of Justice, when we are in a Condition of having Recourse to the Protection of a proper Judge, or Force, if we have no other Way left of righting ourselves. In short, every one knows, that the Laws grant an express Permission, either to all such as depend on the Legislator, or only to some in Particular. From all which it appears, in my Opinion, that the Author had no Reason for excluding *Permission* from the general Idea of the *Law.* To which may be added what I have said on this Subject against PUFENDORF, who is of the same Opinion with GROTIUS, *B.* I. *Chap.* VI. § 15. *Note* 2. By way of Supplement for this Omission, and some others, I am of Opinion that *Law* should be defined as I have already defined it, in a Note on the Abridgment of *The Duties of a Man and a Citizen.* B. I. Chap. II. § 2. of the last Editions: *The Will of a Superior sufficiently notified in some manner or other, by which Will he directs either all the Actions in general of those who depend on him, or at least all those of a certain Kind, so that, in Regard to such Actions, he either imposes on them a Necessity of doing or not doing certain Things, or leaves them at Liberty to act or not act as they shall judge proper.*

6. We have an Example of this in a Law made by *Zaleucus,* inflicting a Penalty on those, who should drink Wine against the Physician's Orders. GROTIUS.

This severe Law made the Offence capital, if we may believe ELIAN, *Var. Hist.* Lib. II. Cap. XXXVII. See PUFENDORF, *B.* I. *Chap.* VI. § 4 in the Text and Notes. To which we may add what ELIAN says of the *Lacedemonians* and *Romans,* Lib. III. Cap. XXXIV. with the Note of the late Mr. PERIZONIUS.

Virtues; tho' otherwise, whatever is conformable to this Right, may also, in a larger Acceptation, be termed [7] *Just.* Of this Right, thus taken, the best Division is that of [8] *Aristotle,* into *Natural* and *Voluntary,* which he commonly calls *Lawful Right;* the Word *Law* being taken in [9] its stricter Sense: Sometimes also [10] an *Instituted Right.* We find the same Difference among the *Hebrews,* who when they speak distinctly, call the Natural Right מצות [11] Precepts, and the Voluntary Right חקים Statutes; the former of which the *Septuagint* call δικαιώματα, and the latter ἐντολὰς.

X. The Law of Nature defined,

X. 1. NATURAL RIGHT *is the Rule and Dictate of* [1] *Right Reason, shewing the Moral Deformity or Moral Necessity there is in any Act, according to its*

7. Thus we say: *It is just to acknowledge Favours, to have Compassion for the Poor, to be liberal to those who want our Assistance, to take a prudent Care of our Health and Fortune,* &c.

8. In his *Ethic. Nicom.* Lib. V. Cap. X. where he makes a Distinction between Δίκαιον Φυσικὸν, and Δίκαιον νομικὸν, as making part of what he calls Δίκαιον πολιτικὸν *Civil Law.* So that his Division is not exactly the same with that of our Author. See my Preface to PUFENDORF, § 24. p. 97, 98. of the second Edition.

9. That is, for a Constitution absolutely depending on the Will of the Legislator.

10. Τὸ ἐν τάξει. The Philosopher makes use of this Expression, when speaking of Injustice. Ἄδικον μὲν γάρ ἐστι τῇ φύσει, ἢ τάξει. *Ethic. Nicom.* Lib. V. Cap. X. p. 68. Vol. II. *Edit. Paris.*

11. Thus *Maimonides,* in his *Guide to the Doubtful,* Lib. III. Cap. XXVI. GROTIUS. See SELDEN, who also adopts this Rabbinical Remark, in his Treatise, *De Jure Nat. & Gent. secundum Disciplinam Hebraeorum,* Lib. I. Cap. X. p. 119, 120. But our Author here gives us to understand, that this Distinction is not always observed, as he expressly acknowledges in his Commentary on St. LUKE i. 6. See Mr. LE CLERC, on *Genesis* xxvi. 5. and in his Additions to Dr. HAMMOND's Notes on *Rom.* viii. 4.

X. (1) PHILO the *Jew,* in his Treatise, where he undertakes to prove that every good Man is free, speaks thus, *Right Reason is an unerring Law, not corruptible or lifeless, written by this or that mortal Man, on Papers or inanimate Pillars, but incorruptible, and engraved by an immortal Nature on an immortal Mind,* p. 871. Edit. Paris. *Will you enquire where the Law of GOD is?* says TERTULLIAN, *when you have a common Law exposed to every one's View, and written on the Tables of Nature?* De Coronâ Militis, *Cap.* VI. The Emperor MARCUS ANTONINUS declares, *The End to be proposed by all rational Creatures, is to follow the Reason and Laws of the most antient Commonwealth,* Lib. II. § 16. See a Fragment of CICERO's Treatise *De Republicâ,* Lib. III. quoted by LACTANTIUS, *Lib.* VI. *Cap.* VIII. St. CHRYSOSTOM has several fine Thoughts on this Subject, in his twelfth and thirteenth Homilies *On the Statues.* What THOMAS AQUINAS says, *Secunda Secundae,* I.VII. 2. and SCOTUS, III. *Dist.* 37. is not unworthy our Notice. GROTIUS.

Suitableness or Unsuitableness to a reasonable Nature, [2] and consequently, that such an Act is either forbid or commanded by GOD, the Author of Nature.

2. The Actions upon which such a Dictate is given, are in themselves either [3] Obligatory or Unlawful, and must, consequently, be understood

divided, and distinguished from such as are not properly called so.

2. Our Annotator adds the Words *ac Sociali, & Sociable* in the Text of his *Latin* Edition, because his Author expresses himself in the same Manner, § 12. *Num.* 1. and in the following Chapter, § 1. *Num.* 3. He thinks it probable, that the Transcriber or Printer omitted those two Words; and that the Author overlooked the Omission, as he has done in several other Places.

3. *Actus debiti, aut illiciti per se.* The Author here supposes we should be under an Obligation of doing or not doing certain Things, even tho' we were not answerable to any one for our Conduct. We are not to be surprized that his Notions on that Subject are not entirely just, since we see at this Day not only the Generality of Philosophers and Scholastick Divines, but also some Authors, otherwise very judicious, and far from being Slaves to the Schools, strenuously maintain, that the Rules of the Law of Nature and Morality do in themselves impose an indispensible Necessity of conforming to them, independently of the Will of GOD. Some however, reason so as to make it seem a mere Dispute about Words. I shall endeavour to put the Question in a clear Light in a few Words, and shew the Foundation of the Negative, which I take against the Author. This Note may be joined to what I have said on the same Subject in my Preface to PUFENDORF, § 6. p. 36. Second Edition. The Question here is not whether we can discover the Ideas and Relations, from which all the Rules of the Law of Nature and Morality are deduced, abstractedly from the Will of an intelligent Being. It must be acknowledged with the Patrons of the Opinion which I oppose, that these Rules are really founded on the Nature of Things; that they are agreeable to the Order conceived necessary for the Beauty of the Universe; that there is a certain Proportion or Disproportion, a certain Fitness or Unfitness between most Actions and their Objects, which give a Beauty to some, and a Deformity to others. But it does not follow from this Concession, that we are, properly speaking, *obliged* to do or not to do such a Thing. The Fitness or Unfitness, which may be termed the *natural Morality* of Actions, is indeed a Reason for acting, or not acting; but then it is not such a Reason as imposes an indispensible Necessity, which is implied in the Idea of an *Obligation.* This Necessity can come only from a *superior,* that is, from some intelligent Being existing without us, who has a Power of restraining our Liberty, and prescribing Rules for our Conduct. If there were any Obligation independently of the Will of a Superior, it must be laid on us either by the Nature of the Things themselves, or by our own Reason. Now the Nature of Things cannot impose any Obligation properly so called. The Relation of Fitness or Unfitness between our Ideas, can of itself only oblige us to acknowledge such a Relation; something more is necessary for obliging us to make our Actions conformable to it. Nor can Reason of itself lay us under an indispensible Necessity of following those Ideas of Fitness or

to be either com-<10>manded or forbid by God himself; and this makes
the Law of Nature differ not only from Human Right, but from a Voluntary Divine Right; for that does not command or forbid such Things

---

Unfitness, which it places to our View, as grounded on the Nature of Things. For,
first, the Passions oppose these abstracted and speculative Ideas with sensible and
affecting Ideas, they shew us in several Actions contrary to the Maxims of Reason, a
Relation of Pleasure, Content, and Satisfaction, which attend them, as soon as we
resolve to perform them. If our Understanding diverts us from such Actions, the
Inclination of our Heart carries us toward them with much more Force. Why then
should we comply with the former, preferably to the latter, if there is no exterior
Principle that obliges us so to do? On this Supposition, are not the Inclinations of
our Heart as natural as the Ideas of our Mind? Do they not arise from a certain Disposition in our Nature? You will say, Reason evidently shews us that we shall act more
conformably to our Interest, by observing the Rules which she prescribes, than in
being guided by our Passions. But the Passions will dispute this Advantage, and even
pretend it lies on their Side, because the Satisfaction which they offer is present and
certain; whereas the Interest to which Reason would engage our Attention, is future
and distant, and perhaps therefore to be looked on as uncertain. Even tho' we were
convinced that, all Things well considered, it would be advantageous to us to listen
to the Dictates of Reason, is not every one at full Liberty to renounce his Interest,
while no other Person is concerned in his acting conformably to it, or invested with
a Right of requiring he should consult it as much as is in his Power? How much soever
a Man acts in contradiction to his real Interest, he will, on this Supposition, be only
imprudent: He will be guilty of no Violation of any *Duty* or *Obligation,* properly so
called. But secondly, what ought to be particularly observed, and which alone is sufficient for proving the Thesis here advanced, is that our Reason, considered as independent on the Being who endowed us with it, is at the Bottom nothing but *Ourselves.* Now no Man can impose on himself an indispensible Necessity of acting or
not acting in such a particular Manner. The very Notion of Necessity implies, that
it cannot cease at the Pleasure of the Person subject to it; otherwise it would be in-
effectual, and reduced to Nothing. If then the Person obliged, and the Person who
lays the Obligation be one and the same, he may disengage himself from it, when,
and as often as he pleases; or rather there will be no real Obligation; as, when a Debtor
succeeds to the Estate and Rights of his Creditor, the Debt ceases. In a Word, as
SENECA very well observes, properly speaking, *No Man owes any thing to himself.* . . .
The Word Owe *takes Place only between two.* De Benef. *Lib.* V. *Cap.* VIII.
       From all which I conclude, that how conformable soever the Maxims of Reason
be to the Nature of Things, and the Constitution of our Being, they are by no Means
obligatory, till this same Reason has discovered the Author of the Existence and Nature of Things, whose Will gives those Maxims the Force of a Law, and imposes an
indispensible Necessity on us of conforming to them, by Vertue of his Right to restrain our Liberty, as he judges proper, and prescribe what Bounds he pleases to the
Faculties we received from him. It is true, GOD can command nothing contrary to

as are in themselves, or in their own Nature, Obligatory and Unlawful; but by forbidding, it renders the one Unlawful, and by commanding, the other Obligatory.

3. But that we may the better understand this Law of Nature, we must observe, that some Things are said to belong to it, not properly, but (as the Schoolmen love to speak) by way of Reduction or Accommodation, that is, to which the Law of <11> Nature is not [4] repugnant; as some Things, we have now said, are called Just, because they have no Injustice

---

the Ideas of Fitness and Unfitness, which Reason shews us in certain Actions, but still the Obligation of regulating our Conduct by those Ideas proceeds only from his Will. The Question is not, Whether that Will be arbitrary or not? It is still that alone which, properly speaking, imposes the Necessity. If, supposing an Impossibility, we could reasonably persuade ourselves that the Divinity is such as he is represented by the *Epicureans,* a Being who does not interest himself in the Actions of Men, requires nothing at their Hands, has no Concern for their living well or ill; whatever Ideas we might entertain of Order, Fitness, and natural Justice, the Consideration of such a Divinity would not be sufficient for imposing an indispensible Necessity of taking those Ideas for our Rule, even tho' we believed he himself acted conformably to them, as far as the Perfection of his Nature requires; for Example is not in itself a solid Foundation of Obligation. In short, that the Will of GOD is the Source of all Duties appears from this Consideration, that when they who are in Possession of a Religion, practise the Rules of Virtue, and the Maxims of the Law of Nature, they ought so to do, not principally and precisely because they acknowledge such Rules conformable to the natural and invariable Ideas of Order, Fitness, and Justice; but because GOD, their Sovereign Master, wills that they should follow them in their Conduct. And, in Reality, it would otherwise be unnecessary for GOD to give any Orders on that Head, because they would be already obliged to act in that Manner: The Will and Authority of GOD would, on this Supposition, be no more than a Sort of Accessory, which, at most, would only make the Obligation stronger. I have treated this Matter more at large in my Reflections on *The Judgment of an anonymous Author;* or the late Mr. LEIBNITZ, printed in 1718, at the End of the fourth Edition of my Translation of the Abridgment of PUFENDORF's Book *Of the Duties of a Man and a Citizen.*

4. He speaks here of such Things as are neither commanded nor forbidden by the Law of Nature, in regard to which we are left to our Liberty to act as we judge proper, unless a lawful Superior makes some positive Law in that Point; as it is in his Power; which is agreeable to the Law of Nature only in the Manner here specified, not being immutable, as our Author observes elsewhere, *B.* I. *C.* II. § 5. *n.* 1. But it is evident from what I have said, *Note* 5. on the preceding Paragraph, that there is a *Natural Law of bare Permission,* as well as one which is *obligatory;* and thus the Things which the Author means, may very well be considered as belonging to *Natural Law,* in the former Acceptation of the Term.

in them; and sometimes by the wrong Use of the Word, [5] those Things which our Reason declares to be honest, or comparatively good, tho' they are not enjoined us, are said to belong to this Natural Law.

4. We must further observe, that this Natural Law does not only respect such Things as depend not upon Human Will, but also many [6] Things which are consequent to some Act of that Will. Thus, *Property* for Instance, as now in use, was introduced by Man's Will, and being once admitted, this Law of Nature informs us, that it is a wicked Thing to take away from any Man, against his Will, what is properly his own. Wherefore [7] *Paulus* the Civilian infers, that [8] *Theft is forbid by the Law of Nature: Ulpian,* that it is [9] *Dishonest by Nature:* And [10] *Euripides* calls it *Hateful to GOD,* as you may see in these Verses of *Helena,*

5. Our Author, in another Part of this Work, mentions *Concubinage, Divorce, Polygamy, B. I. C. II. § 6. n. 2.* the Action of a Person, who discovers to another, what he is not by the Law of Contract obliged to discover: (*B. II. C. XII. § 9. n. 2.*) The Care of declaring War in certain Cases, where it may be omitted without any Violation of Natural Law: (*B. III. C. III. § 6 n. 6.*) The Vow of *Celibacy, Second Marriages,* and the like, (*B. III. C. IV. § 2. n. I.*) as so many Examples of Things belonging to this Class. What we shall say on those Places, and on *B. I. C. II. § 1. n.* 3. will help to explain the Principle here laid down by our Author, and shew wherein he has misapplied or extended it too far. See also PUFENDORF, B. II. C. III. § 22.

6. See PUFENDORF, B. II. C. III. § 15. Note 5. and § 22, 24.

7. *Theft is a fraudulent taking of a Thing, for the Sake of making an Advantage either of the Thing itself, or of the Use or Possession of it: All which is forbidden by the Law of Nature.* Digest. *B.* XLVII. *Fol.* 2. De Furtis, *Leg.* I. § 3.

8. The Words of the Emperor *Julian* on that Subject are, *Besides that, by which we are all convinced, without Instruction, of the Existence of something Divine; there is a second Law, sacred and divine by Nature, which orders us entirely to abstain from another Man's Property, and allows us not to make any Attempt on it, either by Word or Action, or even in our secret Thoughts,* &c. Orat. VII. p. 209. *Edit. Spanheim.* The Philosopher CHRYSIPPUS, as represented by CICERO, said, *There is no Injustice in seeking ones own Advantage; but it is contrary to Equity to take away from another.* De Offic. *Lib.* III. *Cap.* X. GROTIUS.

9. *Theft and Adultery are in their own Nature Evil and Infamous.* Digest. *Lib.* L. *Tit.* XVI. De Verborum significatione, *Leg.* XLII.

10. *For the Deity abhors violence. It is his Will that all Men should remain in quiet Possession of their own Goods; but no Rapine is allowed. Riches unjustly acquired are to be renounced, for the Air and Earth are common to all Men, where, when they increase their Possessions, they are not to detain or take away what belongs to others.* Helen. V. 909, &c.

Μισεῖ γὰρ ὁ θεὸς, &c.

5. As for the Rest, the Law of Nature is so unalterable, that [11] God himself cannot change it. For tho' the Power of God be infinite, yet we may say, that there are some [12] Things to which this infinite Power does not extend, because they cannot be expressed by Propositions that contain any Sense, but manifestly imply a Contradiction. For Instance then, as God himself cannot effect, that twice two should not be four; so neither can he, that what is intrinsically Evil [13] should <12> not be Evil. And this is *Aristotle*'s Meaning, when he says, ἔνια εὐθὺς ὀνόμασται, &c. [14] *Some Things are no sooner mentioned than we discover Depravity in*

---

11. Compare this with what PUFENDORF says, *B.* II. *C.* III. § 5.

12. See Mr. LE CLERC's *Ontology, C.* XIV.

13. The Definition of moral Good and Evil, of Virtue and Vice, being established on the necessary Congruity or Incongruity, which we perceive between certain Ideas, founded on the very Nature of Things; to say the Good becomes Evil, and Evil Good, as long as the Things remain the same, implies a Contradiction. If therefore God should command a Thing in which we find a necessary Incongruity with the Nature of Things; and on the contrary, prohibit a Thing in which we discover a necessary Congruity with the Nature of Things; he would act in Contradiction to himself, because he is the Author of that Nature: Thus he would be wise and not wise at the same Time; he would have all Perfections, and yet want one of the greatest; which is such a manifest Contradiction as can never be the Object of the Divine Omnipotence. If it be said, that God can change the Nature of Things, the Proposition is unintelligible, and when closely examined, implies no less Contradiction. For either the Things would not be the same, tho' called by the same Names; as *Man,* for Example, would be no longer a rational and sociable Creature; or Things remaining still the same, they would no longer be endowed with the same Properties, and the same essential Relations, *i.e.* they would and would not be the same; for the Essence of a Thing, and the Thing itself, differ only in Name.

14. Ethic. Nicom. *B.* II. *C.* VI. The Application of this Passage is not entirely just. *Aristotle* is not here speaking of the Mutability or Immutability of Moral Evil. He means no more than that some Passions and Actions are of such a Nature, that they can be innocent in no Case, nor in what Manner soever they are admitted. Of this Sort are a malicious Joy at our Neighbour's Misfortunes, Impudence, Envy, Adultery, Theft, and Murder; whereas some other Passions and Actions are Good or Evil, as a just Medium is observed, or as we depart from it, and give into either Extreme: Such are Fear, Confidence, Desire, Aversion, Anger, Compassion, Joy, Sorrow, the Actions of giving or receiving, of speaking or being silent, &c. But, whether the moral Evil, always inherent in the former Sort of Actions and Passions, and sometimes in the latter, is absolutely inseparable from them, even by the Will of God, is another Ques-

Cicero in his first Book of Offices [5] remarks, that we do not say *Horses and Lions have any Justice.* And *Plutarch,* in the Life of *Cato the Elder,* νόμῳ μὲν γὰρ, &c. *We by Nature observe Law and Justice, only towards Men.* And *Lactantius,* in his fifth Book, [6] *We find that all Animals, destitute of Wisdom, follow the natural Biass of Self-Love. They injure others to procure themselves some Advantage; for they know not what it is to hurt with a View of hurting, and with a Sense of the Evil that is in it. But Man, having the Knowledge of Good and Evil, abstains from hurting others, tho' to his own Detriment.* [7] *Polybius* having related in what Manner Men first engaged in Society, adds, when they saw any one offending his Parents or Benefactors, they could not but resent it, giving this Reason for it, Τοῦ γὰρ γένους τῶν ἀνθρώπων ταυτῃ διαφέροντος, &c. *For since human Kind does in this differ from other Animals, that they alone enjoy Reason and Understanding, 'tis very unlikely that they should (as other Animals) pass by an Action so repugnant to their Nature, without reflecting on, and testifying their Displeasure at it.*

2. If at any Time [8] Justice be attributed to brute Beasts, it is improperly, and only on the Account of some Shadow or Resemblance of Rea-

---

5. *Nor does our Nature differ in any Thing more from that of Beasts, to which we attribute Strength, as a Horse and a Lion, but never Justice, Equity, or Beneficence; for they have neither the Use of Reason nor Speech.* De Off. B. I. C. XVI. Our Author might have added a Passage from ARISTOTLE, where that Philosopher observes, that *We never say Beasts are temperate or intemperate,* but by a Metaphor, *tho' one Species of Animals differs widely from another, in the natural Desire of Generation, and Greediness in Eating.* Ethic. Nicom. *Lib.* VII. *Cap.* VII. p. 92.

6. *Cap.* XVII. *Num.* 30, 31. *Edit. Cellar.*

7. (POLYB.) *Lib.* VI. *Cap.* IV. In regard to what the Philosopher says of Offences committed against Parents, we have an Example of that Kind in *Ham,* and the Punishment of his Crime, GEN. ix. 22, *&c.* St. CHRYSOSTOM observes, that *We are naturally inclined to join in our Indignation with those who have been injured; for,* says he, *we immediately become Enemies to the Offenders, tho' we have no Share in the Injury.* Hom. XIII. *De Statuis.* The Scholiast on HORACE, *Sat.* III. *Lib.* I. *v.* 97. remarks, that *Our Sentiments of Indignation upon hearing of a Murther, are different from those that arise in our Soul when we are inform'd of a Robbery.* GROTIUS.

8. PLINY, in his *Natural History,* Lib. VIII. Cap. V. speaks of a Sort of Sense of Justice in Elephants, which he terms *divinatio quaedam Justitiae.* The same Writer, *Lib.* X. *Cap.* LXXIV. tells us, on the Credit of another Author, that in *Egypt,* an Asp was known to kill one of its own Young, for having killed the Man's Son who entertained and fed him. GROTIUS.

son [9] in them. But it is not material to the Nature of Right, whether the Act itself, on which the Law of Nature has decreed, be common to us with other Animals, as the *bringing up of* our Offspring, *&c.* or peculiar to us only, as the Worship of God.

XII. Now that any Thing is or is not by the Law of Nature, is generally proved either *à priori,* that is, by Arguments drawn from the very Nature of the Thing; or *à posteriori,* that is, by Reasons taken from something external. The former Way of Reasoning is more subtle and abstracted; the latter more popular. The Proof by the former is by shewing the necessary Fitness or Unfitness of any Thing, with a reasonable and sociable Nature. But the Proof by the latter is, when we cannot with absolute Certainty, [1] yet with very great Probability, con-<14>clude that to be by the Law of Nature, which is generally believed to be so by all, or at least, the most civilized, Nations. For, an universal Effect requires an universal Cause. And there cannot well be any other Cause assigned for this general Opinion, than what is called Common Sense.

There's a Passage in *Hesiod* to this Purpose, very much commended.

Φήμη δ' οὔτις, &c.

[2] *That which is generally reported amongst many Nations is not intirely vain.*

XII. How the Law of Nature may be proved.

9. SENECA says, that wild Beasts are not, properly speaking, *subject to Anger, but have a Sort of blind Impetuosity* in its stead. *Brutes,* says he, *are void of human Passions, but have certain Impulses resembling those Motions.* De Ira. *Lib.* I. *Cap.* III. ORIGEN also observes, that Beasts are not susceptible of Vice, properly so called, but that we find in them something that resembles Vice. *Contra Celsum.* The *Peripaticks* said, *The Lion seems to be angry.* PORPHYR, *De non esu Animalium,* Lib. III. p. 309. *Edit. Lugd.* 1620. GROTIUS.

XII. (1) This Way of proving the Existence of the Law of Nature is of little Use, because only the most general Maxims of that Law have been received by most Nations. Some Practices even contrary to the most evident of them, were long considered as indifferent in the most civilized Countries, as appears from the horrible Custom of exposing Children. See PUFENDORF, *B.* II. *Chap.* III. § 7, 8. and what I have said in my Preface to that Author, § 4.

2. OPP. & DIER. *vers. penult.* But the Passage is not well applied in this Place; for the Poet means only that we ought to endeavour at securing a good Reputation in

Τὰ χοινῇ φαινόμενα πιστά. [3] *That is certain, which universally appears to be so,* [4] said *Heraclitus,* determining λόγον τὸν ξυνὸν, [5] *Common Reason to be the surest Mark of Truth.* And *Aristotle,* [6] κράτιστον πάντας, &c. *'Tis the strongest Proof, if all the World agree to what we say.* Cicero, [7] *The*

---

the World, because false Reports always make some Impression, and prejudice the Person to whose Disadvantage they are spread. Ὀυ πάμπαν ἀπόλλυται, *Are not entirely without Effect.*

3. This is taken from SEXTUS EMTRICUS, [[*sic:* EMPIRICUS]], *Adv. Mathem.* Lib. VII. § 134. p. 399. *Edit. Fabric.*

4. ARISTOTLE maintains, that *What all Men conceive in a certain Manner, is really such as it appears;* and that, *Whoever attempts to discredit such a Belief, will advance nothing much more worthy of Credit.* Ethic. Nicom. *Lib.* X. Cap. II. p. 130. *Edit. Paris.* SENECA, undertaking to prove that no Duty is more evident than that of Gratitude, gives the following Reason for it: *How different soever the Opinions of Men may be on other Subjects, they will all unite in declaring that a proper Return is to be made to those who have deserved well of us.* Epist. LXXXI. QUINTILIAN says, *I will therefore call the Consent of the Learned, the Standard of Language, and the Consent of good Men, the Rule of Life.* Lib. I. Cap. VI. To the same Purpose, JOSEPHUS, the *Jewish* Historian, *There is no Nation in which the same Customs are generally established: One City frequently differs from another in this Point, but Justice is equally proper for all Men, being extremely useful both to the* Greeks *and Barbarians. As our Laws have a strict Regard to that Virtue, they render us, if religiously observed, benevolent and friendly to all Men. This is what we are to require from Laws: Nor are others to profess an Aversion to them, on the Account of the Difference between their Institutions and ours, but rather to consider whether our Laws have a Tendency to promote Probity and Virtue; for this is the common Concern of all Mankind, and is of itself sufficient for maintaining human Society.* Antiq. Judaic. *Lib.* XVI. *Cap.* X. TERTULLIAN says, that *Whatever is equally received by great Numbers of People, is not an Error, but a real Tradition.* De praescript. adv. Haeret. *Cap.* XXVIII. GROTIUS.

None of these Quotations, except the two first, are to our Author's Purpose: That of QUINTILIAN seems rather to insinuate the contrary of what he would prove; for it is well known, that good Men were never the Majority; and that great Master of Rhethoric had a little before declared, that *Custom, if it received its Name from the Practice of the Majority, will give most pernicious Precepts, not only for forming a Stile, but also for regulating our Lives.* The Passage of JOSEPHUS comes to no more than this: That the Practice of Justice is equally useful to all Men; but there is nothing in it that insinuates that all Men entertain the same Ideas of that Virtue.

5. SEXTUS EMPIRIC. *Adv. Mathem.* Lib. VII. § 131, 133.

6. I know not whence this is taken; for I do not find it in any of those Books where it might be supposed that Philosopher has said any Thing of this Nature.

7. TUSCULAN Quaest. Lib. I. Cap. XIII.

Consent of all Nations is to be reputed the Law of Nature. So *Seneca,* [8] *What all Men believe must be true.* Likewise *Quintilian, We allow* [9] *that to be certainly true which all Men agree in.* I with some Reason said, *By the most civilized Nations;* for as [10] *Porphyry* well observes, τίνα τῶν ἐθνῶν, &c. *Some People are savage and brutish,* [11] *whose Manners cannot, with Truth and Justice, be reckoned a Reproach to human Nature in general.* And *Andronicus Rhodius,* παρ᾽ ἀνθρώποις, &c. *That Law* [12] *which is called the Law of Nature, is unchangeable, in the Opinion of all Men who are of a right and sound* <15> *Mind: But if it does not appear so to Men of weak and disturbed Judgments, it argues nothing to the Purpose; for we all allow Honey to be sweet, tho' it may taste otherwise to a sick Person.* To which agrees that of *Plutarch,* in the Life of *Pompey,* Φύσει μὲν, &c. [13] *No Man either was or is by Nature a wild and unsociable Creature, but some have grown so by addicting themselves to Vice, contrary to the Rules of Nature; and yet these, by contracting new Habits, and by changing their Method of living, and Place of abode, have returned to their natural Gentleness. Aristotle* gives this Description of Man, as peculiar to him, ἄνθρωπος ζῶον ἥμερον φύσει, [14] *Man is by* [15] *Nature a mild Creature.* And

8. *Epist.* CXVII.

9. *Instit. Orator.* Lib. V. Cap. X. p. 399. *Edit. Burman.* He instances in the Belief of a Divinity, and the Obligation under which Children lie of loving and obeying their Parents.

10. *Of Abstinence,* Lib. IV. p. 428. *Edit. Lugd.* 1620.

11. JUSTIN MARTYR makes this Exception, *Except such as being possessed with impure Spirits, and corrupted by a bad Education, evil Customs, and unjust Laws, have lost their natural Ideas.* Colloq. cum Tryphone. PHILO the *Jew* observes, that *It is surprizing any Man should be so blind, as not to perceive certain Properties of Things, which are as clear as the Sun.* In his Treatise proving all good Men to be free, p. 871. *Edit. Paris.* St. CHRYSOSTOM cautions us against *forming a Judgment of Things from the Opinion of such as have a corrupt Mind.* In his Homily on the Divinity of JESUS CHRIST. GROTIUS.

12. *Ethic. Nicom.* Lib. V. Cap. X. Num. 2. *Edit. Heins.*

13. In the Life of *Pompey,* Vol. I. p. 633. *Edit. Wech.*

14. *Topic.* Lib. V. Cap. II. p. 228. Vol. I. *Edit. Paris.*

15. St. CHRYSOSTOM says the same in his eleventh Homily *On the Statues.* PHILO the *Jew* is larger on this Point. *Nature,* says he, *when it produced the tamest of all living Creatures, made him sociable, and disposed to Concord. She also gave him the Use of Speech, for promoting an Harmony and a Conformity of Manners.* On the Decalogue,

elsewhere, δεῖ δὲ σκοπεῖν, &c. [16] *To judge of what is natural, we must consider those Subjects that are rightly disposed, according to their Nature, and not those that are corrupted.*

XIII. *Voluntary Right divided into Human and Divine.* — XIII. The other kind of Right, we told you, is the [1] *Voluntary Right,* as being derived from the *Will,* and is either *Human* or *Divine.*

XIV. *Human Right divided into a Civil Right, a less extensive, and a more extensive Right than the Civil: This explained and proved.* — XIV. We will begin with the Human, as more generally known; and this is either a *Civil,* a *less extensive,* or a *more extensive Right than the Civil.* The *Civil* Right is that which results from the Civil Power. The Civil Power is that which governs the *State.* The State is a [1] compleat Body of free Persons, associated together to enjoy peaceably their Rights, and for their common Benefit. The *less extensive* Right, and which is not [2] derived from the Civil Power, though subject to it, is various, including in it the Commands of a Father to his Child, of a Master to his Servant, and the like. But the *more extensive* Right, is the *Right of Nations,* which

---

p. 763. *Edit. Paris.* And in another Place, *Man is the most tractable of Animals, being by Nature endowed with the Gift of Speech, by which the most savage Passions are charmed into Tameness.* Of the Immortality of the World, *p.* 945. GROTIUS.

16. *Polit.* Lib. I. Cap. V.

XIII. (1) This is usually called *Positive Law.* Its Objects are Things in themselves indifferent, or such as are not founded on the Constitution of our Nature, and consequently admit of different Regulations, as Time, Place, and other Circumstances require; all which depend on the Will of a Superior, which is the only Foundation of this Kind of Law, which is therefore called *Arbitrary.* See PUFENDORF, *B.* I. Chap. VI. § 18.

XIV. (1) The Author follows ARISTOTLE in the Addition of this Epithet. That Philosopher considered Civil Society, as a *perfect* Society, αὐτάρκη, containing all that is necessary for living commodiously and happily. *Politic.* Lib. I. Cap. I. See also *Lib.* III. *Cap.* VI. & *Lib.* VII. *Cap.* IV. The Definition of a State may be seen in PUFENDORF, *B.* VII. *Chap.* II. § 13; and the Note on that Place.

2. For there were Parents and Children, Masters and Servants, *&c.* before there were Princes and Subjects. The Authority of a *Father* over his *Child,* that of a *Master* over his *Servant,* &c. is by no Means founded on the Will of the Civil Power, and the Obligations incumbent on Men as Members of a State; but has a different Origin, as shall be shewn in the proper Place. The Sovereign in this Case can only lay a Restraint on that Authority, as far as the Publick Good requires.

derives its Authority from [3] the Will of all, or at least of [4] many, Nations. I say *of many,* because there is scarce any Right found, except that of Nature, which is also called the Right of Nations, common to all Nations. Nay, that which is reputed the Right or Law of Nations in one Part of the World, is not so in another, as we shall shew [5] hereafter, when we come to treat of *Prisoners of War,* and *Postliminy* or the *Right of Returning.* Now the Proofs on which the Law of Nations is founded, <16> are the same with those of the unwritten Civil Law, *viz.* continual Use, and the Testimony of Men skilled in the Laws. For this Law is, as *Dio Chrysostom* well observes, [6] εὕρημα βίου καὶ χρόνου, the *Work of Time and Custom.* And to this purpose eminent Historians are of excellent Use to us.

3. This Positive *Law of Nations,* distinct from *the Law of Nature,* is a mere Chimera. See PUFENDORF *B.* II. *Chap.* III. § 23. with the Notes. I grant there are some Laws common to all Nations, or certain Things which ought to be observed by all Nations, in Regard to one another; and this may very well be termed *the Law of Nations.* But, besides that the Obligation to obey those Laws, does not arise from the Consent of Nations, which cannot take Place here; the Principles and Rules of such a Law, are in Reality the same with those of *the Law of Nature,* properly so called: The whole Difference consists in the Application which may be made in another manner, on the Account of the different Ways taken by Communities for determining Disputes. This is evident from the Example of *Reprisals,* which are founded on that general Maxim of the Law of Nature and Nations, that *Damages ought to be repaired;* for a Man in the State of Nature, cannot demand Satisfaction, for any Injury received from one who lives out of all Civil Society, of any of his Relations or Friends, who are really not concerned in the Affair. As to Customs received by the Generality of Nations, and concerning which the Law of Nature has given no Directions, if we are obliged to submit to them, it is not because they are obligatory in themselves, but because as soon as we know a Thing is generally practised, we are, and may be supposed to conform to such a Custom, while we give no Proof of the contrary. Thus the whole Obligation arises from this tacit and private Agreement, without which the Customs in Question have no Force.

4. See VASQUEZ, II. *Controv. Illustr.* LIV. 4. GROTIUS.

5. *B.* III. *Chap.* VII, IX.

6. Orat. LXXVI. *De Consuetudine.*

by [5] CHRIST. These three Laws do certainly oblige all Mankind, as soon as they are sufficiently made known to them.

XVI. Of all the Nations of the Earth, there was but one, to whom GOD peculiarly vouchsafed to give Laws, which was that of the *Jews,* to whom *Moses* thus speaks, *Deut.* iv. 7. *What Nation is there so great who hath GOD so nigh unto them, as the LORD our GOD is in all Things that we call upon him for? And what Nation is there so great, who have Statutes and Judgments so righteous, as all this Law, which I set before you this Day.* And the Psalmist, cxlvii. 19, 20. *He shewed his Word unto Jacob, his Statutes and Ordinances unto Israel. He hath not dealt so with any Nation, and as for his Judgments they have not known them.* Neither is it to be doubted, but that those *Jews* (among whom *Tryphon* also in his Disputes with *Justin*) do egregiously err, who think that Strangers too, if they would be saved, [1] must submit to the Yoke of the *Mosaick* Law: For a Law

---

from Cruelty towards one another, at a Time when a Tenderness in that Particular was of the greatest Importance for the Multiplication of Mankind. See Mr. LE CLERC's Comment on the Place. Besides, we have not the least Insinuation, that any but the moral Part of this Law was to be obligatory at all Times, and in all Places; and such as pretend it not allowable, even under the Gospel Dispensation, to eat the Blood of any Animal, have been sufficiently confuted. *Secondly,* When GOD says, *Whoso sheddeth Man's Blood, by Man shall his Blood be shed.* This is not a Law, properly so called, but a bare Declaration of the just Punishment which Murtherers are to fear, either from Man or from GOD, by an Effect of the Divine Providence and Vengeance. See the following Chapter, § 5. *note* 2. This is evident from the preceding Words, where God says, *At the Hand of every Beast will I require it:* (the Life of Man) *At the Hand of every Man's Brother will I require the Life of Man.* To which he adds, by way of Confirmation, *Whoso sheddeth,* &c. *For in the Image of GOD made he Man.* From this Passage misunderstood, some Lawyers, as the late Mr. COCCEIUS, Professor of Law at *Francfort* on the *Oder,* (Dissert. *De Sacrosancto Talionis Jure* § 29, *&c.*) infer that even at this Day no human Power can pardon a Murtherer. See a Dissertation of Mr. THOMASIUS, printed at *Hall,* in 1707, and entitled, *De Jure aggratiandi Principis Evangelici in causis Homicidii.* in which he opposes this Error. See also the following Chapter, § 5. *num.* 3.

5. See the following Chapter, § 6 *num.* 2.

XVI. (1) Some Commentators, as well Lawyers or Criticks as Divines, inveigh strongly against this Assertion of our Author; but they only copy the common Places of Scholastick Divinity. They need not have given themselves so much Trouble, had they but considered, that the Question concerning the Salvation of the *Pagans* ought

obliges only those, to whom it is given. And [2] to whom that Law is given, itself <18> declares, *Hear O Israel;* and we read every where that the *Covenant was made with them,* and that *they were chosen to be the peculiar People of GOD,* which *Maimonides* owns to be true, and proves it from *Deut.* xxxiii. 4.

---

not to be brought into this Dispute, as being nothing to the Purpose. For whether the Heathens could or could not be saved without some Knowledge of JESUS CHRIST, either distinct or typical, it is still certain, that the Law of *Moses,* as such, laid no Obligation on the Pagans. This Law was undoubtedly directed only to the *Israelites,* as our Author observes; and an infinite Number of *Pagans,* who neither did or could know that there was such a People in the World, to whom GOD had given particular Laws, being therefore in an absolute Impossibility of having any Acquaintance with them, it cannot be reasonably said, they were under an Obligation of observing them. Thus supposing that the Efficacy of the Sacrifice of JESUS CHRIST cannot be extended to such as have not had the Assistance of Revelation, though through no Fault of their own, how moral soever they may live; they will not be condemned for not submitting to Laws of which they neither had nor could have any Knowledge; but for a Multitude of other Sins. Their being deprived of such a Means of Salvation, which GOD was not obliged to allow them, will be their Misfortune, not their Crime. As to those *Pagans* who lived in the Neighbourhood of *Judea,* and thus had it in their Power to embrace *Judaism,* as GOD did not forbid their being received when they offered themselves, so neither did he command them to be circumcised, to qualify themselves for sharing the Advantages of the *Mosaick* Law. GRONOVIUS was sensible of this, and even gives a Reason for it, which evidently shews the Laws of *Moses,* as such, did not oblige the *Pagans. The Prophets,* says he, *were not to encroach on the Functions of the Messiah, who alone was to unite the Nations, call all Men, and render the Church universal.* EUSEBIUS, in his *Evang. Demonst.* says, *The Law of* Moses *was delivered only to the* Jews, *and that while they remained in their own Country.* Whence he infers, that *therefore there was a Necessity of another Prophet, and another Law.* Lib. I. Cap. I. See Mr. LE CLERC's *Prolegomena to the Eccl. Hist.* Sect. I. Cap. VIII. § 10.

2. The learned GRONOVIUS objects, that the Laws of the Decalogue are universally obligatory, tho' the short Preface which ushers them in is addressed to *Israel,* whom GOD had *brought out of Egypt.* But, beside that the fourth Commandment, relating to the Observation of the Sabbath, was only for the *Jews,* as appears from the whole Tenor of the Words in which it is drawn up; and that the Reason of the Fifth, *that thy Days,* &c. evidently proves the same in regard to that; if the *Pagans* lay under any Obligation to practise the moral Parts of the *Decalogue,* it was not as they were a Set of Laws delivered from Heaven on Mount *Sinai,* but as so many Precepts which all Men may learn from natural Reason. So that ZIEGLER's Criticism does not affect our Author, whom he impeaches of not distinguishing between the *Moral, Ceremonial,* and *Judiciary* Laws.

submitted to the *Levitical* Law, to worship GOD in the Temple at *Je-rusalem,* and to offer Sacrifices; but yet [10] they were obliged to stand in a particular Place, separate from that of the *Israelites,* 1 *Kings* viii. 41. 2 *Macc.* iii. 35. *John* xii. 20. *Acts* viii. 27. Nor do we find that [11] *Elisha*

Strangers to pray and offer Sacrifices in the Temple of *Jerusalem,* only with a view of rendering them in some Manner tributary to the *Jews;* as he permitted that People to carry off the Spoils of the *Egyptians,* and *Hiram* King of *Tyre* to furnish *Solomon* with Materials for building the Temple. But this great Critick did not observe *Sol-omon's* Words at the Dedication of the Temple, 1 KINGS viii. *Moreover, concerning a Stranger that is not of thy People Israel, but cometh out of a far Country for thy Name's sake. . . . Hear thou in Heaven, thy Dwelling-Place, and do according to all that the Stranger calleth to thee for; that all People of the Earth may know thy Name, to fear thee, as doth thy People Israel.* From which it is evident, that GOD accepted of the Homage of Strangers, when offered with pious Dispositions, as *Solomon* supposes they might be; so that GOD had a very different View on this Occasion from what our Commentator pretends: Nor is the Passage quoted from TACITUS, for proving that the *Jews* were enriched by the Offerings and Presents of the *Pagans,* well applied, *Every one of that detestable People sent their Tribute thither, in Contempt of the Religion of the respective Countries in which they lived; and thus the* Jews *grew rich. Pessimus quisque, spretis Religionibus patriis, Tributa & Stipes illuc congerebant; unde auctae* Judaeorum *res.* Histor. *Lib.* V. *Cap.* V. where TACITUS evidently speaks of the Money which the *Jews* themselves dispersed through several Parts of the World, transmitted every Year to *Jerusalem;* Money raised by the Sale of their First-Fruits. That this was their Practice, appears from the Passages of PHILO and JOSEPHUS, quoted by JUSTUS LIPSIUS in one of his Notes, which GRONOVIUS himself has inserted in his Edition of the *Latin* Historian, from whom the Passage is taken.

10. See JOSEPHUS, where he treats of *Solomon's* Temple. GROTIUS.

The Place allotted for Strangers, was called *The Court of the Gentiles.* The *Jewish* Historian, in several Parts of his History, speaks of a Prohibition against passing the Limits of it. See *Antiq. Jud.* Lib. XII. Cap. III. Lib. XV. Cap. ult. *De Bello Jud.* Lib. VI. Cap. XIV. *Contra* APION, *Lib.* II. There is no Mention of this Court in the *Old Testament;* but from EZEKIEL xliv. 7, *&c.* it may be inferred, that there was originally an Inclosure round the *Court of Israel,* where Strangers were allowed to enter, and perform their Devotions. See SELDEN, *De Jure Nat. & Gent. secund. Hebr.* Lib. III. Cap. VI.

11. We have a Reflection to the same Purpose in St. HILARY, on MATT. xii. GROTIUS.

Our Author, in his Treatise of *The Truth of the Christian Religion,* B. V. § 7. joins to these the Example of *Moses,* who did not exhort *Jethro,* his Father-in Law, to embrace the Ceremonies of the Law, which he had delivered to the *Israelites* by Divine Direction. He likewise observes, in a Note on that Place, that some of the *Mosaick* Laws were impracticable to the Generality of other People; as those relating to the

signified to *Naaman* the *Syrian,* nor *Jonah* to the *Ninevites,* nor *Daniel* to *Nebuchadnezzar,* nor the other Prophets to the *Tyrians, Moabites,* and *Egyptians,* to whom they wrote, that there was any Necessity for them to receive the Law of *Moses.*

What I have here said of the whole Law of *Moses,* I would be understood to mean of Circumcision too, which was, as it were, the Introduction to the Law. There is only this Difference, that the Law of *Moses* obliged only the *Israelites;* but that of Circumcision obliged all the Posterity of *Abraham.* Whence we read in the *Jewish* and *Greek* Histories, that the [12] *Idumeans* (the *Edomites*) were compelled by the *Jews* to be circumcised: Wherefore those People who, besides the *Jews,* were circumcised, (as there were many, according to [13] *Herodotus,* [14] *Strabo,* [15] *Phi-<20>lo,* [16] *Justin,* [17] *Origen,* [18] *Clemens Alexandrinus,*

First-Fruits, Tenths, and solemn Feasts; which were to be observed in only one Place in *Judea,* where it was impossible for all the Nations of the World to convene.

12. See JOSEPHUS, *Antiq. Jud.* Lib. XIII. Cap. XVII. PTOLOM. Lib. I. *De Vita Herodis,* as quoted by AMMONIUS under the Word Ἰδουμαῖοι. SELDEN, *De Jure Nat. & Gent. secund. Hebr.* Lib. II. Cap. II. and my 19th Note on this Section.

13. That Father of Historians speaks of the *Egyptians* and *Ethiopians,* and the People of *Colchis,* Lib. II. Cap. XCI, CIV. He asserts that the Use of Circumcision was derived from the *Egyptians* to the other two Nations, as also to the *Phenicians* and to the *Syrians,* who inhabited *Palestine;* by whom he understands the *Jews,* who, according to him, acknowledge the Truth of this Account, as far as it relates to them. See also DIODORUS of *Sicily,* Lib. I. Cap. XXVIII. and Lib. III. Cap. XXXII. p. 17 and 115. *Edit. H. Steph.*

14. See his *Geography,* Lib. XVI. p. 771. *Edit. Paris.* where he treats of the *Cacophagi,* a People of *Ethiopia,* and p. 776. in his Account of the *Troglodytes,* some of whom, he tells us, are circumcised after the Manner of the *Egyptians,* spoken of *Lib.* XVII. p. 824.

15. See his little Piece *On Circumcision,* p. 810, 811. *Edit. Paris.*

16. In his Dialogue with TRYPHON, where he speaks of the Idumeans.

17. In his Answer to CELSUS, *Lib.* V. where he observes, that the *Egyptians,* and the People of *Colchis* had not the same Reason for Circumcision, that obliged the *Jews* to the Practice of that Ceremony; and that the *Jews* themselves made a Distinction between their Circumcision and that used by the *Ishmaelites* of *Arabia,* tho' the People last mentioned were Descendants of *Abraham,* and *Ishmael,* the Founder of their Nation, had been circumcised by the Hands of that Patriarch, *Pag.* 263. *Edit. Cantab.*

18. That Father, in his *Stromata,* Lib. I. Cap. XV. p. 354. *Edit. Oxon.* says that *Pythagoras,* travelling into *Egypt,* was circumcised in that Country, in order to qualify

which the Permission is conceived, that the Thing permitted is conformable or not conformable to the Law of Nature.

The next Observation is not unlike this, *viz.* That Christian Princes may now make Laws of the same Import with those given by *Moses,* unless they be such Laws as wholly related either to the Time of the expected *Messias,* and the Gospel, not then published; or that CHRIST himself has either in [4] general, or in [5] particular commanded the contrary: For, excepting these three Reasons, no other can be imagined, why that which the Law of *Moses* formerly established, should now be unlawful.

The third Observation may be this; whatsoever was enjoined by the Law of *Moses,* which relates to those Virtues that CHRIST requires of his Disciples, ought now as much, if not more, [6] to be observed by us Christians. The Ground of this Observation is, because what Virtues are required of Christians, as Humility, Patience, Charity, *&c.* are to be practised in a [7] more eminent Degree, than under the State of the *Hebrew*

---

4. JESUS CHRIST, for Example, has abolished all the Laws in general, which related to the Distinction of Meats. If therefore any Civil or Ecclesiastical Power pretends to oblige Men to Abstinence from any Sort of Food, on a Principle of Religion, such an Attempt is an open Violation of the Christian Liberty, established by our Saviour. I suppose this done *on a Principle of Religion;* for the Case will be widely different, if the Use of certain Meats are prohibited for good Reasons, founded on the Interest of the State. The Sovereign has an undoubted Power to impose such Abstinence in that View; as he may be allowed to decline making the wisest political Regulations in the *Mosaick* Law his Model, when they are not suited to the Constitution of the State under his Government.

5. Thus JESUS CHRIST having repealed the Husband's unlimited Permission of putting away his Wife for any Cause whatever, and without any other Reason than his own Will; a Christian Prince cannot make a Law, permitting Divorces in that Manner, only obliging the Husband to testify in a Writing delivered to his Wife, that he will have no farther Commerce with her.

6. *Christian Liberty has done no Prejudice to Innocence; the Law of Piety, Sanctity, Humanity, Truth, Fidelity, Chastity, Justice, Mercy, Benevolence, and Modesty, remain intire.* TERTUL. *De Pudicit.* Cap. VI. GROTIUS.

7. *We ought to shew greater Degrees of Virtue, because we have* now *a plentiful Effusion of the HOLY SPIRIT, and the Advantages resulting from the Coming of CHRIST are very great.* CHRYSOST. *De Virginitate.* XCIV. See the same Father, in his Discourse, tending to shew that *Vice is occasioned by Negligence. De Jejuniis* III. And on *Rom.* vi. 14. vii. 5. As also St. IRENAEUS, *Lib.* IV. *Cap.* XXVI. The Author of *Synopsis Sacrae*

Law, and that with good Reason too; because the Promises of Heaven are more clearly proposed to us in the Gospel. Wherefore the old Law, in comparison with the Gospel, is said to be neither perfect nor ἄμεμπτος faultless, *Heb.* vii. 19. viii. 7. And CHRIST is termed the *End* of the *Law, Rom.* x. 5. but the Law only *our Schoolmaster,* or Guide, *to bring us unto CHRIST,* Gal. iii. 24. Thus the old Law concerning the Sabbath, and [8] that relating to Tythes, shew, that Christians are obliged to set apart no less than the seventh Part of their Time for the Worship of GOD, nor no less than the tenth Part of their Income for the Maintenance of those who are employed in Holy Affairs, or for other Sacred and Pious Uses.

Scripturae, among the Works of St. ATHANASIUS, writing of MATT. v. observes, that our *Lord enlarges the Extent of the Precepts of the Law.* GROTIUS.

8. The same Use is made of this Law, in regard to *Christians,* by St. IRENAEUS, *Lib.* IV. *Cap.* XXXIV. And St. CHRYSOSTOM, on the Close of the last Chapter of 1 *Cor.* and on *Ephes.* ii. 10. GROTIUS.

Whether 'tis ever Lawful to make War.

Having viewed the Sources of Right, let us proceed to the first and most general Question, which is, Whether any War be Just, or, Whether 'tis ever Lawful to make War? <24>

[[I.]] *That to make War is not contrary to the Law of Nature, proved by Reason.*

Gel. xii. c.5

I. 1. But this Question, as well as those which follow, is to be first examined by the Law of Nature. *Cicero* learnedly proves, both in the third Book of *His Bounds of Good and Evil,* and in other Places, from the Writings of the *Stoicks,* that there are two Sorts of *natural Principles;* some that go before, and are called by the *Greeks* Τὰ πρῶτα κατὰ φύσιν, *The first Impressions of Nature;* and others that come after, but ought to be the Rule of our Actions, preferably to the former. [1] What he calls *The first Impressions of Nature,* is that Instinct whereby every Animal seeks its own Preservation, and loves its Condition, and whatever tends to maintain it; but on the other Hand, avoids its Destruction, and every Thing that seems to threaten it. Hence comes it, says he, that there's no Man left to his Choice, who had not rather have all the Members of his Body perfect and well shaped, than maimed and deformed. And that 'tis the first Duty of every one to preserve himself in his natural State, to seek after those Things which are agreeable to Nature, and to avert those which are repugnant.

I. (1) CICERO gives this as the Opinion of the *Stoicks,* which he approves of, and confirms, *De Finib.* Lib. III. Cap. V. VI. VII. See also *Lib.* V. *Cap.* VII. and PUFEN-DORF, *B.* II. *Chap.* III. § 14.

2. After that follows, *(according to the same Author)* [2] the Knowledge of the Conformity of Things with Reason, which is a Faculty more excellent than the Body; and this Conformity, in which *Decorum* consists, ought (*says he*) to be preferred to those Things, which mere natural Desire at first prompts us to; because, tho' the first Impressions of Nature recommend us to Right Reason; yet Right Reason should still be dearer to us [3] than that natural Instinct. Since these Things are undoubtedly true, and easily allowed by Men of solid Judgment, without any farther Demonstration, we must then, in examining the Law of Nature, first consider [4] whether the Point in Question be conformable to the first Impressions of Nature, and afterwards, whether it agrees with the other natural Principle, which, tho' posterior, is more excellent, and ought not only to be embraced when it presents itself, but also by all Means to be sought after.

3. This last Principle, which we call *Decorum*, according to the Nature of the Things upon which it turns, sometimes consists (as I may say) in an indivisible Point; so that the least [5] Deviation from it is a Vice: And

2. *As every other Nature only then shews what is its real Good, when it is arrived to Perfection; so what makes the real Good of Man is not to be found in Man, till Reason is perfect in him.* SENEC. *Ep.* CXXIV. GROTIUS.

3. *That is most valuable in every Being, to which it is destined by Nature, and which makes its Excellence. What is most valuable in Man? Reason.* SENECA, *Epist.* LXXVI. See also *Epist.* CXXI. and CXX. V. JUVENAL says, that, according to the Doctrine of ZENO, there are some Things which we ought never to do, even tho' our Life was at stake.

——— *Melius nos*
Zenonis praecepta monent: Nec enim omnia, quaedam
Pro vitâ facienda putat ———
Sat. XV. v. 106, *&c.* GROTIUS.

AULUS GELLIUS, quoted by our Author in his Margin, says, When we are reduced to that Strait, we are obliged to expose ourselves to suffer some exterior Inconveniency or Damage, rather than be wanting to the inviolable Rules of *Decorum*, Lib. XII Cap. V.

4. See our Author's Application of this Principle to the natural Motions of Revenge, *B.* II. *Chap.* XX. § 5. *num.* 1.

5. Thus, for Example, it is never decent (*honestum*) nor, consequently, allowable by the Law of Nature, to fail in Point of Gratitude to a Benefactor; to take another Man's Goods, to which we have no Right; to break a valid Promise or Agreement;

sometimes it has [6] a large Extent; so that if one follows it, he does something commendable, and yet, without being guilty of any Crime, he may not follow it, or may even act quite otherwise: Just as in contradictory Things, one passes immediately from one Extreme to the other; a Thing either is or is not, there is no Medium: But be-<25>tween Things that are opposed after another Manner, as between Black and White, there is a Medium, which either partakes of both Extremes, or is equally removed from both. The last Sort of *Decorum* is most commonly the Subject of Laws both Divine and [7] Human, which by prescribing Things relating thereto, render them obligatory, whereas before they were only commendable. But the Matter in Question is concerning the first Sort of *Decorum.* For, as we have said above, when we enquire into what belongs to the Law of Nature, we would know whether such or such a Thing may be done without Injustice; and by *unjust* we mean that which has a necessary Repugnance to a reasonable and sociable Nature.

Among the first Impressions of Nature there is nothing repugnant to

---

to prejudice any one's Honour; to deprive the Innocent of Life, *&c.* In all which there may be different Degrees of Turpitude, according to the Variety of Circumstances; and as the Ingratitude, the Robbery, the Failure, the Affront, or the Murder, are more or less heinous; but in regard to the Quality of the Actions themselves, the least Fraud, for Example, is not less contrary to the Rules of *Decorum,* and the Law of Nature, than the greatest.

6. The Author does not here speak of the Application of the general Maxims of *Decorum,* and the Law of Nature to particular Cases, as the Commentators on this Work have imagined, who instance in the several Manners of discharging the Duties of Beneficence, Liberality, Friendship, *&c.* referring to *B. II. Chap.* I. § 5. where he treats of the Extent of Time allowed for a just Defence of one's self. The Question in this Place turns on the Nature of Actions in general, as it appears from the Examples to which our Author himself applies his Principle. Thus, independently of any positive Law against Polygamy, it is commendable and decent, according to our Author, to be content with one Wife; but the Man who takes two, commits no Fault: That Action is not contrary to the first Sort of *Decorum,* to which the *Law of Nature,* properly so called, bears a Relation.

7. The Emperor JUSTINIAN congratulates himself, on having given the Force of a Law to a Thing of this Nature, which the antient Lawyers had only advised, *viz.* That neither the Heir, nor any one under his Jurisdiction, should be admitted Witness to a Will. *Institut. Lib.* II. *Tit.* X. *De Test. ordinandis,* § 10. See the THEODOSIAN CODE, *Lib.* III. *Tit.* VIII. *De secundis Nuptiis,* Leg. II. With GODFREY's Comment on that Law, *Vol.* I. *p.* 285.

War; nay, all Things rather favour it: For both the End of War (being the Preservation of Life or Limbs, and either the securing or getting Things useful to Life) is very agreeable to those first Motions of Nature; and to make use of Force, in case of Necessity, is in no wise disagreeable thereunto; since Nature has given to every Animal Strength to defend and help itself. *All Sorts of Animals*, says *Xenophon*, [8] *understand some Way of Fighting, which they learnt no where but from Nature.* So, in a Fragment of *Ovid's* [9] *Halieuticon:* Or, *Art of Fishery, All Animals naturally know their Enemy, and how to defend themselves: They are sensible of the Force and Quality of their Weapons,* And in *Horace, The Wolves assault with Teeth, and the Bulls with Horns: Whence is it but from Instinct?* But *Lucretius* more fully, *Every Animal knows its own Power: A Calf is sensible of its Horns, even before they are grown, and* [10] *will push with its Head, when provoked.* Which *Galen* thus expresses, *We see every living Creature employ his strongest Part in his own Defence: The Calf pushes with his Head, tho' his Horns be not yet grown; the Colt kicks with his Hoofs, tho' yet tender; and the Whelp bites with his Teeth, as yet but weak.* And the same Author tells us, in his First Book *Of the Functions of the Members*, That Man is

---

8. *De Cyri Institut.* Lib. II. Cap. III. § 5. *Edit. Oxon.*

9. This is very well explained by a Passage in PLINY. *For all Animals have this Understanding, and are sensible, not only of their own Advantages, but also of their Enemies Power to hurt them: They know the Use of their own Weapons, the proper Opportunities for an Attack, and the weak Side of their Adversaries.* Hist. Nat. Lib. VIII. Cap. XXV.

10. The same Observation is made by MARTIAL, III. *Epigr.* 58. v. 2.

Vitulusque inermi fronte prurit ad pugnam.

PORPHYRY says, that *Every Animal knows which Part of him is weak, and which strong: That he takes Care of the former, and makes use of the latter; as the Panther of his Teeth, the Lion of his Claws and Teeth, the Horse of his Hoofs, and the Ox of his Horns.* De Abst. Animal. *Lib.* III. p. 268. *Edit. Lugd.* 1620. *Irrational Animals,* says St. CHRYSOSTOM, *carry their Arms on their Bodies; thus the Ox has his Horns, the wild Boar his Tusks, the Lion his Claws: But GOD has given me Arms distinct from my Body, to shew that Man is a tame and sociable Creature, and that I am not to employ those Arms at all Times; for sometimes I quit my Dart, and at others I handle it: That I might therefore be free from Incumbrance, and not be obliged to carry my Arms always with me, he has made them separate from my Nature.* De Statuis, *Hom.* XI. This passage agrees with that quoted from GALEN in the Text. GROTIUS.

as ¹ *Berosus* and ² *Orpheus.* I shall not instance in the seven Nations, whom GOD delivered up to be destroyed by the *Israelites,* because they had a special Commission from GOD to execute this Judgment upon them, for their notorious *Abominations.* Wherefore those Wars in Holy Writ are called, in a literal Sense, *Battles of the* ³ *LORD,* as being undertaken by the Command of GOD, and not the Will of <27> Man. It is more to our Purpose to remark, that the *Israelites,* under the Conduct of *Moses* and *Joshua,* having by Force of Arms repelled the *Amalekites,* who attacked them, *Exod.* xvii. GOD approved the Conduct of his People, tho' he had given no Orders upon that Head before the Action.

And further, GOD himself prescribed to his People certain general and established Rules of making War, *Deut.* xx. 10, 15. thereby plainly shewing, that War might sometimes be just, even without a special Command from GOD; for there he makes a manifest Difference between the Cause of those seven Nations, and that of other People. And since he does not declare the just Reasons of making War, he thereby supposes that they may be easily discovered by the Light of Nature. Such was the Cause of the War made by *Jephtha* against the *Ammonites,* in defence of their Borders, *Judges* xi. and afterwards by *David* against the same People, for affronting his Ambassadors, 2 *Sam.* x. And it is very remarkable,

II. (1) See Josephus *Antiq. Jud.* Lib. I. Cap. VIII. where he quotes the Passage of that profane Historian.

2. Or rather an antient Poet, who assumed the Name of Orpheus Clement of *Alexandria,* Stromat. *Lib.* V. p. 723. *Edit. Potter. Oxon.* And Euseb. *Praep. Evang.* Lib. XIII. Cap. XII. have preserved this Fragment, to which our Author here alludes, and which he himself has quoted in a Note on his Treatise *Of the Truths of the Christian Religion,* Lib. I. § 16. p. 66. *Edit.* 1717. And in his Comment on Matt. v. 31.

3. Our Author found the Expression in this Sense, in 1 Sam. xvii, 47. where *David* says to *Goliath, All this Assembly shall know that the LORD saveth not with Sword and Spear; for the War* (Battle, E. B.) *is the LORD's, and he will give you into our Hands.* But it is more natural to understand by these Words, *The War is the LORD's,* that the Success of the War depends on GOD; as Mr. Le Clerc explains them. Nor does our Author produce any other Passage to the same Purpose; he even gives a different Exposition, at the Close of this Paragraph, to a Text which at first Sight might seem proper to be alledged in this Place. He was thinking of the Rabbinical Distinction between *commanded* and *voluntary* Wars. On which see Cuneus, *De Rep. Hebr.* Lib. II. Chap. XIX. Schickard, *De Jure Regio,* Cap. V. and Selden, *De Jure Nat. & Gent.* &c. *Lib.* VI. *Cap.* XII.

what the Author of the Epistle to the *Hebrews* records, that *Gideon, Barack, Sampson, Jephtha, Samuel,* and others, *by Faith subdued Kingdoms, waxed valiant in Fight, put to flight whole Armies of the Aliens,* Heb. xi. 33, 34. in which Place, (as we may gather from the Context) under the Notion of Faith, is included their assured Confidence, that what they did was pleasing to GOD: And upon this Account *David* is said, by a Woman distinguished for her Wisdom, *To fight the LORD's Battles;* that is, to make just and lawful Wars, 1 *Sam.* xxv. 28.

III. What we have here proved from Holy Writ, may be also confirmed, by the *Consent of all,* or at least the wisest *Nations.* Every Body knows that fine Passage of *Cicero,* where treating of the Right of recurring to Force, in defence of one's Life, he renders this Testimony to Nature, [1] *This* (says he) *is not a written, but a Law born with us, which we have not learned, received, or read, but taken and drawn from Nature itself; a Law to which we have not been formed, but for which we are made; in which we have not been instructed, but with which we are imbued; that if our Lives be brought into Danger by Force or Fraud, either by Robbers or Enemies, all Means that we can use for our Preservation, are* [2] *fair and honest.* And again, *This, Reason has taught the Intelligent, Necessity the Barbarians, Custom the Nations, and Nature herself the wild Beasts, at all Times to repel, by any Means whatsoever, all Force (or Violence) offered to our Bodies, our Members, or our Lives. Caius* the Lawyer says, [3] *Natural Reason allows us*

III. Proved by Consent.

III. (1) *Orat. pro Milone,* Cap. IV. *Ibid.* Cap. XI.

2. SENECA says, *The most secure Means of Defence is always at hand; every Man being charged with the Care of his own Person.* Ep. CXXI. p. 604. *Edit. Gronov. Var.* QUINTILIAN lays it down as a Rule for an Orator, *To speak in his Client's defence, before he attempts to retort the Crime on the Accuser; because our own Safety is naturally preferable to the Destruction of our Adversary.* Inst. Orat. *Lib.* VIII. *Cap.* II. p. 403. *Edit. Obrecht.* SOPHOCLES therefore, speaking of *Hercules,* justly observes, that *Had he defended himself fairly and openly,* (against *Iphitus*) Jupiter *would have pardoned his killing him.* Trachin. v. 281, 282. p. 341. *Edit. Steph.* See also the Laws of the *Wisigoths,* Lib. VI. Tit. I. Cap. VI. GROTIUS. The Quotation from SENECA is not directly to the Purpose.

3. *Therefore if I kill your Servant, who is a Highwayman, and lays Wait for me, I shall be innocent; for natural Reason,* &c. DIGEST. *Lib.* IX. *Tit.* II. *Ad Leg. Aquil.* Leg. IV.

to defend ourselves against Danger. And *Florentinus* the Lawyer, that [4] *It is but just, that whatever any one does in defence of his Body, should be held lawfully done.* [5] *Josephus* observes, *That it is a Law of Nature, fixed in all living Creatures, to be desirous of Life; and that we therefore look on them as our Enemies, who would openly deprive us of it.*

This Principle is founded on Reasons of Equity, so evident, that even in Beasts, which (as I said [6] before) are not susceptible of Right, but have only some slight Resemblance of it, we distinguish between the Attack and the Defence. When *Ulpian* [7] had said, that *An Animal* [8] *without Knowledge,* that is, without the Use of Reason, *is incapable of doing Wrong,* he immediately adds, *When two Rams, or two Bulls fight, and one kills the other, it must be considered,* (according to *Q. Mu-<28> tius*) *whether that which is killed was the Aggressor, or not; in the last Case, the Owner has an Action of Damage against the Master of the other Beast; but in the first he has no Action against him.* Which may be explained by that of *Pliny,* [9] *Lions, as fierce as they are, do not fight with Lions, nor do Serpents bite Serpents; but if Violence be offered them, there are none so tame but will exert their Anger, none so patient of Injury, but, upon receiving Hurt, will make an active and vigorous Defence.*

4. DIGEST. *Lib.* I. *Tit.* I. *De Just. & Jure,* Leg. III.

5. *De Bell. Jud.* Lib. III. Cap. XXV. p. 852. *Edit. Lips.*

6. See § 11. of Chap. I.

7. DIGEST. *Lib.* IX. *Tit.* I. *Leg.* I. § 3, 11.

8. SENECA reasoning in the same Manner on another Occasion, says, that *Beasts, which are not supposed to understand what a Benefit is, or have any Notion of its Value, are gained by constant good Usage.* De Benef. *Lib.* I. *Cap.* III. See the whole Passage, and compare it with that of PHILO the *Jew,* quoted in a Note on § 7. of the *Preliminary Discourse.* GROTIUS.

9. The first Clause only occurs in PLINY, *Hist. Nat.* Lib. VII. but I do not find the following Words in that Author: They probably belong to some antient Author, as far as I can judge by the Stile. This Mixture was occasioned by our Author's taking the Quotation at second hand; for I believe I have discovered whence it was taken. MARCUS LYCKLAMA, in his *Membranae,* a Book published some Years before this, explaining Law III. of the Title in the DIGEST. *De Just. & Jure,* and taking occasion to treat of the natural Right of Self-Defence, *Lib.* VII. *Eclog.* 42. quotes this Passage of PLINY, without specifying the Place, and subjoins what here follows in the Text of GROTIUS.

IV. By the Law of Nature then, which may also be called the Law of Nations, it is plain, that every Kind of War is not to be condemned. History, and the Laws and Customs of all People, fully inform us, that War is not disallowed of by the Voluntary Law of Nations: Nay, [1] *Hermogenianus* declares, that Wars were [2] introduced by the Law of Nations, which I think ought to be interpreted somewhat different from what it generally is, *viz.* That the Law of Nations has established a certain Manner of making War; so that those Wars which are conformable to it, have, by the Rules of that Law, certain peculiar Effects: Whence arises that Distinction which we shall hereafter make use of, between a *solemn War,* which is also called Just, (that is, regular and compleat) and a *War not solemn,* which yet does not therefore cease to be just, that is, agreeable to Right. For tho' the Law of Nations does not authorize Wars *not solemn,* yet it does not condemn them, (provided the Cause be just) as shall hereafter be more [3] fully explained. *By the Law of Nations, (says Livy)* [4] *it is allowed to repel Force by Force.* And *Florentinus* [5] declares it *to be allowed by the Law of Nations to repel Violence and Wrong, and to defend our Lives.*

IV. (1) DIGEST. Lib. I. Tit. I. *De Justitia & Jure,* Leg. V.

2. CORNELIUS NEPOS, in his Life of *Themistocles,* says, that General *freely owned to the* Lacedemonians, *that the* Athenians *had, by his Advice, secured their Temples and Houses with Walls, in order to defend them more effectually against the Enemy; an Action allowable by the common Law of Nations.* Vita Them. *Cap.* VII. *num* 4. *Edit. Cellar.* GROTIUS.

3. See our Author, *B.* III. *Chap.* VI. § 27.

4. *Lib.* XLII. *Cap.* XLI.

5. DIGEST. Lib. I. Tit. I. *De Just. & Jure.* Leg. III. See what I have said on PUFENDORF, *B.* II. *Chap.* III. § 3. *Note* 11. and § 23. *Note* 3. from which it appears, that FLORENTIN, in this Law, spoke of what our Author terms the *Law of Nature,* whether the Question concerns the *Law of Nature* or the *Law of Nations,* in the Manner used by the antient Lawyers in explaining that Distinction. The same is to be said of Law V. of the same Title, quoted by our Author, as the first, *Note* 1. for when the Lawyers refer War to the *Law of Nations,* they only mean, that whereas the *natural Instinct,* common to all living Creatures, prompts Man to defend himself in the best Manner he can; Reason, which is the Principle and Rule of the *Law of Nations,* forbids them to make War, even in their own Defence, without a just Cause, and directs them to keep within certain Bounds. See CUJAS on the Laws in Question. Vol. VII. p. 23, 29, *&c. Edit. Fabrot.*

V. There is a greater Difficulty concerning the *Voluntary Divine Law:* But let none here object, that the Law of Nature being unchangeable, GOD himself cannot decree any Thing against it; for it is true, as to those Things which the Law of Nature either positively forbids or commands, but not as to those that are barely permitted by the Law of Nature; for they, being properly [1] without the Bounds of the Law of Nature, may be either prohibited or commanded, as shall be thought proper. The first Objection then against War, brought by some, is that Law given to *Noah* and his Posterity, *Gen.* ix. 5, 6. where GOD thus speaks, *Surely the Blood of your Lives will I require; at the Hand of every Beast will I require it, and at the Hand of Man; at the Hand of every Man's Brother will I require the Life of Man. Whosoever sheds Man's Blood, by Man shall his Blood be shed; for in the Image of GOD made he Man.* And here some take the Phrase of *requiring Blood* in a general Sense, and the other, that *Blood shall be shed* in its turn, to be a bare Threatening, and not an Approbation; neither of which Explications can I agree to. For the forbidding to shed Blood, reaches no further than that in the Law, *Thou shalt not kill;* which neither disproves Capital Punishments inflicted on Criminals, nor Wars undertaken by publick Authority. Therefore, both the <29> Law of *Moses,* and the Law given to *Noah,* tend rather to explain and renew the Law of Nature, obscured, and, as it were, extinguished by wicked Customs, than to establish any Thing new: So that *the Shedding of Blood,* prohibited by the Law given to *Noah,* ought to be understood in that Sense which implies a Crime; as by Murder we understand not every Act whereby the Life of a Man is taken away, but the premeditated killing of an innocent Person. And that which follows, of *shedding Blood for Blood,* seems to me not so much to denote the bare Fact, or what shall happen, [2] as the Right that Men have to put Murderers to Death.

I thus explain the Case. It is not unjust by the Law of Nature, that a

V. (1) See *Chap.* I. § 9. *Note 5.*
2. See my 4th *Note* on § 15. of the same Chapter.

Man should suffer himself as much Evil, as he has caused (to others); according to that which is called *The* [3] *Law of* Rhadamanthus.

To suffer what one has done, is Just and Right.

And *Seneca* the Father expresses it thus, [4] *It often happens that one suffers, by a most just Retaliation, in the same Manner that one had designed to make another suffer.* From a Sense of this natural Equity, *Cain,* guilty of Parricide, says of himself, *Gen.* iv. 14. *Whosoever finds me shall kill me.* But GOD in those early Days, either upon the Account of the Scarcity of Men, or because there being yet but few Examples of Murder, it was not so necessary to punish it, thought fit to prohibit what was naturally permitted; and ordered that all Intercourse with, and even the [5] Touching of Murderers should be avoided, but that their Lives should be spared. As [6] *Plato* also appointed in his Laws; and [7] *Euripides* informs us, that it was practised by the old *Greeks,* in these Verses,

Καλῶς ἔθεντο, &c.

Our Fathers, in antient Times, had wisely ordered, that whoever embrued his Hands in the Blood of another, should not appear in the Sight of any one in the Country: Banishment was the Punishment inflicted on him for the Murder; but it was not permitted to take away his Life, as he had taken away the Life of another. To which we may refer that of *Thucydides,* * It

---

3. Quoted by ARISTOTLE, *Ethic. Nicom.* Lib. V. Cap. VIII. APOLLODORUS gives the Law of *Rhadamanthus* in this Manner, *Let him who takes his Revenge on an unjust Aggressor escape with Impunity.* Biblioth. *Lib.* II. *Cap.* IV. § 9. *Edit. Th. Gale.* GROTIUS.

4. Controvers. *Lib.* V. Praefat. p. 350. *Edit. Gronov.* 1672.

5. *Contactum ac commercium.* The Author here alludes to the Defilement or Uncleanness, which the Antients thought was contracted by touching a Man who had killed another, even innocently or lawfully. See PUFENDORF, *B.* II. *Chap.* V. §. 16. *Note* 2. And ELIAN, *Var. Hist.* Lib. VIII. Cap. V. with the late Mr. PERIZONIUS's 4th Note; as also EVERHARD FEITH, *Antiq. Homeric.* Lib. 1. Cap. VI. But these confused and obscure Ideas were not in Being in *Cain*'s Time.

6. *De Legib.* Lib. IX. p. 864, &c. Vol. II. *Ed. H. Steph.*

7. ORESTES, *v.* 511, *&c.*

*In Lib. III. *De Bell. Pelopon.* § 45. *Edit. Oxon.* SERVIUS, on 1 B. of VIRGIL's *Aeneid.* v. 136, 140, observes that *All the Punishments inflicted by the Antients were*

was an [11] antient Law against incestuous Marriages, tho' not mentioned by *Moses* in its proper Place. Among those Commands of GOD to the Sons of *Noah,* they say [12] this was one, that not only Murders, but also Adulteries, Incests, and Rapines should be punished with Death, which the Words of *Job* seem to confirm; and even the Law of *Moses* gives Reasons for these capital Punishments, [13] which Reasons suit no less with other Nations, than with the *Hebrews* themselves; and particularly it is said of Murder, that the Land cannot be cleansed but by the Blood of the Slayer. Besides, it would be absurd to think, that whilst the *Jews* were allowed to secure their publick and private Safety by capital Punishments, and to defend themselves by War, all other Nations and Powers should be denied the same Privilege; and yet that the Prophets should never have intimated to those Nations and Powers, that GOD condemned every Kind of War, and all Use of the Sword of Justice, as they frequently admonished them of other Sorts of Sins which they were guilty of. <31>

Nay on the contrary, is it not most evident, that since the Laws of *Moses,* with respect to criminal Matters, carry so visible a Character of the Divine Will, the other Nations would have done very well to take them for a Model? It is even probable, that the *Greeks* at least, and particularly [14] the *Athenians,* did so: Whence proceeds so great an Agreement of the old *Attick* Law, and from thence of the *Roman* [15] in the *Twelve Tables,* with the *Hebrew* Laws. This is enough to prove, that the Law given to *Noah* is not to be taken in that Sense which they imagine, who would thence conclude all Wars to be unlawful.

Job xxxi. 11.

Lev. xviii. 24, 25, 27, 28. Ps. ci. 5. Prov. xx. 8. Numb. xxxv. 31, 33.

---

11. See *B.* II. *Chap.* V. § 13.

12. See SELDEN, *De Jure Nat. & Gent. secund. Hebr. Disciplinam.*

13. I find nothing in or near these two Texts, relating to the Subject in Hand.

14. See our Author's Treatise, *On the Truth of the Christian Religion,* Lib. I. § 15. with Mr. LE CLERC's Note, p. 28. *Edit.* 1717.

15. An antient Lawyer has drawn a Comparison between the Laws of *Moses* and the *Roman* Law, under this Title, *Collatio Mosaicarum & Romanarum Legum.* PETER PITHOU published that Work for the first Time, at *Paris,* in 1572; of which we have lately been presented with a beautiful Edition, in the *Jurisprudentia Ante-Justinianea,* by Mr. SCHULTING, a learned Professor of Law at *Leiden.*

VI. The Arguments brought out of the New Testament against War are more plausible; in examining which, I shall not suppose that, which others do, that there is nothing in the Gospel (except Points of Faith, and the Sacraments) but what is injoyned by the Law of Nature; for that, in the Sense that most Divines take it, I cannot think true.

1. This I freely grant, that there is nothing commanded us in the Gospel, which is not agreeable to natural Decorum; but I see no Reason to allow, that the Laws of CHRIST do not oblige us to any Thing but what the Law of Nature already required of itself.

2. And those, who are of that Opinion, are strangely embarrassed to prove, that certain Things which are forbid by the Gospel, [1] as *Concubinage, Divorce, Polygamy,* are likewise condemned by the Law of Nature. Indeed these are such that Reason itself informs us it is more Decent to refrain from them, but yet not such, as (*without* the Divine Law) would be criminal. The Christian Religion commands, that we should lay down our Lives one for another; but who will pretend to say, that we are obliged to this by [2] the Law of Nature. *Justin Martyr* says, [3] *To live only according to the Law of Nature, is to live like an Infidel.*

3. Neither shall I follow them, who supposing another Principle very considerable, if it were true, pretend that CHRIST, in the Precepts he gives in the fifth and following Chapters of St. *Matthew,* only interprets

VI. *Certain Cautions concerning the Question, whether War be contrary to the Law of the Gospel.*

1 John iii. 16.

VI. (1) The Author, in a Note on this Place, quotes a Passage from St. JEROM, which I at present omit, because he gives it more at large on *B.* II. *Chap.* V. § 9. *Num.* 4.

2. This Instance is not altogether just. The Law of Nature, rightly understood, requires us in certain Cases to sacrifice our Lives for others, when a considerable Advantage may result from such an Action to the Publick. Thus we find the wise Pagans thought it their Duty to die for their Country. The Christian Religion therefore, only furnishes us with much more powerful Motives for the Practice of this Duty, by proposing the certain Hope of a Life to come, which will make us ample Amends for the Loss of the present. It is the Will of JESUS CHRIST, that we suffer Death for the Gospel; but this is no more than an Extension or Application of the Law of Nature, because nothing is more advantageous to Society, than a sincere and judicious Profession of the Christian Religion, and consequently, than the couragious Resolution of such as sacrifice their Lives for the Interest of its holy Doctrines.

3. *Epist. ad Zenam.* We meet with a like Thought in ORIGEN's *Philocalia.* GROTIUS.

nor to defend the Subject by Arms against Highwaymen and Pyrates, there would of Necessity follow a terrible Inundation of Crimes, and a Deluge of Evils, [12] since even now that Tribunals are erected, it is very difficult to restrain the Boldness of profligate Persons. Wherefore if it had been the Design of CHRIST to have introduced a new Kind of Regulation, as was never heard of before, he would certainly have declared in most distinct and plain Words, that none should pronounce Sentence of Death against a Malefactor, or carry Arms in Defence of one's Country, which we no where read that he did; for what is brought to this Purpose, is either very general or obscure. But Equity itself, and common Sense, teaches us to restrain Words that are general, and favourably to explain those that are ambiguous, and even to recede somewhat from the Propriety and common Acceptation of the Words, in <35> order to avoid that Sense which may bring along with it the greatest Inconveniencies. [13]

(5.) *Arg.*   5. The fifth Argument may be this, that it cannot by any good Reason be proved, that the Laws of *Moses,* which regarded the Punishments of Crimes, were abolished, 'till the City of *Jerusalem* was destroyed, and with it the Form of the State, without any Hope of re-establishment. For neither is there in the Law of *Moses* any Term fixt to that Law; neither does CHRIST or his Apostles ever speak of the abolishing of that Law, unless so far as it may seem comprehended (as I said) in the Destruction of the *Jewish* Government. Nay, on the contrary, St. *Paul* says, that the High Priest (*at that Time*) was appointed to judge according to the Law

Acts xxiii. 3.   of *Moses.* And CHRIST himself in the Preface to his Precepts, said, that
Matt. v. 17.   he came not to destroy the Law, but to fulfil it; which is easily understood to refer to the ceremonial Part; for the Lines of a rough Draught are compleated, when the Picture appears in all its Perfection. But as to the

12. St. CHRYSOSTOM says, that *To this End Tribunals were erected, Laws made, Punishments appointed, and various Kinds of Penalties enjoined.* Serm. ad Patrem fidel. GROTIUS.

13. To which add, that if the Gospel absolutely condemned War and capital Punishments, such Christians as observed the Precepts of their Religion with the greatest Exactness, would thereby be inevitably exposed to become a Prey to Villains and Usurpers; which is not agreeable to the Goodness and Wisdom of GOD.

Judaical Law, how can it be true, if CHRIST, as some imagine, abolished it at his Coming? And if the Obligation of that Law continued as long as the *Jewish* State subsisted, it follows, that the *Jews,* even such as turned Christians, if [14] they were called to the Magistracy, could not avoid it, nor judge [15] otherwise than *Moses* had prescribed.

Having thoroughly consider'd all Things, I cannot indeed find the least Reason, why any pious Man, that heard our Saviour pronounce those Words, should take them in any other Sense. I own, that before the Time of the Gospel, some Things were tolerated (either as to outward Impunity, or even in regard to Conscience, which I have not now Occasion or Leisure strictly to examine) which CHRIST did not allow to his Followers; as, for Instance, to put away a Wife for every Offence, and a Person injured to seek Reparation by Course of Law: But tho' between CHRIST's Precepts and those Permissions, there is a certain Difference, yet there is no Contradiction: For he that keeps his Wife, and he that parts with his Right of taking Vengeance, does nothing contrary to the

14. Either there is some Omission in this Place, (tho' all the Editions agree) or our Author expresses himself improperly. If the Political Law continued in force, it follows indeed, that the *Jews,* when converted to Christianity, ought, if Magistrates, to judge according to those Laws; but it by no Means follows, that they could not on any Account, or for any Reason, decline the Magistracy. The Author probably means, that they cannot decline it merely because the Exercise of it was attended with the Obligation of passing Sentence of Death for certain Crimes. I find nothing, at least in the Books of the Old Testament, from whence it can be inferred, that every one called to the Magistracy was obliged to accept of that Charge. The *Jews* acknowledged no such Obligation, as appears from a Passage of the *Talmud,* quoted by BUXTORF, in his *Florileg. Hebraic.* p. 183. where it is said, that the antient Sages declined publick Offices, and excused themselves from undertaking the Function of a Judge, 'till they saw none else would accept of it; and that even then they did not take Place in the Council, but at the earnest Intreaty of the People and Elders.

15. The *Jews* however in our Saviour's Time, had not the Power of Life and Death, but were under a Necessity of obtaining the *Roman* Governor's Permission for executing a Criminal. See our Author's Commentary on MATT. v. 22. and on JOHN xviii. 31. So that they only declared, according to their Law, such or such a Person guilty of a capital Crime; which supposes, however, that JESUS CHRIST had not abolished the political Laws, and, consequently, is sufficient for our Author's Purpose, whatever that passionate and injudicious Divine OSIANDER may say.

to protect the Good, and restrain the Wicked. [19] *Tacitus* speaks appositely to this Purpose, *Nations can have no Peace without Arms, no Arms without Pay, and no Pay without Taxes.* To which agrees that of St. *Austin,* [20] *For this Cause we pay Tribute, that Soldiers may have Money to buy them Necessaries.* <37>

(10.) *Arg.*
Acts xxv. 11.
10. The tenth Argument is taken from that Place of the *Acts,* where St. *Paul* pleads thus, *If I have wronged any Man, or done any Thing worthy of Death, I refuse* [21] *not to die.* Whence I conclude, that St. *Paul* did believe, that even after the publishing of the Evangelical Law, there were some Crimes which Equity allowed, and even required, to be punished with Death: Which also St. *Peter* teaches. But if it had then been GOD's Will, that capital Punishments should be no longer used, St. *Paul* might indeed have cleared himself; but he ought not to leave such an Opinion in the Minds of Men, as if to punish Offenders with Death had been now no less lawful than formerly. But having proved that capital Punishments were justly inflicted after the Coming of CHRIST, I think it also proved, that some Wars may be lawfully made, as against a Multitude of armed Offenders, who are to be overcome by Arms, [22] before they can be brought to a Trial. Indeed the Forces of Criminals, and the

1 Pet. ii. 19, 20.

---

no Room for Criticism; and that Mr. VANDER MUELEN has done Justice to the Author in this Place.

19. The Historian puts this Speech in the Mouth of PETILIUS CEREALIS, *Hist.* Lib. IV. Cap. LXXIV. Num. 2.

20. *Contra Faust.* Lib. XXII. Cap. LXXIV. p. 299. Tom. VI. *Edit. Eras. Basil.* 1528. This Passage (in which our Author writes *propter necessaria militi,* instead of *propter bella necessario militi,* as the Words stand in the Edition here specified, which probably he used) is quoted in the *Canon Law, Caus.* XXIII. *Quaest.* I. *Can.* IV. but not exactly in the same Terms, and among some short Extracts of what goes before, or follows.

21. The same Apostle says elsewhere, *There was no Cause of Death in me,* that is, *I had done nothing worthy of Death.* Acts xxviii. 18. JUSTIN MARTYR makes this Declaration in his second *Apology;* addressed to the Emperor, the Senate, and the whole Body of the *Roman* People, *But we desire that such as do not live conformably to the Precepts of JESUS CHRIST, and are only nominal Christians, may be punished, even by your Authority.* GROTIUS.

22. The Author here alludes to a Passage in TACITUS, relating to PISO, as the learned GRONOVIUS has observed on this Place. *Petitam armis Rempublicam; utque reus agi posset, acie victum.* Annal. *Lib.* III. *Cap.* XIII.

Boldness wherewith they resist, may have some Weight, in considering whether it be proper to pursue them with the utmost Rigour; but still that lessens nothing of the Right itself.

11. The eleventh Argument is, that [23] in the *Revelation* of St. *John,* some Wars of the Righteous are foretold, with manifest Approbation, *Chap.* xviii. 6. and elsewhere.

(11.) Arg.

12. The twelfth Argument may be this, that the Law of CHRIST did only abolish the Law of *Moses,* in regard to those Things which separated the *Jews* from the *Gentiles;* but what Things were accounted honest by the Law of Nature, or by the tacit Consent of civilized Nations, it was so far from abrogating, that it comprehends them under the general Precept *to think on every Thing that is honest and vertuous.* Now the Punishment of Crimes, and repelling Injuries by Arms, are by Nature reputed laudable, and referred to the Virtues of Justice and Beneficence. And here, by the by, we may observe the Error of them, who pretend that the *Israelites* had a Right to make War, only because GOD had given them the Land of *Canaan.* Indeed this is a just Cause, but not the only one. For even before those Times, holy Men did make War by following the Light of Reason; and also the *Israelites* themselves afterwards, upon other Occasions, as *David,* for the affronting of his Ambassadors. Besides, what every man possesses, by Vertue of human Laws, is not less his own, than if GOD had (immediately) given it to him; and that Right is not taken away by the Gospel.

(12.) Arg.

Eph. ii. 14.

Phil. iv. 8.
1 Cor. xi. 14.

23. This eleventh Argument occurs both in the first Edition of the Work before us, and in that of 1632, which the Author assures us he had carefully revised. I make this Observation, because it is omitted in several Editions, which was probably the Printer's Fault, who skipped over two Lines, being misled by the Resemblance of the Words *Undecimum* and *Duodecimum.* This Article was wanting in the Edition of 1642, the last published in the Author's Life Time; but it had been restored before my Edition appeared.

VIII. Let us now see the Reasons for the contrary Opinion, that the pious Reader may more easily judge which are the most weighty.

1. First they alledge the Prophecy of [1] *Isaiah,* who foretold, *That the Nations should beat their Swords into Plow-Shares, and their Spears into Pruning Hooks. Nation shall not lift up Sword against Nation, neither shall they learn War any more.* But this Prophecy is to be understood, either conditionally, as many others are, as that should be the State of Affairs, if all Nations would [2] submit to the Law of <38> CHRIST, and live up to it, whereunto there should nothing be wanting on GOD's Part; for it is certain, if all were Christians, and lived like Christians, there would be no Wars: Which [3] *Arnobius* expresses thus, *If all Persons who look upon themselves as Men, not so much from the Shape of their Bodies, as because they are endowed with Reason, would lend an Ear to his salutary and peaceable Lessons, and not presumptuously follow their own Fancies rather than his Exhortations, the whole World would long since have enjoyed profound Peace, and lived in perfect and indissoluble Union. Iron would have been employed for gentler Purposes, and converted into less dangerous Instruments*

VIII. (1) St. CHRYSOSTOM explains this Prophecy of the universal Peace established by the Foundation of the *Roman* Empire at the Time of our Saviour's Birth. *It is foretold,* says that Father, *not only that this Religion shall be well established, and immoveable, but also that it shall bring much Peace on the Earth; that the several Aristocracies and Monarchies shall be destroyed; and that there shall be one Kingdom raised above all the others, the greatest Part of which shall enjoy Peace in a more perfect Manner than before: For formerly Artificers and Orators bore Arms, and went to the Wars. But since the Coming of CHRIST, that Practice has been abolished, and military Employments are confined to a particular Rank of Men. Discourse on the Divinity of CHRIST.* We have exactly the same Explication in EUSEB. *De Praep. Evang.* Lib. I. Cap. X. p. 8. *Edit. Rob. Steph.* GROTIUS.

2. In Reality, as JUSTIN MARTYR observes, Christians have no Enemies among themselves to fight with, Ὀυ πολεμοῦμεν τοῖς ἐχθροῖς. Which is exactly what PHILO the *Jew* said of the *Essenes, You can find among them no Artist who makes Javelins, Darts, Swords, Helmets, Cuirasses, Shields, or any Sort of Armour or Machines.* In his Treatise proving *every good Man is free,* p. 877. *Edit. Paris.* St. CHRYSOSTOM likewise says, *If Men loved one another as they ought to do, there would be no capital Punishments.* GROTIUS.

3. *Adversus Gentes,* Lib. I. p. 6. *Edit. Lugd. Salmas.*

than what it has hitherto served for. And [4] *Lactantius* thus, *What would be the Consequence, if all Men would unite in Concord? Which certainly might be done, if banishing their deadly and impious Rage, they would resolve to live innocently and justly.* Or this Place is to be understood literally; and then, it is plain that this Prophecy is not yet fulfilled; but that the Accomplishment of it, and of the general Conversion of the *Jews,* is yet to be expected. But take it which Way you will, there can be nothing hence inferred against the Lawfulness of War, as long as there are those who will not suffer others to live in Quiet, and who insult such as love Peace.

Several Arguments are drawn from the fifth of St. *Matthew,* to judge of which it is necessary, that we remember what was said a little before, *viz.* If CHRIST had intended to have abolished all capital Punishments, and the Right of (*making*) War, he would have done it in most plain and exact Terms, on Account of the great Importance and Novelty of the Thing; and so much the more, because none of the *Jews* could imagine but that the Laws of *Moses,* concerning Judgments and other political Affairs, ought to preserve their Force in regard to the *Jews,* as long as their Government subsisted. After this general Remark, let us examine these Places in order.

2. The second Argument brought to defend their Opinion is out of those Words. *You have heard it has been said, an Eye for an Eye, and a Tooth for a Tooth; but I say unto you, resist not Evil,* (לרשע which answers to the *Greek* Word τῷ ἀδικοῦντι him that injures thee); *but if any Man strike thee on the one Cheek, turn to him the other also.* From hence some infer, that no Injury is to be repelled or revenged, either publickly or privately; but this the Words do not imply; for CHRIST does not here speak to Magistrates, but to those that are injured; nor of all Injuries

(2.) *Arg.*
Ex. xi. 13.
Matt. v. 38, 39.
Acts vii. 27.

4. It is where he reproaches the Pagans with the Deification of their Conquerors; on which Occasion he reasons thus, *If Immortality can be acquired only by shedding Blood, Who will have Gods, if an universal Concord was established in the World? And this certainly might be effected, if Men would lay aside their pernicious and impious Rage, and become innocent and just. Will no one be worthy of Heaven, on this Supposition? Will Virtue lose its Existence, merely because Men are not allowed to give a Loose to their Passions, and destroy one another?* Instit. Div. *Lib.* I. *Cap.* XVIII. *Num.* 16. *Edit. Celler.*

neither, but of slight ones, as a Box on the Ear, for the Words following limit those that go before, however general they may at first appear. So in the following Precept, *If any Man will sue thee at the Law, and take away thy Coat, let him have thy Cloak also.* [5] Our Saviour does not forbid absolutely to have Recourse to Law, or to take Arbitrators in order to decide a Difference. This is evident from the Interpretation of St. *Paul,* who does not prohibit every Kind of Law-Suit, but only would have Christians not go to Law with one another before the Heathen, <39> and that from the Example of the *Jews,* amongst whom it was a received Maxim, that *He that brings the Cause of an* Israelite *before Strangers, profanes the Name of GOD;* but CHRIST, to exercise our Patience, would not have us dispute for Things that may be easily recovered, as a Coat, or a Cloak with a Coat, if one run a Risque of being deprived of both; nor prosecute our Right according to Law, however well founded it may be. *Apollonius Tyanaeus* [6] said, *It was not like a Philosopher to sue for a little Money. The Praetor* (said *Ulpian* [7]) *does not disapprove the Action of*

1 Cor. vi. 4.

---

5. St. CYPRIAN explains the Text thus, JESUS CHRIST commands you, *not to demand the Restitution of what is taken from you.* De Patientia. And St. IRENAEUS says, that our Lord here commands us, *not to be sorrowful, like Men who cannot bear to be defrauded; but to be chearful, as if we had freely given what is taken from us.* And if any Man shall compel thee to go a Mile, go with him two. *That is,* says the same Father, *that you should not follow him like a Slave, but go before him like a Freeman.* Lib. IV. Cap. XXVI. LIBANIUS, who had read the Gospels, commends those who did not go to Law for the Recovery of a Coat or a Cloak, *Orat. de Custodiâ Reorum.* St. JEROM says, that *When any Man would sue us, and take away our Coat by litigious Chicanry, the Gospel directs us to grant him our Cloak also.* Dialog. I. Adv. Pelag. Tom. II. p. 274. *Edit. Basil.* GROTIUS.

The Passage of St. CYPRIAN, here quoted by our Author, is in his Treatise *De Bono Patientiae,* p. 216. *Edit. Fell. Brem.* But it does not fully appear, that that Father designed it as an Explanation of the Words of the Gospel that follow.

6. *Vit. Apol. Tyan.* Lib. II. Cap. XV. (XXXIX. *Edit. Olear.*)

7. DIGEST. *Lib.* IV. *Tit.* VII. *De alienat. judicii, mutandi causâ factâ.* Leg. IV. § 1. This Law considered in itself, does not relate to the Action of sacrificing some Part of our Property, rather than engage in a Suit of Law. The Case is widely different; for the Person here supposed to avoid the Multiplication of Law-Suits, is in Possession of the Goods of another Man, who sees the Proprietor disposed to recover them into his own Hands. See Mr. NOODT's excellent Commentary on the first Part of the DIGEST. p. 203, 204; for I should be too long in this Place, if I undertook to give the

a Man, who had rather lose his Substance than be engaged in a Multiplicity of Law-Suits, for the Recovery of it; for this Aversion to Suits of Law is not to be condemned. What *Ulpian* here says to be approved of by good Men, is what CHRIST himself commands, chusing the Subject of his Precepts from Things most honest and commendable: But we cannot justly infer from hence, that a Parent or Tutor ought not to defend by Law, when he is forced to it, what his Child or Pupil cannot subsist without. For a Coat or Cloak is one Thing, and one's whole Maintenance another. In *Clement's* Constitutions, it is said of a Christian, if [8] he have a Suit depending, *Let him endeavour to make it up, tho' it be somewhat to his Loss.* What therefore uses to be said of moral Things in general, may be applied here, that they do not consist in an indivisible Point, but have in their way a certain Extension.

So in that which follows, *If any Man shall compel thee to go with him one Mile, go with him two:* Our Lord did not say a hundred Miles, which might draw one too far from his necessary Business, but *one,* and if occasion be, *two,* which is only a kind of a Walk, and the Trouble and Hindrance occasioned by it almost nothing at all. The Meaning then is, that in Things which will not incommode us much we must not insist with Rigour upon our Right; but rather [9] yield more than is desired, that our [10] Patience and good Nature may be known unto all.

Our Saviour adds, *Give unto him that asks of thee,* [11] *and from him that would borrow of thee, turn not away.* If these Words were understood

---

Grounds of this Explication, which supposes an Acquaintance with the Niceties of the *Roman* Law.

8. *Lib.* I. *Cap.* XLV.

9. CICERO recommends *making large Abatements of our Right, and avoiding Law-Suits and Quarrels, even sometimes to our own Prejudice.* De Offic. *Lib.* II. *Cap.* XVIII.

10. JUSTIN MARTYR says, that our Saviour's Design in laying down this Precept, is to engage us to the Practice of Patience and Civility to all Men, and to avoid Passion. Apol. II. GROTIUS.

11. The same Father explains this of that Chearfulness with which we ought to *divide our Substance with the Indigent; and the Care we ought to take to avoid Ostentation in all our Actions.* Apol. II. And in another Place, *communicating our Goods to every needy Person.* St. CYPRIAN says, *We are to refuse our Alms to no one.* Testim. *Lib.* III. *Cap.* I. GROTIUS.

absurd than, when he had bid them abstain from capital Punishments, to add immediately, that the publick Powers were ordained by GOD to this End, to execute Punishment in GOD's Stead?

(5.) Arg.   5. The fifth Place, which some alledge is, *Tho' we walk in the Flesh,*
2 Cor. x. 3. *we do not war after the Flesh; for the Weapons of our Warfare are not* [38] *carnal, but mighty, through GOD, to the pulling down of strong Holds,* &c. But this Place makes nothing to the Purpose; for both what goes before, and what follows, shews that by the Word *Flesh* St. *Paul* there meant the weak State of his Body, as to outward Appearance, upon which Account he was contemned. To this St. *Paul* opposes his own Weapons, that is, the Power given to him as an Apostle, to punish the Refractory, which he used to *Elymas* the Sorcerer, the incestuous *Corinthian, Hymenaeus,* and *Alexander.* He therefore denies this Power to be carnal, that is, weak; nay, on the contrary, he affirms it to be most strong. What is this to the Right of capital Punishments, or of War? Nay, on the contrary, because the Church at that Time was destitute of the Assistance of the publick Powers, GOD raised up that miraculous Power for its Defence; which began to cease almost as soon as the Church had Christian Emperors; as the Manna ceased as soon as the *Israelites* were come into a fruitful Country. <43>

(6.) Arg.   6. The sixth Place produced is, *Put on the whole Armour of GOD, that*
Eph. vi. 11, 12. *ye may be able to stand against the Wiles of the Devil; for we wrestle not against Flesh and Blood,* (add *only,* after the Manner of the *Hebrews*) *but against Principalities,* &c. He speaks of that Warfare which Christians have, as Christians, not of that which they may have in common with other Men upon certain Occasions.

(7.) Arg.   7. The seventh Place that is brought is, *From whence come Wars and*
James iv. 1, *Fightings among you? Come they not hence, even from your Lusts, that war*
2, 3. *in your Members? Ye lust, and have not: Ye envy, and desire to have, and cannot obtain: Ye fight and war, and yet ye have not, because ye ask not; ye ask and receive not, because ye ask amiss, that ye may consume it upon your*

38. St. CHRYSOSTOM is of Opinion, that by *carnal Weapons* in this Place, are understood *Riches, Glory, Power, Eloquence, Address, Intrigue, Flattery,* and *Hypocrisy.* GROTIUS.

Lusts. This contains no general Maxim, which absolutely condemns the Use of Arms; it only says, that those Wars and Fights with which the dispersed *Jews* were at that Time miserably harassed among themselves (part of which History we meet with in *Josephus*) did arise from wicked Causes; and that the Case is the same still, we know, and lament. That of *Tibullus* has a Meaning not unlike this Passage of St. *James.* [39] *Gold is the Cause of so many Quarrels: There were no Wars whilst People drank out of wooden Goblets.*
And we find it remarked [40] often in *Strabo,* that those Nations [41] lived

---

39. *Divitis hoc vitium est auri; nec bella fuerunt,*
    Faginus adstabat quum scyphus ante dapes.
       Lib. I. Eleg. XI. v. 7, 8. *Edit. Brockhuys.*

40. See, for Example, *B.* VII. *p.* 300. *Edit. Paris. B.* XIV. *p.* 656. and *B.* XV. *p.* 713.

41. PHILO the *Jew* makes the same Remark, in his Treatise *Of a contemplative Life,* p. 892. *Edit. Paris.* upon quoting that Verse of HOMER, *Iliad.* B. XIII. v. 6.

   Γλακτοθάγων, ἀβίωντε, δικαιοτάτων ἀνθρωπῶν.

Men who live on Milk, and in great Poverty; but are remarkable for their Probity. JUSTIN, having told us that the *Scythians* made a Profession of *Despising Gold and Silver as much as other Men idolized them,* observes, that *The Innocence of their Morals and Freedom from Avarice proceeds from this excellent Disposition;* FOR, says he, *where the Use of Riches is known, there Covetousness is found. B.* II. Ch. II. Num. 8, *&c.* NICEPHORUS GREGORAS says something like this of the same People, *B.* II. The Passage is worth reading. PLUTARCH, in his Life of *Alexander the Great,* p. 698. Vol. I. *Edit. Wechel.* introduces *Taxiles,* an *Indian* King, speaking thus to that Prince, *What Necessity is there of Fighting and Wars between us, if you neither come to deprive us of our Water, nor necessary Food; for which only reasonable Men are obliged to take Arms?* DIOGENES the Philosopher said, that *Robbers and Warriors were not to be found among such as lived on* Water-gruel. PORPHYRY looks on *a simple and cheap Diet, as what contributes very much towards establishing Piety, and making it common among Men.* Of Abstinence from Animal Food, *B.* II. p. 144. *Edit. Lugd.* 1620. GROTIUS.
In the Verse quoted from HOMER, at the Beginning of this Note, our Author, following the common Explanation, takes Ἀβίων for an Epithet; whereas it is the proper Name of some of the antient *Scythians,* as the Author of the short *Scholia* observes, tho' he has given Occasion to this false Interpretation. Upon consulting STRABO's *Geography,* B. VII. p. 296, 300. *Edit. Paris.* ARRIAN's Account of *Alexander's Expedition.* B. IV. Ch. I. Q. CURTIUS, *B.* VII. *Chap.* VI. *Num.* 11. And STEPHANUS, *De Urbibus,* under the Word Ἄβιοι, it will appear, that the Poet here speaks of the *Abians,* as a particular People; and it is surprising, that Madam DACIER is the

one hand are always commendable, excellent, and in their own Nature agreeable to GOD: And on the other, left entirely to the Liberty of every Man; so that they can in no Case be obligatory. Now, upon a careful Examination of the very Examples, here alledged by our Author from the ancient Fathers, which are the most considerable of those made to regard the Evangelical Counsels, it will appear that they turn on things, which either are neither good, nor evil in their own Nature, or are really obligatory in relation to certain Persons, and in certain Circumstances. 1. Let us begin with *second Marriages* and *Celibacy* in general, which our Author elsewhere ranks in this Class. *B*. III. *Chap*. IV. §. 2. *numb*. 1. It is certain that whether a Person marries or lives single, he does neither Good nor Evil in that, considering the thing in itself. As the married State does not necessarily engage to Vice, so neither is an unmarried Life an infallible Means for practising Virtue.

A Man may be good or bad in a married State; as he may likewise be either in Celibacy. It is but too evident from Experience that those, who have made a Vow of Celibacy, or laid themselves under the same Tie in regard to a second Marriage, have generally fallen into one of these two Inconveniences, *viz*. either they have not lived chastly, or have not proved less subject to other Passions and Vices very unworthy of a Christian, such as Anger, Covetousness, Hatred, Pride, the Spirit of Domination, Sloth, *&c*. even though a Man's Constitution will easily allow him to forego Marriage, if while he lives in Celibacy, he does not for that Reason become more useful to Society, and more capable of discharging his Duty, the Matter is then entirely indifferent. But if one has good Reason to believe he shall be able to employ his Time better, and do the Publick more Service in a single Life (which depends on the Condition and Circumstances of each Person, of which they must judge for themselves) he is then under an indispensible Obligation not to marry, supposing he believes himself entirely secure from Temptations of Impurity; or not to marry a second Time, especially when he may thus make a better Provision for his Family. 2. In regard to forbearing Law Suits, and chusing rather to lose one's Property, than sue the Person, who has taken it from us or detains it unjustly; it is a general Maxim, that we are obliged to make some Abatement in our Right, whenever that can be done without great Prejudice to ourselves, or occasioning any other Inconvenience. The View of promoting Peace, and Prudence equally require such a Cession. So that Law-Suits bring commonly so many pernicious Sources of Hatred, Animosities, Divisions, Discontent, Perplexities, Expences, *&c*. we are to avoid them as much as possible, and expose ourselves to a slight Loss rather than engage in all unhappy Consequences, which attend the pursuit of our most just Rights. This is not a Counsel, but a real Precept, both the Gospel, and the Law of Nature, especially when certain particular Circumstances demand such a Moderation. This was the Case in the Infancy of Christianity, when, to avoid giving an ill Opinion of that Religion, and its Votaries, it was highly improper for Christians to go to Law in the Courts of *Pagan* Judges. See what our Author says, Paragraph 8. of this Chapter, *num*. 4. But, if no such Inconvenience to ourselves or others is to be apprehended, and some considerable Interest is at Stake, it is so far from being a very commendable Action, quietly to permit our Property to be taken away, or detain'd, that it would even be a bad one; for thus ill-designing

Men would be encouraged to do evil; and such a Moderation would be the more blameable, as it might add to the Inconveniences of one's self or one's Friends. So that Patience in the Case before us, is either useless or prejudicial; and then it cannot deserve Commendation; or it is a real Duty. Almost the same may be said of declining War. Thirdly, when the primitive Christians refused the Edileship or Praetorship, it was, according to GRONOVIUS, because those who accepted of these Posts were obliged to exhibit publick Shews for the Entertainment of the People, in which there was some Mixture of Idolatry. But the extravagant Ideas they had of several other things, give us room to believe, that many of the antient Doctors of the Church condemn'd all in general, who sought for or accepted of Honours and Dignities. In regard to the thing its self, the Honours in question are either vain Titles and frivolous Distinctions, which suppose no Merit in the Persons who receive them, and have no Tendency to promote the Good of Society: Or it is requisite that they, on whom they are conferred, should be possess'd of certain commendable Talents and Qualities, for the worthy Discharge of the Functions annexed to them. There is no great Virtue in neglecting or rejecting the former: And as there is great Danger they will inspire us with Sentiments of Pride, even that ought to be a Reason for avoiding them. In regard to the latter, either the Candidate is Possess'd of the Qualifications requisite for acting in a publick Character, or he is not. If not, or even if there are other Candidates who are possess'd of them, in a much greater Degree, he commits a Fault in pursuing, or even barely accepting of the Dignities in Question, for which a Man can never be too well qualified. But if one is convinced not only in one's own Opinion, in which one may deceive himself; but also by the impartial Judgment of understanding Persons, that one is much more capable of acquitting one's self of an honourable Employ, to which one is called, than others who aspire at them, it would be either Sloth or false Modesty to decline it, and it could not be reasonably done, but when the Person is engaged so to do by some stronger Obligation, or knows he has great Reason to apprehend the Influence of Temptations to Vanity, which might prompt him to frequent Abuses of the Power and Privileges with which he would be invested. Fourthly, LACTANTIUS does not allow a Christian to trade by Sea. *For why should he go to Sea,* says that Father, *or what should he seek for in a foreign Country, when his own furnishes him with all Necessaries?* Lib. V. Cap. XVII. But the Apostle St. JAMES manifestly supposes it lawful *to go from Coast to Coast for the sake of Traffick and Gain.* Chap. iv. *v.* 13, 14. The thing therefore is in itself indifferent; so that as we may Trade either innocently, or in a manner contrary to some Virtue; to abstain from trading, unless it be with a View of avoiding an insatiable Avidity of Gain, to which a Man finds himself disposed, or some other dangerous Temptation, has nothing in it deserving Commendation. In this Case it is no longer a pretended Counsel of extraordinary Perfection, but an indispensible Obligation incumbent on every Christian. Fifthly, taking an Oath is sometimes indispensibly necessary, as when things which regard the Glory GOD, or the Good of Mankind are concerned; or when the Magistrate for just Reasons requires it. As to these Cases, where our Interest only is concerned, and where the Distinction of *Counsels* and *Precepts* might take Place most, we are to judge of them by the Principles already laid down in regard to Law-Suits.

Sixthly, to all these Examples given by GROTIUS, let us add one alledged by Dr. HAM-MOND, who, out of respect to Ecclesiastical Antiquity, had likewise adopted the Distinction of *Counsels* and *Precepts,* as appear from his long Note on *Colos.* ii. 23. It is taken from St. PAUL's Generosity, in preaching the Gospel without receiving any Salary. 1 *Cor.* ix. 15. 18. But on a close Examination of the Matter, we shall find nothing in it relating to a *Counsel* properly so call'd. Though the Apostle glories in not having made use of his Power of demanding a Salary, and *expects to be rewarded* for his Conduct, it does not thence follow that the said Act was entirely free in regard to him, and had no relation to his Duty. He himself clearly gives us to understand the contrary, when he says, that if he had not made use of his Power, it was *that the Gospel might be without Charge.* In Reality, it was a Matter of the last Importance, that the first Preachers of the Gospel should carefully avoid all that could give the least Suspicion of their publishing the Christian Religion for their own Profit and Advantage: And it may be said in general that all who undertake to instruct others in that holy Religion, can never appear too disinterested, or be too humble. Thus, though the Persons to whom the Apostles preached, could with no shew of Reason require them to do it without some Salary; and that, strictly speaking, St. PAUL was not obliged to do it; yet as soon as he was persuaded his Ministry would by that Means prove more efficacious (which probably he had room to conclude from some particular Reason unknown to us; and he seems elsewhere to insinuate that he had one, 2 *Cor.* xi. 9, 10, 11, 12, 13.) he lay under a real Obligation so to do; an Obligation founded on the general Engagement, which requires every Man to seek and employ all Means necessary for acquitting himself of an important Charge, in the best manner he is able. However, as in such Cases Persons make an Abatement of their Right in Favour of those with whom they have to do; and therefore a greater Stock of Virtue is requisite for resolving on such a Sacrifice, than barely refusing to take what others have in Rigour a Right to demand, we have likewise more Reason to congratulate ourselves on so happy a Disposition, and may expect from the Divine Goodness a greater Recompence. Besides, the Apostle here considers the Disinterestedness, for which he applauds himself, as a Duty, not formally enjoin'd him by particular Order from Heaven, or at least not necessarily join'd with the Exercise of the Evangelical Ministry, in Opposition *to the Necessity imposed on him of preaching the Gospel,* v. 16. for which he had received an express Command from our Lord JESUS CHRIST, *Acts* xxii. 14, 15. See what GROTIUS himself has said on this Point, in his Notes on LUKE xvii. 10. And this leads us to what gave Occasion to this false Distinction of *Precepts* and *Counsels,* which comes now to be consider'd. The Apostles made use of the Word *Counsel,* when speaking to *Christians* of the Conduct they ought to observe in certain Circumstances, in regard to things either indifferent in themselves, or concerning which they had neither any particular Order from JESUS CHRIST, nor any general Rule in the Gospel, imposing an evident and indispensible Obligation of acting or not acting in such or such a manner. Thus St. PAUL, 1 *Cor.* vii. treating of Marriage, and considering the Afflictions and Persecutions, to which *Christians* were then exposed, says, that in Reality such as are not favour'd with the Gift of Continence might, and even ought to engage in that State, and that married Persons ought not to refuse one another the Marriage Debt, unless it be done by mutual Consent; nor separate, even though one of the Parties were not a Christian, But that he had rather those who had never been married, and those whose conjugal Tie had been dissolved by the Death of one or the other, should remain as they are. He declares, however, that *he has no Commandment of the Lord,* concerning that Matter; but that *he gives his Judgment,* or Counsel, *as one who hath obtain'd Mercy of the Lord to be faithful, and who hath the Spirit of the Lord,* v. 25. 40. that is as a good Interpreter of the Will of GOD, in determining what was to be done in regard to the Circumstances of those Times. In which, however, he could not avoid laying down some general Rules, which each Person was to apply for his own Use and Direction, according to his State and Condition, *v.* 17. so that as he was obliged to leave the Matter to each Man's Judgment and Conscience, he therefore calls his Exhortations bare *Counsels,* or *Advice.* He does the same, when he admonishes the *Corinthians* to practise Liberality to the Poor, the Exercise of which Virtue ought to be voluntary and proportion'd to each Man's Abilities, 2 *Cor.* viii. 10. Hence some have, without sufficient Grounds, taken Occasion to imagine there are some things, which, though of an excellent Nature, and in themselves highly agreeable to GOD, are left to every one's Liberty, so that there is no evil in the neglect of them, nor any Reason to be apprehensive of Punishment for such Omission; but if any Man forms the noble Design of aspiring to them, he arises to an extraordinary degree of Perfection, and performs such Acts of Virtue as merit a singular Reward. Another Reason, not unlike this, which may have given Birth to the Distinction under Consideration, is, that as GOD requires of Men more extensive Duties and in greater Number, in Proportion to their Knowledge and Assistance on the Practice of them; these are certain virtuous Acts, and even certain Virtues, not expected from great Numbers, because there are but few in Circumstances will oblige them to such Practices. It has been particularly observed that GOD requires greater Sanctity from *Christians,* than he demanded of the *antient Jews.* But it ought to be consider'd that, if any one, under the *Jewish* Dispensation, had by Force of Meditation and Reflection, acquired as exact and extensive a Knowledge of his Duties, as that to be found in the Gospel, which might have been done by a careful Examination of the Principles, dispersed through the Writings of MOSES and the other Prophets; such a *Jew* would then have been obliged to as regular and holy a Conduct, as that of true *Christians.* Lastly, it is to be observed that the Distinction of *Counsels* and *Precepts,* is so far from having any Tendency toward making Men virtuous, that in certain Cases, it may divert them from the Practice of Virtue. As Men are fond of the Wonderful, and of every thing that flatters their Vanity; they are in great Danger of being dazzled with the pompous Ideas of an imaginary Perfection, which raises them above the common level; and, while in pursuit of such Chimeras, neglecting several Branches of their real Duty, the Practice of which their Passions sometimes render more difficult, than the Sacrifice they make by abstaining from Things permitted. It is even possible for Man, under Pretence of extraordinary Sanctity, to deceive himself grosly in regard to plain and common Duties, and imagine himself excused the Practice of them, to make himself Amends for the Violence committed on his Inclinations; by this Abstinence from certain Things. Experience shews the

as good Counsel, [19] and tending to a more sublime Life, but not as an absolute Precept. Thus many of the Primitive Fathers condemn'd [20] all Oaths, without any Exception; whereas [21] St. *Paul* himself did swear in Matters of Consequence. A Christian in *Tatian* said, *I refuse the Pretorship.* In *Tertullian, A Christian is not* [22] *ambitious of the* Aedile's *Office.* *Lactantius* maintains, that a just Man (such he would have a Christian to be) should not make War; [23] but at the same time says, that he should not go to Sea. How many of the Primitive Fathers dissuade Christians from second Marriages? All which, as they are commendable, excellent, and highly pleasing to GOD, so they are not required of us by the Necessity of any Law. These Remarks will suffice to answer all Objections founded on Ecclesiastical Antiquity.

X. [1] Now to confirm our own Opinion, first we want not Writers, and even more ancient ones than those that are opposed to us, who believed that the Practice of inflicting capital Punishment, and that of making War, the Innocence of which depends on the Justice of the former, are not inconsistent with Christianity: *Clemens Alexandrinus* says, that a Christian, if he be called to the Government, should be <49> (as *Moses*) a living Law to the Subjects, reward the Good, and punish the Bad. And

---

Truth of this Reflection in such as make Vows of Celibacy and Poverty. See Mr. LE CLERC's Addition to Dr. HAMMOND's Note, already cited; as also his Notes on the second Epistle of SULPICIUS SEVERUS. *Edit. Leipsic.* 1709.

19. The fourth Council of *Carthage* forbids Bishops to go to Law for temporal Concerns, even though actually attacked. See St. AMBROSE, *de Offic.* Lib. II. Cap. XXI. and GREGORY *the Great,* Lib. II. Ind. XI. Epist. LVIII. GROTIUS.

20. See our Author's Notes on MAT. v. 34. and TILLOTSON's XXII. Sermon.

21. In *Rom.* i. 9. 2 *Cor.* i. 18. 23. *Gal.* i. 20. *Philip.* i. 8. 1 *Thes.* ii. 5.

22. *Apolog.* Cap. XLVI.

23. *For why should he (the just Man) go to Sea, or what should he look for in a foreign Country, who is supplied with all he wants in his own? Why should he go to War, and engage in other Men's mad Quarrels, whose Soul is always at Peace with all the World?* Instit. Divin. *Lib.* V. *Cap.* XVII. *num.* 12. *Edit. Cellar.*

X. (1) Our Author's Thoughts were probably on what that antient Doctor says in his *Stromata,* Lib. I. Cap. XXVI, XXVII. p. 420. and of *Edit. Oxon.* where we meet with the Sense, but not expressed in the same Words.

in another Place, [2] describing the Habit of a Christian, he says, it would become him to go *barefoot,* unless he should happen to be a Soldier. In the Constitutions, intitled, *The Constitutions of* Clemens Romanus, we [3] read, *Not that all Killing is unlawful, but only that of the Innocent; provided that this Right of putting to Death be reserved to the Magistrate alone.*

But setting aside private Opinion, let us come to the publick Authority of the Church, which ought to be of the greatest Weight. I say then, that Soldiers were never denied Baptism, or Excommunicated by the Church, (*because they were Soldiers*) which yet ought to have been done, and would have been done, if the military Profession had been repugnant to the Conditions of the new Covenant. In the aforesaid Constitutions, the same Writer treats of those who formerly used to be admitted to Baptism, and those who used to be rejected, [4] *Let a Soldier that desires to be baptized, be exhorted to abstain from Wrongs and Oppressions, to be content with his Pay: If he complies with these, let him be admitted.* *Tertullian* in his Apology, speaking in the Person of Christians, says, [5] *We go to Sea, and fight together with you.* He had said a little before, [6] *We are but of a few Days standing, and yet we have filled all your Empire, Islands, Castles, Towns, Councils, and your very Armies.* In the same Book he had [7] told that Rain had been obtained in favour of the Emperor *Marcus Aurelius,* by the Prayers of his Christian Soldiers. In his Book *Of a Crown,* he says, that the Soldier who had thrown away the Garland, was more brave than the rest of his Fellows; and he [8] informs us, that he had many Christian fellow Soldiers.

We may add, that some Soldiers that had suffered Torments and

2. *Paedag.* Lib. II. Cap. XI. p. 240.
3. *Lib.* VII. *Cap.* III.
4. *Lib.* VIII. *Cap.* XXXII.
5. *Apolog.* Cap. XLII.
6. *Ibid.* Cap. XXXVII.
7. *Cap.* V. Father PAGI, in his Criticisms on BARONIUS, *Tom. I.* has shewn that this Story has a great Mixture of Fables. But it is sufficient for our Author's Purpose, that *Marcus Aurelius* had Christians in his Army; a Fact which can never be disputed, and which has given Occasion to all the Wonders invented concerning the *thundering Legion,* as it is called by EUSEBIUS, and others.
8. *Cap.* I.

Death for the Sake of CHRIST, received from the Church the same Honour with other Martyrs; among whom are recorded [9] three of St. *Paul*'s Companions: *Cerialis,* who suffered Martyrdom under *Decius; Marinus,* under *Valerian;* fifty under *Aurelian; Victor, Maurus,* and *Valentinus,* a Lieutenant-General under *Maximian:* About the same Time, *Marcellus* the Centurion, *Severian* under *Licinius. Cyprian* concerning *Laurentius* and *Ignatius,* both *Africans,* says, [10] *They also were once Soldiers in the Armies of this World, but were truly the Soldiers of GOD in the spiritual Warfare, whilst they vanquished the Devil by the Confession of CHRIST, and obtained by their Martyrdom, the Palms, and glorious Crowns of the LORD.* Hence it is plain, what the common Opinion of the primitive Christians was concerning War, even before the Emperors were Christians.

If the Christians in those Times did not willingly appear at [11] Trials for Life, it ought not to be thought strange, since for the most part Christians themselves were to be tried. Besides, the *Roman* Laws in other Things, were more severe than Christian Lenity could allow of; which sufficiently appears in the single Instance of the [12] *Silanian* Decree of the

9. Add to all these a Soldier, baptized by *Cornelius,* mentioned by ADO, in his Martyrology. GROTIUS.

10. *Epist.* XXXIX. *Edit. Oxon.* (34. *Pamel.*)

11. *Capitalibus suppliciis.* Thus the Words stand in all Editions; but what follows makes it evident that the Author design'd to have said *Capitalibus Judiciis, at Trials for Life.* The Question is about acting as a Judge, not as a bare Spectator of the capital Executions, as TESMAR ridiculously explains this Passage, who quotes QUINTILIAN and SENECA. It appears from TERTULLIAN, that the Obligation of being present at such Trials, was one of the Reasons why the primitive Christians made a Difficulty of bearing Arms; and that Father uses the very Terms which I have placed here, pursuant to my Author's Meaning. *De Idol.* Cap. XIX. GROTIUS has before quoted what follows, and immediately precedes that Sentence, to which he probably alludes.

12. By this *Senatus Consultum,* or Decree of the Senate, it was ordered, that if a Master happened to be assassinated in his own House, all the Slaves under the same Roof should be put to Death; even tho' no Proof appeared of their being concerned in the Murther, or having heard any Thing when the Blow was given. We have an Example of the Case in TACITUS, *Annal.* Lib. XIV. Cap. XLII, *&c.* The Emperor *Adrian,* as our Author has observed in a Note, softened the Rigour of that Decree, by ordering that only they should be racked, who were near enough to the Place, where the Master was killed, to hear some Noise. SPARTIAN, *Vita Hadriani,* Cap.

Senate. But yet, after that *Constantine* embraced, <50> and begun to promote, the Christian Religion, capital Punishments did not thereupon cease. Nay, *Constantine* himself, among other Laws, made also this [13] of sowing up Parricides in a Leather Sack; tho' otherwise he was so very mild towards Criminals, that he is [14] blamed by many Historians, for too much Indulgence. He had also a great many Christians in his Army, (as History informs us) and caused the Name of CHRIST to be put [15] on his Standard: From that Time also the military Oath was changed to that Form extant in *Vegetius,* [16] *By GOD, and CHRIST, and the HOLY GHOST, and the Majesty of the Emperor, which, next to GOD, ought to be loved and reverenced by Mankind.* Neither at that Time, among so many Bishops, some of whom had suffered very severely for Religion, do we read of so much as one, that exhorted *Constantine* not to put any Criminal to Death, or to engage in any War, or that dissuaded the Christians from serving in Wars, out of Fear of GOD's Wrath; tho' most of those Bishops were very strict Observers of Discipline, and far from dis-

---

XVIII. Our Author says likewise, in the same Note, we may add to the too rigorous Laws of the *Romans,* that which forbids admitting the Evidence of a Slave, but when he persisted in it on the Rack. *See Cod.* Lib. VI. Tit. I. *De servis fugitivis, &c.* Leg. IV. and Mr. NOODT's *Probabilia Juris,* Lib. I. Cap. XIII.

13. *If any one is guilty of the Death of his Parent, or Son, or any other Relation, which falls under the Denomination of Parricide,—Let him be sewed up in a Sack, with a Dog, a Cock, a Viper, and an Ape—and thrown either into the neighbouring Sea, or a River,* Lib. IX. Tit. XVII. *De his qui parentes aut liberos occiderunt.* Leg. ult. It is well known this was the antient Manner of punishing Parricides among the *Romans;* but the Use of it was abolished. Such Criminals were burnt, or obliged to engage with wild Beasts, for the Entertainment of the Publick. See the Commentators on the *Institutes,* Lib. IV. Tit. XVIII. *De publicis Judiciis,* § 6. and the *Receptae Sententiae* of PAUL the Lawyer. *Lib.* V. *Tit.* XXIV. with Mr. SCHULTHIG's Notes.

14. He used to say, *The distempered and rotten Limb must be cut off, that it may not communicate the Infection to those that are sound; but not a sound one, or one that began to heal.* ZON. *Vit. Constantini,* Lib. IV. Cap. XXXI. And this his Historian represents as the Result of his Tenderness for such as reformed their Lives. As the *Christians* complained of that Prince's Excess of Clemency, the *Danes* did the same in relation to their King *Harold,* as we learn from SAXO the *Grammarian. Northern* Hist. *Lib.* XI. p. 193, 194. *Edit. Wechel.* 1576. GROTIUS.

15. See the late Mr. CUPER's Notes on LACTANTIUS, *De Mortibus Persecutorum,* Cap. XLIV.

16. VIGET. *De Re Militari,* Lib. II. Cap. V. *Edit. Plantin. Scriver.*

sembling those Things, which related either to the Duty of the Emperors, or other Persons: Such was St. *Ambrose,* in the Time of *Theodosius,* who in his seventh Sermon speaks thus, [17] *To go to War is no Fault; but to do it purely for Plunder is a Sin.* And in his Offices, [18] *Valour, which either defends our Country by Arms from Barbarians, or protects the Weak at Home, or our Companions from Robbers, is compleat Justice.* This Argument seems to me of so great Weight, that I will seek for no other.

I am not ignorant, that Bishops, and other Christian People, have [19] often interceded in favour of Criminals, especially such as were condemned to Death, and that Custom was introduced, that they who [20] took Sanctuary in a Church, should not be delivered up, but upon *promise* to save their Lives; and that about *Easter,* [21] those who were committed to Prison should be released. But he that carefully considers all these and such like Things, will find that they are only the Effects of

17. We find a like Saying of St. AUGUSTIN, inserted in the *Canon Law,* Caus. XXIII. Quaest. I. Can. V. as taken from his Book, *De verbis Domini,* Tract or Sermon XIX. And our Author quotes the same Words elsewhere, under the Name of that Father, B. II. *Chap.* XXV. § 9.

18. *De Offic.* Lib. I. Cap. XXVII. This Passage occurs also in the *Canon Law* already quoted; where we have several of the like Thoughts of other Fathers of the Church.

19. St. AUGUSTIN says, *It is a Priest's Duty to intercede for Criminals.* Several Instances of such Acts of Goodness may be seen in that Father's Epistles. GROTIUS.

The very Passage, here quoted by our Author, occurs in that Father's fifty-fourth Epistle, addressed to *Macedonius,* a Judge, *You ask me,* says he, *Why we say it is a Duty annexed to our sacerdotal Character to intercede for Criminals?* &c. This is followed by his Reply to that Magistrate's Objections.

20. See St. CHRYSOSTOM, *Homil.* XVI. *De Statuis.* The Council of *Orleans,* Cap. III. and the Laws of the WISIGOTHS, *Lib.* VI. *Tit.* V. 16. *Lib.* IX. *Tit.* II. *Cap.* III. GROTIUS.

21. *As soon as the first Day of the Paschal Feast is come, let no Man remain in Prison; let every ones Chains be loosed.* COD. *Lib.* I. *Tit.* IV. *De Episcopali audentiâ, &c.* Leg. III. This, however, took Place only in regard to some certain Crimes, as appears from the rest of the Law. *See Observationes divini & humani juris,* printed at *Paris* in 1564. p. 43, *&c.* They were written by BARNABAS BRISSON, a President famous for his great Learning. Besides, the Custom under Consideration had been before received by the *Jews,* as any one may perceive from what he reads in the Gospels. Our Author, in his Notes on MATT. xxvii. 15. conjectures that this Privilege was granted them by *Augustus.*

Christian Goodness, which eagerly embraces all Opportunities of Mercy; and not <51> the Consequences of a fixed and settled Opinion, which condemns in general all capital Punishments; and therefore, those Favours were not universal, but limited to certain Times and Places, and even the Intercessions themselves were moderated [22] with certain Exceptions.

Here some object against us, the 12th Canon of the Council of *Nice*, which runs thus, [23] *Whoever being called by Grace, have at first shewed their Zeal and Faith, and quitted their military Employment; but have afterwards returned like Dogs to their Vomit; so that some shall give Money, and make Interest, to be taken into the Service: They shall lye prostrate (in the Church) for ten Years, after having been for three Years bare Hearers (of the Word). But in regard to all these, it must be observed what Disposition they are in, and in what Manner they do Penance. For whoever, by Fear, by Tears, by Patience, and by good Works, testify the Sincerity of their Conversion, these fulfilling the appointed Time of Hearing, shall at Length assist at publick Prayers, and afterwards it shall be lawful for the Bishop to treat them somewhat more favourably. But whosoever shall look on their Punishment with Indifference, and shall think the Form of their entering into the Church to be sufficient for their Conversion, these shall fulfil the whole appointed Time.* The very Term of thirteen Years Penance, sufficiently declares, that the Matter in Question is not about a small or doubtful Sin, but a heinous and incontestable Crime. The Crime here meant, was undoubtedly [24] Idolatry; for the Mention which was made of the Times of *Licinius,* in the 11th Canon immediately preceding, ought to be supposed tacitly repeated here, as the Sense of the following Canon often

---

22. These Exceptions may be seen in CASSIODORE, *Var.* Lib. XI. Cap. XL. See also the *Decretals,* Lib. III. Tit. XLIX. *De immunitate Ecclesiarum, Caemeterii, &c.* Cap. VI. GROTIUS.

23. SIMEON LE MAITRE expresses the Sense of this Canon thus, *Let such as (having at first resisted the Violence used on them) have afterwards yielded to Iniquity, and engaged in the Army again, be excluded from Communion for ten Years.* BALSAMON, ZONARAS, and RUFINUS, *Lib.* X. *Cap.* VI. give this Canon the same Sense. GROTIUS.

24. TERTULLIAN, in his Treatise *Of Idolatry,* Cap. I. calls it, *The most enormous Crime which Man can commit: The Heighth of Guilt.* And St. CYPRIAN, *gravissimum & extremum Delictum.* Ep. XI. (XV. *Edit. Oxon.*) GROTIUS.

that required continual Application, such as the Service in War, and the Exercise of certain Civil Employments; for which Reason the first Canon provided, that no Bishop, Priest, or Deacon, should meddle in secular Affairs; and the 80th, that he should not be concerned in the administration of publick Affairs. And the sixth of the *African* Councils, that he should not act either as an [33] Attorney or an Advocate. So St. *Cyprian* holds it [34] unlawful for them to be appointed Tutors or Guardians.

But we have the express Judgment of the Church for our Opinion, in the first Council of *Arles,* which was held under *Constantine;* for the third Canon of that Council runs thus, *As to those who throw away their Arms in Time of Peace, we have thought fit to exclude them from the Communion;* that is, they who quit their military Employment, when there was no Persecution. For the Christians by the Word [35] *Peace* meant so, as appears from *Cyprian* and others. Let us add the <53> Example of the Soldiers under *Julian,* who had made so great Progress in Christianity,

33. See St. JEROM's Epistle to *Nepotian.* GROTIUS. The Canon here quoted, is not the VI. but the VII. as ZIEGLER observes on this Place.

34. *Whoever has attempted to divert the Priests and Ministers of the Church, from the Service of the Altar, deserves not even to be mentioned in the Priest's Prayers at the Altar: For which Reason,* Victor, *who, in Opposition to the Regulation lately made in a Council, dared appoint a Priest to the Charge of a Guardian, is not to be allowed any Oblation among you, for the Repose of his Soul;* (pro Dormitione ejus) *nor is any Prayer to be offered in the Church in his Behalf.* Lib. I. Epist. IX. (*Edit. Oxon.* Ep. I.) Addressed to the Priests, Deacons, and Laity at *Furni.* See also JUSTINIAN's *Code,* Lib. I. Tit. III. *De Episcopis & Clericis, &c.* Leg. LII. GROTIUS.

The Passage of St. CYPRIAN, to which our Author barely refers, occurs in the *Canon Law,* Distinct. LXXXVIII. *Can.* XIV. and *Caus.* XXI. *Quaest.* III. *Can.* IV. From which it appears, that, according to that Father, the deceased deserves some Kind of Punishment even after Death, for having dared to name a Priest Guardian; because he, on that Account, forbids Oblations, or publick Prayers to be offered in his Name, on the Anniversary of his Death, according to the Custom then introduced, which afterwards paved the Way to Superstition. See Bishop FELL's Note on this Passage; and DODWELL's fifth *Dissertation on St.* Cyprian. To which may be added, Mr. LE CLERC's Life of St. *Cyprian,* in his *Biblioth. Univers.* Tom. XII. p. 234, *&c.*

35. Examples of this Acceptation of the Word may be seen in TERTULLIAN, *De Idololatria,* Cap. XIX. in his Treatise, *De fuga Persecut.* Cap. III. CYPRIAN, *Epist.* X. (XVI. *Edit. Oxon.*) XXII. XXXI. (XXX. *Edit. Oxon.*) *De Lapsis,* p. 123. SULPICIUS SEVERUS, *Hist. Sacra,* Lib. II. Cap. XXXII. Num. 1 & 2. *Edit. Vorst.* Cap. XXXIII. Num. 3. and at the Beginning of his Hist. *Lib.* I. *Cap.* I. *Num.* 3. GROTIUS.

that they were ready to seal the Truth of the Gospel with their Blood; of whom St. *Ambrose* speaks thus, [36] *The Emperor* Julian, tho' an Apostate, yet had under him Christian Soldiers, to *whom when he said, March (against the Enemy) in defence of the State, they obeyed him; but when he said, March against the Christians, then they acknowledged the Emperor of Heaven.* Such was the *Thebean* Legion long before, which in the Reign of *Dioclesian* the Emperor were instructed in the Christian Religion, by *Zabda,* the thirtieth Bishop of *Jerusalem,* and afterwards left a memorable Example of Christian Constancy and Patience to all Ages, which I shall speak of hereafter.

Let it suffice, in this Place, to mention that Speech of theirs, which expresses accurately, and in few Words, the whole Duty of a Christian Soldier, [37] *We offer you our Service against any Enemy whatever, yet hold it a most heinous Crime to embrue our Hands in the Blood of Innocents: They can act vigorously against the Impious, and the Enemies of the State; but have no longer Force, when the Business is to massacre the Pious, and our fellow Citizens. We remember that we took up Arms for the Defence of our Countrymen, and not against them. We have always fought for Justice, for Piety, for the Preservation of the Innocent; these have been hitherto the Recompence of our Dangers. We have fought with Fidelity. How should we present it to you,* (the Speech is made to the Emperor) *if we neglect it towards GOD?* And St. *Basil* speaks thus of the antient Christians. [38] *Our Ancestors never accounted Slaughters committed in War, as Murders, excusing them who fought for Virtue and Piety.*

36. (*The Emperor* Julian, &c.) This Passage does not belong to St. AMBROSE, tho' attributed to him in the *Canon Law,* Caus. XI. Quaest. III. Can. XCIV. where it has been observed, that St. AUGUSTIN has something like it, on Psalm cxxiv. which is also produced in *Can.* XCVIII. See Mr. PITHOU's Note. Our Author himself elsewhere quotes a Passage not unlike this, from the Father last named, in a Note on *B.* II. *Chap.* XXVI. § 3.

37. This Declaration is taken from the Account of the Martyrdom of the *Thebean Legion,* attributed to St. EUCHERIUS, Bishop of *Lyons.* But Mr. DUBOURDIEU, Minister of the *French* Church in the *Savoy,* at *London,* published a Dissertation in 1705, shewing that Relation to be a spurious Piece, and that the *Thebean Legion* never had any real Existence.

38. Our Author says nothing that can assist us in guessing from what Part of St. BASIL's Works these Words are taken.

CHAPTER III

The Division of War into Publick and Private.

An Explication of the supreme Power.

I. *The Division of War into publick and private.* I. The most general and most necessary Division of War is this, that one War is private, another publick, and another mixed; that is a publick War, which is made on each Side by the Authority of the [1] Civil Power. Private War is that which is made between private Persons, without publick Authority. Mixed War is that which is made on one Side by publick Authority, and on the other by mere private Persons. But let us first speak of private War, which is the most antient. <54>

That some Sort of private War may be lawfully waged, as far as respects the Law of Nature, I think has been fully proved by what I have said above, where it was shewn, that it is not repugnant to the Law of Nature, for any one to repel Injuries by Force. But perhaps some will think, that it is not lawful, at least since the establishment of publick Judges; for tho' Courts of Justice are not from Nature, but human Ap-

---

I. (1) *Auctore eo, qui jurisdictionem habet.* By the Authority of the *Civil Power.* The Reason of his expressing himself so, is, because on one hand, by the Term *War,* he understands all taking of Arms with a View of deciding a Quarrel, in opposition to the Way of terminating a Difference, by Recourse to a common Judge; and on the other, includes under the Name of *Publick War,* even that which is carried on by an inferior Power, without the Orders of the Sovereign Power; as appears from what he says, § 4 and 5. Thus all the Criticisms of the Commentators fall to the Ground; who do not consider, that our Author was at full Liberty to define his Terms as he pleased; provided he always fixes the same Ideas to them, and reasons on them conclusively.

pointment; yet, since it is much honester, and more conducive to the Peace of Mankind, that Differences should be decided by a third Person that is disinterested, than that every Man should be allowed to do himself Justice in his own Cause, wherein the Illusions of Self-Love are much to be apprehended: Equity itself, and natural Reason, advise us to submit to so laudable an Institution. *Paulus* the Lawyer says, [2] *That is not to be allowed to private Persons, which may be done publickly by a Magistrate; lest it be the Occasion of great Troubles.* The Reason why Laws were invented, says King *Theodorick, is,* [3] *that none should use Violence, and do himself Justice; for wherein does War differ from Peace, if private Persons determine their Disputes by Force?* And Laws call that *Force, whensoever* [4] *a Man would take that which he thinks is due, without having Recourse to a Judge.*

II. Undoubtedly, the Liberty allowed before is now much restrained, since the erecting of Tribunals: Yet there are some Cases wherein that Right still subsists; that is, when the Way to legal Justice is not open. For the Law which forbids a Man to pursue his Right any other Way, ought to be understood with this equitable Restriction, that one finds Judges to whom he may apply. Now the Way to legal Justice may fail, either for some Time or absolutely. It fails *for some Time only,* when the Judge cannot be waited for [1] without certain Danger or Damage. It fails *absolutely,* either by Right or Fact: By Right, if a Man be [2] in Places not inhabited, as on the Seas, in a Wilderness, in desart Islands; and any other Places where there is no Civil Government. By Fact, if Subjects will not

II. That all private War, by the Law of Nature, was not unlawful, after the erecting of Tribunals of Justice, defended, with some Examples.

2. DIGEST. *Lib.* L. *Tit.* XVII. *De Diversis Reg. Juris,* Leg. 176. See JAMES GODFREY'S Comment on that Law.

3. CASSIOD. *Var. Epist.* Lib. IV. Ep. X. See also the *Edict* of THEODORIC, *Cap.* X. and CXXIV. GROTIUS.

4. DIGEST. *Lib.* IV. *Tit.* II. *Quod metûs causa, &c.* Leg. XIII. This is what the *Latins* call, in the Law Stile, *Injicere manum, To lay Hands on;* as is remarked by SERVIUS, the antient Commentator on VIRGIL. In *Aeneid.* X. v. 419. GROTIUS.

II. (1) As when a Man is attacked either in the Night, or even by Day, in private Places; or when such as see us in Danger, will not, or cannot, assist us, and bring the Aggressor to Justice. See *B.* II. *Chap.* I.

2. See *B.* II. *Chap.* XX. § 8. *Num.* 6, 7.

submit to the Judge, or the Judge refuse [3] openly to take Cognizance of Matters in Dispute.

What we said before, that even since Tribunals of Justice were erected, every private War is not repugnant to the Law of Nature, may be gath-

Ex. xxii. 2. ered from the Law given to the *Jews,* where GOD thus speaks by *Moses, If a Thief be found breaking up,* (that is, by Night) *and be smitten, that he dies, there shall no Blood be shed for him; but if the Sun be risen upon him, there shall be Blood shed for him.* For this Law so accurately distinguishing *the Cases,* seems not only to import an Impunity; but also to explain the Law of Nature; and that it is not founded on any particular Divine Command, but on common Equity; whence we see that other Nations have followed the same Principle. That of the Twelve Tables is well known, which was undoubtedly taken from the [4] old *Attick* Law; [5] *If a Thief commit a Robbery in the Night, and if a Man kill him, he is killed lawfully.* So is he reputed innocent by the Laws of all known Nations, who by Arms defends himself against him that assaults his Life; which so manifest a Consent is a plain Testimony, that there is nothing in it contrary to the Law of Nature. <55>

III. *Nor by the Evangelical Law, with an Answer to the Objections.*

III. There is more Difficulty concerning the *Divine positive Law,* more perfect than the Law of Nature, I mean *the Gospel.* I doubt not but GOD, who has more Right over our Lives than we ourselves, might have required Patience of us to such a Degree, that being brought privately into Danger, we ought rather to suffer ourselves to be killed, than to kill. But our Question is, Whether he has thought fit to tye us up so far? Two

---

3. This was the Case of MOSES, when he saw one of his Brethren (that is, an *Israelite*) *suffering Wrong, he defended him, and avenged him that was oppressed, and smote the* Egyptian. *Exod.* ii. *Acts* vii. 24. For at that Time the *Israelites* had no Room to expect Justice from the *Egyptian* Judges.

4. SOLON's Law runs thus, *If any Man steals in the Day-Time, above the Value of fifty Drachms, he shall be brought before the Council of the Eleven: But whoever steals any Thing by Night, it shall be lawful to kill him, or wound him in the Pursuit.* DEMOSTHENES Orat. against *Timocrates,* p. 476. *Edit. Basil.* 1572. See hereafter, *B.* II. *Chap.* I. § 12. where the Reason of the Law is more fully considered. GROTIUS.

5. This Law is preserved by MACROBIUS, who urges it as a Proof, that the Word *Nox* is by the Antients taken for *Noctu.* Saturnal. *Lib.* I. *Cap.* IV.

Places (of Scripture) are wont to be brought for the affirmative Opinion, which we have already explained, when we examined whether War in general was lawful. *But I say unto you, resist not him that doth Thee an Injury. Dearly beloved, avenge not yourselves;* the *Latin* Version has it, *Defend not yourselves.* There is also a third Place, in those Words of CHRIST to *St. Peter, Put up thy Sword into the Sheath; for they that take the Sword shall perish by the Sword.* Some also add the Example of CHRIST himself, who died for his Enemies.

Matt. v. 39.
Rom. xii. 19.

Matt. xxv. 52.
Rom. v. 8, 10.

Amongst the primitive Christians there are some, who indeed did not disallow of publick Wars, but believed Self-defence between private Persons to be unlawful. I have already cited some Passages of St. *Ambrose,* in favour of the Innocence of War: We find in St. *Austin* many more on that Subject, and more clear, which every Body knows. Yet the same St. *Ambrose* said, [1] *Perhaps CHRIST therefore said to* Peter, *upon his shewing him two Swords, It is enough; as if it had been lawful to (the Time of) the Gospel, to make Use of the Sword; that the Doctrine of Equity might be in the Law, and the Perfection of Goodness in the Gospel.* And in another Place, [2] *A Christian, tho' he be attacked by a Highwayman, is not to strike him again, lest in defending himself he offend against Piety.* And St. *Austin,* [3] *I do not dislike that Law, which allows those* (Robbers, and other violent Aggressors) *to be killed; but how I shall defend them who kill them, I know not.* And again, [4] *I do not approve of the Maxim of killing him, by whom one is apprehensive of being killed one's self; unless he happen to be a Soldier, or publick Officer, so that he does not do it for himself, but for others, by Vertue of a lawful Authority.* And it plainly appears, that St. *Basil* was of the same Mind, from his [5] second Epistle to *Amphilochius.*

But the contrary Opinion, as it is more common, so it seems to me more reasonable, that we are not obliged to such a Patience; for we are commanded in the Gospel to love our Neighbours as ourselves, not be-

III. (1) Lib. X. *in Lucam.* Cap. XXII. p. 1782. *Edit. Paris.* 1569.

2. *De Offic.* Lib. III. Cap. IV.

3. *De Lib. Arbitrio,* Lib. I. Cap. V.

4. *Epist. ad Publicolam,* CLIV.

5. *Cap.* XLIII. LV. See also a Canon of the Council of *Orleans,* cited by GRATIAN, in the Canon Law, *Caus.* XIII. *Quaest.* II. *Can.* XXXII. GROTIUS.

the very Connexion of the Words plainly shews, for the Words going before are *Render to no Man Evil for Evil;* but this is the Description of Revenge, not of Defence. St. *Paul* also supports his Exhortation from that Place of *Deuteronomy, Vengeance is mine, I will repay it:* Where 'tis in the *Hebrew* לונקם, which in its proper and natural Sense signifies Vengeance; and it is evident, Self-Defence cannot be meant in that Place.

Now what was said to St. *Peter,* does indeed contain a Prohibition to use the Sword, but not in the Cause of Defence; for he had no Need to defend himself: CHRIST had already said concerning his Disciples, *Suf-* John xviii. 8, 9 *fer these to go away;* and this, *That the Saying might be fulfilled which he spake, of those thou hast given me I have left none.* Nor was it necessary to defend CHRIST; for he would not be defended. Therefore he gives this Reason in St. *John* for forbidding it, *The Cup which my Father hath given* Ver. 11. *me, shall I not drink it?* And he says in St. *Matthew, How then should the Scriptures be fulfilled, that thus it must be?* St. *Peter* being then of a fiery Temper, thought of Revenge, and not of Defence. Besides, he would have taken up Arms against them who came with publick Authority, which whether it be lawful in any Case to resist, is a particular Question, that shall be handled in its proper Place. But what CHRIST also adds, *All they that take the Sword, shall perish by the Sword;* is either a proverbial Saying, which signifies, that Blood causes Blood; and therefore, that the Use of Arms is never free from Danger: Or, according to the Opinion of *Origen, Theophylact, Titus,* and *Euthy-*<57>*nius,* it shews, that we should not incroach upon GOD's Right, by anticipating the Vengeance Rev. xiii. 10 which He, in his own due Time, will fully requite. In which Sense precisely, it is said, *He that killeth with the Sword, shall be killed by the Sword: Here is the Patience and Faith of the Saints.* With which agrees that of *Tertullian,* [10] *GOD is a fit Depository of thy Patience; if thou layest thy Injuries in his Hand, he is thy Avenger; if thy Losses, he is thy Surety; if thy Grief, he is thy Physician; if thy Death, he is thy Reviver: What ought not Patience to do, that has GOD for its Debtor?* Moreover, in these Words of CHRIST there seems to be included, a Prophecy of those Punish-

10. *De Patientia,* Cap. XV.

ments which the Sword of the *Romans* would take of the Blood-thirsty *Jews.*

As to the Example of CHRIST, who is said to have died for his Enemies, it may be answered; that all CHRIST's Actions were indeed full of Virtue, that we may laudably imitate them, as far as 'tis possible; and that Imitation will certainly be rewarded; but yet they are not all such, as either result from an Obedience to an indispensible Law, or constitute a Law to us. For that CHRIST died for his Enemies, and the Ungodly, he did it not by any Law, but as it were by a special Covenant and Agreement with the Father; who, upon his doing it, did not only promise him the most exalted Glory, but also a People that should endure forever. Isa. liii. 10. Besides, this Fact of CHRIST was, as it were, singular, of which we can hardly find any Example; as St. *Paul* shews: And CHRIST himself com- Rom. v. 7. mands us to expose our Life to Danger, not for every one, but for our Brethren, [11] who profess the Christian Religion. 1 John iii. 16.

In fine, the Passages quoted from Christian Doctors, either seem to give an Advice of extraordinary Perfection, rather than to establish an express Command; or contain only the Opinion of some private Persons. For in those most antient Canons called Apostolical, he only was to have been [12] excommunicated, who with the first Blow killed his Adversary

11. *Who profess the Christian Religion.* This is the Signification of the Word Brother, here used by the Apostle. He at the same time supposes, without Doubt, that the Persons, in whose Favour we hazard our Lives, deserve so great a Sacrifice at our Hands, and that we have good Grounds to believe such an Action will procure them some considerable Advantage; which cannot be said in regard to a Highwayman, or any other unjust Aggressor.

12. *If an Ecclesiastick strikes a Man in a Quarrel, and kills him with one Blow, let him be deposed for his Rashness. If a Layman is guilty of the same Fault, let him be deprived of the Communion,* Can. LXIV. Our Author, in his Margin, quotes two Canons from the *Decretals;* one, which orders that if a Layman wounds an Ecclesiastick, in his own Defence, or on finding him in Bed with his Wife, Mother, Sister, or Daughter, he shall not incur the Sentence of Excommunication. *Lib.* V. *Tit.* XXIX. *De Sent. Excom.* Cap. III. Another, which makes several Distinctions, in Cases where a Man kills an Aggressor, and supposes, as the former does, that he may be killed, *Cum moderamine inculpatae tutelae. With the Moderation of an innocent Defence.* Lib. V. Tit. XII. *De Homicidio voluntario, vel casuali.* Cap. XVI. In both of them it is laid down, as a Fact, that *all Laws allow of repelling Force by Force.*

in a Quarrel, *through an* [13] *Excess of Passion.* And St. *Austin* himself, whom we quoted before on the other Side, seems yet to approve [14] of this Opinion.

IV. Publick Wars are either [1] *Solemn, according to the Law of Nations,* or *not solemn:* What I here term *Solemn* is generally called *Lawful,* or *made in Form,* in the same Sense as a *Will* is termed *Lawful,* in [2] Opposition to a *Codicil;* or a *Mar-<58>riage Lawful,* in Opposition of the [3] *Cohab-*

13. St. AMBROSE, on the Advice of our Saviour, *to sell our Coat and buy a Sword,* has these Words: *Lord, why do you forbid me to strike, since you command me to purchase a Sword? Why am I order'd to carry a Weapon, which I am not allow'd to draw! Unless perhaps that I may be provided for my own Defence, not arm'd for Revenge.* Lib. X. in *Lucam.* Cap. XXII. p. 1782. *Edit. Paris.* GROTIUS.

14. Our Author finds this in *Quaest.* LXXXIV. on the Book of *Exodus.* But St. AUGUSTIN in that Place only gives the Reason, why the Law of MOSES, allow'd of killing a Thief in the Night, but not in the Day. *Because,* says he, *after Sun rising a Man might distinguish, whether the Thief came to kill or barely to steal; and in the latter Case, he was not to be kill'd.* That Father makes no other Distinction; nor does he speak of what the Evangelical Law permits or requires in this Case.

IV. (1) See *B.* III. *Cap.* III.

2. The Epithet *Lawful* is taken in this Sense in the very Definition of a *Will* or *Testament,* given by the Civil Law. A *Testament* is there called, *A Declaration of our* (last) *Will, made in Form;* which is expressed by *Justa,* the very Word used by our Author. DIGEST. *Lib.* XXVIII. *Tit.* I. *Qui Testamentum facere possunt,* &c. *Leg.* I. See also the Fragments of ULPIAN, *Tit.* XX. § 1. I do not know that the Terms *Justum Testamentum* occur in the Body of the Civil Law, precisely in Opposition to *Codicils.* For in the Law quoted from DIGEST. *Lib.* XXIX. *Tit.* II. *De acquir. vel amitt. Haereditate.* Leg. XXII. *Justum Testamentum* is opposed to *Non justum Testamentum,* that is, to a Will not made in Form; and this only is meant in the Title, *Injusto, rupto, initio facto Testamento.* Lib. XXVIII. Tit. III. It is well known, that certain Formalities are required even in *Codicils;* tho' not so many as to make a Will good and valid; at least when no Will has been made before or after, which gave them Force.

3. *Contubernium,* and a Woman cohabiting with a Slave was called *Contubernalis:* Even when a Freeman cohabited with a Slave, it was not reckoned a lawful Marriage. *Inter Servos & Liberos* Matrimonium *contrahi non potest,* Contubernium *potest.* JUL. PAULUS, *Recept. Sent.* Lib. II. Cap. XIX. § 6. Contubernales, *quoque servorum, id est, uxores, & natos, instructo fundo contineri verum est.* DIGEST. *Lib.* XXXIII. *Tit.* VII. *De instructo, vel instrum. legato.* Leg. XII. § 33. *Cum Ancillis non potest esse Coannubium; nam ex ejusmodi* Contubernio *servi nascuntur.* COD. *Lib.* V. *Tit.* IV. *De incertis & inutilibus nuptiis.* Leg. III. VARRO calls the Wives of Slaves *Conjunctae.* De Re Rusticâ. *Lib.* I. *Cap.* XVII. And such Cohabitation is expressed by the Word *Consortium,* in the *Institutes,* Lib. III. Tit. VII. *De servili cognatione.*

itation of Slaves: [4] Not because it is not allowed a Man, if he pleases, to make a Codicil, and a Slave to cohabit with a Woman; but because a

4. Even among such as were Citizens, and consequently free, there were *non-legitimate Marriages,* which produced *illegitimate Children.* PAULUS, *Sentent.* Lib. II. Tit. XIX. and DIGEST. *Lib.* XLVIII. Tit. V. *Ad Leg. Jul. de Adulterio.* Leg. XIII. § 1. SENECA, *De Vitâ Beatâ,* Cap. XXIV. and SUETONIUS, *in Octav.* Cap. XL. likewise speaks of a Sort of *illegitimate Liberty.* GROTIUS.

The *non-legitimate Marriages,* which our Author here means, are those contracted by Children, who being under the Power of their Father, married without his Consent; for, according to him, such Marriages were not dissolved, when once contracted; they only wanted the Effects of Law, which they would have had, if authorized by the Father's Approbation. Thus he explains the following Words of the Lawyer PAULUS, *Eorum, qui in potestate Patris sunt, sine voluntate ejus Matrimonia jure non contrahuntur; sed contracta non solvuntur.* In which he follows the Opinion of CUJAS, *Observationes Juris,* Lib. III. Cap. V. But there is abundant Reason to believe the *Roman* Lawyer speaks only of Fathers being deprived of the Power of dissolving the Marriages of their Children under their Jurisdiction, even with their Consent. See Mr. SCULTING's Notes, Page 300 of his *Jurisprudentia Ante Justinianea.* As to the *Uxor injusta,* mentioned in Law XIII. § 1. DIGEST. *Ad Leg. Jul. de Adulter.* CUJAS seems to have retracted in another Part of his Work, where he conjectures, that the Law under Consideration speaks of a Woman who has not been married with the ordinary Formalities. *Observ.* Lib. VI. Cap. XVI. *Quae non solemniter accepta est aquâ & igni.* For among the antient *Romans,* when those Formalities, which consisted in what they called *Confarreatio & Coemptio,* had been omitted, a young Woman, tho' brought home to the House of her intended Husband, was not reckoned married fully, and according to Law: She was not yet a Member of the Family, nor placed under the Man's Power, which they expressed by *In manum Viri convenire:* She had no Right of Succession to his Estate, either in the Whole, or in Conjunction with the Children proceeding from such a Cohabitation. In order to supply the Defect of the Formalities required, she was obliged to live a whole Year with her Husband, without lying three Nights out of his House, according to the Law of the *Twelve Tables,* preserved by A. GELLIUS, *Noct. Attic.* Lib. III. Cap. II. and MACROBIUS, *Saturnal.* Lib. I. Cap. XIII. 'Till that Time she was called *Uxor injusta,* as the President BRISSON has explained this Matter, in his Treatise, *Ad Leg. Jul. de Adulteriis,* published before the sixth Book of CUJAS's *Observations;* that is, she was considered not as a Concubine but a real Wife, tho' something was still wanting in that Union, for investing her with all the Rights and Privileges of a legitimate Marriage. Whereas Matrimony contracted without the Father's Consent, or that of the Person under whose Power the Father himself lived, was absolutely null and illegitimate; in the same Manner as incestuous Marriages, and such as were contracted between a Guardian and his Ward, between a Governor of a Province and a Woman of the same Province, *&c.* And our Author himself, *B.* II. *Chap.* V. § 14. *Note* 11. suspects that the last Words of the Passage, quoted from PAUL's *Receptae Sententiae,* were added by ANJAN, Referendary to the

Will, and a Marriage in Form, have [5] some peculiar Effects, by the Civil
Law; which it is convenient to observe; for many, misunderstanding the
Word *Lawful,* think all Wars are condemned as unjust and unwarrantable, to which that Epithet does not agree. Two Things then are requisite
to make a War solemn by the Law of Nations. First, that it be made on
both Sides, by the Authority of those that have the Sovereign Power in
the State: And then, that it be accompanied with some Formalities; of
which we shall treat in its proper Place. These Conditions are equally
necessary, so that if the one be wanting, the other is needless.

But a publick War not Solemn, may be made both without any Formality, and against mere private Persons, and by the Authority of any
Magistrate whatever. And indeed if we consider the thing without respect to the Civil Law, every Ma-<59>gistrate [6] seems to have as much

---

King of the *Wisigoths.* It is certain, at least, that the *Roman* Lawyer says the direct
contrary in another Place, *A Marriage cannot be good, without the Consent of all, that
is, of those who contract, and of those under whose Power they are.* DIGEST. *Lib.* XXII.
Tit. II. *De Ritu Nuptiarum.* Leg. II. The *Libertas non justa,* alledged by our Author
in this Place, was a Sort of Freedom, neither intire nor irrevocable. See the learned
TORRENTIUS on that Point, in his Commentary on the Passage of SUETONIUS, above
quoted; and J. LIPSIUS, on TACITUS, *Annal.* Lib. XIII. Cap. XXVII. as also, Mr.
NOODT on DIGEST. *Lib.* I. *Tit.* V. *p.* 33.

5. Thus a Man could not, by a Codicil, directly appoint an Heir, or disinherit
those who had a Right to the Succession. *Institut.* Lib. II. Tit. XXV. *De Codicillis.*
§ 2. A Slave had not the Right of paternal Power over his Children; nor even a Freeman over those born to him of his Wife, who was a Slave, *&c.*

6. PUFENDORF criticises this Opinion, *B.* VIII. *Chap.* VI. § 10. But it is easy to
reconcile our two Authors. GROTIUS fixes a more general Idea to the Term War, as
appears by his Definition of it, *Chap.* 1. § 2. See my first *Note* on that Chapter. According to him also, when an inferior Magistrate takes Arms for the Maintenance of
his Authority, and to reduce those to their Duty, who refuse to submit; he is supposed
to act with the Approbation of the Sovereign, who by entrusting him with a Share
in the Government of the State, invested him at the same Time with the Power necessary for the Exercise of his Charge. The Question therefore is only, whether every
Magistrate, as such, stands in need of an express Order from the Sovereign in this
Case, so that the Frame of civil Societies in general require it, independently of the
Civil Law of each particular State. Now I ask, if such a Magistrate has a Right to
employ Arms for the Reduction of one Person, of two, three, ten or twenty, who
refuse him Obedience, or attempt to hinder the Exercise of his Jurisdiction, why may
he not make use of the same Means against fifty, a hundred, a thousand, two thousand, *&c.?* The larger the Number is, the more he will stand in need of Force for

Right, in case of Resistance, to take up Arms in order to execute his Jurisdiction, as to defend the People committed to his Protection. But since by War the whole State is endangered, therefore it is provided, by the Laws of almost all Nations, that it be undertaken only by the Order or with the Approbation of the Sovereign. There is such a Law in [7] *Plato's* last Book *de Legibus.* And by the *Roman* Law he was reckoned [8] guilty of High Treason, who without Commission from the Prince presumed to make War, list Soldiers, or raise an Army. And the *Cornelian* Law, [9] enacted by *L. Cornelius Sylla,* says, without Commission from the People. In the Code of *Justinian,* there is a Constitution extant, made by *Valentinian* and *Valens,* thus, [10] *Let no Man use any Sort of Arms without*

---

conquering the Resistance. Now this is what our Author includes under the Term *War.* If it be objected, that it would be dangerous to allow an inferior Magistrate so much Power, this only proves that Legislators do well in setting Bounds to what would otherwise be a Consequence of the very Design of placing the Magistrate in his Post, in order to proceed in a Manner attended with fewer Inconveniences, so that the Commentators on our Author have no good Reason for falling on him in this Place, as if he weaken'd and destroy'd the first Principles of publick Law.

7. *If any Man makes Peace or War, by his own private Authority, without the Order of the State, let Death be his Punishment? But if any Part of the State makes Peace or War of their own Heads, let the Officers of the Army convene the Authors of such an Attempt before a Council of War; and let the Criminal, on Conviction, suffer Death. De Legib.* Lib. XII. p. 955. Vol. II. *Edit. H. Steph.*

8. DIGEST. *Lib.* XLVIII. *Tit.* IV. *ad Leg. Jul. Majest.* Leg. III.

9. This Law is by Conjecture only ascribed to *L. Corn. Sylla.* All we know of the Matter is grounded on a Passage of CICERO, where the Orator speaks of a *Cornelian Law,* relating to Treason. *I take no notice of his going out of the Province, heading an Army, making War by his own private Authority, going to a Kingdom without the Order of the People and Senate; which Actions as they are prohibited by several ancient Laws, so are they most expresly forbidden by the* Cornelian Law *Majestatis, and the* Julian *de pecuniis repetundis.* Orat. in Pison. Cap. XXI.

10. *Lib.* XI. *Tit.* XLVI. *Ut armorum usus, inscio principe, interdictus sit.* This Law has no manner of Relation to the Power of making War, in whatever Sense the Word is taken. The Emperors VALENTINIAN and VALENS forbid such as are not Soldiers by Profession, to carry Arms on a Journey. See GODFREY's learned Comment on Law I. of the same Title, in the *Theodosian Code,* Lib. XV. Tit. XIV. Tom. V. p. 419. where he gives a very good Explication of that Law; and shews that *movere arma,* the Phrase here employ'd, signifies only to *carry* Arms, whether a Person makes use of them or not.

the Dangers to which the State would inevitably be exposed, if every Magistrate should pretend to judge of the Usefulness or Necessity of War.

Livy, I. 38.
Cap. 45, &c.

Cneius Manlius was not therefore injuriously accused by his Lieutenants, because he had made War upon the *Galatians,* without the Order of the People of *Rome;* for tho' the *Galatians* had supplied *Antiochus* with some Troops; yet, as Peace had been made with that Prince, it did not belong to *Manlius,* but to the People of *Rome,* to determine whether that Injury was to be revenged on the *Galatians.* [4] *Cato* would have had

---

4. SUETONIUS says, in one Place, that *Cato had frequently declared on Oath, that he would impeach him* (Caesar) *as soon as he was divested of the Command of the Army.* Cap. XXX. And in another Place, he speaks in general of *some Persons who were for giving him into the Hands of the Enemy.* Cap. XXIV. But PLUTARCH relates the Fact, with its several Circumstances: He tells us, that after the Victory gained by *Caesar* in the *Belgick Gaul,* over the *Usipetes,* and the *Tenchterians,* who had passed the *Rhine,* in Order to settle themselves, *the Senate decreed publick Rejoicings and Sacrifices,* to express their Gratitude to the Gods, and do honour to the General. Whereupon *Cato delivered it as his Opinion, that Caesar should be delivered up to the Barbarians,* (that is, the *Germans*) *to expiate his Perfidy, and divert the Curse from the State, which that Action might draw on it.* Vit. Caes. *p.* 718 *Tom.* II. *Edit. Wechel.* Where PLUTARCH produces the Authority of TANUSIUS GEMINUS. Τανύσιος δὲ λέγει; for that is the true Reading, and justified by a MS. not Γαγύσιος. See also what he says in his Parallel of the Lives of *Crassus* and *Nicias,* p. 567. So that *Cato* proposed giving *Caesar* into the Hands of the Enemy, not because he had made War on the *Germans* without the express Orders of the Commonwealth, but because that General had attacked the *Germans,* against the Promise and Assurance given them, and seized several of their Deputies; as appears from what he himself says in his Commentaries. *Bel. Gall.* Lib. IV. Cap. XI. *&c.* He does indeed endeavour to put a Gloss on his Conduct; but there is good Reason for believing that he here, as on other Occasions, disguises Things, in order to turn them to his own Advantage. See his Commentators on this Place, in Mr. DAVIES's Edition; and FREINSHEIM's Supplement to LIVY, *Lib.* CV. *Cap.* LI. *&c. Edit. Cleric.* The Manner in which *Cato* gives his Opinion is sufficient for forming a Conjecture, that they were persuaded at *Rome* that *Caesar* had not dealt fairly and honestly in the Matter under Consideration. But, whatever becomes of this Question, it is evident from the Authority alledged, that our Author has not given the true Reason for *Cato*'s voting for delivering *Caesar* into the Hands of the *Germans.* He likewise confounds the Defeat of the *Usipetes* and the *Tenchterians,* which happened before *Caesar* laid the first Bridge over the *Rhine,* with the Victory he gained over those of *Treves* about two Years after; for *Caesar* did not till that Time carry the War into the Country of the *Germans,* in order to take his Revenge on them, as he himself says, for sending Succours to those of *Treves. Bell. Gall.* Lib. VI. Cap. IX. And this

C. Caesar delivered up to the *Germans,* for making War on <61> them: I believe not so much in respect to Justice, as to free the City from the Fear of a Man that wanted to render himself absolute. For the *Germans* had assisted the *Gauls,* declared Enemies to the People of *Rome,* and therefore could have no Reason to complain of any Wrong done them, if the *Romans* had just Cause to make War against the *Gauls.* But *Caesar* ought to have been contented with beating the *Germans* out of *Gaul,* the Province appointed to him, and not to have pushed the War on the *Germans* in their own Country, especially when there was no Danger to be feared from thence, without first consulting the People of *Rome.* The *Germans* therefore had no Right to demand *Caesar* to be delivered up to them, but the People of *Rome* had to punish him; as the *Carthaginians* plainly answered the *Romans,* [5] *The Question is not whether* Hannibal

---

Expedition took up but little Time, and was far from being considerable. At *Caesar's* Approach the Enemy retired into their Forests; and the *Roman* General being apprehensive he should fall short of Provisions for his Army, repassed the *Rhine* a few Days after. *Ibid.* Cap. XXIX. Tho' DION CASSIUS attributes this Motion to his Fear of the Enemy. *Lib.* XL. *p.* 151. *Edit. II. Steph.* But several of our Author's Expositors have confounded Matters still more, by understanding what he here says of *Caesar's* war with *Ariovistus,* when that Prince had possessed himself of Part of the Country of the *Sequani,* related *Bel. Gal.* Lib. I. The learned OBRECHT is one who gives in to this Mistake, as appears not only from his Notes on this Work, published by one of his Scholars without his Knowledge; but also from a Corollary placed at the End of his Dissertation *De Censu Augusti,* which is the ninth of the Collection printed in 1704. For he there makes PLUTARCH say, Caesar's *War with* Ariovistus *being ended,* Cato *gave his Opinion,* &c. And he maintains, *that the* Roman *People had at that Time no Right to punish* Caesar, *but that the* Germans *had a Right to demand his Delivery into their Hands.* Mr. BUDDEUS makes the same Supposition, in his *Jurisprudentiae Historicae specimen.* § 110. Even in the Application which they both make of *Cato's* Vote, the last Proposition advanced by OBRECHT is as false as the first is true; as I shall shew in another Place, where I shall have Occasion to speak after our Author of the War made on *Ariovistus.* B. III. Chap. III. §10.

5. LIVY, *Lib.* XXI. *Cap.* XVIII. *Num.* 6. The learned GRONOVIUS thinks this Way of reasoning, employed by the *Carthaginians,* was a mere Piece of Chicanry; because *Hannibal,* by attacking the City of *Saguntum* by his own private Authority, had violated a Clause of the Treaty between the *Romans* and *Carthaginians.* It is true here was a real Infraction of the Treaty, as I shall shew elsewhere, in Opposition to our Author, *B.* II. *Chap.* XVI. § 13. But then that was the very Thing in Question; and till they were convinced of that, they might say with Reason, that the *Romans* had

of Magistrates. 3. Judgments. To the first he refers the Power of making War or Peace, of concluding or breaking Treaties and Alliances, of enacting or repealing Laws; to which he adds, the inflicting of Death, Banishment, Confiscation of Goods, and the Punishment of Peculation and Extortion: That is, in my Opinion, the Judgments that relate to publick Crimes; whereas, in the third Class, by *Judgments* he means those that concern Crimes committed directly against private Persons. *Dionysius Halicarnassensis* chiefly takes Notice of these [4] three Things, 1*st,* The Right to create Magistrates. 2*dly,* The Right to [5] make Laws and repeal them. 3*dly,* The Right of making Peace or War. In another Place he adds, the Right of Judging as a [6] <63> Fourth; and again, elsewhere, [7] the Right of Regulating the Affairs of Religion, and of calling Assemblies.

But if any one would divide it right, he may easily find all Things relating to it; so as that nothing may be wanting or superfluous. For he that governs a State, does it either by himself or by another. What he does himself respects either general Affairs or particular; what concerns general Affairs relates to the making or repealing of Laws; which extends as well to sacred Things (as far as he has a Right to meddle in them) as

4. The *Greek* Writer is there speaking of the *Roman* People, *Who,* he says, *were from the very Beginning possessed of three great and most necessary Branches of Power,* viz. *that of creating civil Magistrates, and Officers for the Army; that of enacting and abrogating Laws; and that of regulating whatever belonged to Peace and War.* Antiq. Rom. *Lib.* IV. *Cap.* XX. *p.* 215. *Edit. Oxon.* See likewise *Lib.* II. *Cap.* XIV.

5. The Grammarian SERVIUS describes the Power of the *Romans* in the same Manner, *Omni Ditione.* Omni *in this Place,* says he, *is better than* omnis, *to express their enjoying all Power, in regard to Peace, War, and Laws.* GROTIUS.

6. In a Speech made by *Manius Valerius,* where he requires, that the People *should be allowed a Share in the Administration of Justice, especially in Causes which nearly concern the Good of the Commonwealth; as when a Person is accused of raising Sedition, endeavouring to enslave his Country by the Exercise of despotick Power, or betraying it to the Enemy.* Antiq. Rom. *Lib.* VII. *Cap.* LVI. *p.* 445. *Edit. Oxon.*

7. Our Author has his Eye on the Place where the *Grecian* Writer speaks of the Power given by *Romulus* to the Kings, which was reduced to the following Heads, 1. *The Direction of what related to the Sacrifices, and other Parts of Religious Worship.* 2. *The Maintenance of both the Natural and Civil Laws, with the Cognizance of the most considerable Violations of both.* 3. *The Convening of the Senate, Assembling of the People, giving their Votes first, and putting in Execution whatever was carried by a Plurality of Voices.* 4. *The Command of the Armies.* Lib. II. Cap. XIV.

to profane. *Aristotle* calls this Ἀρχιτεκτονικὴ, the [8] *chief Art* of Government. The Particular Affairs are either directly publick or private, but considered as they relate to the publick Good. Those which are directly publick, concern either certain Actions, as the making of Peace, War, Treaties, Alliances; or certain Things, as Taxes, and such like, in which is comprehended that [9] eminent Dominion which a State has over its Subjects, and their Goods, for the publick Use. *Aristotle* calls this Art by the general [10] Name Πολιτικὴ, *Political,* and by another (Βουλευτικὴ) that signifies the *Art of Deliberating.* Private Affairs are here the Differences of private Persons, so far as the Repose of the Society requires the Decision of them by publick Authority: And this Art *Aristotle* calls [11] Δικαστικὴ, *Judicial.* Those Things which are dispatched by another, are either done by Magistrates, or other Ministers, among whom we may put Embassadors. In these then consists the Civil Power.

VII. That is called Supreme, whose Acts are not subject to another's Power, so that they cannot be made void by any other human Will. When [1] I say, by any other, I exclude the Sovereign himself, who may change his own Will, as also his Successor, who enjoys the same Right, and consequently, has the same Power, and no other. Let us then see what this Sovereign Power may have for its Subject. The Subject then is either common or proper: As the Body is the common Subject of Sight, the Eye the proper; so the common Subject of Supreme Power is the State; which I have before called a perfect Society of Men.

VII. What Power is supreme.

Cacheranus Decis Pedem. 139. n. 6.

We then exclude the Nations, who are brought under the Power of another People, as were the *Roman* Provinces; for those Nations are no longer a State, as we now use the Word, but the less considerable Members of a great State, as Slaves are the Members of a Family. Again it

8. *Ethic. Nicom.* Lib. VI. Cap. VIII.
9. See *Chap.* I. § 6.
10. *Ethic. Nicom.* Lib. VI. Cap. VIII.
11. *Ibid.*
VII. (1) What PUFENDORF says, *B.* VII. *Chap.* V. may serve as a Comment on all this. As to our Author's Definition of the *Sovereign Power,* see a Treatise *De Jure Imperii,* written by RABOD HERMAN SCHELIUS, *p.* 132. &c.

Vict. de jure
belli. n. 7. happens sometimes, that divers People have one and the same Head, and yet each of those People make a compleat Society; for it is not in the moral Body, as 'tis in the natural, where one Head cannot belong to several Bodies; for there the same Person may be head, under a different Consideration, to several distinct Bodies; of which this is a certain Proof, [2] that upon the Extinction of the reigning Family, the Sovereign Power reverts to each People. So it may also happen, that several States may be linked together in a most strict Alliance, and make a [3] Compound, as *Strabo* more [4] than once calls it; and yet each of them continue to be a perfect State, which is observed both by others, and by [5] *Aristotle* in several Places.

The State then is, in the Sense I have just mentioned, the common Subject of Sovereignty. The proper Subject is one or more Persons, according to the Laws <64> and Customs of each Nation, Ἡ πρώτη ἀρχή, the first Power of the State, in *Galen, Lib. 6. de placitis, Hyppoc. & Plat.*

VIII. *The*
Opinion

VIII. 1. And here we must first reject their Opinion, [1] who will have the Supreme Power to be always, and without Exception, in the People; so

---

2. See *B.* II. *Chap.* IX. § 8.

3. Pufendorf treats of this at large, *B.* VII. *Chap.* V. § 16, *&c.* It is worth while to consult him on the Subject.

4. He makes use of the Term σύστημα, when speaking of the *Amphictyons,* Lib. IX. p. 643. *Ed. Amst.* (420 *Paris.*) and of the *Lycians,* Lib. XIV. p. 980. *Edit. Amster.* (664. *Paris.*)

5. He calls those Bodies Συμμαχίαι, *Alliances, Polit.* Lib. II. Cap. II. p. 313. *Edit. Paris.* Tom. II. and Lib. III. Cap. IX. p. 348. because such Sort of Confederacies are commonly formed chiefly with a View of mutual Defence against the common Enemy.

VIII. (1) See my Remarks on Pufendorf, *B.* VII. *Chap.* VI. § 5. *Note* 2. The late Mr. Hertius has left us a whole Dissertation on this Question, which is the eighth in his first Volume of *Commentationes & Opuscula, &c.* Where we have a particular and exact Account of the Books published on both Sides of this Question. It must be owned, there has been much Misunderstanding in regard to the whole Subject of the respective Rights of the Sovereign and People. The first who wrote on it with any Extent, having only confused Ideas of the Law of Nature, were not sufficiently acquainted with the Topick of such Questions. Add to this the particular Interests and Passions, which in this, as in other Cases, have carried the Disputants on both Sides into vitious Extremes. But if we examine Things without Prejudice, I believe we shall that they may restrain or punish their Kings, as often as they abuse their Power. What Mischiefs this Opinion has occasioned, and may yet occasion, if once the Minds of People are fully possessed with it, every wise Man sees. I shall refute it with these Arguments. It is lawful for any Man to engage himself as a Slave to whom he pleases; as appears both by the *Hebrew* [2] and *Roman* Laws. Why should it not therefore be as lawful for a People that are at their own Disposal, to deliver up themselves to any one or more Persons, and transfer the Right of governing them upon him or them, without reserving any Share of that Right to themselves? Neither should you say this is not to be presumed: For the Question here

refuted which holds that the supreme Power is always in the People, and the Arguments answered.

Ex. xxi. 6.
Instit. l. I. tit.
3. de jure per-
son. § 4.

---

find it not very difficult to establish certain Principles, which neither favour Tyranny, nor the Spirit of Independence and Rebellion. It is certain, that as soon as a People in any Manner submits to a King, really such, they are no longer possessed of the Sovereign Power; for it implies a Contradiction, to say we confer a Power on any one, and keep it still in our own Hands. But it does not thence follow, that we have conferred it so as not to reserve a Right to reassume it in any Case. This *Reserve* is sometimes *expressed;* and there is always a tacit one, the Effect of which appears, when the Person on whom the Power has been conferred abuses it in a Manner directly, and remarkably, contrary to the End for which it was conferred. See our Author, in the following Chapter, § 11. For I do not know any Man has ventured to maintain, that a Prince entirely forfeits his Right for the least Abuse of the Sovereign Authority. Princes being Men, as well as the meanest private Person, and consequently, subject to Faults, that Consideration is supposed to be taken in, when they are invested with their Power. And it is certain, that the People pardon them a great Number of crying Injustices, before they think of recovering their natural Liberty.

2. In the Margin of the Original, we have here a Quotation from A. GELLIUS, which is not only faulty in all the Editions before mine, but also misapplied, as has been observed by GRONOVIUS, in a Note on that antient Writer, tho' he is entirely silent in this Place. The Passage in Question is as follows,

Diogenes *the* Cynick *was a Slave; but he was sold into Slavery, and so lost his Liberty.* Noct. Attic. *Lib.* II. *Cap.* XVIII.

Our Author by this designs to let us know, that among the antient *Grecians* every Man had a Right to sell his own Liberty directly; as appears from his *Florum Sparsiones ad Jus Justinianeum.* Tit. *De Jure Personarum.* p. 14. *Edit. Amstel.* where he makes use of this Passage for proving the pretended Difference between the *Grecian* and *Roman* Laws in this Particular. But the *Latin* Compiler of *Miscellaneous Observations* only means, that *Diogenes* from a Freeman became a Slave; for he was taken by Pirates, who sold him; as appears from the Passages of DIOGENES LAERTIUS, alledged by GRONOVIUS on that Place. A Passage from DION of *Prusa,* quoted by our Author, *B.* II. *Chap.* V. § 27. *Num.* 1. would have been more to his Purpose.

is not, what may be presumed in a Doubt, but what may be lawfully done? In vain do some alledge the Inconveniences which arise from hence, or may arise; for you can frame no Form of Government in your Mind, which will be without Inconveniences and Dangers. [3] *Either you must take the one with the other, or* [4] *refuse both,* says the Comedian.

But as there are several Ways of Living, some better than others, and every one may chuse which he pleases of all those Sorts; so a People may chuse what Form of Government they please: Neither is the Right which the Sovereign has over his Subjects to be measured by this or that Form, of which divers Men have divers Opinions, but by the Extent of the Will [5] of those who conferred it upon him. <65>

There may be many Causes why a People should renounce all Sovereignty in themselves, and yield it to another: As when they are upon the Brink of Ruin, and they can find no other Means to save themselves; or being in great Want, they cannot otherwise be supported. For if the *Campani* formerly, obliged by Necessity, submitted themselves to the *Romans* in this Form, [6] *We yield up, O ye Senators, the People of* Campania, *and the City of* Capua, *our Fields, Temples, and all that we have,*

3. TERENCE, *Heautontim.* Act II. Scene II. Ver. 84.

4. CICERO speaking of the Power of the *Tribunes* of the *Roman* People says, *You see plainly,* Quintus, *that the Tribuneship is exposed to many Abuses. But it is unjust, in the Prosecution of any Accusation, to enumerate Inconveniencies, and place Abuses to View, without taking any Notice of the Advantages resulting from the Thing under Consideration—But we should not enjoy the Advantage sought for, without that Mixture of Inconveniencies.* De Legibus, *Lib.* III. *Cap.* X. GROTIUS.

5. The City of *Augsbourg* petitioned *Charles* V. that the Resolutions of their Senate might be allowed no Force, without the Assent of the Masters of the Tribes of the People. The *Norimbergers* desired the direct contrary. GROTIUS.

Our Author is mistaken here, in attributing to *Charles* the Fifth, what the Historians say of *Sigismund;* as has been observed by WAGENSEIL, *De Norimbergae rebus notabilibus.* Cap. XXIII. p. 179; for which he quotes MELANCTHON, *Chron. Carion.* Lib. II. p. 206. I am beholden to Mr. HERTIUS for this Remark. See his Dissertation *De specialib. Rom Germ. Imperii Rebus publicis, &c.* § 23. in Tom. II. of his *Commentationes & Opuscula, &c.*

6. LIVY, *Lib.* VII. *Cap.* XXXI. *Num.* 4.

both Divine and Human, into your Power. [7] And some People, when they offered to submit themselves to the Power of the *Romans,* were refused, as [8] *Appian* relates: What hinders, but that any People may, after the [9] same Manner, yield up themselves to one powerful Prince. We read in *Virgil,*

Nec cum se, &c.

It may also happen, that a Master of a Family having large Possessions, will suffer no Body to dwell in them upon any other Condition; or one may have a great many Slaves, and make them free, upon Condition of acknowledging him for their Sovereign, and paying some Taxes: Of which we have many Instances. *Tacitus* speaks thus of the *German* Slaves, [10] *Every one has his Dwelling, and governs his own House. The Master de-*

---

7. The *Falisci* and the *Samnites* did the same. See LIVY, *Lib.* V. *Cap.* XXVII. and *Lib.* IX. *Cap.* XLII. Thus likewise the *Epidamnii,* being abandoned by those of *Corcyra,* surrendered themselves to the *Corinthians,* to engage that People in their Defence against the *Taulantii,* the *Illyrians,* and the *Exiles,* who had joined them. THUCYDIDES, *Lib.* I. § 24, 25. *Edit. Oxon.* GROTIUS.

8. See APPIAN's Preface, *p. 6. Edit. Tol.* The same Author instances in the *Libyans,* p. 7. *Edit. Toll.* (3 *H. Steph.*)

9. This Passage of VIRGIL is nothing to the present Purpose, as has been observed by the Commentators of the Work before us. It is taken from the fourth Book of the *Aeneid,* v. 618, 619. where *Dido,* among the Imprecations with which she loads *Aeneas,* wishes that, after having made a disadvantageous Peace, he may enjoy neither Kingdom nor Life,

——— *Nec cùm se sub leges pacis iniquae*
Tradiderit, regno aut optatâ luce fruatur;
Sed cadat ante diem, ———

Our Author, by changing the Punctuation, and the Sense, makes the unfortunate Lover say,

——— *Nec, cùm se sub leges pacis iniquae*
Tradiderit regno.

A remarkable Example how far the Memory imposes on such as depend on it too much.

10. *De moribus Germanorum,* Cap. XXV. See a Dissertation by Mr. THOMASIUS, *De hominibus propriis Germanorum,* § 66, &c. Where he explains that Historian's Account of the several Sorts of Slaves among the antient Germans. The *Liti* or *Lidi,* in the middle Age, are also brought as an Example on this Occasion. See the late Mr.

very poor, or Strangers, the Women and young Folks, were excluded from publick Councils. There are also some People that have other [20] Peo-<67>ple under them, who are no less subject to them than if they were under Kings. Whence arose that Question, [21] *Are the Collatine People in their own Power?* And when the *Campani* had delivered themselves up to the *Romans,* they [22] are said to have passed under a foreign Do-

---

to place it to the Account of his Expositor, who is in other Respects a very great Critick, but here on this and other Subjects, has often made strange Mistakes, in explaining an Author whose Principles he did not thoroughly understand; as I have long since observed in my Notes on PUFENDORF, and as appears from what I have said in my *Latin* Edition of this Work of GROTIUS.

20. Thus *Salamis* depended on the *Athenians,* from the Time of *Phileus,* and *Eurysaces* the Son of *Ajax,* as PLUTARCH informs us in the Life of *Solon,* p. 83. Tom. I. *Edit. Wech.* The Emperor *Augustus* took that Island from the *Athenians; as Adrian* afterwards did *Cephalenia.* XIPHILINUS. The Country of *Atarnes* in *Mysia,* formerly belonged to those of *Chios,* as we learn from HERODOTUS, *Lib.* I. *Cap.* CLX. and the *Samians* were Masters of several Towns on the Continent, according to STRABO, *Lib.* XIV. *p. 639. Edit. Paris.* Anactorium in the Gulph of *Ambracia,* was partly in the Hands of the *Corinthians,* and partly in those of the *Corcyrans.* THUCYD. *Lib.* I. *Cap.* LV. *Edit. Oxon.* In a Treaty of Peace concluded between the *Romans* and *Etolians,* it was stipulated that the City of *Oeneades,* with its Territories and Inhabitants, should belong to the *Acarnanians.* LIVY, *Lib.* XXXVIII. *Cap.* XI. *Num.* 9. PLINY speaks of seven (GROTIUS says six) Cities given to those of *Halicarnassus,* by *Alexander* the Great, *Hist. Nat.* Lib. V. Cap. XXIX. The same Writer says, the Island of *Lindus,* and the City of *Caunus* belonged to the *Rhodians,* Lib. XXXIII. Cap. IV. and Lib. XXXV. Cap. X. which is also attested by CICERO, *Ep. ad Quintum Fratrem,* Lib. I. Ep. I. The *Romans* gave several Towns to the same *Rhodians,* in return for their Assistance in the War with *Antiochus.* EUTROP. *Lib.* IV. *Cap.* II. *Num.* II. *Edit. Cellar.* Those were Towns in *Caria* and *Lysia,* which the Senate afterwards took from them. See POLYB. *Exc. Legat.* Cap. XXV. and XCIII. GROTIUS.

Besides that this Note is superfluous, which gives such a Number of Instances of what is well known, there are several Mistakes in it. First, *Augustus* did not take *Salamis* from the *Athenians.* STRABO, who flourished under *Augustus* and *Tiberius,* expressly tells us, that the Island in Question depended then on the *Athenians.* Geogr. *Lib.* IX. p. 603. *Edit. Amst.* (394. *Paris.*) Our Author has confounded *Salamis* with *Egina;* for XIPHILIN says, Augustus *distressed the* Athenians, *and took* Egina *from them,* p. 75. *Edit. H. Steph.* Secondly, Neither did *Adrian* take the Island of *Cephalenia* from the *Athenians.* On the contrary, they received it from that Emperor, as we learn from the Author here quoted, *p.* 264. Thirdly, there is no such Island as *Lindos,* which is the Name of a City in *Rhodes,* as PLINY assures us, *Lib.* V. *Cap.* XXXI.

21. LIVY, *Lib.* I. *Cap.* XXXVIII. *Num.* 2.

22. *Idem.* Lib. VII. Cap. XXXI. Num. 6.

minion. As *Acarnania* and *Amphilochia* are said to have been under the Power of the *Aetolians: Peraea* and *Caunus* under that of the *Rhodians*. *Pydna* was given by *Philip* to the *Olynthians*. And those Towns which had been under the *Spartans,* when they were delivered from their Government, were called *Eleutherolacones, (freed Laconians).* The City *Cotyora* is said to have belonged to the People of *Sinope,* in *Xenophon. Nice* in *Italy* was adjudged to the People of *Marseilles,* in *Strabo:* And the Island of *Pithecusa* to the *Neapolitans.* So we read in *Frontinus,* that the Town *Calatia* was adjudged to the Colony of *Capua, Caudium* to the Colony of *Beneventum,* with their Territories. *Otho* gave the Cities of the *Moors* to [23] the Province of *Boetica,* as it is in *Tacitus.* All which were absolutely void, if we allow, that the Right of Government is always at the Discretion and Will of the Persons governed.

But both sacred and profane History do testify, that there are some Kings who do not depend on the People, considered even as a Body, *If thou shalt say,* (said GOD to the *Israelites*) *I will set a King over me.* And to *Samuel, Shew them the Manner of the* [24] *King that is to reign over them.* Hence the King is said to be *anointed over the People;* and *over the Inheritance of the LORD;* and *over Israel. Solomon* is called King over all *Israel.* So *David* thanks GOD, that he had subdued the People under him: And CHRIST says, *The Kings of the Gentiles exercise Lordship over them.* That Passage of *Horace* is well known,

[25] *Regum timendorum,* &c.

Formidable Kings have Dominion over their own People; but Kings themselves are subject to the Dominion of Jupiter.

Seneca thus describes the three Forms of Government, [26] *Sometimes we have Reason to fear the People; sometimes the Persons of Credit in a Council, when the greatest Part of Publick Affairs are in the Hands of that*

Liv. 1. 26. c. 24
xxxviii. c. 3.
xxxii. c. 33.
xlv. c. 25.
Strab. xiv.
Diod. xvi.
Paus. I. iii.
Exp. Cyri I. v.
Strab. I. iv.
— v.

Deut xvii. 14.
1 Sam. viii. 4. 9
— ix. 16.
— x. 1.
— xv. 1.
2 Sam. xv. 2
1 Kings iv. 1.
Ps. cxliv. 2.
Luke xxii. 25

23. This Example is nothing to the Purpose; for it speaks of a Province of the *Roman* Empire, which of Course could not have a Sovereign Power over those Cities, without the Emperor's Will and Pleasure.

24. See what is said on the following Chapter, § 3.

25. Hor. *Lib.* III. *Ode* I.

26. *Epist.* XIV.

Council; and sometimes one single Person, who is invested with the Power of the People, and over the People. Such are those who [27] *Plutarch* says, *Not only command according to the Laws, but even command the Laws themselves.* And in *Herodotus, Otanes* thus describes Monarchy, *A Power to command as one pleases, without being accountable to any Person.* And *Dion Prusaeensis* describes *Royalty: So to govern, as not to give Account to another. Pausanias* to the *Messenians, opposes regal Government to that which must give Account of its Actions.*

Aristotle says, there are some Kings who have the same Power as the whole Nation has in another Place over their Persons and Goods. So after the chief Men of *Rome* began to assume to themselves the Regal Power, the [28] People are said to have <68> bestowed all their Dominion upon them, and Power even over themselves; as [29] *Theophilus* expounds it. Hence is that Saying of *Marcus Antoninus* the Philosopher, [30] *No one but GOD only can be the Judge of a Prince;* and [31] *Dion,* B. 53. of such a

---

27. This Passage of PLUTARCH is not very well applied. The Historian speaks there of *Philopemenes,* General, not Sovereign of the *Achaeans,* and observes, that *He was so great a Master of the Art of War, that he understood not only how to command according to the Laws, but even how to command the Laws themselves, when the Good of the State required it; that he did not stay till the Command was given him, but took it when Opportunity offered; being persuaded, that the Person who had better Skill and Judgment than those at the Helm, was their General, rather than he whom they chose.* Compar. Vit. Philopoem. & Flamin, *p.* 382. *Tom.* I. *Edit. Wech.*

28. *The Prince's Pleasure has the Force of a Law; for by the* Lex Regia, *made by his Authority, the People conferr'd on him all the Authority and Power.* DIGEST. Lib. I. Tit. IV. *De Constit. Principum,* Leg. I. See the learned GRONOVIUS's Oration *De Lege Regia,* which I have translated into *French,* and illustrated with Notes. That Piece was published in 1714, in the second Edition of Mr. NOODT's Discourse on *The Power of Sovereign Princes, and Liberty of Conscience.*

29. *The* Lex Regia *gave the King all Manner of Power over the People.* Ad *Institut.* Lib. I. Tit. II. § 6. p. 22. *Edit. Fabroti.*

30. XIPHILINUS, in Marc. Anton. *p.* 271. *Edit. H. Steph.* See MILTON's Exposition of this Passage, *Defens. pro Pop. Anglic.* Cap. II. *p.* 49. Mr. DE TILLEMONT, in his *History of the Emperors,* Vol. IV. *p.* 644. *Edit. Bruxelles,* joins and explains that Prince's Words, as if he meant to say, *He feared not the Mutinies of the Soldiers, because GOD alone is the Master of Empires.* GRONOVIUS gives them the same Sense.

31. This is said in Justification of *Augustus's* Conduct, whom he thought discharged from all Obligation of Obedience to the Laws, *Lib.* LIII. *p.* 591. *Edit. H. Steph.*

Prince, *He is free, Master of himself, and of the Laws, so that he does what he pleases, and what he doth not please he need not do.* Such a Kingdom was that of the [32] *Inachidae* antiently in *Greece* at *Argos;* for in the *Argive* Tragedy *of Suppliants,* the People thus address the King in *Aeschylus.* [33]

32. These are the *Anakim* עֲנָקִים, mentioned *Deut.* ii. 10. Hence the Name of the Goddess Ὄγκα עֲנָקָה, to whom *Cadmus* built a Temple at *Thebes,* and whom the *Grecians* called *Pallas.* ESCHYLUS says, the *Inachidae* were *Pelasgi,* that is, Exiles, for the *Syriac* Word פֻּגל. The first Inhabitants of *Lacedemonia* were *Pelasgi;* for which Reason the *Lacedemonians* called themselves Descendents of *Abraham,* 1 *Maccab.* xv. 21. Now as the Kings of *Argos* were arbitrary, in Imitation of those of the *East,* from whence they came, so were the Kings of *Thebes,* who descended from the *Phoenicians.* This appears from the Words of *Creon,* in SOPHOCLES, and those of the *Theban* Herald, in the *Suppliants* of EURIPIDES. GROTIUS.

In regard to the *Anakim,* and the Origin of *Inachus,* see BOCHART, *Chanaan.* Lib. I. Cap. I. and Mr. LE CLERC's *Compendium of Universal History,* p. 13, 14. Second Edition. For what concerns the Goddess Ὄγκα consult SELDEN, *De Diis Syris.* Syntagm II. Cap. IV. The Passage of SOPHOCLES, referred to by our Author, as tending to prove the Kings of *Thebes* in *Boeotia* absolute, is taken from that great Poet's AN-TIGONE. The new King is introduced speaking like a most absolute Prince, in relation to his Prohibition of burying *Polynice.* ANTIGONE owns *It is one of the many Advantages of a Tyrant,* that is, of a *King,* according to the Language of those Times, *to do and say what he pleases;* and affirms, that is the Reason why the *Thebans* dared not open their Mouths, tho' they were persuaded in their Hearts, that *Creon's* Edict was unjust and inhuman, *v.* 516, *&c.* See also *v.* 748, *&c.* That Prince, in another Place, falling on the common Place of the Necessity of Subordination and Obedience in a State, says, *The Will of him whom the People has placed at their Head, is to be obeyed, when he commands Things of small Consequence, what is just or unjust.* v. 681, 682. He then asks, whether *he was guilty of a Fault, in supporting the Honour of his Authority?* The *Theban* Herald in EURIPIDES speaks thus, *The State from which I am deputed, is governed by one Man, not by the People.* v. 410, 411. And THESEUS, who thence takes Occasion to harangue on the Advantages of a popular Government, as was that of *Athens,* in Opposition to Monarchy, observes, among other Things, that in a Kingdom there are *no common Laws,* made by the People, *but one Person's Will is the only Law.* v. 429, *&c.* PAUSANIAS plainly tells us, that the Kings of *Thebes* were absolute, when he speaks of the Revolution that happened after the Demise of *Xanthus,* the last *Theban* King, *From that Time,* says he, *the* Thebans *judged it better to be governed by a Number, than to let every Thing depend on one Man.* Boeotic. *Cap.* V. *p.* 287. *Edit. Wechel.* But we cannot say quite the same of the Kings of *Argos.*

33. But, as MILTON observes, in his *Defens. pro Pop. Anglic.* Cap. V. p. 174. The Poet puts those Words into the Mouth of some foreign Women, who desiring the King of *Argos's* Protection and Assistance against the *Aegyptian* Fleet in Pursuit of them, flatter him with an absolute Power, which did not belong to him; as is evident from that Prince's own Words, *I have already told you, I will not do it, without the*

Sir, you are the City and the Publick; you are an independent Judge. Seated on your Throne, as upon an Altar, you alone govern all by your absolute Commands.

Quite otherwise than King *Theseus* himself speaks of the State of *Athens* in [34] *Euripides, This City is not governed by a single Person, but it is a free City, where the People reign, by establishing new Magistrates every Year, as they think fit.* For *Theseus,* as [35] *Plutarch* explains it, was only their General in Time of War, and the Guardian of their Laws; in other Things upon [36] a Level with the Citizens. Hence it comes to pass, that Kings who are accountable to their People, are said to be called Kings improperly. So after *Lycurgus,* and especially after the *Ephori* were constituted, the *Lacedemonian* Kings are said by [37] *Poly-<69> bius,* [38] *Plutarch,* and [39] *Cornelius Nepos,* to be Kings only in Name, and not in Reality; which Example others also followed in *Greece.* Thus [40] *Pausanias* says (of the *Argives*) to the *Corinthians, The* Argives, *of old great Lovers of Equality and Liberty, have limited the Regal Power as much as possible; so that they have left to the Sons and Posterity of* Cisus, *nothing but the bare*

Consent of the People, even tho' it was in my Power. Conformably to this Declaration, he convenes the People, and having obtained their Approbation, promises the Petitioners to comply with their Request. See also the Passage of PAUSANIAS, quoted by our Author, *Note 40.*

34. *Supplic.* v. 404, *&c.*

35. *Vit. Thes.* p. 11. Tom. I. *Edit. Wech.*

36. *Demophoon* the Son of *Theseus,* speaks thus in one of EURIPIDES's Tragedies, *I am not invested with absolute Power, like the Kings of the Barbarians; but if I govern with Justice, I shall be treated as I deserve.* Heraclid. v. 424, 425. GROTIUS.

37. That Historian speaks only of the Manner how the Kings of *Lacedemonia* were limited. *Lib.* VI. *Cap.* VIII. which is the Place our Author had in View.

38. It is where he speaks of *Cleomenes,* who, as he observes, *had only the Name of King, but the whole Power was lodged in the Hands of the* Ephori. Vit. Agid. & Cleomen. *p.* 805. *Edit. Wech.*

39. His Words are these, *For it has long been a standing Custom among the* Lacedemonians, *to have two Kings, who are such more in Name than Authority, chosen out of the two Families of* Proclus *and* Euristhenes, *&c.* Vit. Agesil. *Cap.* I. *Num.* 2. *Edit. Cellar.* And *Cap.* XXI. *De Regibus,* Num. 2. *But* Agesilaus, *like the other* Spartans, *was King of the* Lacedemonians, *in Name, not in Power.*

40. *Corinthiac.* Cap. XIX. p. 61. *Edit. Wech. Graec.*

Name of King. So also *Plutarch* [41] observes, That the Senate had Power to judge Kings among the *Cumaeans.* [42] *Aristotle* denies that such King-doms constitute any proper Form of Government, because they do but make Part of an Aristocratical or Democratical State.

Nay, even among Nations, which are not always under Kings, we meet with some Instances of a Sort of temporary Monarchy, which is not sub-ject to the People. Such was the Power of the [43] *Amymones* among the *Cnidians,* and of the Dictators [44] in the first Ages at *Rome,* from whom there was no Appeal to the People; whence a Dictator's Edict was held

41. *The Officer who had the Care of the Prison, used to bring the Kings before the Senate by Night, and not give them their Liberty till they were cleared by that Body.* PLUTARCH, *Quaest. Graec.* p. 291, 292, Tom. II. *Edit. Wech.*

42. The Philosopher does not say such Kings made Part of an Aristocratick or Democratick State; but *that there may be, even in Democracy and Aristocracy, Generals invested with as large a Share of Authority in Military Affairs, as the Persons who bear the Title of King.* Polit. *Lib.* III. *Cap.* XVI. *p.* 359. *Edit. Paris.*

43. *Amymones.* Our Author, and some others, miscall this People, as GRONOVIUS observes; for *Amnemones* is the true Reading, which he shews from PLUTARCH, *Quaest. Graec.* 292. But I am surprized that no one has taken Notice of the Misapplication of this Example. For the sixty chosen Men, there mentioned, who governed in the most important Affairs with absolute Authority, held their Office during Life, (διὰ βίου). So that this cannot be alledged as an Instance of temporary Sovereignty. But our Author, trusting his Memory on this Occasion, thought PLUTARCH wrote δί ἔτους, were chosen *annually.* Or perhaps, having read BODIN, who makes the same Mistake in his Treatise *Of the Commonwealth,* Lib. I. Cap. VIII. p. 126. *Edit. Lat. Francof.* 1622. he took it from that Writer, without consulting the Original. I am inclined to believe this was the Case, because they agree in giving the Magistrates of *Cnidos* the Appellation of *Amymones.* But whatever led him into this Error, our Au-thor might have produced a more suitable Example nearer Home, which is that of the Government of *Friesland,* where the Senators, who compose the supreme Council of State, and are elected every Year, have had, during that Time, so absolute an Au-thority ever since the Year 1629, that they do what they please, without consulting any one, or being obliged to answer for their Conduct when out of Office; nor can any Act of theirs be abrogated. This I learnt from a Lawyer of that Country, who has been successively Professor and Member of that Sovereign Council; from whence he was called into the Academy of *Franecker.* See ULRIC HUBER, *De Jure Civitatis,* Lib. I. Sect. VIII. Cap. II. Num. 3, *&c.*

44. See § 11. where the Author treats professedly of the *Dictators.* I have transposed a Note of the Author to that Place; because it contains an Example taken from the *Roman* History, relating to what he says of the Power of those extraordinary Magistrates.

Justice to the People. But it does not therefore follow, as they infer, that the People are superior to the King: For Guardianship was undoubtedly designed for the Benefit of the Pupil; and yet it gives to the Guardian [54] a Power over the Pupil. Neither does it avail, that a Guardian may be removed if he does not manage his Charge well; and therefore there ought to be the same Power over a King. For as to a Guardian, it is to be considered, that he has a Power superior to him: But in Civil Governments, because there must be some dernier Resort, it must be fixed either in one Person, or in an Assembly; whose Faults, because they have no superior Judge, GOD declares, that he takes Cognizance of; who either punishes them, if there be a Necessity for it; or tolerates them, for the Chastisement or Trial of a People.

Jer. xxx. 12.

It is admirably said of [55] *Tacitus, You must bear with the Luxury or Covetousness of Princes, as you do Barrenness, Storms, and the other Inconveniences of Nature: There will be Faults, as long as there are Men; but the Evil is not perpetual, and* <71> *is compensated by the Good which happens from Time to Time.* And [56] *M. Aurelius* said, the Magistrates are to judge of private Persons, Princes of Magistrates, and GOD of Princes. There is a remarkable Place in *Gregory* of *Tours,* where that Bishop thus [57] addresses the King of *France, If any one of us (O King!) should transgress the Bounds of Justice, he may be punished by you: But if you yourself should*

Station; for the first Kings were properly no more than Judges, who had no Power to inflict Punishments by their own Authority, and without the Consent of the People. *Theog.* v. 83, &c.

54. *Guardianship,* as Servius defines the Term, *is a Power over a free Person,* &c. *Instit.* Lib. I. Tit. XIII. *De Tutelis,* § 1.

55. *Hist.* Lib. IV. Cap. LXXIV. Num. 4.

56. The Author has the Passage of Xiphilin in View, which I have quoted *Note* 30 of this Paragraph. He sets it down in a Note on this Place; where he also quotes two Expressions of two other Princes, to the same Purpose. *King* Vitigis, (in Cassiodorus) declares, *that what regards the Royal Power* (he should have said *Dignity*) *is to be judged by the Powers above; since it is derived from Heaven, and is accountable to Heaven alone.* In the same Author a King says, *We cannot be subject to another, because we have no Judges.* This last Passage is in the *Formula Praefecturae Urbanae,* Var. VI. 4. The first Words of the former are taken from *Lib.* X. 31. But I do not know where our Author found, *Since,* &c.

57. *Hist.* Lib. V.

offend, Who shall call you to Account? When we make Representations to you, if you please, you hear us; but if you will not, who shall condemn you? There is none, but he who has declared himself to be Justice itself. Among the Maxims of the *Essenes, Porphyry* mentions this, [58] *That it is not without a particular Providence of GOD, that the Power of Commanding falls to the Lot of some Persons.* And [59] *Irenaeus* says excellently, *By whose Orders* [60] *Men are born; by his Command also are Kings ordained, proper for them who are governed by them.* We have the same Thought in [61] the Constitutions of *Clement, You shall fear the King, knowing that he is chosen of GOD.*

Neither is it an Objection to what I have said, that we read of some People punished for the Offences of their Kings; for this does not happen, because they do not punish or [62] restrain their King, but because they seem to give, at least a tacit Consent to his Vices; or perhaps, without

1 Kings xiv 6.
2 Kings xvii.
7, &c.

58. *De Abstin.* Lib. IV. p. 389. Josephus the *Jewish* Historian, who, with Philo, is our best Guide in what relates to the *Essenes,* says exactly the same, *De Bello Judaic.* Lib. II. Cap. XII. So that it would have been more proper to have quoted the original Author.

59. *Lib.* V. *Cap.* XXIV. This Passage, and those quoted both in the Text and the following Note, mean no more than that such or such Princes reign by the Permission of Providence. But this is not to the present Purpose: For the Question here is about *Right,* not *Fact.* Besides, Do not the worst of Tyrants exercise their Power by the Permission of Providence?

60. Homer says, *Dignity is derived from* Jupiter. *Iliad.* Lib. II. v. 197. The *Aegyptians,* according to Diodorus of *Sicily, were of Opinion, that Kings did not attain the Sovereign Power without a Divine Providence.* Lib. I. Cap. XC. *Ed. Steph.* St. Augustin says, *The same who gave the Empire to* Flavius *and* Titus Vespasian, *Princes of the greatest Lenity, bestowed it on* Domitian, *remarkable for his Cruelty; in short,* Julian, *the Apostate, received it from the same Hand which conferred it on* Constantine, *the Christian Emperor,* De Civit. Dei, *Lib.* V. *Cap.* XXI. Cassiodorus makes King Vitigis say, That *every Promotion to Dignity is to be considered among the Gifts of the Divinity;* and that *this is true in a particular Manner, in regard to that of a Sovereign.* Var. X. 31. The Emperor *Titus* declared, that *The Powers were established by Fate.* Epitom. Aurel. Victor. *Cap.* X. *Num.* 10. Or, as it is expressed by Suetonius, that *The Dignity of Princes was bestowed by Fate.* In Vit. Titi. *Cap.* IX. Grotius. See what I have said in the foregoing Note.

61. *Lib.* VII. *Cap.* XVII.

62. This Reason may sometimes take Place. See Mr. Le Clerc's Reflections on the Famine with which GOD punished the *Israelites,* on the Account of *Saul's* exterminating the Descendants of the antient *Gibeonites,* 2 Sam. xxi.

respect to this, GOD may make use of that Sovereign Power which he has over the Life and Death of every Man, to chastise their King, in regard to whom it is a great Punishment to lose his Subjects.

IX. *Mutual Subjection refuted.* IX. There are others, who fancy to themselves a reciprocal Dependence between the King and the People; so that, according to them, the People ought to obey the King whilst he makes a good Use of his Power; but likewise, when he abuses it, he becomes in his Turn dependent on the People. Now if by what they say, they mean only, that our Duty to our Sovereign does not oblige us to do any Thing manifestly unjust, they say but the Truth; but this implies no Right to compel [1] the King, or to command him. But suppose they had a Design to divide the Government with the King, (of which we shall say something [2] hereafter) there ought to be Bounds assigned to the Power of each Party, according to the Difference of Places, Persons, or Affairs, that the Extent of their respective Jurisdictions might be easily discerned. <72>

But the Goodness or Badness of an Action, especially in Civil Concerns, which are liable to frequent and intricate Discussions, are not fit to distinguish those Limits; from whence would necessarily follow the utmost Confusion; because, [3] under Pretence that an Action appeared

IX. (1) That is, while he remains really a King, and has not so far abused his Power, as to give just Occasion to consider him no longer in that Character. For this Restriction is always to be understood.

2. See § 17. of this Chapter.

3. That is, if the People had a Right to consider themselves as independent of the King, and proceed against him authoritatively, as often as the King should do any Thing that seems unjust, or prejudicial to the publick Good, a perpetual Source of Quarrels and Disorders would be opened, because it might easily happen, that the People, at certain Times would judge some Things unjust or prejudicial, which are not really so. So that the King, on such Occasions, being persuaded he had not abused his Power; and the People thinking the contrary; and no Judge being to be found for deciding the Difference; they must necessarily come to an open War. It is better therefore, that the Sovereign should sometimes do Things really Evil, with Impunity; and the Inconvenience on this Side is less than that on the other. But then it does not follow, that the People can never judge of the King's Actions, and that they are obliged to submit to, and suffer every Thing. This is contrary to the natural End of all Society, and to the Obligation under which whole Nations, as well as each Man, lye of preserving themselves.

Good or Bad, the King and People would each, by Vertue of their Power, assume to themselves the Cognizance of one and the same Thing; which Disorder, no Nation (as I know of) ever yet thought to introduce.

X. Having confuted these Errors; it remains that we give some Cautions, in order to direct us how to judge rightly, to whom the Sovereign Power in every Nation belongs. Let this then be the first, That we be not deceived by the Ambiguity of Words, or the Shew of outward Things. For Example, Tho' among the *Latins,* a Kingdom and a Principality are generally Opposites; as when *Caesar* said, [1] the Father of *Vercingetorix* had obtained the Principality of *Gaul,* but was slain for aspiring to the Royalty: And when *Piso,* in *Tacitus,* said, [2] that *Germanicus* was the Son of a Prince of the *Romans,* not of a *Parthian* King: And *Suetonius,* [3] that *Caligula* wanted but little of changing the Ornaments of a Prince into those of a King: And *Maroboduus* is said in [4] *Velleius* not to have been contented with the Principality, which he possessed with the Consent of those that depended on him, but ambitiously to have affected the Regal Power.

Yet we see these two Words often confounded together; for the *Spartan* Chiefs descended from *Hercules,* after [5] they were subjected to the *Ephori,* were yet called Kings (as we have [6] seen above). And in antient *Germany,* there were some Kings, who, as *Tacitus* says, [7] governed by the Deference paid to their Counsels, rather than by any Power they had of commanding. *Livy* relates, [8] that *Evander* reigned more by the Esteem

X. *Cautions in judging of the Sovereign Power.*

X. (1) *De Bell. Gall.* Lib. VII. Cap. IV.

2. *Annal.* Lib. II. Cap. LVII.

3. *Vita Calig.* Cap. XXII.

4. *Lib.* II. *Cap.* CVIII. p. 115. *Edit. Oxon.* 1711.

5. The Kings of *Lacedemonia,* as the learned GRONOVIUS observes on this Place, were not subject to the *Ephori,* but the *Ephori* were established to oppose the Kingly Power, when it degenerated into Tyranny: As the *Tribunes of the People,* among the *Romans,* were set up to check the Consular Power. This we learn from VALERIUS MAXIMUS, *Lib.* IV. *Cap.* I.

6. See the 39th *Note* on Paragraph 8.

7. *De Morib. Germanor.* Cap. XI. Num. 6.

8. *Lib.* I. *Cap.* VII. *Num.* 8.

People had for him, than by his own Authority. *Aristotle,* [9] and *Polybius,* [10] and *Diodorus,* [11] gave the Title of Kings to the *Suffetes,* or Judges of the *Carthaginians:* And *Hanno* is so called by *Solinus.* [12] *Strabo* [13] speaks of *Scepsis* in *Troas,* that having incorporated the *Milesians* into the State, it formed itself into a Democracy, leaving the Name of King to the Descendants of their antient Kings, and something of the Dignity. <73>

The *Roman* Emperors, on the contrary, after they exercised openly, and without any Disguise, a most absolute monarchical Power, were nevertheless called Princes. There are also some Republicks, where the chief Magistrates [14] are honoured with the Ensigns of Royalty.

On the other Side, the States of a Kingdom, that is, the Assembly of those who represent the People, divided into three Orders, according to *Gunther,* [15] *Praelati, proceres, missisque potentibus Urbes. Prelates, Nobles, and Deputies of Towns.* Those States, I say, in [16] some Places, are only,

---

9. *Politic.* Lib. II. Cap. IX. p. 334.

10. The *Carthaginians,* says that Historian, had Kings, and a Senate invested with Aristocratical Power. *Lib.* VI. *Cap.* XLIX.

11. He tells us the *Carthaginians* conferred the Title of King on their General *Mago.* Biblioth. Hist. *Lib.* XV. *Cap.* XV. p. 465. *Edit. H. Steph.* The same Title is given him twice or thrice in the same Place.

12. XENOPHON, *of* Lampsacus, *relates that* Hanno, *King of the* Carthaginians, *travelled into those Islands,* Cap. LVI. The Author here adds, in a Note, a Passage from the Writer of *Hannibal*'s Life. He means CORNELIUS NEPOS, whose *Lives of illustrious Generals,* at that Time passed under the Name of AEMILIUS PROBUS; but the Learned very much doubted their being the Work of that Grammarian of the middle Age: *For two Kings were chosen yearly at* Carthage, *as the Consuls were at* Rome. *Cap.* VII. *Num.* 4. *Edit. Cellar.* He likewise observes, that we may rank among those Kings, improperly so called, the Princes on whom their Fathers, who were real Kings, bestowed the Title of King, without divesting themselves of the Sovereign Power. Such was *Darius,* whom *Artaxerxes* condemned to die for a Conspiracy against him; as we learn from PLUTARCH, *Vit. Artax.* p. 1026. Tom. II. *Ed. Wech.*

13. It had before been formed into an Aristocracy; as appears from the Words immediately preceding those quoted by our Author. *But afterwards they* (the *Scepsians*) *were changed into an Oligarchy, &c.* Geogr. *Lib.* XIII. *p.* 904. *Edit. Amst.* (607. *Paris*).

14. As the *Doge* of *Venice,* who is crowned, and has the Title of *Serene;* tho' not a Sovereign Prince.

15. In *Ligurin.*

16. See PUFFENDORF, *B.* VII. *Chap.* VI. § 12.

as it were, the King's Great Council, by whose Means the Complaints of the People, which the Members of his Privy-Council often conceal from him, come to his Ear; and the King has nevertheless a Power afterwards to ordain whatever he thinks fit, in regard to the Matters in Question. But in other Countries they have a Right to take Cognizance of the Actions of the Prince, and also to prescribe Laws, which shall oblige the Prince himself.

Many think, that in Order to know whether a Prince be Sovereign or not, we need only consider whether he mounts the Throne by Right of Succession, or by Means of Election; for according to them, successive Kingdoms only are Sovereign. But it is certain, that Maxim is not generally, and without Restriction, true. For Succession is not a Title that determines the Form of the Government, and the Extent of the Power of him that governs: It imports only a Continuation of the Rights of him, to whom one succeeds. When a Family is chosen to reign, the Right conferred upon it passes from Successor to Successor, with the same Power that the first Election had given, and no more. Among the *Lacedemonians* the Kingdom was Hereditary, even after the constituting of the *Ephori.* And of such a Kingdom, that is, of the chief Dignity of the State, *Aristotle* speaks, [17] Τούτων τῶν Βασιλειῶν αἱ μὲν κατὰ γένος εἰσὶν, αἱ δὲ αἱρεταί. *Of those Kingdoms; some are Hereditary, others Elective.* The same Author, [18] and *Thucydides,* [19] and *Dionysius* [20] of *Halicarnassus,* observe, that in the Times of the Heroes, most of the Kingdoms of *Greece* were so. On the contrary, the *Roman* Empire, even after all Power was taken from the Senate and People, [21] was conferred by Election.

XI. Another Caution may be this, We must distinguish between the Thing itself, and the Manner of enjoying it; which takes Place not only

XI. *The second Caution.*

---

17. He there speaks of such as had only the perpetual Command of the Armies. *Polit.* Lib. III. Cap. XIV. p. 256. *Edit. Paris.*

18. *Ibid.* p. 357.

19. *Lib.* I. § 53.

20. See the Passage quoted at Length, on PUFENDORF, *B.* VII. *Chap.* I. § 7. *Note* 1.

21. This Point of History is treated at large, *B.* II. *Chap.* IX. § 11.

cause it was not perpetual: For the Nature of moral Things is known by
their Operations, wherefore those Powers, which have the same Effects,
should be called by the same Name. [6] Now the <75> Dictator, during

6. If therefore the People confer all the Right of exercising all the Parts of Sovereignty on any one for a Time, without consulting any one, or being accountable
for his Conduct; it may be said he is a Sovereign during that Time. I do not understand why several Authors so obstinately maintain that there can be no Sovereignty
for a Time. Either this is a mere Dispute about Words, or the Reasons alledged are
no better than so many different Ways of begging the Question. The Power of commanding, even absolutely, is of such a Nature that it may be conferred for a Time,
without ceasing to be such. If a private Person sells his Liberty for a Term of Years
only, he will be as effectually a Slave during that Time, as if he had taken a Master
for Life. It is true, in that Case the Master has no Right to sell him; but the Power of
Alienation is not, according to the Law of Nature alone, a necessary Consequence of
Slavery, much less of Sovereignty in general. It is pretended that the Limitation of
Time destroys the Nature of Sovereignty; but then it is falsely supposed that all Sovereignty ought to be perpetual. It is said that a sovereign Power conferred for a Time,
is of Course dependent; which I deny. It is indeed conferred by the People, and they
designed to confer it only for a Time; but the Moment the Person, on whom it is
conferred, is actually invested with it, he is above the People, and is no more dependent on them, during the Time fixed, than a Prince established for Life; all the Difference is, that when the Time is expired, his Superiority and Independence are at an
End. It is farther objected, that such a Limitation confines the Sovereignty to certain
Acts of Sovereignty. But it is sufficient that the Person established Sovereign for a
Time, is thereby possessed of a Power of exercising all the Acts and Parts of the Sovereignty, as he shall judge proper, and according to the Exigency of Circumstances,
it is not necessary that he should actually have Occasion to exercise them all. If this
is not granted, a King, who either has reigned, or, according to the Course of Nature,
can reign but a very short Time, would not be a Sovereign. Those, who maintain that
Perpetuity of Duration has a necessary Connection with the Nature of Sovereignty,
are not aware that this Assertion will carry them farther than they would wish. For
it would follow, that all Sovereignty ought to extend as far as it is possible, and consequently must be successive; because that is the only Way to render it perpetual,
while Princes are under the same Necessity of dying, as the meanest of their Subjects.
It would likewise follow, that however a Sovereign behaves himself, he cannot be
deposed, even though he should carry his Tyranny to the utmost Excess; or at least,
that a Prince, who is deposed, was not a Sovereign during the Time of his good Administration. But our Antagonists agree with us in owning that, in that Case, the
most absolute Princes forfeit the Sovereignty; and as all Princes may commit such
Abuses, it is evident that on that Account all Sovereignty is for a Time. Now if it is
not contrary to the Nature of Sovereignty, that it should end at a Time, which indeed
was not limited, but which might come, and was considered as possible to come, I
do not see why it may not end at a fixed and determined Time. There are several

the whole Time of his Office, [7] exercised all the Acts of civil Government, with as much Authority as the most absolute King; and nothing he had done could be annulled by any other Power. And the Continuance of a

---

other Conditions, on which we may conceive that the sovereign Authority is expressly so conferred on a Person, that the Execution or Defect of such Conditions may render it a Power for a Time. Let us suppose, for Example, that in an elective Kingdom, where it is not thought proper to establish a Regent, the People desirous of settling the Crown on the late King's Son, who is a Minor, choose another King, on Condition that he shall resign the Crown to the young Prince, if he lives to the Time of his Majority. This would certainly be a Sovereignty for a Time. Hence we may conclude, if such a Sovereignty, because not perpetual, is therefore less advantageous to the Possessor, and is esteemed less glorious; it is not in itself a less real Sovereignty. All that remains therefore is to enquire whether the Instances alleged are to the Purpose or not. See the following Note.

7. So that, says our Author in a Note on this Place, the People were obliged to have Recourse to Intreaties, for saving the Life of *Q. Fabius Maximus Rullianus,* General of the Cavalry (*Magister Equitum*) whom *L. Papirius Cursor,* the Dictator, had condemned for giving Battle without his Orders. Livy. *Lib.* VIII. *Chap.* XXIX, XXXV. The Author, who had before spoken of the Dictatorship, as an Instance of temporary Sovereignty, (§. 8.) observes likewise in a Note, which I have reserved for this Place, that when *M. Livius Salinator* was Censor, he disfranchised all the Tribes (*aerarias reliquit*) except one, and thus shewed he had a Power over the whole People. Liv. *Lib.* XXIX. *Cap.* XXXVII. *num.* 13. But how considerable soever the Power of the *Censors* was in certain Respects, it was not universal like that of the *Dictators.* Perhaps our Author made this Remark only with a View of shewing that, if the *Censors* were absolute, and above the whole People in what concerned their Office; much more ought we to consider the Dictators as such. But whatever was his Design, I think he has Reason to mention the *Dictators,* as a sort of temporary Sovereigns by distinguishing, as he does, between the Power of the Dictators, such as it was originally in the first Ages of the *Roman* Commonwealth, and that which they enjoyed in later Times, when it had suffered such gradual Changes, as divested it of the Character of intire Independence. In Regard to the former, which is here under Consideration, ancient Authors, both *Latin* and *Greek,* give us an Idea of a real Sovereignty for a Time. We have already (§. 8. *Notes,* 45, 46.) produced Passages from Livy on that Subject. Dionysius Halicarn. speaking of *Titus Lartius,* the first Dictator, stiles him a *Monarch.* He says, *he had an absolute, independent Power in Affairs of War and Peace, and all others.* That *he was called Dictator, because he might command and prohibit what he pleased.* That *the* Romans *did not think it proper to give him a Title* (that of *King*) *which was odious to a free State, and conveyed an Idea of Oppression.* That *the very Appellation of* Dictator *expressed the Extent of his Authority;* and that *the* Dictatorship *was in Reality an elective Tyranny,* or Royalty. *Lib.* V. *Cap.* LXXIII. He had before observed that *the Senate decreed that* this extraordinary Magistrate *should be accountable to none for his Conduct:* That *his Authority should be equal to that of Ty-*

when they served under Kings, were never attacked in War, nor besieged by an Enemy, but being a free People should be besieged by the Hetrurians; and in another Place, *The People of* Rome *are not now under a King but at Liberty.* And again in another Place, he opposes those Nations that were free, to them that lived under Kings; and [3] *Cicero* said *Either the Kings should not have been expelled, or the People should have had their Liberty in Deed, and not in Words.* And after them [4] *Tacitus, The City of* Rome *was at first under Kings; but* L. Brutus *brought in Liberty, and the consular Government.* And elsewhere, *The Liberty of the* Germans *is more severe than the regal Power of* Arsaces. And [5] *Arrian* Βασιλεῦσι καὶ τῆσι πόλεσιν ὅσα αὐτόνομα. *To the Kings and free Cities, (those that live after their own Laws.)* And *Caecina* in [6] *Seneca, The regal* <77> *Thunderbolts are those whose Force affects either the Assembly of the States, or the chief Places of a free City: The Meaning whereof is that the State is threatened with a regal Power.* So those *Cilicians* who were not under Kings were called *Eleuthero Cilices,* [7] *free Cilicians.* And [8] *Strabo* says of *Amisus,* (a City of *Pontus*) that it was sometimes free, and sometimes under Kings. And every where in the *Roman* Laws, that treat of War, and Judgments

3. *De Legibus. Lib.* III. *Cap.* X.

4. *Annal.* Lib. I. *Cap.* I. *num.* I. Idem *De Morib. German.* Cap. XXXVII. num. 6.

5. *Histor. Indic.* Cap. XI. *Edit. Gronov.*

6. *Natur. Quaest.* Lib. II. Cap. XLIX. We have an Instance of this Presage in the History of *Genoa,* by PETER BIZAR. *B.* XIX. The Author, in a Note on this Place, produces the following additional Passages to prove that the ancient *Greek* and *Latin* Writers opposed *Liberty* to *Monarchical Government. This* Teres, *the Father of* Sitalces, *was the first who enlarged the Kingdom of the* Odrysae *so much, that he exceeded the other Kings of* Thrace; *for great Part of* Thrace *is free.* THUCYD. *Lib.* II. *Cap.* XXIX. *Edit. Oxon. Men are not to speak their Minds in the same Matter in a free State, as under Kings,* SENECA Pater *Suasor* I. p. 4, 5. *Edit. Elziv.* 1672. JOSEPHUS distinguishes between *Kings* and *free States,* Antiq. *Lib.* XIII. *Cap.* XVII. CICERO says he *had procured the Assistance of free States, and confederate Kings.* Ad Famil. *Lib.* XV. *Epist.* IV. And PLINY speaking of some Nations as *free,* adds, that they were *not subject to Kings,* Hist. Nat. *Lib.* VI. *Cap.* XX.

7. *Free Cilicians.* CICERO mentions them *Ad Fam.* Lib. XII. Ep. IV. & *ad Attic.* Lib. V. Ep. XX.

8. *Geograph.* Lib. XII. p. 822. *Edit. Amsterd.* (547. *Paris.*)

of [9] Recovery, Foreigners are distinguished into [10] Kings and free People. It is said even of those, who do not enjoy this publick Liberty, as well as of those who are deprived of personal Liberty, that *they are not their own Masters;* but that they *belong* to those on whom they depend. Hence that in [11] *Livy, which Cities, which Lands, which Men were once under the Power of the* Aetolians. And again, [12] *Are the People of* Collatia *their own Master?* The Argument then which is here used, is not to the Purpose, since [13] the Question does not relate to personal but civil Liberty. But properly, when a People is alienated, it is not the Men themselves, but the perpetual Right of governing them, as they are a People. Thus when a Freed-

9. See Paragraph 21.

10. In the Law Definition of *Postliminium,* which is called *the Right of recovering a Thing lost, and restoring it to its former State, established between us, free Nations and Kings, by Laws and Customs.* DIGEST. *Lib.* XLIX. *Tit.* XV. *De Captivis & Postliminio,* &c. Leg. XIX.

11. LIVY, XXXVIII. *Cap.* XI. *Num.* 9.

12. *Idem.* Lib. I. Cap. XXXVIII. *Numb.* 2.

13. Our Author's Argument, which is not delivered very clearly, stands thus. When it is said, that free Persons are not to be sold, this is to be understood of single Persons, not of the whole Body of a People. Now single Persons who are Members of a People, are *free,* though the whole People is not so; for the Liberty of a Man consists in his having no particular Master, who has a Power of commanding his Actions, and even to dispose of his Person, and Estate; and those, who are Members of a People not free, have, as such, but one common Master, who has a Right to command them as his Subjects. Thus when a King alienates his Crown, we cannot say he disposes of his Subjects, considering each of them in particular; for, after he has sold or given away his Kingdom, each Subject is still as free as before, and has only another Sovereign. As to the Body of the People, barely by having a King, really such, it ceases to be free; and thus, even according to the Maxim objected against our Author, such a People may be sold, their own Way, that is, the Prince, invested with a full Right to govern them as long as he lives, may transfer his Right to another; for in this consists the Alienation of the Sovereignty. But then it must be observed that our Author does not pretend that every Sovereign Prince has, as such, a full Right to alienate the Sovereignty; he confines this Power to some only, that is, to such as have acquired the Kingdom by just Conquest, or by making his Advantage of a pressing Necessity, which obliged the People to put themselves under his Dominion without Reserve or Restriction; as is evident from what he says, § 11, and § 14. But we have shewn, in *Note* 4 on § 11, that this Distinction of our Author is not well grounded; no Sovereign having a Right to alienate his Dominions, without a Concession from his Subjects, either formal, or tacit, but clear, in what Manner soever he obtained the Crown.

Thus we read, that *Hercules* having conquered the City of *Sparta*, [23] gave the Sovereignty of it to *Tyndareus*, on Condition, that if *Hercules* left any Children of his own, he should restore it to them. So *Amphipolis* [24] was given in Marriage Dowry to *Acamas* Son of *Theseus;* and [25] *Agamemnon* promises in *Homer* to give *Achilles* seven Cities. King *Anaxagoras* gave two Parts of his Kingdom to *Melampus*. And [26] *Justin* tells us of *Darius, that he bequeathed by Will his Kingdom to* Artaxerxes, *and to* Cyrus *the Cities, of which he was Governor.* Thus, the <79> Successors of *Alexander* the Great [27] are to be considered as having succeeded him, every one in his allotted Part, in the full Right of Property, by Vertue whereof he governed those Nations, which had been formerly under the *Persians,* or else as having acquired that Sovereignty themselves, by Right of Conquest; therefore it is not to be wondered at, that they claimed to themselves the Right of Alienation.

Text, not *restored*) were the same he had received as a Gift from the King of the *Hebrews*. See Mr. LE CLERC's Commentary of the Passages, quoted in the Margin.

23. The same *Hercules* having conquered the *Dryopes*, whose Country was situated near *Parnassus*, made a Present of them to *Apollo;* as we learn from SERVIUS on *Aeneid*. IV. v. 146. *Aegimius,* King of the *Dorians,* gave *Hercules* part of his Dominions, as a Reward for his Assistance, in the War against the *Lapithae*. APOLLODOR. *Biblioth.* Lib. II. Cap. VII. § 7. *Edit. Paris. Cychreus* King of *Salamis,* dying without Issue, left his Kingdom, by Will, to *Telamon. Idem.* Lib. III. Cap. XI. § 7. *Peleus* received a third Part of the Dominions of *Eurytion* King of *Phthia,* as a Portion with his Daughter. *Idem.* Lib. III. Cap. XII. § I. *Porca* King of *Alba* bequeathed his Kingdom to *Numitor,* his eldest Son. LIVY, *Lib.* I. *Cap.* III. *Num.* 10. GROTIUS.

24. This Fact is recorded by DEMOSTHENES, in his Oration *De malè obita legatione,* p. 251. *Edit. Bas.* 1572.

25. *Iliad.* Lib. IX. v. 149, *&c.* See SERVIUS on VIRGIL, *Ed.* VI. v. 48. and PAUSANIAS, *Corinthiac,* Cap. XVIII. p. 60. *Edit. Wech.* Thus likewise in HOMER, *Jobates* gave his Daughter to *Bellerophon,* with *half his Royal Honours;* which SERVIUS explains, *with Part of his Kingdom.* On *Aeneid.* v. 118. *Peleus* gave *Phenix* the Country of the *Dolopes,* lying on the Borders of *Phthia,* as PHENIX himself testifies. *Iliad.* Lib IX. v. 479, 480. *Lanassa* marrying *Pyrrhus,* King of *Epirus* had for her Portion the City of *Corcyra,* conquered by her Father *Agathocles,* King of *Syracuse.* PLUT. *in Pyrrho.* GROTIUS.

26. *Lib.* V. *Cap.* XI. *Num.* 2.

27. AMMIAN. MARCELLINUS, speaking of *Persia,* says, tho' not conformably to the Truth of History, that *Alexander the Great* bequeathed that whole Kingdom to one of his Successors. *Lib.* XXIII. *Cap.* VI. p. 398. *Edit. Vales. Gron.* GROTIUS. See HENRY DE VALOIS's Note on that Passage.

When King *Attalus,* [28] the Son of *Eumenes,* had made, by his Will, the People of *Rome* Heir to his Goods, they, under the Name of Goods, possessed themselves of his Kingdom. Of which *Florus* [29] thus speaks, *Therefore the* Romans *entering upon it as Heirs, reduced it into the Form of a Province, not by Force of Arms, but in a fairer Way, by Right of Inheritance.* And afterwards, when *Nicomedes,* King of *Bithynia,* had made the People of *Rome* his Heir, they immediately reduced the Kingdom into the Form of a Province. And [30] *Cicero,* in his second Oration against *Rullus,* says thus, *We have got a good Inheritance, the Kingdom of* Bithynia. So that Part of *Libya,* called *Cyrenaica,* was left by King *Apion,* by Will, to the *Romans. Tacitus,* in his fourteenth *Annal,* mentions some Lands [31] which formerly belonging to King *Apion,* were, together with

Appian Bell. Mithridat. & Bell. Civil.

Eutrop. 1. 6.

28. VALERIUS MAXIMUS tells us, *Attalus* did this out of a Principle of Gratitude, *Lib.* V. *Cap.* II. *Num.* 3. SERTORIUS affirmed, that on that Account, *the* Roman *People had a very good Title to that Country.* PLUT. *Vit.* Sertor. p. 580. *Tom.* I. *Edit. Wech.* GROTIUS.

29. *Lib.* II. *Cap.* XX. *Num.* 3.

30. *Orat.* II. *De Lege Agrar. contra Rull.* Cap. XV. p. 413. *Edit. Graev.*

31. APPIAN of *Alexandria* tells us, that *Apion, a Bastard of the Race of the* Lagides, *left the Country of* Cyrene, (to the *Roman* People) *by his Will.* De Bell. Mithridat. AMMIAN. MARCELLIN. speaks of this Legacy, *Lib.* XXII. *Cap.* XVI. *We became possessed of the drier* Libya, *by the Disposal of King* Apion; *we received* Cyrene, *and the other Cities of* Libya Pentapolis *from the Liberality of* Ptolomy: For that King of *Cyrene* was called both *Apion* and *Ptolomy.* See Breviar. LIV. *Lib.* LXX. That Prince himself came to the Throne by his Father's Will, as we learn from JUSTIN, *Lib.* XXXIX. *Cap.* V. *Num.* 2. EUSEBIUS in his *Chronicle* at the Year 1952, speaks of another *Apion,* mentioned by AMMIAN. MARCELL. who had made the *Roman* People Heirs of the *Dry Libya.* [But see HENRY DE VALOIS's Notes on that Place.] To these may be added the following Examples. King *Arsaces,* by his Will, divided *Armenia* in such a Manner, that the greater Part of it fell to his Son *Arsaces,* and the smaller to *Tigranes.* PROCOP. *De Aedificiis,* Lib. III. Cap. I. We learn from JOSEPHUS, that the Emperor *Augustus* having allowed *Herod* to leave the Kingdom of *Judea* to which of his Sons he pleased, that Prince altered his Will several Times, *Antiq. Jud.* Lib. XV. XVI. Among the *Goths* and *Vandals* the Kings disposed of their Conquests by Will. *Gizeric,* King of the *Vandals,* followed this Custom in Regard to his *Spanish* Dominions. PROCOP. *Vandalic.* Lib. I. Cap. VII. *Theuderic,* King of the *Ostrogoths,* gave his Sister *Amalesfrida* the Country of *Lilybaeum,* in *Sicily,* for her Portion. *Ibid.* Cap. VIII. We find the same Practice established in other Nations. *Pepin* having conquered *Aquitain,* divided it among his Children. FREDEGAR, *Chron.* We have Testimentary Disposals of *Burgundy,* in AIMONIUS III. 68, 75. The King of *Fez* bequeathed *Fez* to his

his King-<80>dom, bequeathed to the *Romans*. And in [32] *Cicero, Every Body knows that the* Romans *are become Masters of the Kingdom of* Aegypt, *by Vertue of the Will of the King of* Alexandria. *Mithridates, in Justin,* speaking of *Paphlagonia,* says, [33] *Which fell to his Father, not by Force, and the Superiority of his Arms, but by a testamentary Adoption.* The same

Lib. 42. c. 4. Author also relates, *that* Orodes *King of* Parthia, *was a long while de-*

---

second Son. Leo *Afer,* Lib. III. See also what the same Historian says of *Bugia,* Lib. V. The Sultan *Aladin* left *Ozmin* several Cities by his Will. Leunclav. *Hist. Turc.* Lib. II. The King of *Germianum,* who married his Daughter to *Bajazet,* gave her what he possessed in *Phrygia.* Idem. *Lib.* V. *Musal* divided the *Turkish* Dominions in *Cappadocia* among his Children. Nicetas, Lib. III. *Chuschin Bega* gave *Murat* the Cities lying near the *Euxine* Sea. Leunclav. *Lib.* I. *Bajazet* gave *Stephen* the Cities of *Servia,* in Honour of his Wife, Sister to the said *Stephen.* Idem. *Lib.* VI. The Sultan *Mahomet* bequeathed his Kingdom to *Murat.* Idem. *Lib.* XII. *Jacup Beg,* Prince of *Germianum,* appointed the Sultan *Murat* Heir of his Dominions. *Idem.* Lib. XIV. *Mahomet,* Emperor of the *Turks,* had thought of leaving his *European* Dominions to his Son *Amurat,* and those in *Asia* to his other Son *Mustapha.* Chalcocondyl, *Lib.* IV. The Emperor *Basil Porphyrogennetus* was by *David Curopalates* made Heir to his Possessions in *Iberia.* Zonar. in *Basil Porphyrog.* I now come to the Practice of such Christians as were victorious in the *East: Michael Despota* divided *Thessaly* among his Children. Nicephor. Gregoras, *Lib.* IV. The Prince of *Etolia* left *Athens* to the *Venetians,* and sold *Boeotia* to *Anthony.* Chalcocondyl. *Lib.* IV. The Prince of *Arcadia* gave his Daughter, *Messina, Ithome,* and those Parts of *Arcadia* that bordered on the Sea, for her Portion, on her Marriage with the Son of *Thomas* the *Grecian* Emperor. *Idem.* Lib. V. Prince *Charles* made a Will, by which he divided *Acarnania* among his natural Sons; and gave several Parts of *Etolia* to his Mother's Relations. *Id.* Thus the Kingdoms of *Jerusalem* and *Cyprus* were partly bequeathed by Will, and partly alienated by Contracts. Consult Bembo, *Hist. Ital.* Lib. VII. and Paruta, *Lib.* I. for what relates to *Cyprus.* The City of *Castro* in *Sardinia,* and others depending on *Cagliari,* were Gifts to the *Genoese.* Bizar, *De Bello Pisano,* Lib. II. *Robert* gave *Dyrrachium* and *Aulone* to *Baimund,* his younger Son. Anna Comnena, *Lib.* V. *Cap.* II. *Alphonso,* King of *Arragon,* who had conquered the Kingdom of *Naples,* left it to *Ferdinando,* his natural Son: And *Ferdinando* bequeathed some Cities in that Kingdom to his Grandson. Mariana, *Hist. Hisp.* Lib. XXX. Grotius. See *Note* 20. on this Paragraph.

32. The Passage stands thus in Cicero, *Orat.* II. *De Lege Agrar. contra Rull.* Cap. XVI. p. 415. *For who among you does not know it is said, that that Kingdom fell to the* Roman *People by the Will of King* Alexander?

33. *Which* (Paphlagonia) *became hereditary to his Father, not by Force, or Superiority of Arms, but by Vertue of a Will, by which he had been adopted, and by Default of Heirs of the Family.* Lib. XXXVIII. Cap. V. Num. 4.

bating, to which of his Sons he should leave his Kingdom. And *Polemo,* Prince of the *Tibarenians,* (a People of *Cappadocia*) and of the Country adjoining, left his Wife Heiress of his Dominion; which also *Mausolus* had formerly done in *Caria,* tho' he had several Brothers alive.

Strabo, I. 12.
Id. I. 13.

XIII. But as to Kingdoms which were originally established by the full and free Consent of the People, I confess [1] it cannot be presumed, that it was ever their Design to allow the King to alienate the Sovereignty. Wherefore what *Crantzius* observed in *Unguinus,* as a Thing never heard of, that by his Will he had bequeathed *Norway,* [2] we have no Reason to blame, since he might have in View the Customs of the antient *Germans,*

XIII. Some are held not so fully.

Hist. Dan. l. 2 cap. 4.

XIII. (1) *Vopiscus,* a *Roman* Senator, declared that the Empire ought not to be left by Will, like Lands and Slaves. TACIT. *Cap.* VI. SALVIAN, speaking of *Nebuchadnezzar,* King of *Babylon,* makes the following Observation, *For he* (the Prophet) *spoke to the King; to the King not of one single City, but, as was then supposed, of the whole World; who therefore could not bequeath the Nations which he governed, to the Poor; bestow the several barbarous People under his Jurisdiction, on the Needy, like Money; or convert his extensive Kingdom into a Patrimony for the Indigent.* Break off thine Iniquities, *says he,* by shewing Mercy, *that is, give the Poor Money, because you cannot bestow your Kingdom upon them: Distribute your Substance among them, because you cannot dispose of your Crown.* Ad Eccl. Cathol. *Lib.* I. p. 356. *Edit. Paris.* 1645. GROTIUS.

I have set down the last Passage at Length, which our Author has quoted in such a Manner, that if I had not found it by Chance, after a long Enquiry, it would not have appeared whether SALVIAN was speaking of Kings in general, or of some one in particular. But that Author's Argument, thus considered intire, and the Passage of DANIEL, *c.* iv. which gave Occasion to it, will shew us that it is possible he never thought of the Subject in Question. It is very probable he only means, that a Prince is not obliged to sell his Subjects, in order to raise Money for the Relief of the Poor; and that it would not be proper or possible for him to leave them his Dominions; that therefore the King of *Babylon* ought to give Alms, not as a King, but as a very rich Man: Whence the good Priest concludes, in a Manner worthy of the Age in which he lived, that since *Daniel* exhorts the King, in general Terms, to *redeem his Sins by Alms,* without excepting any Thing in his Possession, that could be given to the Poor, he by these Words directed the King to employ his whole Treasure in Alms, *When he only does not command him to give what he could not bestow, he seems to have commanded him to give his All.* So that no Consequence can be drawn from those Words for deciding whether Kings in general, and those of *Babylon* in particular, had, according to SALVIAN, a Power of alienating their Dominions at Pleasure.

2. The Author here has HOTOMAN in View, who, in his *Quaestiones illustres,* Cap. I. criticises on the *German* Historian's Observation.

amongst whom the Kings had no Power to alienate their States. For as to what is related of *Charles* the Great, *Lewis* the Pious, and also others afterwards among the *Vandals* and *Hungarians,* the testamentary Dispositions, which they made, were rather bare Recommendations to [4] the People, who were to choose their Successors, than a true Alienation. And of *Charles, Ado* expressly remarks, that he much desired to have his Will [5] confirmed by the chief Nobles of *France.* <81> The like is reported of *Philip* King of *Macedon,* that when he designed to disinherit his Son

4. [[Barbeyrac's notes are wrongly numbered at this point. He introduces a note 3, which does not correspond to any number in his text. It contains the note that Grotius himself put at the point where Barbeyrac put note 4.]] See the *Capitularies* of CHARLES *the Bald,* Cap. XII. *Conventus ad Carisiacum.* To this Purpose is the Will of *Pelagius,* by which he left *Spain* (or the Kingdoms of *Leon, Asturias,* and *Castille*) to *Alphonso* and *Ormisinda;* as also some Particulars in SAXO GRAMMAT. relating to *Denmark.* We are not therefore to be surprized that the Wills of some Princes have been set aside, because not ratified by the People; as that of *Alphonso,* King of *Arragon,* MARIANA, *Hist. Hisp.* Lib. X. p. 499. and that of *Alphonso,* King of *Leon,* by which he had appointed his Daughters his Heirs, exclusive of his Sons. *Idem.* Lib. XII. p. 577. GROTIUS.

ZIEGLER, on this Place, quotes the very Words of *Charlemagne's* Will, which we find after his Life, written by an anonymous Monk of *Angoulême,* and published by P. PITHOU, *p.* 203, *&c.* As likewise in the large Collection of MELCHIOR GOLDAST, *Ann.* 806. In which that Prince evidently supposes the Approbation of the People absolutely necessary: *But if either of those three Brothers shall have a Son, whom the People shall elect to succeed his Father,* &c. The Historians say also that *Charlemagne,* toward the Close of his Life, assembled the Grandees of all his Dominions, and that with their Approbation he associated *Lewis* King of *Aquitain,* afterwards called the *Pious,* or the *Debonnaire,* and declared him his Successor. EGINHART, in *Vita Caroli Magni,* Cap. XXX. See also ANSELM, *Annal. Francor.* Ann. 813, and THEGANUS, *De Gestis Ludov. Imper.* Cap. VI.

5. He made them confirm his Will by an Oath, as EGINHART assures us in another Work, or in his *Annals.* The learned BOECLER, who quotes the Passage in his *Short History of the ninth and tenth Ages,* Tom. III. *Dissert.* p. 20. is of Opinion that the Succession was fixed and constantly observed at that Time; in which he is joined by several other Authors. But it is not easy to reconcile this with all the Precautions taken by *Charlemagne,* and his Successors, for securing the Disposals they made. The Matter was carried so far, that Religion, or rather Superstition was called in to their Assistance. *This Proposal* (of *Charlemagne*) *was received with great Satisfaction by all present; for they thought him divinely inspired on this Occasion, for the Good of the Kingdom;* says EGINHART, *De Vit. Car. Mag.* Cap. XXX. See the other Authorities alledged by Mr. SCHMINKRE, in his last Edition of that Work.

Perseus, and settle the Crown upon *Antigonus,* his Brother's Son, [6] he went over all the Cities of *Macedon* to recommend *Antigonus* to the Princes, as [7] *Livy* informs us. In Regard to what is said of *Lewis* the Pious, that he restored the City of *Rome* to Pope *Paschal,* [8] it is nothing to the

6. We have something like this in CASSIODORE, *Lib.* VIII. *Epist.* III, *&c.* Thus the Agreements made between *Sanches* and *James,* concerning the mutual Succession to the Crown of *Aragon,* were confirmed by the Nobility; as we learn from MARIANA, *Hist. Hisp.* Lib. X. p. 512. That Historian says the same of the Will of *Henry* King of *Navarre,* by which he made *John* his Heir, *Lib.* XIII. *p.* 597. And of that of *Isabella* Queen of *Castille,* Lib. XXVIII. (or *Append. Hist. Hisp.* p. 243). GROTIUS.

7. *Lib.* XL. *Cap.* LVI. Num. 7.

8. Several Objections may be made in this Place. *First,* The Fact itself is false. We find no Account of this pretended Donation, either in AIMONIUS, in EGINHART'S *Annals,* in ANASTASIUS, or in THEGANUS, *De Gestis Ludov. Imp.* nor in the uncertain Author of that Emperor's Life. The Whole is founded on a spurious Act, of which two different Copies are produced; one, which RAPHAEL VOLATERRAN (*Geogr.* Lib. III.) tells us, he took from the *Vatican* Library; the other appears in the *Canon Law,* Distinct. LXIII. *Laïci, etiam principes magni, Episcopos non eligant,* Cap. XXX. See Mr. DU PLESSIS MORNAY'S *Mystery of Iniquity,* pag. 336, *&c. Edit. Saumur,* 1612. as also HERMAN CONRING, *De Germ. Imperio Rom.* Cap. VII. and GRONOVIUS'S Notes on this Place. *Secondly,* It appears from History, that the Popes were not Sovereigns of the City of *Rome,* and its Dependencies 'till long after the Time of *Lewis the Debonnaire.* The Donation of *Constantine* is a Fable, as is owned by the most understanding and sincere Authors of the *Romish* Communion. Among others, see LAUR. VALLA'S Oration, *De falsò creditâ & ementitâ Const. M. Imp. Rom. donatione,* published in 1517, and dedicated to *Leo* X. When the Popes had engaged those Cities of *Italy,* which remained in the Hands of the Emperors of the *East,* to shake off the Yoke of those Princes, tho' they had found Means to make themselves Masters of the Revenues, and temporal Government of the City of *Rome,* and Places adjacent: This was not done in Quality of real Sovereigns, acknowledged as such. And when *Pepin* came in to their Assistance against the *Lombards,* he bestowed the City of *Rome,* and the other Parts of the Exarchate of *Ravenna* on the Popes, on that Foot only. Some Authors say that the *Romans* had promised *Pepin* the Imperial Crown. See the Life of *Charlemagne,* by BOECLER, in his History *De Reb. Saec.* IX. & X. Tom. III. p. 23. of the Collection of his Dissertations. *Charlemagne* confirmed the Donation made by his Father, and even before he was declared Emperor, took Cognizance of the Affairs of *Leo* III. who immediately after his Promotion to the Pontificate, had presented that Prince with the Keys and Standard of *Rome,* intreating him to depute a Person for receiving the Homage of the *Romans,* and giving an Oath of Allegiance; as appears by the very antient Annals of *France,* Ann. 796. See the Notes on EGINHART, *Cap.* XXVIII. last Edition. In the Will of *Charlemagne,* as given us by EGINHART, *Cap.* XXXIII. *Rome* is mentioned as one of the metropolitan Cities of his Dominions. See HENN. ARNISAEUS, *De Subjectione & Exemptione Clericorum, &c. Item de Translatione*

the Father, or nearest Kindred shall chuse. Thus we see in the Kingdom of [3] *Epirus,* which had been founded by the Consent of the People, Guardians were nominated by the People to their young King *Aribas;*

---

absent, and it was impossible for him to give any Orders; as for Example, if he was a Prisoner in the Hands of an Enemy, and could find no Means of signifying to whom he would have the Care of the Government committed. The people may and ought to be supposed to have reserved to themselves this temporary and provisional Right; and if the King refuses them the Exercise of it, he has no more to do than to take proper Measures in good Time, for settling the Regency as he pleases. Neither those of the Royal Family, nor even the Mother of the King under Age, have any Privilege in this Case, exclusive of the People. The Mother may indeed act as Guardian to her Son, in what concerns his Education, and the Administration of his private Patrimony; but the Administration of the Government is of a very different Nature; and as even those Princes, who have a Power of alienating their Dominions, can never do it in a Manner disadvantageous to their Subjects, so neither can they deprive the People of the Right of providing for their own Preservation and Interest, during a Minority, when the deceased King has made no Provision of that Kind. As to the other Relations of the Royal Minor, who have a Right to the Succession, according to their respective Ranks, that Right cannot yet operate, because it is only in Expectation; and even the Interest of the actual Heir requires that the Administration of the Government should not be regulated absolutely by their Will; because this might prompt them and give them an Opportunity, to anticipate the Time of their Succession. What I have here laid down ought with more Reason to take Place in Kingdoms established by an entirely free Consent of the People, and without any Concession of a Power of Alienation: For even in such Kingdoms, the People may allow the King a Right to regulate the Regency, where there is no fundamental Law relating to the Affair. See *Note* 6. on this Paragraph. And thus the different Manner, of establishing a Regency, is of itself of no Service toward proving the Distinction of *patrimonial,* and *usufructuary Kingdoms;* as our Author pretends. But, to do him Justice, it should be observed that he speaks only of the Regency of a Kingdom *(Tutela Regni)* not of the Guardianship of a King under Age, or of the Power to direct his Actions, and take Care of his private Patrimony. These two Rights are indeed usually united; but they may be separated, and lodged in different Hands. So that, the Objection of some Commentators on this Place doth not affect our Author, *viz.* That, according to his Principles, a private Person will have more Power than a King, in Relation to the Guardianship of his Children. "It is neither new, nor singular (said a Gentleman, some Years ago, in the Parliament of *Paris*) to see, in private Families, the Education of Minors, separated from the Regulation and Administration of their Estates; and History is full of Instances, where the Regency of a Kingdom, and the Guardianship of the Royal Minors have been entrusted in different Hands." *Recueil General des Pieces touchant l' Affaire des Princes Legitimes & Legitimez.* Tom. I. p. 66.

3. JUSTIN. *Lib.* XVII. *Cap.* III. *Num.* 10.

and by the Nobles of [4] *Macedon* to the posthumous Son of *Alexander* the Great: But in *Asia* the Less, that was won by the Sword, [5] *Eumenes* appointed his Brother Guardian to his Son *Attalus:* So did *Hiero* in *Sicily* nominate [6] such as he thought fit to be Guardians to his Son *Hieronymus.*

Plut. de Amore
Fratern.

4. *Idem.* Lib. XIII. Cap. II. Num. 14.

5. The learned GRONOVIUS finds Fault with our Author, for having ranked the *Lesser Asia,* where *Eumenes* reigned among the patrimonial Kingdoms, acquired by Right of Conquest; for, says he, that Prince did not conquer *Asia,* but received it as an Inheritance from his Father *Attalus,* and his Dominions were enlarged by the *Romans,* in return for his Assistance, in the War with *Antiochus.* But our Author does not pretend that *Eumenes* himself conquered the *Lesser Asia;* he only means that that Country was originally a Conquest. *In* Asiâ Minore, *bello parta, Rex* Eumenes Attalo, *filio suo, fratrem suum tutorem dedit.* That is, *In the* Lesser Asia, *which had been gained by Conquest, King* Eumenes, *&c.* Now it is certain, that *Alexander the Great* had conquered *Asia,* and that, after his Death, it descended to his Successors with the same Right; and consequently, was a patrimonial Kingdom, according to our Author's Principles. See STRABO, *Geograph.* Lib. XIII. p. 925, 926. *Edit. Amst.* (623, 624. *Edit. Paris.*) To which it should be added, that what the *Romans* gave *Eumenes,* they had acquired by Force of Arms; and in making that Donation, they transferred their Right to him. The Commentator's Criticism therefore is ill grounded; but he might have made one more just, by observing, that, according to PLUTARCH, quoted by our Author in his Margin, *Eumenes* not only appointed his Brother *Attalus* Guardian to the Heir of the Crown, and Regent of the Kingdom during the Minority, but really and absolutely left him the Kingdom itself, and obliged him to marry his Widow. For which Reason the Philosopher gives it, as an excellent Instance of fraternal Friendship, that *Attalus,* the Brother here mentioned, would not prefer any of the Children which he had by his Sister in Law, then his Wife, but took Care of his Nephew's Education, and, as soon as he came to Age, placed him on the Throne, *Tom.* II. *p.* 489, 490. This Want of Exactness in our Author is therefore the more remarkable, because the Fact thus related, conformably to the Sense of the *Greek* Writer, was still more to his Purpose, as it shews what Liberty Kings, who looked on the Kingdom as their own Patrimony, took in disposing of it. STRABO indeed relates the Matter in a different Way; he speaks of *Attalus* as having been named Guardian only of the King's Son, and Regent of the Kingdom; but he tells us that *Attalus* dying, after a Reign of twenty one Years, left the Crown to his Nephew. *Geogr.* Lib. XIII. p. 926. *Edit. Amst.* (624. *Edit. Paris.*)

6. The Author takes this Fact from LIVY, *Lib.* XXIV. *Cap.* IV. The learned GRONOVIUS takes Notice of two Mistakes on this Occasion. *First,* That this *Hieronymus* was Grandson to *Hiero;* as appears from the very Words of the *Roman* Historian; for *Gelo,* the Father of *Hieronymus,* was dead. *Secondly,* That the Kingdom in Question was not patrimonial, since this *Hiero,* the second of that Name who had reigned in *Sicily,* was made King by the formal and express Consent of the People; as we learn

But whether the King is Proprietor of every particular Spot of Ground
in his Kingdom, as the Kings of *Aegypt*, after the Times of *Joseph*, or as
the Kings of *India*, according to *Diodorus* and *Strabo*, or whether he is
not, this is extrinsick to Sovereignty, and has no Relation to the Nature
of it: Thus there neither results from it another Form of Sovereignty, nor
another Manner of holding it.

Gen. xlvii.

Lib. 2.
Lib. 15.

XVI. The third Observation is this, That [1] Sovereignty is not less Sovereignty, tho' the Sovereign at his Inauguration solemnly promises some
Things to GOD, or to his Subjects, even such [2] Things as respect the
Government of the State. I do not here speak of the Observation of the
natural and divine Law, or even of the Law of Nations, to which all Kings
stand obliged, tho' they have promised no-<84>thing; but of the Observation of certain Rules, to which they would not be obliged but by
their Promise. The Truth of what I say appears by the Example of a
Master of a Family, who has promised his Family something that regards
the Direction of it: For tho' he is bound to perform his Promise, yet he
does not therefore cease to be the Head, and in some Manner, the Sovereign of his Family, as far as the End and Constitution of that little

*XVI. Sover-
eignty not lost
by any Promise
made of Things
which belong
not to the Law
of God or
Nature.*

---

from JUSTIN, *Lib.* XXIII. *Cap.* IV. *Num.* 1, 2. So that Instance is so far from confirming our Author's Principles, that it actually destroys them.

XVI. (1) See PUFEND. *B.* VII. *Chap.* VI. § 10, *&c.*

2. The Emperor *Trajan*, when he was chosen Consul by the free Votes of the
People, took an Oath that he would discharge that Office faithfully, SUBMITTING
*himself and his whole Family to the Divine Vengeance, if he knowingly and wilfully vi-
olated the Laws.* PLINY, *Paneg.* Cap. LXIV. Num. 3. *Edit. Cellar.* Adrian *swore he
would never punish a Senator, till he had been condemned by the Senate.* SPARTIAN. *Vit.
Hadrian.* Cap. VII. The Emperor *Anastasius* took an Oath to observe, and put in
Execution, the Decrees of the Council of *Chalcedon;* as we learn from ZONARAS,
CEDRENUS, and other Writers. The later *Greek* Emperors took an Oath to the
Church. See ZONARAS, in the Life of *Michael Rangabes*, and elsewhere. We have an
Example of the Promises made by the *Gothic* Kings in CASSIODORUS, *Var.* Lib. X.
16, 17. GROTIUS.

All the Instances here alledged by the Author, are not to his Purpose. For the
Question is into what Engagements Princes enter before they are actually invested
with the Sovereign Authority, or when they ascend the Throne, not what Promises
they make after that Time, which may be less binding.

Society permits. A *Husband* likewise loses nothing of his Authority over his Wife, for having promised her somewhat, which he stands obliged to fulfill.

Yet I must confess, where such Promises are made, Sovereignty is thereby somewhat confined, whether the Obligation only concerns the Exercise of the Power, or [3] falls directly on the Power itself. In the former Case, whatever is done contrary to Promise, is unjust; because, as we shall shew elsewhere, every true Promise gives a Right to him to whom it is made. [4] In the latter, the Act is unjust, and void at the same Time, B. 2. ch. 11.

3. Our Author's Meaning, and the Grounds of his Distinction, are these: Sometimes the People require, for Example, that the King shall raise Taxes only on certain Things, as on Lands or Commodities. In which Case the King has a Power of raising Taxes, which is a Branch of the Sovereign Authority; he is not obliged to consult the People, or enquire whether they think it necessary to impose extraordinary Taxes, or raise them in this or that Quantity; but then he can lawfully lay them only on such Things as are specified by the fundamental Laws. So that then the Limitation falls on the *Exercise of the Power,* not on the Power itself. The same is to be said, when the People have stipulated, that the King shall, in all civil and criminal Cases, cause the Laws of the Country to be observed, without depriving him of a Power to make others, which shall not be contrary to them: That he shall chuse him Magistrates only out of a certain Rank of Men: Or that he shall enter into no Offensive War, but on certain Conditions, and in certain Cases. But sometimes the People stipulate, that the King shall levy no Taxes, make no Laws, chuse no Magistrates, or engage in no War, without the Consent of the People; and then the Limitation of the Royal Authority affects the *Power itself.* For, tho' the Prince is possessed of all the Parts of the Sovereignty, there are some which he cannot exercise without the People's Consent. This deserves particular Notice; because the Commentators understand our Author's Words as if he supposed a Division of the Sovereignty. Such a Division is mentioned in the following Paragraph; and the Difference is, that when the Sovereignty is really divided, the People exercise that Part of it which they have reserved to themselves, independently of, and without any Obligation to consult the King; whereas, in the Case under Consideration, the People cannot, for Example, make War of their own Heads; but have only a Right to require that the King shall not enter into one without their Consent; and when such a Consent is given, the King, not the People, makes the War.

4. I see no Ground for this Distinction. All that the King doth in both Cases, contrary to his Engagements, seems to me equally unjust, and void in itself. The King, for Example, hath no more Right to impose Taxes on Commodities, or other Things excepted by the fundamental Laws, than to raise any without the Consent of the People, when he hath entered into a solemn Obligation to observe that Condition, which limits one Part of the Sovereignty. The Engagement is as real, and as strong,

through the Defect of Power. It does not however follow from thence, that the Prince who makes such Promises, depends on a Superior; for the Act is not made void in this Case, by a superior Authority, but by Right itself. Among the *Persians* their [5] Monarch was, Ἀυτοκρατὴς καὶ ἀναπεύθυνος, absolute, and accountable to none, as *Plutarch* declares, and adored as [6] an Image of the Divinity; nor, as it is in *Justin,* [7] was he changed but by Death. He was a King that spoke thus to the *Persian* Nobility, [8] *I have called you together, that none might think I have followed only my own Counsel, but remember it is your Duty to obey, rather than advise.* And yet upon his Accession to the Crown he took an Oath, as [9] *Xeno-<85>phon* and [10] *Diodorus Siculus* observe; and it was not [11] allow-

in the former as in the latter Case; and consequently, the King has no more Right to violate one than the other: So that, if what he hath done is not annulled, it is either for want of sufficient Strength in the People, or the Effect of their tacit Toleration and Ratification, who may wave their Right for Peace sake, or on other Considerations.

5. PLUTARCH, *De trib. generib. Rerum. pub.* Tom. II. p. 826.

6. PLUTARCH makes *Artabanus* a General under King *Artaxerxes,* speak thus, *Tho' we have a great Number of good Laws, the most excellent of all is to honour the King, and adore him as the Image of GOD, who preserves all Things.* Vit. Themistoclis, *Tom.* I. *p.* 125. *Edit. Wech.* See BARN. BRISSON. *De Regno Persarum,* Lib. 1. p. 22, *&c. Edit. Sylburg.*

7. *Lib.* X. *Cap.* 1. *Num.* 2.

8. VALERIUS MAXIMUS, from whom our Author takes this Fact, gives it as an Example of great Insolence, *Lib.* IX. *Cap.* V. *extern.* Num. 2. See BRISSON, *De Regno Pers.* Lib. I. p. 24. *Edit. Sylburg.*

9. The Passage here meant by our Author occurs in the *Cyropaedia,* where the Historian tells us that *Cambyses,* having declared *Cyrus* his Successor in the Presence of the Nobility, whom he had convened for that Purpose, made that Prince *promise on Oath to defend the* Persians *against their Enemies and maintain their Laws, to the utmost of his Power;* and engaged the *Persians,* in the same solemn Manner, *to support and defend the Crown and Dominions of* Cyrus *against all Attempts.* To which he adds, that the Persians *and their Kings entered into the same Engagements in his Time.* Lib. VIII. Cap. V. § 12, 13. *Edit. Oxon.* It is surprizing that the learned BRISSON should omit this Circumstance in his Collection *De Regno Pers.*

10. I do not know where DIODORUS of *Sicily* mentions this Oath; and very much doubt his saying any Thing of it.

11. JOSEPHUS, in his Account of Queen *Vasthi (Vasta)* tells us *there was a Law that would not allow the King to be reconciled to her.* Antiq. *Lib.* XI. *Cap.* VI. p. 374. *Edit. Lips.* Such Laws were called *Laws of the Kingdom,* as is observed by Rabbi JACCHIADES,

able for him to change the Laws that had been made in a certain Manner, as both *Daniel*'s History and [12] *Plutarch* in his Life of *Themistocles* inform us. [13] *Diodorus Siculus* too, B. xvii. and a long Time after, [14] *Procopius* in his first Book of the *Persian* War, [15] where there is a remarkable Story to this purpose. *Diodorus Siculus* [16] says the same Thing of the Kings of *Aethiopia*. The same Author tells us, [17] that the Kings of *Egypt*, who doubtless exercised a Sovereign Authority no less than the other *Eastern*

---

on DANIEL vi. 13. See MARIANA, *Hist. Hisp.* Lib. XX. concerning the Laws of the Kingdoms of *Spain.* GROTIUS.

Mr. BRISSON has also omitted this remarkable Circumstance. Our Author, in his Notes on the Book of ESTHER, *Chap.* i. v. 18. supposes that the Formality required for making the Laws and Ordinances of the *Persian* Monarchs immutable, consisted in their being sealed not only by the King, but also the Grandees of the Kingdom; and grounds his Conjecture on what is related in *Daniel*'s Revelations, *Chap.* vi. v. 17.

12. *Plutarch* in the Life of *Themistocles.* We have no such Life in PLUTARCH. I am very much mistaken, if he had not his Eye on a Passage in that of *Artaxerxes.* The Fact is this. The *Persians* had a Law that when the King had nominated and solemnly declared his Successor, the Person so named should have a Power of making what Demands on him he pleased, and the King should be obliged to comply with him, if what he asked was possible. *Darius,* being thus appointed by his Father *Artaxerxes,* making Use of that Privilege, demanded *Aspasia,* one of the King's Concubines. The King was displeased at the Request; *however,* as the Historian observes, *he delivered the Lady, being compelled to it by the Law; but took her again soon after.* Tom. II. 1025. *Edit. Wech.*

13. Here our Author only refers to the XVII Book of DIODORUS of *Sicily;* but probably he had the following Passage in View; where the *Greek* Writer makes a Remark on a Thing that *Darius* did out of Fear, after he had lost the Day near the River *Issus.* His Horses being frighted carried him in his Chariot into the Midst of his Enemies; whereupon he laid hold of the Reins himself, and thus *was forced to put himself into a Posture unsuitable to his Dignity, and contrary to the Laws, which the Kings of* Persia *were obliged to observe.* Hist. Lib. XVII. Cap. XXXIV. p. 580. *Edit. H. Steph.*

14. The Law, here meant by our Author, and reported by PROCOPIUS, *Lib.* I. *De Bell. Persico,* Cap. V. forbad leaving the Crown to a Person, who had any bodily Imperfection or Deformity; or I am rather inclined to believe he was thinking of another Law, against depriving a Family of an Office, to bestow it on a Stranger. *Ibid.* Cap. VI.

15. The same Historian speaks of a Law relating to the Fort of *Lethe,* which was altered by the King of *Persia;* but doth not approve of the Change. *Ibid.* Cap. V. GROTIUS.

16. *Lib.* III. *Cap.* V. p. 102. *Edit. H. Steph.*

17. See *Lib.* I. *Cap.* LXX, *&c.* p. 44, 45. *Edit. H. Steph.*

Kings, were obliged to observe many Things, which if they did not perform, they could not during their Lives be called to an Account; yet after
their Deaths, their [18] Memories might be arraigned, and being found
guilty were refused *solemn* Burial; as [19] the Bodies of wicked Princes
amongst the ancient *Hebrews*, were not interred in the *Royal* Sepulchres;
by this wonderful Temperament, the *Sacredness* of *sovereign Majesty* was
preserved, and yet their *Kings* were *restrained* from breaking their Engagements for fear of a future Condemnation. [20] *Plutarch* also <86> tells

2 Chr. xxiv. 25
— xxviii. 27.

18. By the *Roman* Laws, *the Bodies of Tyrants were to remain unburied;* as we learn
from APPIAN, *De Bello Civili.* Lib. III. p. 873. *Edit. Toll.* (537. *H. Steph.*) The Emperor
Andronicus Paleologus forbad the Burial of *Michael,* his Father, for having embraced
some Doctrines of the *Latin* Church. NICEPH. GREG. *Lib.* VI. GROTIUS.

19. See JOSEPHUS, speaking of the two *Jehorams;* the one King of *Judah,* the other
King of *Israel.* Antiq. *Lib.* IX. Cap. III, V. And what he says of *Joash,* King of *Judah;*
ibid. *Cap.* VIII. GROTIUS.

This Circumstance of the Burial of the three Kings is recorded, of the first in 2
CHRON. xxi. 20. of the second, in 2 KINGS, ix. 26. of the third, in 2 CHRON. xxiv. 25.
But we read in 2 KINGS, xii. 21. that Joash *was buried with his Fathers in the City of
David.* Our Author endeavours to reconcile these two Accounts in his *Notes on the
Old Testament,* by saying that the Words last quoted mean that some Honour was
shewn to his Corpse, but not the greatest usually bestowed on such as had always
reigned well; which was to be buried in the Sepulchre of the Kings. The Commentators on the Work before us pretend that this Custom was not constantly observed;
and that, when it was practised, it was not always by Way of Punishment, inflicted
by Men. Their Opinion is founded on this Observation; that very few of the many
Kings of *Judah* and *Israel,* spoken of in the sacred History, obey'd GOD's Com-
mandments, and yet it is not probable that only such as did were buried in the Sepulchre of the Kings, some of them, say they, even seem to have given Orders for their
being deposited in other Places; on which Occasion they quote 2 KINGS, ix. 28. and
xxi. 18, 26. But besides that those Princes were wicked, though some more so than
others, there may have been some particular Reasons, why the Bodies even of those
whose Crimes deservedly reflected Dishonour on their Memory, might not actually
be treated in this Manner. But, however that may be, it is certain that the sacred
History represents it as a Punishment on the *Jewish* Kings, that they were not buried
with their Ancestors. One of the Prophets expressly declares it such to *Jeroboam; thy
Carcass,* says he, *shall not come unto the Sepulchre of thy Fathers,* 1 KINGS, xiii. 22. [these
Words are not directed to *Jeroboam;* but spoken by one Prophet to another]. See also
the following Chapter, *v.* 13.

20. His Words are these: *At* Passaron, in the *Territories of* Molossia, *it was cus-
tomary for the Kings to sacrifice to* Jupiter Ἄρειος, *and take an Oath to the People of*
Epirus, *to govern according to the Laws; and for the People to maintain his Power, according to the same Laws.* In Pyrrh. p. 385. *Tom.* I. *Edit. Wech.* GROTIUS.

us in the Life of *Pyrrhus,* that the Kings of *Epyrus* were accustomed to take an Oath, that they would govern according to the Laws.

But what shall we say of Promises, accompanied by this Clause, that if the King breaks his Faith, he shall forfeit the Crown? Even in that Case, the Power does not cease to be supreme, but the Manner of holding it will be limited by such a Condition, and the Sovereignty will not be unlike a temporary one. *Agatharchides* said, a King of the *Sabaeans, was* ἀναπεύθυνος, *the most absolute Prince in the World,* and yet if he were found without his own Palace, he might be stoned to Death; which *Strabo* also observes out of *Artemidorus.*

Thus, Lands held as *Feoffments of Trust* are no less our own, [21] than if we possessed them with full Property; but yet they are capable of being lost. Such a commissory Clause may be added not only in Compacts between the People and the King, on whom they confer the sovereign Authority, but also in other Contracts. We see [22] some Treaties of Alliance made on that Condition with neighbouring Nations: or even by those Treaties it is stipulated, that the Subjects [23] shall not assist their King, nor obey him, if he violates his Engagements.

XVII. The fourth Observation is this, Though the sovereign Power be but one, and of itself undivided, consisting of those Parts above mentioned, with the Addition of Supremacy, that is, τῷ ἀνυπευθύνῳ, ac-

See an Example in Crantzius His. Suec. 1. 9.

Ap. PHOTIUM. L. 16.

XVII. It may sometimes be divided.

---

21. *Est quidem Fundus, non minùs quàm, &c.* Thus the Passage stands in all the Editions of the Original before mine; where I have inserted the Word *noster* after *fundus;* which the Sense evidently requires; and then it runs thus: *Lands held as Feoffments of Trust are no less our own, than if we possessed them with full Property,* &c. I am very much mistaken, or our Author had that Law of the DIGEST in his Mind: *Non ideo minûs rectè* quid NOSTRUM *esse vindicabimus, quòd* ABIRE A NOBIS DOMINIUM SPERATUR, si CONDITIO *Legati aut Libertatis extiterit,* Lib. VI. Tit. I. *De rei vindicat.* Leg. LXVI.

22. Our Author himself elsewhere asserts that this *commissory* Clause is tacitly included in all Treaties of Alliance. B. II. *Chap.* XV. § 15.

23. See MARTIN CROMER. *Polonic.* Lib. XIX, & XXI. We have likewise an Instance of this Sort of Stipulation in the Chronicle of LAMBERT DE SCHAFNABURG, on the Year 1074. in the Reign of *Henry* IV. Emperor of *Germany.* GROTIUS.

countable to none, (¹) yet it sometimes happens, that it is divided, either into *subjective Parts,* as they are called, or *potential; (that is, either amongst several Persons, who possess it jointly; or into several Parts, whereof one is in the Hands of one Person, and another in the Hands of another).* Thus though there was but one *Roman Empire,* yet it ² often happened, that one ruled in the *Eastern* Part, and another in the *Western;* nay, and sometimes the Empire was divided among three. So also it may happen, that the People in chusing a King, may reserve certain Acts of Sovereignty to themselves, and confer others on the King absolutely and without Restriction. This however does not take place, (as I have shewed already) as often as the King is obliged by some Promise; but only then, when either ³ the Partition is expressly made, (of which also we have treated above) or when the People being (as yet) free, shall require certain Things of the King, whom they are chusing, by way of a perpetual Ordinance; or if any Thing be added, whereby it is implied, that the King may be compelled or punished. ⁴ For every Ordinance flows from a Superior, at least in Regard to what is ordered. And Compulsion is not always indeed an Act of a Superior, for naturally every Man has Power to compel his Debtor; but it is repugnant to the State of an Inferior; therefore from Compulsion there at least follows an Equality, and consequently a Division of the sovereign Power. <87>

Many alledge here a great Number of Inconveniencies, to which the

XVII. (1) See what I have said on PUFENDORF's *Law of Nat.* &c. B. VII. Chap. IV. § 1. and on the Abridgment of *The Duties of a Man and a Citizen.* B. II. Chap. VII. § 9. *Note* 1. in the third and fourth Editions.

2. This Example is not well applied. See PUFEND. *B.* VII. *Chap.* V. § 15. who has given some more exact.

3. In the Reign of the Emperor *Probus,* the Senate confirmed the Laws made by the Prince; took Cognizance of Appeals; created Proconsuls; and assigned the Consuls their Deputies. VOPISCUS, in *Probo.* Cap. XIII. See also GAILIUS, *Lib.* II. *Observ.* LVII. *Num.* 7. and Cardinal MANTICA, *De tacitis & ambiguis conventionibus,* Lib. XXVII. Tit. V. *Num.* 4. GROTIUS.

The last Words of the original Passage are *Legatos Consulibus darent.* But as the learned SALMASIUS has shewn in a Note on that Place, the true Reading is *Legatos ex consulibus darent;* that is, *named the Consular Lieutenants,* for Governing even those Provinces which were reserved to the Emperor.

4. See on this Subject PUFEND. *B.* VII. *Chap.* IV. § 14.

State is exposed by this Partition of Sovereignty, which makes of it as it were a Body with two Heads; but in the Matter of civil Government, it is impossible to provide against all Inconveniencies; and we must judge of a Right, not by the Ideas that such or such a Person may form of what is best, but by the Will of him, that conferred that Right; as we have already observed. A very ancient Example of this Division is brought by *Plato* in his third Book of Laws. For the [5] *Heraclidae* (the Posterity of *Hercules*) being settled at *Argos, Messena* and *Lacedemon,* their Kings were obliged to govern according to Laws prescribed to them; and whilst they did so, the People were bound to continue the Kingdom to them and their Posterity, and not to suffer any one to take it from them. Moreover, besides the reciprocal Engagement of each People and their King, the three Kings [6] stood engaged one to the other, the three Nations one to the other, and each King to the two neighbouring Nations, as also each Nation to the two neighbouring Kings; all of them together promising mutual Assistance.

XVIII. But they are much mistaken, who suppose, because Kings will not allow some of their Acts to be of Force, till they are ratified by the Senate, or some other Assembly, that there is a Partition of Sovereignty. For whatever Acts are thus annulled, ought to be reputed as annulled by the King's Authority, who by that Means ([1]) would take Care, that noth-

XVIII. Ill inferred from this, that some Princes will have their Acts confirmed by the Senate.

5. *De Legib.* Lib. III. p. 683, 684. Tom. II. *Edit H. Steph.* The Commentators pretend that the Example is not well applied; because as they tell us, it turns only on an Alliance. But on a careful Examination of it, we shall find that, pursuant to the Alliance, the Subjects had a Power of exercising some Acts of Sovereignty, independently of their Prince.

6. We have several Examples of this Sort in the History of the Northern Nations. See JOANNES MAGNUS, *Hist. Sued.* Lib. XV. & XXIX. CRANTZIUS, *Sued.* Lib. V. PONTANUS, *Hist. Dan,* Lib. VIII. GROTIUS.

XVIII. (1) It is very probable, however, that in those Kingdoms, where a certain Assembly must approve of the Edicts and Ordinances of the Prince, this Approbation had originally more Force, and was a Kind of Limitation of the legislative Power, wisely established for preventing Abuses. But in Process of Time, the Kings found Means to reduce it to a *Verification,* that is, to a bare Formality; none of the Members of the Assembly daring to give his Opinion on such Edicts; of which sometimes only the Titles are read, and to which no one pretends to make Objections, for Fear of incurring the Prince's Displeasure, who requires a blind Obedience.

² which he calls παμβασιλείαν, (the same is παντελὴς Μοναρχία in *Soph-ocles*'s *Antigone;* αὐτοκρατὴς βασιλεία, καὶ ἀνυπεύθυνος, in *Plutarch;* ἐξουσία αὐτοτελὴς, in Strabo) and a Kingdom like that of *Lacedemon,* which is only the first Dignity of the State; of such a Mixture we have an example (I think) in the *Israelitish* Kings, for without Doubt in most Things they ruled with an absolute Power. For the People desired a King, ³ *such* a one as the neighbouring Nations had; but the Power of the *Eastern* Kings was very absolute. Thus *Aeschylus* brings in *Atossa* speaking to the *Persians* of their King, οὐκ ὑπεύθυνος πόλει, *not accountable to the* L. xxxvi. *State for his Actions.* And that of ⁴ *Virgil* is well known, *The* Egyptians, *Lydians,* Parthians *and* Medians, *have not a more profound Respect for their King.* And in ⁵ *Livy: The* Syrians, *and People of* Asia *are Men born to Slavery;* ⁶ <89> to which agrees with that of *Apollonius* in ⁷ *Philostratus,*

---

hereditary, only as far as the People allowed them to be so. But, whatever becomes of that Question, it appears from the Passages already quoted that the Kingdoms, mentioned by ARISTOTLE, as being of a middle Sort between the *Spartan Kingdoms* and *absolute Monarchy,* did not admit of a real Division of the Sovereignty, like those Governments, which our Author distinguishes by the Appellation of *Mix'd.*

2. Ἀυτοκρατὴς βασιλεία. DIONYS. of *Halicarn.* Speaking of the *Lacedemonians,* says they were not αὐτοκράτορες, *absolute, and independent,* Lib. II. Cap. XIV. p. 85. *Edit. Oxon.* (87 Sylb.) GROTIUS.

3. The People, to use the Words of JOSEPHUS, *thought it not absurd or unreasonable to submit to the same Form of Government, as was established among the neighbouring Nations.* Antiq. Lib. VI. Cap. IV. p. 174. *Edit. Lips.* GROTIUS.

4. This is spoken of the Bees. *Georg.* Lib. IV. *v.* 2100, *&c.*

5. *Lib.* XXXVI. *Cap.* XVII. *Num.* 5.

6. CICERO speaks of the *Jews* and *Syrians* as *People* born to Slavery. De Prov. Consular. *Cap.* V. EURIPIDES says that *among the Barbarians, all are Slaves except one Man.* Helena, 2. 283. In which he imitates a Thought of ESCHYLUS, who declares *no one is free but* Jupiter *alone.* Prometh. vinct. which LUCAN applies to *Caesar.* Lib. II. *v.* 280, 281. SERVIUS & PHILARGYRIUS, on VIRGIL, *Georg.* IV. *v.* 210. quote a Passage from SALLUST, where that Historian observes, that the Eastern Nations *have naturally a profound Veneration for the Name of a King.* The Emperor *Julian* speaks of the servile Temper of the *Syrians, Persians, Parthians,* and all the Barbarians of the *East* and the *South,* who were governed by despotic Princes, in Opposition to the Love which the ancient *Germans* had for Liberty. In S. CYRIL. p. 138. *Edit. Spanhem.* CLAUDIAN tells the Emperor *Honorius,* that he commands a free People, and not such as the *Arabians, Armenians* and *Syrians.* De IV. Consulatu Honorii. *v.* 306. GROTIUS.

7. He makes *Apollonius* of *Tyana* say, that *Damis being an* Assyrian, *and a Neigh-*

Ἀσσύριοι καὶ Μῆδοι τας τυραννίδας προσκυνοῦσι: *The* Assyrians, *and* Medes *adore arbitrary Government;* and that of *Aristotle,* οἱ περὶ τὴν Ἀσίαν ὑπομένουσι τὴν δεσποτικὴν ἀρχὴν, οὐδὲν δυσχεραίνοντες: *The Asiaticks submit to despotick Power without Difficulty;* and in *Tacitus,* that of *Civilis Batavus* to the *Gauls, Let* Syria *and* Asia *serve, and the East accustomed to Kings.* For at that Time there were Kings in *Germany* and *Gaul;* but as the same Author observes, they governed in a precarious Manner, more by a persuasive, than commanding Power.

Polit. 1. 3.
c. 14.
Hist. iv.

We have also observed before, that the whole *Hebrew* Nation depended on their King; and *Samuel* describing the Right of Kings, fully shews, that there remained [8] no Power in the People against the Injuries of their Kings, which the [9] Ancients rightly gather from that of the *Psalm-*

---

bour to the Medes, *who adored arbitrary Government, entertained no noble Sentiments of Liberty.* Vit. Apollon. *Lib.* VII. *Cap.* XIV. *Edit. Oxon.*

8. But see the following Chapter, § 3.

9. St. JEROM, on this Place, observes, that as David *was a King, he feared no Man.* To which he elsewhere adds; he had *no Superior.* Epist ad Rusticum, *de Paenitentiâ.* Tom. I. p. 221. *Edit. Erasm. Basil.* St. AMBROSE reasons in the same Manner on this Passage: *For he was a King, and obliged by no Laws; for Kings cannot transgress* (against Men) *and being secure under their own Power, can be punished by no Laws: He did not therefore sin against Man, to whom he was not subject; but tho' his Post secured him, he was subject to GOD by the Ties of Faith and Religion.* Apol. David. *Cap.* X. See also ARNOBIUS the younger on the same *Psalm,* and ISIDORE of *Pelusium,* Lib. V. Epist. 383, in the late Edition of his Works. *Vitiges,* King of the *Goths,* said, *The Actions of Kings are to be judged at the Tribunal of GOD; for as their Power is derived from Heaven, so they are obliged to justify themselves to Heaven alone.* CASSIODORE. See § 8. *Note* 56. GROTIUS.

I am surprized that our Author, both here and in his Treatise *De imperio summarum Potestatum circa sacra,* Cap. IX. § 20. could adopt so unreasonable an Explication of DAVID's Words, as that given by the Fathers of the Church, and the loose Conclusion, they draw from them. To speak with MILTON, in his *Defensio pro Pop. Angl.* Cap. II. p. 51. and the learned RABOD HERMAN SCHELIUS in his posthumous Treatise *De jure Imperii,* p. 255, is there any Probability that *David,* when he spoke these Words, penetrated with Sentiments of Humiliation and Repentance, thought of the Prerogative of Kings; and that he intended to boast of a pretended Power, which authorized the Commission of Rapin, Murder, and Adultery, and left his Subjects no Room for Complaint? I cannot think the most zealous Defenders of arbitrary Power, how extravagantly soever they may compliment Kings with Impunity, and however strong an Obligation they may impose on Subjects of Non-Resistance, would venture to maintain, that a Prince, who takes away the Life of an innocent

did [15] of themselves take Cognizance of some criminal Affairs, in which *Maimonides* prefers them [16] to the Kings of the ten Tribes of *Israel;* and that plainly appears from many Examples, as well in Holy Writ, as in *Hebrew* Authors; but it seems that the Cognizance of some Causes was not allowed to them, as concerning Crimes committed by a Tribe, or by

Luke xiii. 33.
the High [17] Priest, or by a Prophet; and this is plain from the Story of the

Jer. xxxviii. 5.
Prophet *Jeremy,* whom when the Princes demanded to put to Death, the King answered them, *Behold he is in your Power, and the King can do* [18] *nothing against you,* that is, in such sort of Affairs. Moreover, when any

Joseph. Antiq.
one had been accused before the *Sanhedrim,* upon any other Account whatsoever, it was not in the King's Power to screen him from the Judgment of that Tribunal: and therefore *Hyrcanus,* finding there was no Way to hinder *Herod* from being tried, sought out Expedients to elude the Sentence. <91>

In *Macedonia,* those that descended from *Caranus,* as *Callisthenes* says in *Arrianus:* [19] οὐ βίᾳ ἀλλὰ νόμῳ Μακεδόνων ἄρχοντες διετέλεσαν,

15. And this was carried so far, that he ordered the Execution of the Criminals, without any Formality of Justice. *David* exercised the same Severity on the Man, who boasted of having killed *Saul.* 2 *Sam.* i. 15. and on the Assassins of *Isbosheth,* ibid. iv. 15.

16. See SELDEN, *de Synedriis.* Lib. II. Cap. XIV. § 1.

17. But do we not read that *Solomon* deposed *Abiathar,* the High Priest. 1 *Kings* ii. 27. Our Author, and those whom he has followed, confound the Government of the *Hebrews* before the *Babylonish* Captivity, with the State of the Commonwealth of *Israel* under the *Asmonean* Princes, who, though they wore the Crown, and had assumed the Title of King, were obliged, for confirming their Authority, to share it with the *Sanhedrim,* which had been established since the *Jews,* having shook off the *Syrian* Yoke, began to be governed by the High Priests, in Conjunction with the Heads of their own People; according to the judicious Conjecture of Mr. LE CLERC in his Dissertation, § 7. In Regard to Crimes committed by a whole Tribe, or by the High Priest, or by a false Prophet. See SELDEN, *de Synedriis.* Lib. III. Cap. IV. *&c.*

18. The Question there is not concerning the Rights of the Royal Power, as has been observed by Commentators. *Zedekiah* only declares that, in that Conjuncture, he is obliged to yield to the importunate Demands of the Heads of the People, who looked on *Jeremiah* as a Traitor, and one, who held a Correspondence with their Enemies the *Chaldeans.*

19. *De Expedit. Alexandri.* Lib. IV. Cap. XI. The Author speaks rather of the Manner, how *Alexander*'s Predecessors had acquired the Throne, *viz.* without Usurpation or Violence, than of the Manner how they exercised the Royal Authority.

reigned according to the Laws, and not by Force; and *Curtius,* [20] in his fourth Book, *though the* Macedonians *were used to regal Government, yet they lived in a greater Appearance of Liberty than other Nations:* For the King himself could not judge of capital Crimes: And the same Author in the 6th Book, [21] *By an ancient Custom amongst the* Macedonians, *the Army took Cognizance of capital Crimes, in Time of War; and the People in Time of Peace; so that in this Respect the Kings had no Power, but by the Way of Persuasion.* There is also in another Place of the same Author another Instance of this Mixture, [22] *The* Macedonians *decreed, that according to the Custom of their Nation, their King should never hunt on Foot, or without being attended by some of the Nobles and of his Favourites.* And *Tacitus* of the *Goths, They were under the Government of* [23] *Kings, who kept them a little more in Subjection, than those of other Nations in* Germany, *but so as not to leave them an entire Liberty.* He had said before (*in speaking of the* Germans *in general*) that their Kings, who were only the chief or principal Men of the State, [24] governed rather by Persuasion, than by their Authority. But elsewhere he describes an absolute Monarchy in these Words, [25] *They (the* Suiones) *are under the Dominion of a Prince, whose Authority is absolute, and not precarious.* And *Eustathius* describing the Republick of the *Corcyreans,* [26] said it was *a Mixture of*

---

20. This Passage is followed by the ensuing Words: *They opposed* him *(Alexander) in his Pursuit of Immortality with more Vigour than was expedient either for themselves or the King.* Lib. IV. Cap. VII. *Num.* 31.

21. *Lib.* VI. *Cap.* VIII. *Num.* 25.

22. *Lib.* VIII. *Cap.* I. *Num.* 18. PUFENDORF, in a Dissertation *De rebus gestis Philippi,* which appears among his *Academical Dissertations,* § 16. pretends that from those Passages it follows only that the Power of the Kings of *Macedon* was limited. But, on a careful Examination of those Authorities, and others which he quotes, it will, in my Opinion, appear that they suppose somewhat more than a bare Limitation; at least if we consider the Origin of those Customs, and the Manner how they had been long practised.

23. *German.* Cap. XLIII. *Num.* 7.

24. *Ibid.* Cap. XI. *Num.* 6.

25. *Ibid.* Cap. XLIV. *Num.* 3.

26. On *Odyss.* Lib. VI.

even before they knew what would be resolved in it, as *Livy* [38] and *Dionysius* observe. To conclude, *Isocrates* pretends that the Government of *Athens* was, in the [39] Time of *Solon, A Democracy mixed with an Aristocracy.* These Things being premised, let us examine some Questions, which are often produced on this Subject.

XXI. *A Confederate on unequal Terms may have the Supreme Power.*

Justin, l. 43. c. 5.

Valer. Max. l. 5. c. 2.

XXI. The first is, Whether a Power inferior to any other by Vertue of a Treaty of *unequal Alliance,* may have the Sovereignty? [1] By *unequal Alliance* I mean, not such as is made between two Powers whose Strength is unequal; as when [2] the City of *Thebes* in the Time of *Pelopidas* made a League with the King of *Persia,* and the *Romans* with the *Massilians,* and afterwards with King *Masinissa;* nor such as stipulates some transient Act, as when an Enemy is reconciled, upon paying the Charges of the War, or performing any other Thing once for all. But I mean, when by the express Articles of the League, some lasting Preference is given from one to the other; or whereby the one is obliged to maintain the Sovereignty and Majesty of the other; as it was in the [3] League between

---

38. *Lib.* I. *Cap.* XVII. *Num.* 9. DIONYSIUS of *Halicarnassus* says, that in his Time *the Resolutions of the People had the Force of a Law, without the Cognizance of the Senate; but that the Orders of the Senate were subject to the People's Determination,* Antiq. Rom. *Lib.* II. *Cap.* XIV. Our Author means to speak of those Times, when § 19. he maintains, against POLYBIUS, *that the Government of* Rome *was Democratical:* So that some of his Commentators have unjustly accused him of contradicting himself in this Point. We may see in GRONOVIUS's Observations on *B.* I. *Chap.* XXV. how the People by degrees incroached on the Right of the Senate, and at last swallowed it up. It will not be improper to read a Dissertation of PUFENDORF, already quoted, *De formâ Reip. Rom.* tho' he does all in his Power for saving the Authority of the Senate. See also PAUL MERULA, *De Leg. Romanor.* Cap. II. § 12. and *Cap.* III. § I. And RABOD HERMAN SCHELIUS, *De Jure Imperii,* p. 41, *&c.*

39. In his *Panathenaic* Oration, where he says that *Lycurgus* copied that Form of Government, as much as was possible.

XXI. (1) See PUFENDORF on this Subject, *B.* VIII. *Chap.* IX. § 3, 4. compared with our Author, *B.* II. *Chap.* XV. § 7. *&c.*

2. PLUTARCH, from whom the Author has certainly taken this Fact, says that *Artaxerxes* granted, among other Things, *That the* Thebans *should be considered as the King's hereditary Friends.* In Vit. Pelopid. *p.* 294. *Edit. Wech.*

3. LIVY, who gives an Account of this Treaty, adds, that this was to be done, *sine dolo malo, without Fraud,* Lib. XXXVIII. Cap. XI. Num. 2.

the *Aetolians* and the *Romans*, that is, to hinder any Attack on their Sovereignty, and to make <93> their Dignity, which is denoted by the Word Majesty, to be respected; *Tacitus* [4] calls that *the having a Reverence for the* Roman *Empire;* which he thus explains, *Tho' placed on their Banks, and beyond the Limits of our Empire, yet in Mind and Will they act with us.* So *Florus,* [5] *Other People, who were not under the Dominion of the* Romans, *were sensible of their Grandeur, and reverenced the Conquerors of Nations.*

[6] *Andronicus Rhodius* rightly observes after *Aristotle,* that this is proper to Friendship between Unequals, that the more Honour be given to the more powerful, and the more Assistance to the more weak.

To the Inequality in Question may be referred some of those Rights, which are now called Right of [7] Protection, Right of [8] Patronage, and

---

4. *De morib. German.* Cap. XXIX. Num. 3, 4. Neither this Passage, nor that in the following Note, speaks of any Alliance, but only of the Impression made by the *Roman* Grandeur on other Nations.

5. *Lib.* IV. *Cap.* XII. *Num.* 61.

6. Paraphr. *Lib.* VIII. *Cap.* XVIII. *p.* 567. *Ed. Hein.* 1617.

7. *Protectionis.* This Term is used when one Prince or State takes another less powerful Prince or State under *Protection,* and engages in its Defence, either without any Consideration, or on Condition of receiving a certain Tribute. We have several Examples of this Kind in the *German* Empire, and elsewhere. See the late Mr. HERTIUS's Dissertation *De specialibus Romano-Germ. Imperii Rebus pub. &c.* § 34. in the second Volume of his *Comment. & Opusc.* and his *Paraemiae Juris Germanici,* Lib. II. Cap. V.

8. *Advocatia. Advocati* were those who engaged to defend a Church or a Monastery. See the Origin of this in the *Bibliotheque Universelle,* Tom. I. p. 97, *&c.* The learned GRONOVIUS on this Place, quotes several Authors who treat on this Subject. We have likewise a great Number of curious and instructive Observations on the same, in a Dissertation written by the late Mr. HERTIUS, *De consultationib. legib. & judiciis in specialib. Rom. Germ. Imperii Rebus pub.* § 17. Tom. II. of his *Commentationes & Opusc. &c.* It will be sufficient to produce one considerable Example of this Kind of *Patronage,* which comes to our Author's Purpose; which is that of the Emperor of *Germany,* who stiles himself *Supreme Patron of the* Roman *Church,* tho' he is not supreme Head of that Church, and has long had no Right over the Temporalities of the Pope. See likewise the *Jus Ecclesiastic. Protestantium,* by Mr. BOHMER, Professor of Law at *Hall,* Lib. III. Cap. V. § 36, 37. where he gives a compendious History of the Right of *Patronage,* and points out such Authors as treat of it most satisfactorily.

Allies. To which agrees that of *Scipio Africanus* the Elder, [19] *The People of* Rome *had rather engage Men by Kindness than by Fear, and gain foreign Nations by Protection and Alliance, than subject them by hard Bondages;* and what *Strabo* [20] relates of the *Lacedemonians* after the Coming of the *Romans* into *Greece, they continued free, contributing nothing but what they were obliged to do as Friends and Allies.* As private Protection takes not away personal Liberty, so publick Protection does not the Civil, which cannot be conceived without Sovereignty. Therefore you may see *Livy* opposes the State of those who [21] are under the Protection of another People, to that of those who are under their Dominion. And *Augustus* threatned [22] *Syllaeus* King of the *Arabians* (as *Josephus* <95> relates) if

19. LIVY, *Lib.* XXVI. *Cap.* XLIX. *Num.* 8.

20. *Geograph.* Lib. VIII. p. 562. *Edit. Amst.* (865, *Paris.*)

21. *In fide & in ditione.* Thus, speaking of the *Sidicinians, who were neither under the Protection (in fide) of the* Roman *People, nor subject to their Jurisdiction, (nec ditione)* Lib. VIII. Cap. I. Num. 10. And elsewhere, *in fidem se tradere,* is opposed to *in servitutem;* as when *Pheneas,* who appeared at the Head of the Embassy sent from the *Etolians,* said to a *Roman* Consul, *Non in servitutem, sed in Fidem tuam nos tradimus; we do not offer ourselves as your Slaves, but put ourselves under your Protection,* Lib. XXXVI. Cap. XXVIII. Num. 4. But the Consul soon let the World know, that in those Days the *Romans,* by *in fidem tradere* understood surrendering at Discretion, and submitting to their Jurisdiction. See SPANHEIM's *Orbis Rom.* Exercit. II. Cap. X. p. 299. That Expression became ambiguous, as the *Romans* began to act like Masters with their Allies. See our Author's Observation, *B.* III. *Chap.* XX. § 50. in which there is no Contradiction, as BOECLER would insinuate, who shewed me the Passages here quoted. He himself observes, that the *Latin* Writers, when they would speak justly, make an Addition of some Word, for avoiding the Ambiguity; as in the following Passages, *Quorum in Fide, & Clientelâ Regnum* (Numidia) *erat.* FLORUS, *Lib.* III. *Cap.* I. *Num.* 3. *Manus ad* Caesarem *tendere & voce significare coeperunt* (Bellovaci) *sese in ejus Fidem & Potestatem venire.* CAESAR *De Bello Gall.* Lib. III. Cap. XIII. Bellovacos *omni tempore in Fide atque Amicitiâ Civitatis* Aeduae *fuisse.* Idem. *Ibid.* Cap. XIV. But the first of these Expressions, according to SPANHEIM, in his *Orbis Rom.* as above quoted, p. 307. signifies as much as the second.

22. Here are several Mistakes in this Sentence, which the learned GRONOVIUS has observed. *First, Syllaeus* was not King of the *Arabians,* but only Minister or General to *Obodas,* King of Part of *Arabia. Secondly,* This Menace regards *Herod,* whom *Syllaeus* had accused to *Augustus,* concerning his Expedition into *Arabia;* whereupon *Augustus* wrote to the King of the *Jews,* that *he had till then treated him like a Friend, but for the future would use him as a Subject.* JOSEPHUS, *Antiq. Jud.* Lib. XVI. Cap. XV. p. 572. *Thirdly,* Our Author doth not give us a just Idea of the Condition of the Kings of *Arabia;* for those Kings, as well as all the others from the *West* to *Euphrates,*

he did not leave off injuring his Neighbours, he would take Care that he should be made a Subject of a Friend; which was the Condition of the Kings of *Armenia,* who, as *Paetus* writes to *Vologeses,* [23] were under the *Roman* Jurisdiction, and consequently more Kings in Name than Reality; as were also the Kings of *Cyprus,* and some others, formerly Subjects [24] to the *Persian* ὑποταγέντες, as *Diodorus* calls them.

Here may be objected what *Proculus* adds, [25] *Those who are Members of confederate States are summoned to appear before us; they are tried at our*

---

at that Time depended on the *Romans* so much, that they received the Crown from them; and even a Son could not succeed his Father without their Consent. JOSEPHUS, in the very Place I have quoted, and in the following Chapter, tells us how much *Augustus* was provoked at *Aretas,* for entering on his Reign, after the Demise of *Obodas,* without waiting for his Approbation; and what Submission that Prince was obliged to make for appeasing the Emperor. It is well known likewise, that *Archelaüs,* Son to the *Herod* already mentioned, went to *Rome* immediately after his Father's Death, to solicit the Confirmation of the Kingdom of *Judea,* which he gained only under the Title of *Ethnarch;* and some Years after, on the Complaints of the *Jews,* the Emperor banished him to *Vienna.* See the late Mr. PERIZONIUS's Dissertation, *De Angusteâ Orbis terrarum Descriptione,* § 3, 5, 6.

23. TACITUS, who relates this Fact, makes *Paetus say, The* Armenians *had always been subject to the* Roman *Power, or to a King chosen by the Emperor.* Annal. *Lib.* XV. *Cap.* XIII. *Num.* 4. FLORUS tells us, that *after the Defeat of* Tigranes, Pompey *required no other Subjection of the* Armenians, *than that of receiving their Governors from the* Romans, *Lib.* IV. *Cap.* XII. *Num.* 43. See SPANHEIM's *Orbis Romanus,* p. 452.

24. *Biblioth. Hist.* Lib. XVI. Cap. XLVI. p. 534. *Edit. H. Steph.*

25. DIGEST. *Lib.* XLIX. *Tit.* XV. *De Captiv. & Postlimin. &c.* Leg. VII. § 2. See what PUFENDORF says to this, *B.* VIII. *Chap.* IX. § 4. in the first Note, where I have joined what he had written in two different Places. The Difficulty will vanish on reading SPANHEIM's *Orbis Rom.* Exercit. II. Cap. X. The *Alliance* and *Liberty* of the Kings and People in Question, were widely different from what our Author conceives them to have been. The Inequality of those Alliances, implied not a bare *Inferiority of Respect,* but a real *Dependence* and *Subjection;* as is evident from several Places in LIVY, who makes a clear Distinction between *Foedus aequum,* and *Foedus iniquum.* When the People of *Campania* applied to the *Romans* for their Assistance against the *Samnites,* and at the same Time a perpetual Alliance, they said, *had they made this Application at a Time when Fortune was favourable to them, as the Alliance would have been of a more early Date, so it would have been bound by a weaker Tye: For then, as they should have remember'd they contracted it on equal Terms, (ex aequo) they perhaps had been as truly Friends, but less subject and devoted (minus subjecti atque obnoxii) to the* Romans. *Lib.* VII. *Cap.* XXX. *Num.* 2. The Rest of their Speech speaks this Dependence, tho' they had not yet declared their Disposition to put themselves at

Tribunals, and are punished by Vertue of the Sentence passed against them.
But to make this more plain, we must know there are four Kinds of
Differences, or Subjects of Complaint. First, If the Subjects of the King
or State under Protection, are accused of having done any Thing contrary to the Treaty of Alliance. Secondly, If the King, or the States themselves be accused. Thirdly, If the Allies under the <96> Protection of the

---

Discretion under the *Roman* Power; which they had Orders to do, only on a Refusal
of forming an Alliance with them on the Terms proposed. The same Historian informs us, that *the* Apulians *gained an Alliance (Foedus) not on equal Terms, (neque
aequo foedere) but on Condition that they should be subject to the* Roman *People, (in
ditione Populi Romani).* Lib. IX. Cap. XX. Num. 8. It was only in the Time of the
first Consuls, and before the *Sicilian* War, that the *Romans* made Alliances, not prejudicial to the Sovereignty of their Allies; but from that Time they were only nominally
such. The People, whom they termed *Free, Allies* and *Friends,* were so called, because
the *Roman* People, with the Property of their Lands, gave them a Permission to be
governed by their own Laws, and the proper Magistrates of their respective Countries.
But then they were to acknowledge that all this was a Concession from the *Roman*
People; and that People made this Dependence appear by diminishing or taking away
that Liberty as they pleased. In *Note* 22 on this Paragraph we have given an Example
of their Manner of treating Kings; and the Lawyer SCEVOLA makes it Treason *maliciously to hinder the King of a foreign Nation from obeying the* Roman *People.* DIGEST.
Lib. XLVIII. *Tit.* IV. *Ad Leg. Jul. Majestatis,* Leg. IV. A plain Proof that the *Romans*
considered the allied Kings, and much more the Cities and Nations called Free and
Allied, as dependent on them. Those People could neither undertake a War, or enter
into an Alliance, without Permission from the *Romans:* They were obliged to find
Quarters and Provisions for their Generals and Armies, and from Time to Time receive such Governors as were sent to regulate Affairs: They paid Tributes and Imposts,
unless they had obtained a particular Exemption, and even that Exemption did not
secure them from paying in certain extraordinary Cases. Add to all this, that those
Nations, as well as the allied Kings, were obliged to furnish the *Romans* with Troops
on every Demand; and this was the Reason why *all the World was to be enrolled,* LUKE
ii. 1. On which see Mr. PERIZONIUS's Dissertation, already quoted. We are not to be
surprized therefore, that the *Romans,* when they thought proper, took Cognizance
of Charges brought against the Members of allied Cities or Nations, and exercised
the Power of Life and Death on them. It must be owned however, that the Lawyer,
whose Words gave Occasion to the Objection discussed by our Author, lays down a
bad Definition of the Liberty of the People in Question, as being really independent,
(*qui nullus alterius potestati subjectus est*) and, consequently, all our Author's Distinctions are superfluous, in the Application he makes of them; so that it is sufficient
to examine them in themselves.

same King or State do quarrel among themselves. Fourthly, If Subjects complain of Injuries done by their Sovereign.

As to the First, If any Thing has been committed contrary to the Articles of Treaty, the King or State are obliged either to punish the Offender, or to deliver him up to them that are injured; which takes Place not only between unequal Confederates, but also equal; and even between such as are not engaged in any League, as we shall shew in [26] another Place. The Sovereign is also obliged to endeavour to have Satisfaction made, which in *Rome* was called the [27] Delegate's Office. And *Gallus Aelius* in *Festus* says, A Recovery *is when the Law decides between King and People, Nations and Foreign States; how Things may be restored by the Assistance of a Judge Delegate, how they may be recovered, and how private Mens Cases may be prosecuted among themselves.* But one of the Confederates has no Right directly to seize or punish the Subject of another; therefore *Decius Magius,* a *Campanian,* being seized by *Hannibal,* and sent to *Cyrene,* and from thence to *Alexandria,* declared, that he was seized by *Hannibal* contrary to the Articles of the League, and thereupon was set at Liberty. Livy, l. 23.

As to the second, The superior Ally has a Right to compel the inferior to stand to the Articles of the Treaty, and upon refusal to punish him. But neither is this peculiar to unequal Alliances; the same Thing takes Place between equal Allies. For, to have a Right to punish any one that has rendered himself guilty, it is sufficient that one is not subject to him; which [28] shall be treated of elsewhere; wherefore Kings or Nations not allied, have also that Right in regard to one another.

As to the third Case, As in an equal Confederacy, Controversies are generally referred to [29] a Convention of the Associates, who are not in-

---

26. *B.* II. *Chap.* XXI. § 4.

27. *Reciperatores.* See TORRENTIUS's Commentary on SUETONIUS, *in Nerone,* Cap. XVII. and that of THEOD. MARCILLY, on the Life of *Vespasian,* Cap. X.

28. *B.* II. *Chap.* XX. § 3.

29. This Sort of Assembly is called Κοινοδικίον, in an antient Inscription, where we find the Articles of a Treaty between the *Priansii* and the *Hieropotamii,* by which those People reciprocally bestowed the Right of Citizens one on the other. GROTIUS. He should have said *Hierapytnii.* Mr. JOHN PRICE, a learned *Englishman,* first

terested in the Affairs in Question, as we find was formerly practised amongst the *Greeks, Latins,* and *Germans,* or to the Decision of Arbitrators, or even to the Judgment of the chief of the Confederacy, as to a common Arbitrator: So in an unequal Confederacy, it is commonly agreed that the Things in Dispute shall be determined before him, who is the Head of the League. Therefore this does not imply any Jurisdiction; for even Kings have often their Causes tried before Judges appointed by themselves.

As to the fourth and last, Associates have no Right of Judging: When therefore *Herod* accused his own Sons before *Augustus* of certain Crimes, they replied, [30] *You might have punished us by your own Right, both as a Father, and as a King.* And when *Hannibal* was accused at *Rome* by some *Carthaginians,* [31] *Scipio* told the Senate, it did not belong to them to meddle in Affairs belonging to the Republick of *Carthage.* And 'tis in this [32] *Aristotle* says an *Alliance* differs from a *State,* that 'tis the Business of *Allies* to take Care that no Injuries be done by one to the others, but not that the Subjects of a confederate State do not injure one another.

It may again be objected, that Historians make use of the Word *to command,* in speaking of the Prerogatives of a superior Ally; and that *to obey,* in speaking of the Engagements of the inferior Ally. But this should not affect us; for this is, when the Things concern either the common Good of the Allies, or the private Advantage of the Superior in the League. As to Things of common Concern, when the Assembly does not sit, even in an equal League, he that is chosen Prince of the League (נְגִיד בְּרִית, *Dan.* xi. 22.) commonly commands the other Allies, as *Agamemnon* did the *Grecian* Princes; and afterwards the *Lacedemonians* did the *Grecians,* and after them the *Athenians.* We read in [33] *Thucydides's*

---

published this curious Inscription, in his Notes on APULEIUS's *Apology,* p. 59, *&c. Edit. Paris.* 1635. It is also found among the *Oxford Marbles,* p. 116. See SPANHEIM's *Orbis Rom.* Exercit. I. *Cap.* IV. and Exercit. II. *Cap.* XVI.

30. *Antiq. Jud.* Lib. XVI. Cap. VIII.

31. VALERIUS MAXIMUS, *Lib.* IV. *Cap.* I. *Num.* 6. See another Instance in POLYBIUS, *Excerpt. Legat.* CV. GROTIUS.

32. *Politic.* Lib. III. Cap. IX. p. 348. *Edit. Paris.*

33. *Lib.* I. *Cap.* CXX. *Edit. Oxon.*

Oration of <97> the *Corinthians. The Chiefs of an Alliance ought not to challenge any Advantage in what concerns their particular Interest: But it is just, that in the Administration of common Affairs they have the Pre-eminence.* Isocrates says, that the antient *Athenians,* whilst they were the Chiefs of *Greece,* [34] *were contented to take Care of common Affairs, but as for the Rest, they left to every People their Liberty:* And elsewhere, [35] *being persuaded that they ought to have the Command of the War, and not to rule over their Allies.* And again, *Managing their Affairs like Confederates, not despotically.* The *Latins* express by the Word *imperare, to command,* that Right of the principal Ally; but the *Greeks* more modestly use the Term τάσσειν, *to regulate.* The *Athenians* having the Conduct of the War against the *Persians,* as [36] *Thucydides* relates it, *did regulate which Cities should contribute Money against the Barbarians, and which Ships.* So they who were sent from *Rome* into *Greece,* [37] are said to be *sent to regulate the State of the free Cities.* But if he, who is only chief of the Confederacy, governs the common Affairs in the Manner I have now said, we must not wonder, that in an unequal Alliance, the superior Ally does the same Thing. Therefore *Imperium,* in this Sense, that is, Ἡγεμονία, *chief Command,* does not take away the Liberty of others. The *Rhodians,* in their Oration to the *Roman* Senate, extant in *Livy,* thus addressed them, [38] *The* Grecians *formerly were strong enough to command: Where the Command is now, they wish it may be forever; they are contented to defend their Liberty with your Arms, not being able to do it with their own.* Thus *Diodorus* tells us, after the taking the Fort of *Cadmea,* by the *Thebans,* many *Grecian* Cities [39] joined in a League, *to maintain in common their Liberty, under the Conduct of the* Athenians. *Dion Prusaeensis,* speaking of those

34. *In Panegyr.* p. 62. *Edit. H. Steph.*
35. *Ibid.* p. 56, 62.
36. *Lib.* I. *Cap.* 96. *Edit. Oxon.*
37. As the younger PLINY says to one of his Friends, *Remember you are sent into the Province of* Achaia,—*that you are sent to regulate the State of free Cities.* Lib. VIII. Ep. XXIV. Num. 2. *Edit. Cellar.* See SPANHEIM's *Orbis Rom.* p. 311, 381, 394, 395.
38. *Lib.* XXXVII. *Cap.* LIV. *Num.* 24.
39. *Lib.* XV. p. 471. *Edit. H. Steph.*

very *Athenians* in the Time of *Philip* of *Macedon,* said, [40] *Having at that Time abandoned the Command in War, they only retained their own Liberty.* Thus [41] *Caesar* calls those People Confederates, whom a little before he had said were under the Command of the *Suevians.*

But as to those Things which respect the particular Interest of each Ally, if the Demands of the superior Ally are often called *Commands,* that does not imply any Right to require such Things with Authority; but that Way of Speaking is used, because those Demands produce the same Effect, as Commands properly so called, and the same Regard is paid to them. In this Sense the Intreaties of a King are called *Commands,* and the Advices of a Physician *Prescriptions.* [42] Before this *Consul* (C. Posthumius) *no Body,* says *Livy,* B. 42. *was ever chargeable, or any Ways burdensome to our Confederates; our Generals were abundantly supplied with Mules, Tents, and all Baggage necessary for War, that they should not* COMMAND the *Allies to furnish them.*

In the mean Time it is true, that it often happens, that if he who is superior in the League, be much more powerful than the Rest, he by [43] Degrees usurps a Sovereignty, properly so called, over them, especially if the League be perpetual, and that he has a Right to plant Garrisons in their Towns; as the *Athenians* did, when they suffered their Allies to appeal to them, [44] which the *Lacedemonians* <98> never did. Whereupon

40. I do not know in what Piece of the *Gretian* Orator these Words occur.

41. *Sub imperio Suevorum.* These People are here mis-named. CAESAR calls them *Nervii.* De Bello Gall. *Lib.* V. *Cap.* XXXIX. The learned GRONOVIUS observes also, that the Word *Imperium* is not to be taken in an improper Sense, because the Nations here mentioned, were really subject to the *Nervii,* but that of *Allies, (Socii)* which the *Romans* sometimes gave to the People of their own Provinces.

42. *Lib.* XLII. *Cap.* I. *Num.* 9.

43. I find THUCYDIDES making this Observation on the *Athenians,* who seeking one specious Pretext to Day, and another to Morrow, and having gained the *Ionians* with their Allies, induced those People to intrust them with the Command of a War on the *Medes.* Lib. VI. Cap. LXXVI. *Edit. Oxon.*

44. The learned GRONOVIUS suspects that the Author's Memory failed him on this Occasion, and that he attributes to the *Athenians* what PAUSANIAS says of the *Romans, viz.* that after the War with *Perseus,* they obliged several of the *Achaians* to appear at *Rome,* and answer to the Charges exhibited against them, of having favoured that vanquished Prince. Whereupon the Historian observes, that this Way of pro-

Isocrates compares the Rule which the *Athenians* exercised over their Confederates [45] to that of Kings. Thus the [46] *Latins* complained, that under the [47] *Pretence* of a Confederacy with the *Romans,* they were

---

ceeding seemed strange to the *Grecians;* since nothing of that Nature had been attempted by the *Macedonians;* who when at the Height of their Power and Grandeur, referr'd such Cases to the *Amphictyons,* or States General of *Greece.* Achaic or *Lib.* VII. *Cap.* X. *p.* 216. *Ed. Wech.* I am persuaded our Author has really committed a Mistake, and that his Commentator has discovered what gave Occasion to it. It might be observed, that our Author probably imagined he had read what he relates, in ISOC-RATES, whom he afterwards quotes. But the *Greek* Orator is so far from saying any Thing like it, that he maintains, on the contrary, that in regard to the Practice in Question, and several other Things of which the *Athenians* were accused, *he could make it appear, that the* Lacedemonians *had acted much worse, and more oppressively than they.* To which he adds, that *the* Lacedemonians *had put more* Grecians *to Death, without the Formality of a Trial, than had been impeached and tried by the* Athenians *since they inhabited that City.* Orat. Panath. *p.* 245, 246. *Edit. H. Steph.*

45. Our Author probably had his Eye on a Passage in his *Oration on Peace,* where he reproaches his Countrymen, the *Athenians,* with *pretending to be of Opinion, that Tyranny,* or Monarchical Government, *was oppressive, and pernicious, not only to the Subject but even to the Prince himself;* and at the same Time acting as if they looked on the Empire of the Sea as productive of the greatest Advantages, tho' in Reality, it differs not in the least from a Monarchy.

46. The Author in his Margin quotes DIONYSIUS of *Halicarnassus,* Lib. VI. but almost the same Words he uses may be found in LIVY, *Lib.* VIII. *Cap.* IV. *Num.* 2. where the Historian makes a Praetor of the *Latins* say, *For if we can now bear Slavery, under the Shadow of an equal Alliance,* &c.

47. Thus PLUTARCH says of *Aratus,* the *Athenian* General, that *he was accused of imposing Masters on the Cities* (of *Achaia*), *giving them the soft Appellation of Allies.* Vit. Arat. (*Tom.* I. *p.* 1045. *Edit. Wech.*) *Dillius Vocula,* Lieutenant-General of the *Roman* Forces, speaking of some People of the *Belgick Gaul,* says they had till that Time been under an *easy* Slavery, *molle Servitium.* TACIT. *Hist.* Lib. IV. (Cap. LVII. Num. 4.) FESTUS RUFUS, (or as he is called by others, SEXTUS RUFUS) speaking of the *Rhodians,* (and the Inhabitants of other Islands) observes that, *at first they enjoyed Liberty; but in Process of Time accustomed themselves to obey the* Romans, *who engaged them to it by kind Usage.* Cap. X. *Edit. Cellar.* JULIUS CAESAR, having spoken of some People as Friends and Clients of the *Aedui,* tells us, *they had formerly been under the Jurisdiction (of those of* Auvergne, *Bell. Gall.* Lib. VII. Cap. LXXV.) To which may be added, FREDERIC MINDANUS, *De processibus,* Lib. II. Cap. XIV. Num. 3. ZIEGLER, (*ad auream Praxim* CALVOLI) §. *Landassii,* Conclus. I. Num. 86. GAILIUS, *Lib.* II. *Observ.* LIV. *Num.* 6. See also AGATHIAS, *Lib.* I. where the *Goths* are informed what they may expect of the *Francs* in Time. GROTIUS.

In the Passage, here quoted from CAESAR's *Commentaries,* there is no Mention of *Friendship.* Perhaps he at the same Time was thinking of another Place, which is as

brought into Servitude. So did the *Aetolians,* [48] that they had nothing left but the bare Shadow, and empty Name of Liberty; and the [49] *Achaeans* afterwards, *that they had a League in Show; but in Reality a precarious Slavery.* So in [50] *Tacitus Civilis Batavus* complains of the same *Romans, that they used them not as at first, like Confederates, but as mere Slaves:* And in another Place, [51] *they falsely called that Peace, which was indeed a miserable Slavery. Eumenes* also, in *Livy,* [52] said the Confederates of the *Rhodians* were only so in Name, but really their direct Vassals. Also the [53] *Magnesians* complained that *Demetrias* was free in Shew; but in Effect all Things were managed as the *Romans* pleased; and *Polybius* [54] remarks, that the *Thessalians* were in [55] Appearance free, but in Truth under the Dominion of the *Macedonians.*

When Things go in that Manner, and Usurpation is changed at last into Right, by the tacit Concession of those who suffer it, of which we shall treat in another Place; [56] then those who had been Allies become Subjects, or at least there is made a Partition of the Sovereignty, which, as I said before, may happen some-<99>times.

---

much to his Purpose, and where that Word is inserted, *De Bell. Gall.* Lib. VI. Cap. XII. The Passage of AGATHIAS, here referred to, is in *Lib.* I. *Cap.* XI. But the Writer doth not say *the* Goths *were informed,* &c. He speaks of *Aligernes,* a *Gothick* Prince, who being desirous of siding with the *Romans,* is determined to take that Step from the Consideration of the servile State to which he saw his Countrymen were on the Point of being reduced by the *Francs,* under the Shadow of an Alliance and Protection.

48. *He* (Alexander *Prince of the* Etolians) *accused the* Romans *of Fraud, who under the pompous but empty Name of Liberty, kept Garrisons in* Chalcis *and* Demetrias. LIVY, *Lib.* XXXIV. *Cap.* XXIII. *Num.* 8. *They were now loaded with more splendid and heavier Chains,* &c. *Lib.* XXXV. *Cap.* 38. *Num.* 10.

49. *Idem.* Lib. XXXIX. Cap. XXXVII. Num. 13.

50. *Histor.* Lib. IV. Cap. XIV. Num. 5.

51. *Ibid.* Cap. XVII. Num. 3.

52. *Lib.* XXXVII. *Cap.* 53. *Num.* 4.

53. LIVY, *Lib.* XXXV. *Cap.* XXXI. *Num.* 12.

54. *Hist.* Lib. IV. Cap. LXXVI.

55. Such were the *Lazi,* a People of *Colchis,* in the Reign of the Emperor *Justinian.* PROCOP. *Persic.* Lib. II. (Cap. XV.) GROTIUS.

See SPANHEIM's *Orbis Romanus.* Exercit. II. Cap. XVII. p 447, 448.

56. See *B.* II. *Chap.* IV. § 14.

XXII. There are also Powers, [1] who pay something to another, either to secure themselves from their Insults, or to get Protection, ξύμμαχοι φόρου ὑποτελεῖς, [2] *Tributary Confederates*, as it is in *Thucydides;* such were the [3] Kings of the *Jews*, and of the [4] neighbouring Nations, after

XXII. (1) The Emperor *Justinian* paid the *Persians* a certain Sum yearly. See Procop. *Persic.* Lib. II. (Cap. X.) and *Gothick.* Lib. IV. (or *Hist. Miscellan.* Cap. XV.) This was in soft Terms called *A Tribute for securing the* Caspian *Gates.* The *Turks* give the *Arabians* of the Mountains Money, to secure them from their Incursions.

See to the same Purpose Casaubon's Note on Spartian, *in Hadriano,* Cap. VI. and what Mr. Hertius says, partly after him, though he doth not mention his Name, in his *Elementa Prudentiae Civilis,* Part I. Sect. XII. § 11. and Part II. Sect. XX. § 9.

2. *Lib.* I. *Cap.* XIX. *Edit. Oxon.*

3. *De Bello Civil.* Lib. V. p. 1135. *Edit. Amsterd.* 715. H. Steph. Josephus tells us that *Marcus Antonius,* speaking of *Herod,* declares *it was not reasonable that Prince should be called to Account for what he had done, as King; for then he would not be a King: and that it was just that those, who invested him with that Dignity and Power, should allow him to enjoy them.* Antiq. Jud. *Lib.* XV. *Cap.* IV. p. 516. *The* Jews, says St. Chrysostom, *on their Declension, and Subjection to the* Romans, *were neither entirely free, as before, nor absolutely Slaves, as now. They were ranked among the Allies of that People; paid Tribute to their own Kings, and received Governors of their Nomination. They likewise followed their own Laws, and punished their Delinquents according to the Custom of their own Country.* De Eleemosyna II. Grotius.

The Example of the Kings of the *Jews,* and those of the neighbouring Nations, is not well applied. For at that Time the Authority of all those Princes was merely precarious. See my 22d and 25th Notes on § 21. The very Passages, alledged by our Author in this Place, are directly against him. What is here related of *Marcus Antonius* was said on Occasion of some Complaints laid before him against *Herod,* on the Account of the Death of *Aristobulus,* his Brother-in-Law; and it is evident from those very Words, that all that Prince's Power was dependent on the *Romans;* tho' in the Case then under Consideration, *Anthony,* being gained by Presents, would not take Cognizance of the Charge urged against *Herod,* tho' but too well grounded; and that is the Reason why he laid so much Stress on the Quality of King, in Regard to *Herod*'s Subjects. St. Chrysostom expressly says, the *Jews* were subject to the Command of the *Romans,* Ὑπὸ τὴν τῶν Ῥωμαίων ἐτεθησαν ἀρχὴν, and that they had no more than the specious Title of Allies, in the Sense already explained. After all, Josephus expressly observes, that after *Jerusalem* was taken by *Pompey,* the *Jews* lost their Liberty, and became Subjects (ὑπήκοοι) to the *Romans.* Antiq. Jud. *Lib.* XIV. *Cap.* VIII. See Spanheim's *Orbis Rom.* Exercit. II. Cap. XI.

4. The Kings of those neighbouring Nations were not more independent than those of the *Jews.* See Note 22 on the foregoing Paragraph. But the learned Gronovius quotes an Author who has produced more exact Instances of Princes, who, without ceasing to be Sovereigns, paid Tribute to foreign Nations, to prevent In-

the Time of *M. Anthony,* ἐπί φόροις τεταγμένοις, as *Appian* speaks; yet I see no Reason to doubt, but that such Sort of Allies may have Sovereignty, tho' the acknowledging their Weakness takes off something from their Dignity.

XXIII. *Of those that hold their Dominions by a* Feudal *Tenure.* XXIII. Many think it more difficult to determine, whether feudatory Princes may be Sovereign? But that Question may be easily decided by what has been said before. For in this Contract, ¹ (which is peculiar to the *German* Nation, and no where found but where they have planted themselves) two Things are to be particularly considered, First, The personal Obligation of the Vassal. Secondly, The Right of the Lord to the Thing itself.

The personal Obligation is the same, whether a Man holds the Sovereignty by a feudal Right, or any Thing else, tho' lying ² in another Place. But such an Obligation, as it takes not from a private Man personal Liberty, so neither does it lessen the Sovereignty in a King or State, which is Civil Liberty. Which may be plainly seen in *Franc Fiefs,* which consist in personal Obligation only, but ³ give <100> no Right to the

---

cursions into their Countries. See AMM. MARCELL. *Lib.* XXV. *Cap.* VI. *p.* 468. *Edit. Vales. Gron.* with FRID. LINDENBROGIUS's Note on the Place.

XXIII. (1) See my 4th Note on PUFENDORF, *B.* IV. *Ch.* 8. § 12.

2. As when the Kings of *England* paid Homage to those of *France,* for the Provinces they possessed in that Kingdom. See BODIN, *De Repub.* Lib. I. Cap. IX. p. 171, 172. *Edit. Francof.* 1622.

3. *Nullo jure in rem. Without any Right to the Thing itself.* What our Author says here, agrees neither with the Idea which the Feudists give of *Franc Fiefs,* nor with the Nature of Fiefs in general. By the Term *Franc Fief* is meant, that which is exempt from all Charges and Services, which require considerable Labour or Expence; so that the Obligation of the Vassal is reduced to *Fidelity* and *Loyalty,* which consist only in honouring the Lord, under whom he holds, securing him from Damage, and doing him all the Good in the Vassal's Power, as it is specified in the Form of the Oath of Fidelity. FEUDOR, *Lib.* II. *Tit.* VI. *De formâ Fidelitatis,* and *Tit.* VII. *De novâ formâ Fidelitatis.* But this Exemption from Charges and Services doth not deprive the Lord of a *Franc Fief* of a Right to the Thing itself, which the Vassal holds in *Fief,* or hinder it from returning to him, when the Vassal is guilty of Felony, or leaves no Heirs. The Exclusion of such a Right destroys the very Nature of a *Fief,* properly so called. Tho' the Vassal of a *Franc Fief* had a Power to alienate the Thing without the Consent of the Lord, which the Doctors do not allow, still the Right of the latter would be per-

Thing itself. For these are nothing else but a Species of that unequal League, of which we have treated already, wherein one promises Services, and the other Defence and Protection. But suppose a Vassal has prom-

---

petual over those, in whose Favour the Fief should be alienated. I am very much mistaken, if our Author has not here, and elsewhere, (as *B.* III. *Chap.* XX. § 44.) confounded what are called *Franc Fiefs,* with certain Engagements improperly termed *Fiefs,* on the Account of some Resemblance between them in the Respect and Homage paid. An ingenious Gentleman, who has published curious Extracts from RYMER's *Foedera,* observes, as a certain Fact, *that Homage was frequently paid for simple yearly Pensions, without expressing the Cause of such Homage. We have Examples of this Kind,* says he, *in the first Volume of this Collection,* p. 1. *and in some other Places, in Regard to the Counts of* Flanders, *who paid Homage to the Kings of* England, *for a Pension of 400 Marks. Bibliotheque Choisie,* Tom. XX. p. 99, 100. By the Agreement made *May* the 17th, 1101, between *Henry* I. King of *England,* and *Robert* Count of *Flanders,* the King obliges himself to give him 400 Marks of Silver yearly *in Fief,* on Condition that *Robert* should be obliged to send 500 Horse into *England,* for the King's Service, when he should have Occasion for them. *Biblioth. Choisie,* Tom. XVI. p. 10, *&c.* I find BODIN had long ago made a like Observation. *Our Ancestors,* said he, *abused the Word* Liege *in all their ancient Treaties of Alliance and Oaths. I remember I have seen 48 Treaties of Alliance and Forms of Oaths, collated with the original Records, by which the three Electors on this Side of the* Rhine, *and several other Princes of the Empire, entered into Obligations with the Kings* Philip de Valois, John, Charles the Fifth, Sixth, and Seventh, *and* Lewis the Eleventh, *promising and swearing, in the Presence of the King's Deputies, to serve him in his Wars against all Powers, except the Emperor and King of the* Romans, *acknowledging themselves Vassals and Liege-Men of the King of* France: *Some of them stiling themselves Counsellors, others Pensioners, and all Liege Vassals, except the Archbishop of* Treves, *Elector of the Empire, who only calls himself Confederate. And yet they held nothing from the Crown; for only the Pensioners of* France *took an Oath to serve the King, in the Things, and on the Conditions specified in the Instrument. The Oath of the Duke of* Guelders *and the Count of* Juliers *runs thus,* Ego Devenio Vasallus ligîus CAROLI, Regis Francorum, pro ratione quinquaginta millium scutorum auri, ante festum D. Remigii mihi solvendorum. *That is,* I become the Liege Vassal of CHARLES, King of the Francks, on the Consideration of fifty thousand Crowns of Gold, to be paid me before the Feast of St. Remigius. *This Instrument is dated in the Month of* June, 1401. *This same Way of speaking was used even between Sovereign Princes; as in the Treaty of Alliance made between* Philip de Valois, *King of* France, *and* Alphonso, *King of* Castille, *in the Year 1336, on which Occasion Proxies appeared from both Parties, to require and give Assurance of mutual Homage and Fidelity. But this is an Abuse of the Words* Vassal *and* Liege; *for which Reason they are no longer admitted into the Oaths taken by the King's Pensioners, nor into Treaties.* De la Repub. B. I. *Chap.* IX. *p.* 175, 176. the *French* Edition, printed in 1608. I have set down this Passage at length, as it is of singular Use for explaining our Author's Meaning, and discovering the Origin of his Mistake, which none of his Commentators have ob-

See *Bald.*
Prooem.
Digest. *Natta,*
Consil. 485

ised his Lord to serve him against all and every Man, which they now
call [4] *Feudum Ligium,* (for formerly that Word was of a larger Signification) that takes off nothing [5] from the Right of Sovereignty which the
Vassal has over his own Subjects; not to mention, that there is always a
tacit Condition supposed, *viz.* that the War undertaken by the Lord [6]
be just: Of which we shall treat in another Place.

As to the Right of the Lord to the Thing itself, enjoyed by a feudal
Title, it is such indeed, that if the Family of the Vassal be extinct, or if
he falls into certain Crimes, he may lose the very Right of Sovereignty:
Yet the Power he has over his Subjects does not cease to be Sovereign;
for as I have often said, there is a Difference between the Thing, and the
Manner of holding it. And I find many Kings constituted by the *Romans*
with this Condition, that upon the failing of the Royal Family the Sovereignty should return to themselves; as *Strabo* observes of *Paphlagonia,*
and some other Kingdoms. [7] <101>

Lib. 12.

---

served. Since I penned this Note, I have found something in another Work of our
Author to confirm my Conjecture. It is in *Chap.* V. of his Treatise, *De antiquitate
Reip. Batav.* where he maintains, that even tho' the old Counts of *Holland* were Vas-
sals of the Empire of *Germany,* the *Hollanders* would still be a free and independent
People. To prove this Proposition he observes, that according to the Lawyer *Proculus,*
Clients are not the less free, because not equal in Dignity to their *Patrons;* nor a People,
because obliged by a Clause in a Treaty of Alliance to reverence the Majesty of their
Ally, provided they are not subject to his Dominion. *Hence,* says he, *comes the Name
of* Franc Fief. *But our Counts never owned themselves subject to this Sort of Obligation
of Fief.*

4. *Ligius Homo,* or *Lidges,* a Term supposed to be derived from the *German Ledig,*
empty, originally signified no more than a Vassal. See Vossius, *De Vitiis Sermonis,*
Lib. III. Cap. XX. under the Word *Liga;* and the late Mr. Hertius's Treatise *De
Feudis oblatis,* Part II; § 6. in Vol. II. of his *Comment. & Opusc. &c.* But in Process
of Time it has stood for a *Liege-Man,* or *Liege-Vassal,* one who entered into an Engagement to respect his Lord more than all other Men, and serve him against every
other; so that such a Vassal cannot be Vassal to two Masters in the same Manner, and
ought to acknowledge no other Sovereign.

5. In Reality, such an Engagement no more prejudices the Sovereignty of the Vassal Prince, than when a Prince, by a Treaty of Alliance, promises another, to whom
he is not feudatary, to assist him in all his Wars.

6. See *B.* II. *Ch.* XV. § 13. and *Ch.* XXV. § 4.

7. But those Kingdoms were more than Feudatary. See *Notes* 22 and 25, on § 21.
Strabo calls the Kings meant by our Author, *Subjects* (Ὑπήκοοι) to the *Romans,*

XXIV. We must also distinguish in *Sovereignty,* as well as *Property,* between the Right itself, and the Exercise of that Right, or between the
first Act and the second. [1] For as a King, when an Infant, has a Right to
govern, but cannot exercise that Right; so has a Prince that is Lunatick,
or a Prisoner, or that lives in a foreign Country, so that he is not at Liberty
to exercise himself the Acts of Sovereignty: For in all such Cases they
have their Lieutenants or Vice-Roys to act for them. Therefore *Deme-trius,* living confined under *Seleucus,* forbad any Credit to be given to
his Letters, or Seal, but ordered that all Things should be administred
as if he were dead.

Lib. VI. p. 440. *Edit. Amst.* I shall set down the whole Passage, because it is corrupted
in one Place, where I do not find any one has observed the Fault. The Geographer
plainly distinguishes between the Kings of *Asia,* whose Families were extinct, and
those who, revolting from the *Romans,* and being conquered by that People, had given
them Occasion to reduce their Dominions into the Form of *Roman* Provinces. Among
the former he reckons the Kings of *Pergamus,* those of *Syria, Paphlagonia, Cappadocia,*
and, as it is in the original Text and the *Latin* Version, those of *Egypt.* The Examples
of the latter are *Mithridates,* surnamed *Eupator,* and *Cleopatra,* Queen of *Egypt.* Τὰ
δ' ὅμοια καὶ περὶ τὴν Ἀσίαν συνέβη. Καταρχὰς μὲν ὑπὸ τῶν Βασιλέων διωκεῖτο
ὑπηκόων ὄντων. ὕστερον δ' ἐκλιπόντων ἐκείνων, καθάπερ τῶν Ἀτταλικῶν Βασιλέων,
καὶ Σύρων, καὶ Παφλαγόνων, καὶ Καππαδόκων, και Ἀιγυπτίων, καὶ (I add this
Particle, which is absolutely necessary) ἀφισταμένων, καὶ ἔπειτα καταλυομένων,
καθάπερ ἐπὶ Μιθριδάτου συνέβη τοῦ Ἐυπάτορος, καὶ τῆς Ἀιγυπτίας Κλεοπάτρας,
ἅπαντα τὰ ἐντὸς Φασίδος καὶ Ἐυφράτου, πλὴν Ἀράβων τινῶν, ὑπὸ Ῥωμάιοις ἐστὶ,
&c. I am of Opinion, that instead of Ἀιγυπτίων STRABO wrote Βιθυνῶν. It is well
known, at least, that the *Romans* inherited *Bithynia* by the Will of *Nicomedes,* the
last King of that Country; as they in the same Manner acquired the Kingdom of
Pergamus, whose Kings are here termed Ἀτταλικοὶ Βασιλεῖς. See § 12. of this Chapter, where these two Facts are quoted on the Credit of good Authors.
    XXIV. (1) See *B.* III. *Chap.* XX. § 3. of this Work.

CHAPTER IV

Of a War made by Subjects against their Superiors.

1. The Question stated.

2 Sam. x.

Gen. xiv.

I. Private Men may certainly make War against private Men, as a Traveller against a Robber, and Sovereign Princes against Sovereign Princes, as *David* against the King of the *Ammonites;* and so may private Men against Princes, but not their own, as *Abraham* did against the King of *Babylon,* and other neighbouring Princes; so may Sovereign Princes against private Men, whether their own Subjects, as *David* [1] against the Party of *Ishbosheth,* or Strangers, as the *Romans* against Pirates. <102>

I. (1) This Example is criticised by Commentators, who will not allow it to be just. *Ishbosheth,* say they, had been acknowledged King by the eleven Tribes, over which he reigned two Years, 2 SAM. ii. 10. *David* himself was so far from considering him as a rebellious Subject, that he gives him the Character of *a just Man.* Ibid. iv. 11. and punishes his Murtherers. The Promise, which GOD had made of transferring the Crown to *David,* and his Descendents, specifies no fixt Time; nor was it to be fulfilled 'till after the Death of *Saul* and *Ishbosheth.* Hence it is concluded, that those who sided with *Ishbosheth* were his Subjects, and not *David*'s. But it appears from the sacred History, that tho' *David* had been privately appointed by *Samuel,* and that but Few were at first acquainted with the Will of GOD, who designed he should succeed *Saul;* it afterwards became publickly known, and reached the Court of the Prince on the Throne. *Jonathan* says to *David,* in the Wilderness of *Ziph, Thou shalt be King over* Israel, *and I shall be next unto thee; and that also my Father* Saul *knoweth.* 1 SAM. xxiii. 17. *Saul* himself makes the same Declaration, when he acknowledges the Generosity of the Man, whom he had persecuted with so much Rage and Cruelty, *I know well that thou shalt surely be King, and that the Kingdom of* Israel *shall be established in thy Hand: Swear now therefore unto me by the LORD, that thou wilt not cut off my Seed after me, and that thou will not destroy my Name out of my Father's House.* Ibid. xxiv. 20, 21. From which Words it is evident, that he looked on *David* as the Man who was to be his immediate Successor, according to a Promise from Heaven.

The only Question is, whether private or publick Persons may lawfully make War against those that are set over them, whether as supreme, or subordinate. First, it is agreed on all Sides, that they that are commissioned by the higher Powers may make War against their Inferiors, as *Nehemiah* did by the Authority of *Artaxerxes,* against the neighbouring petty Princes. Thus the [2] *Roman* Emperors allowed the Proprietor of an Heritage to drive away Harbingers or Quarter-masters. But the main Question is, What is lawful for Subjects to do against their Sovereign, or those that act by his Authority. This is allowed by all good Men, that if [3] the civil Powers command any Thing contrary to the Law of Nature, or the Commands of God, they are not to be obeyed. For

Nehem. Ch. ii. & iv.

When the eleven Tribes made their Submission to *David,* they owned they knew the Lord had said to him, *Thou shalt feed my People* Israel, *and thou shalt be a Captain over* Israel. 2 SAM. v. 2. So that, by Vertue of that Divine Election, all who were acquainted with it, were obliged to receive *David* as their lawful King, on *Saul*'s Demise. For the Case was not the same among the *Hebrews,* as among other People, who being directed by no extraordinary Revelation, bestowed on their Kings all the Power they had over them. The *Israelites* were but lately come out of the *Theocracy;* and though GOD, in Compliance with their imprudent and obstinate Demand, had granted them a Change of that happy Form of Government into a Human Monarchy, he did not thereby divest himself of the Right of making the immediate Choice of their Kings, when he pleased. It was thus that *Saul* the first King of *Israel* ascended the Throne. *David,* therefore, having been anointed by *Samuel,* in *Saul*'s Life-time, had an incontestible Title to the Succession; and consequently, the eleven Tribes, who owned *Ishbosheth,* might be considered as so many rebellious Subjects against the lawful Sovereign; and the more so, because they need only have consulted their usual Oracle, the URIM and THUMMIM, in Order to know the Will of GOD. If *David* punished the Murtherers of *Ishbosheth,* as having killed a *just,* or innocent, *Man;* it was not because he did not look on him as an Usurper of his Right; but he calls him *innocent* in Regard to *Rechab* and *Baanah,* who had dispatched him by their own private Authority, without any Injury received from him. And he himself would spare the Lives of *Saul*'s Children, on the Account of the Oath he had taken to their Father; in Consideration of which he pardoned *Ishbosheth,* and would never have hurt him. See Mr. LE CLERC, on 2 Sam. iv. 11.

2. *Licentiam enim Domino* (Praedii) *actori, ipsique plebi Serenitas nostra commisit, ut eum, qui praeparandi gratiâ ad possessionem venerit, expellendi habeat facultatem, nec crimen aliquod pertimescat: quum sibi arbitrium ultionis suae sciat esse concessum; rècteque sacrilegum prior arceat, qui primus invenit.* COD. Lib. XII. Tit. XLI. *De Metatis & Epidemeticis.* Leg. V.

3. See *Book* II. *Chap.* XXVI. § 3.

Acts iv. 19.
— v. 29.
the Apostles, when they alledged, that we must obey God rather than Man, did but appeal to a Principle of Reason, engraved on the Minds of Men, which [4] *Plato* expresses almost in the very same Words. But if for this, or any other Cause, any Injury be done us by the Will of our Sovereign, we ought rather to bear it patiently, than to resist by Force.

II. *War against Superiors, as such is unlawful by the Law of Nature.*

II. Indeed all Men have naturally a Right to secure themselves from Injuries by Resistance, as we said before. But civil Society being instituted for the Preservation of Peace, there immediately arises a superior Right in the State over us and ours, so far as is necessary for that End. Therefore the State has a Power to prohibit the unlimited Use of that Right towards every other Person, for maintaining publick Peace and good Order, which doubtless it does, since otherwise it cannot obtain the End proposed; [1] for if that promiscuous Right of Resistance should be allowed,

4. In *Socrates*'s Apology, where he makes that Philosopher express himself in the following Manner: *I honour and love you;* [speaking to the *Athenians*] *but will obey GOD, rather than you.* Tom. I. p. 29. *Edit. H. Steph.*

II. (1) We are here to consider, first *single Persons,* and then the *Body of the People.* In Regard to *single Persons,* it is certain that the End of civil Society in general requires that each of them should not have a Right to resist the supreme Power, as often as he thinks himself aggrieved by it. For, besides that a Superior may be wrongfully accused on that Article, whoever submits to human Authority, must be sensible that the Person, in whose Favour he divests himself of part of his Liberty, is and always will be Man, that is, subject to Mistakes, and Failures in the Discharge of his Duty; and is therefore to be supposed to acknowledge him for his Master on that Foot. Consequently, he at the same Time grants him a Right, not to treat him in any Manner unjustly (no Man can ever give or have a real *Right* to commit the least *Injustice*) but to require that he shall not be divested of his Authority, for every Abuse of it. A Man, who never abuses his Power, ought to be considered as a Man not to be found; and no Authority would be lasting, or sufficient for producing the Effect, for which it is designed, if it could be so easily lost. But it doth not thence follow, that a particular Person either doth or ought necessarily to engage to suffer every Thing from his Superiors, without ever opposing Force with Force. Were it so, those who enter into any Society, where they are to obey; would without Dispute be in a worse Condition, than before; and nothing could oblige them to divest themselves of that natural Liberty, of which every Man is so jealous. Even such as submit to a Conqueror, would have done better, had they continued in a State of War with him. We must distinguish therefore between *doubtful,* or *supportable Injustices,* and *manifest* or *insupportable Injustices.* The former are to be born; but, strictly speaking, there is no Obligation to bear the latter; and if we sometimes ought to bear them, it is by no Means

<103> there would be *no longer a State*, but a Multitude without Union, such as the [2] *Cyclops* were, *every one gives Law to his Wife and Children.* A Mob where *all are Speakers, and no Hearers.* Or the [3] *Aborigines*, whom *Sallust* mentions as a wild and savage People, without Laws, without

out of Regard to the Person, who commits them, but for the Good of Society. So that, if there is no Room to apprehend that Resistance will occasion greater Evils and Disorders, than those to which the Society already is exposed, or those to which it is in Danger of being exposed, we may safely employ our whole Right against the Man, who, by an Excess of Madness, has disengaged us from the Tie of Subjection, and entered into a State of War with us. Now, that there are some manifest and enormous Injustices, in regard to which a private Person cannot deceive himself, and conceive an unwarrantable Prejudice against his Prince will be easily granted, if we enquire well into the Nature of Things, and the Conduct of Sovereigns, become Tyrants. Who can doubt, for Example, whether a Prince, who attempts to kill one of his Subjects, or deprive him of his Goods, without any Crime committed by the Sufferer, and without the Formality of a Trial, for no other Reason but his own good Pleasure, or for some Reason evidently unjust, as for his refusing to believe what he knows to be false, particularly in Matters of Religion; who, I say, can doubt that this is one of those enormous and insupportable Abuses of the supreme Authority, the Toleration of which, is so far from being necessary for the Sake of preserving Order, and for the public Peace, that it is directly contrary to and destructive of both? Have we not even commonly very great Reason to believe, that a Prince who proceeds those Lengths in Regard to one or more particular Persons, will not stop there, and that the rest may expect the like Treatment? If the public Interest requires those, who obey, should suffer some Thing, it no less requires that those, who command, should be afraid of putting their Patience to the utmost Trial. A Man, who imagines himself allowed to do what he pleases to his Inferiors, is capable of doing every Thing. It is true, indeed, that commonly speaking, one, or some few particular Persons, would resist to no Purpose, and only draw greater Evils on their own Heads. But this is a prudential Consideration, which makes no Diminution in their Right, to oppose a Superior, who by enormous and insupportable Acts of Injustice, and the Violation of his Engagements to them, has discharged them of their Obligations to him. What I have already laid down, takes Place, and that much more, in Relation to a whole People, or the greater Part of it. The greater the Number of the Oppressed is, the more the Oppressor deserves to be brought to Reason. The Tyrant in that Case has less Reason to complain, as hardly any Thing but a horrible Excess of Ambition and Madness could have obliged the Body of the Nation to rise against him. See what I have said on PUFEND. *Book* VII. *Cap.* VIII. § 6. *Note* I.

2. *Odyss.* Lib. IX. *v.* 114, 115. EURIP. In *Cyclop. v.* 120.

3. *Bell. Catalin.* Cap. VI.

Hence it is, that the Majesty (that is, the Dignity and Authority) of the Sovereign, whether it be King or State, is fenced with so many Laws, and so many Penalties; which Authority could not be maintained, if it were lawful to resist. [13] If a Soldier resist his Officer that corrects him, if he lays hold on the Cane, he is degraded; but if he wilfully break it, or strike again, he is punished with Death. And in *Aristotle*, [14] *If a Magistrate strikes, he shall not be struck again.*

III. *Nor allowed by the Hebrew Law.*

Jos i. 18.
Deut. xvii. 12.
1 Sam. viii. 11.
Deut. xvii. 14.

III. By the *Hebrew* Law, he that was disobedient, either [1] to the High-Priest, or to the extraordinary Governor appointed by God, was to be put to Death. But that which in *Samuel* is spoken of the Right of Kings, [2] to him that thoroughly considers it, appears not to be understood of a true Right, that is, of a Power to do honestly and justly, (for a far different

---

pro C. Rabirio Postum. *Cap.* XI. Our Author, in a Note on this Place, refers us to a Passage of Josephus, which he had before quoted, in *Note* 3. on § 22. of the foregoing Chapter.

13. Digest. *Lib.* XLIX. Tit. XVI. *De Re Militari.* Leg. XIII. § 4. See Ruffus's *Leges Militares.* Cap. XV. published with Vegetius. by *Plantin,* in 1607.

14. *Ethic. Nicom.* Lib. V. Cap. VIII. p. 64. *Edit. Paris.* This Passage is not intirely to the Purpose. The Philosopher is treating of the Penalty of *Retaliation;* to shew that it would be sometimes contrary to Justice, he instances in the Case of a subaltern Magistrate, who should, without just Cause, strike one of his Inferiors; and maintains that it would not be suitable to the Character of such a Person, that he should be sentenced to receive Correction in the same Manner. It can be inferred only by Way of Consequence, from this Example, and that of Military Discipline, before alledged, that, commonly speaking, Inferiors ought not to resist the supreme Power, or subaltern Officers, acting in his Name, and by his Authority.

III. (1) The Law speaks of such as should *insolently* despise (for so it is in the Text) the Decision of the Judges established by GOD, for explaining and applying the Laws of *Moses,* in doubtful Cases. So that this is wide of the Question in Hand, where we must always suppose a manifest Injustice. See Mr. Le Clerc on Deut. XVII. 12.

2. Our Author, with several Interpreters, supposes that, when *Samuel* told the *Israelites* how Kings would treat them, he spoke of *Right,* and not only of *Fact.* Pufend. in *B.* VII. *Chap.* VI. § 9. gives us a Paraphrase on the Words of the Prophet, in which he explains them to us so as to make them mean no more than what a King, whether absolute or not, may lawfully require. But in Order to perform this to his Mind, he is obliged to soften the Force of the original Expressions, contrary to the Rules of Criticism. We need only consider the following Words: *He* (the King) *will take your Fields, and your Vineyards, and your Oliveyards, the best of them and give them*

Way of living is prescribed to a King, in that Part of the Law which treats of a King's Duty) nor of barely what he will do; for that would not have been extraordinary in him, when even private Men do likewise Injuries [3] to private Men; but it is to be understood of an Action, <105> whether just or not, as has in it some Effect of Right, that is, it implies the Obligation [4] of Non-resistance. Therefore it is added, when People are thus

---

to his Servants. v. 14. These are manifest Acts of Tyranny; and the Story of *Naboth* sufficiently shews, that the most abandoned Princes dared not maintain that Subjects were obliged to suffer the Seizure of their Goods or Estates, even though they are paid for them beyond their just Value. Whence it appears, that it was not thought that *Samuel* in any Manner design'd to fix the Right of a King, or the Obligation of the Subject, but only to let the People know to what Calamities they would be exposed by the Abuse of the royal Power and Strength. The Prophet's View, which was to divert the *Israelites* from persisting in their Demands, requires no more; and the original Word, usually rendered *Right, jus,* frequently signifies in Scripture the *Manner of Proceeding,* or *Custom.* The Example, which I have given, after the Commentators, on PUFENDORF, as before quoted, is sufficient for putting this beyond Dispute. Besides, the divine Goodness and Sanctity do not, I think, allow us to imagine he designed to give the least Insinuation, which might give Kings Occasion to believe themselves warranted to do what they pleased, and neglect the Duties so clearly prescribed in the Law. This would be a sort of Contradiction, unworthy of an infinitely perfect Being.

3. True; but then there is a wide Difference between the Injuries, which private Persons may do one to another in a State, where the Laws are observed, and that which a wicked Prince may do to his Subjects. For, as it has been observed, and as every one plainly sees, the Strength lodged in the Hands of Princes puts them in a Condition of oppressing their Subjects a thousand Ways, which are out of the Power of private Persons. Shall a Citizen, for Example, seize on his Neighbour's Field or Vineyard, with Impunity? Shall he take away his Children, or Servants by Force?

4. Or rather a physical Inability to resist. The *Israelites,* as Mr. LE CLERC observes on the Passage under Consideration, never were of Opinion that no one, even the Body of the People, could not lawfully resist the King. This is evident from the Manner, in which the ten Tribes shook off the Yoke of *Rehoboam,* and the Example of several Tyrants, who were killed in the same Kingdom of *Israel.* Our Author, in a Note on this Place, quotes what PHILO makes the *Jews* of *Alexandria* say, when they place their own Conduct in Opposition to that of the Natives of the Country. *When were we suspected of Faction? When did not all the World look on us as a peaceable People? Is not our daily Behaviour irreproachable, and such as tends to promote Concord, and the Good of Society?* In Flaccum, *pag.* 978. *Edit. Paris.* But it doth not thence follow that the *Jews,* even after the Captivity, were of Opinion, that Resistance is never allowable. The Example of the *Macchabees,* and the whole History of that Nation, manifestly shew the contrary. See MILTON, *Defens.* Cap. IV. pag. 115, *&c.* When they were vi-

oppressed, they should cry unto GOD for Help, [5] as if no Remedy were to be expected from Man. It is then a Right, in the same Sense as it is said that [6] *the Pretor renders Justice, even when he pronounces an unjust Sentence.*

IV. *Nor by the Law of the Gospel, as proved by Scripture.*

IV. Where *Christ* in the New Testament commands to give to *Caesar* the Things that are *Caesar's,* he certainly intended, that his Disciples should yield as great, if not a greater Obedience (both active and passive) to the higher Powers, than what the *Jews* were bound to pay to their Kings. Which St. *Paul* (who could best interpret the Words of his Lord)

Rom. xiii.

largely describing the Duties of Subjects, says among other Things, *He that resists the Power, resists the Ordinance of God, and they that resist, shall receive unto themselves Damnation.* And a little further, *for he is the Minister of God to thee for Good.* And again, *Wherefore ye must needs be subject, not only for Wrath, but also for Conscience Sake.* He includes in Subjection

---

olently harassed by the *Roman* Governours, they submitted because they were not in a Capacity of resisting; though, to shew their Innocence, and appease their Persecutors, they sometimes valued themselves on their forced Patience, as when *Petronius* went with an Order from *Caligula* to place that impious Prince's Statue in the Temple. See JOSEPHUS, *Antiq. Jud.* Lib. XVIII. Cap. XI. and PHILO, *De Legat. ad Caium,* pag. 1025, 1026. But I do not find in either of these Historians the Words quoted by the *English* Author, already mentioned, as an Acknowledgement made by the *Jews* themselves of their own Weakness. Πολεμεῖν μὲν οὐ βουλόμενοι, διὰ τὸ μήδ᾽ ἀνδύνασθαι: *that they would not fight, because they were not able,* pag. 133. I only observe that JOSEPHUS says, that when *Petronius* was on his March for *Judea* at the Head of three Legions, and a Body of auxiliary Troops from *Syria,* the *Jews* either could not imagine they were to be employed against them, or were sensible of their own Inability to defend themselves. *De Bell. Jud.* Lib. II. Cap. XVII.

5. But the *Israelites* frequently implored the Divine Assistance, in the Time of the *Judges,* when oppressed by any neighbouring King or People; and will any one say they were then forbidden to resist the Oppressor, when it was in their Power? The Prophet certainly means no more than that GOD, to punish them for demanding a monarchical Form of Government, at any Rate, and in some Manner against his Will, would not change it, by his Providence, when they came to feel the grievous Inconveniencies attending it. And the Prediction was justified by the Event. See Mr. LE CLERC on the Place.

6. DIGEST. *De Justitiâ & Jure.* Lib. I. Tit. I. Leg. XI.

the Necessity [1] of Non-resistance, not only such as arises from the Apprehension of a worse Evil, but such a one as flows from the Sense of our Duty, whereby we stand obliged not only to Man, but to GOD also: He adds two Reasons for it; *First,* because GOD has approved of this *Ordinance* of *commanding* and *obeying,* both formerly in the *Jewish* Law, and now in the *Evangelical,* wherefore the publick Powers are to be esteemed by us, as ordained by GOD himself; for we make those Acts our own, which we support and countenance by our Authority. *Secondly,* because this *Ordinance* tends to our *Advantage.* But some may say, to bear Injuries is not advantageous; to which others, more truly, than pertinently to the Apostle's Meaning, as I suppose, say, these Injuries are also advantageous to us, because such a Patience shall not lose its Reward. The Apostle seems to me to have regarded the general End proposed in this *Ordinance,* which is the [2] publick Peace, wherein is comprehended that also of every particular Person. And certainly this Advantage we <106> commonly receive from the sovereign Powers: For no Body ever wished ill to himself, and the Happiness of the Prince depends on the Happiness of his Subjects, *sint quibus imperes, leave some to reign over,* [3] said one to *Sylla.* The *Hebrews* have a Proverb, [4] *If there were no sovereign Power, we should swallow up one another alive.* To which agrees that of [5] St. *Chrysostom, Take away the Governors of States, Men would be more savage than Brutes, not only biting but devouring one another.*

IV. (1) True; but the Apostle doth not here direct us how we are to behave ourselves toward the Powers, in all Cases, and however they act. So far from that, that he supposes a Magistrate who acts like a true *Minister of* GOD, and employs his Authority for the Good of those whom he governs.

2. St. Chrysostom says very well that the Prince *labours in Concert with* a Preacher of the Gospel. Grotius.

3. *Fursidius* to *Sylla.* Florus. *Lib.* III. *Cap.* XXI. *num.* 25. See Plutarch in *Sylla.* p. 472. and St. Aug. *De Civit. Dei.* Lib. III. Cap. XXVIII. Grotius.

4. It occurs in the Pirke Aboth, or sentences of the *Jewish* Doctors; and is attributed to the Rabbi *Hananias. Pray,* says he, *for the Peace of the Kingdom; for, if there was no Fear* (of the Magistrate) *Men would eat one another alive.* Cap. III. p. 42. *Edit. P. Fagii.* 1541.

5. *De Statuis.* Hom. VI. That Father repeats the same Thought in two or three other Places. *If you take away the Courts of Judicature, you at the same Time take away all Order of Life,* ibid. *Tell me not of Persons, who have abused their Authority; but*

If the supreme Magistrate sometimes, through Fear, Anger, or some other Passion deviates from the straight Path, that leads to publick Tranquillity; it ought to be considered as a rare Case, and an Evil which, as *Tacitus* [6] observes, is made up by good Offices. It is enough for the Laws to regard that which generally happens, as [7] *Theophrastus* said, and to which we may apply that of [8] *Cato, No Law can be convenient for every particular Person, it is enough, if it be beneficial in general, and to the greater Part.* But as to such Cases, which rarely happen, they ought to be submitted to the general Rules. For though the Reason of the Law does not take Place in such or such a particular Case, yet it subsists in its Generality, to which particular Cases ought to make no Exception; because that is much better, than to live without Law; or to allow every Man to be a Law to himself. *Seneca* speaks pertinently to this Purpose. [9] *It is better not to admit of an Excuse, though just, from a few, than that all should be allowed to make what Excuse they please.*

Here we shall cite that remarkable [10] Saying of *Pericles* in *Thucydides.* [11] *I esteem it better, even for private Men, that the State in general flourish,*

---

consider the Beauty of the Establishment itself, and you will see the great Wisdom of the first Author of it, ibid. *If you take away them* (the Magistrates) *all is ruined. We shall then have no Cities, no Lands, no Market-Place, or any Thing fix'd and certain. All Things will be turned Topsy-turvy, and the Stronger will devour the Weaker.* In Epist. ad Romanos. We have another Passage to the same Purpose on the Epistle to the *Ephesians.* GROTIUS.

6. HIST. *Lib.* IV. *Cap.* LXXIV.

7. DIGEST. Lib. I. Tit. III. *De Legibus, &c.* Leg. VI. See also *Lib.* V. *Tit.* IV. *Si pars hereditatis petatur.* Leg. III.

8. *Satis commoda omnibus* &c. *sufficiently accommodated to all,* &c. LIVY, *Lib.* XXXIV. *Cap.* III. *num.* 5.

9. The Philosopher says this in Regard to Laws concerning insolvent Debtors; on which Occasion he asks: *Do you suppose our Forefathers not prudent and judicious enough to understand it would be the highest Piece of Injustice to treat a Man, who has thrown away what he borrowed in Gaming and Debauchery, in the same Manner, as one who has lost both another Man's Substance and his own by Fire, Robbery, or any other sad accident? They admitted of no Exception,* says he, *that Men might know they were obliged to keep their Word. For it were better,* &c. De Benefic. *Lib.* VIII. *Cap.* XVI.

10. *Lib.* II. *Cap.* LX. *Edit. Oxon.*

11. Thus likewise St. AMBROSE lays it down for a Maxim, *that the Interest of each particular Person is the same with that of the Public.* De Offic. *Lib.* III. (Cap. IV.) The

though they themselves do not thrive in it, than that they should flourish in their Affairs, and the Publick suffer. For let a Man's private Affairs be never so prosperous, yet if his Country be lost, he must perish with it. On the contrary, if the State flourish, a Man in bad Circumstances may mend his Condition. Since then the State can relieve private Persons in their Misfortunes, but private Persons cannot do the same Thing in regard to the State; ought not every one to concur in defending it, instead of acting like you, who, being overwhelmed with your domestick Losses, abandon the Care of the publick Safety? Which *Livy* speaks in short, [12] *If the Commonwealth flourish, it secures every Man's private Estate, but by betraying the Publick, you will never preserve your own.* And *Plato* observed, [13] τὸ μὲν γὰρ κοινὸν ξυνδεῖ, &c. *That which is the Bond of States, is the Care of the publick Good, and that which destroys them is the minding only one's private Advantage; therefore it concerns both the State and private Men, to prefer the Interest of the publick to that of particular Persons.* And *Xenophon,* [14] ὅστις ἐν πολέμῳ, &c. *He that* <107> *mutinies against his General in War, offends against his own Safety.* And *Jamblichus,* [15] *private Interest is inseparable from the Publick, each particular Advantage is included in the Publick; for as in the natural Body, so in the political, the Preservation of the Parts depends on that of the Whole.*

Now, in publick Matters there is nothing more considerable than the Order of Government I have spoken of, which is incompatible with the Right of Resistance left to private Persons. I shall explain this out of an

---

Lawyers hold the same in the contract of Partnership: *For that is always to be done which is to the Advantage of the whole Company, not what is for the private Interest of one of the Partners.* DIGEST. *Lib.* XVII. *Tit.* II. *Pro Socio.* Leg. LXV. § 5. See also COD. *Lib.* VI. *Tit.* LI. *De Caducis tollendis.* Leg. unic. § 14. GROTIUS.

12. *Lib.* XXVI. *Cap.* XXXVI. *num.* 9.

13. *De Legib.* Lib. IX. p. 875. Tom. II. *Edit. H. Steph.*

14. *De Exped. Cyri.* Lib. VI. Cap. I. § 19. *Edit. Oxon.*

15. Our Author has quoted this Passage in *Latin* only. I have not been able to find it either in JAMBLICHUS's Life of *Pythagoras,* nor in his *Protrepticon.* Perhaps he has used the Name of that Philosopher for that of some other. However, we have a Thought very like it in HIEROCLES. *Wherefore we are not to separate the public from the private Good, but consider them as one and the same. For what is advantageous to our Country, is common to all, and shared by each in particular; for the whole, considered as separate from the Parts, is nothing.* In STOB. Serm. XXXIX.

excellent Place in *Dion Cassius*, οὐ μέν τοι καὶ ἐγὼ, &c. [16] *I think it neither decent for a Prince to submit to his Subjects, nor can one ever be in Safety, if those who ought to obey pretend to command. Do but consider what a strange Disorder it would cause in a Family, if Children should be allowed to despise their Parents, and what in Schools, if Scholars should slight their Masters; what Health for Patients that will not be ruled by their Physicians? Or what Security for those in a Ship, if the Sailors will not follow the Orders of the Pilot? For Nature has made it necessary, and useful to Mankind, that some should command, and some should obey.*

1 Ep ii. 17, 18, 19, 20. To the Testimony of St. *Paul*, we shall add that of St. *Peter*, whose Words are these, *Honour the King; Servants be subject to your Masters, with all Fear, not only to the Good and Gentle, but also to the Froward; for this is thank-worthy if a Man for Conscience toward GOD endure Grief, suffering wrongfully. For what Glory is it, if when ye be buffeted for your Faults, ye shall take it patiently? But if when ye do well, and suffer for it, ye take it patiently, this is* [17] *acceptable with GOD.* He immediately confirms this by the Example of *CHRIST.* And *Clement* in his Constitutions, expresses the same Sense in these Words, ὁ δοῦλος, &c. *Let the Servant love his Master with the Fear of God, though he be wicked and unjust.* Here we may observe two Things. First, that what is said of Submission to Masters, however froward they are, ought [18] to be applied to Kings. For that which follows, being built upon the same Foundation, respects the Duty

16. This is Part of *Julius Caesar*'s Speech to his mutinous Soldiers at *Plaisance*. Lib. XLI. pag. 189. *Ed. H. Steph.*

17. TERTULLIAN says that *in fearing Men we honour* GOD. *De Poenit.* GROTIUS. *Chap.* VII. But the Discourse there turns on a different Subject.

18. This Consequence can be drawn only by Accommodation; and even then it will not follow that the Subject is obliged to suffer every Thing, since even a Slave has a Right to the Protection of the Laws, when he meets with insupportable Treatment from his Master. See Mr. NOODT's Discourse on *the Power of Sovereigns*, p. 254. second Edition of the *French* Translation. Besides, the Precepts here laid down by the Apostle, were partly grounded on particular Circumstances, as we shall shew in the 24th Note on the 7th Paragraph. In short, one may say of those general Precepts, which recommend Submission to the sovereign Power, what our Author himself says of those which relate to the Submission of Slaves to their Masters, *Book* II. *Chap.* V. § 29. See likewise SCHELIUS's Interpretation of these Passages of St. *Peter*, and St. *Paul*, in his Treatise *De Jure Imperii*, p. 316, &c.

of Subjects as well as of Servants; and secondly, that the Submission, to which we are bound, implies an Obligation to bear Injuries with Patience; as it is usually said of Parents, [19] *Love your Parent if he is just; if not, bear with him.* [20] A young Man of *Eretria,* who had been long a Disciple to *Zeno,* being asked, what he had learnt, answered, ὀργὴν πατρὸς φέρειν, *To bear my Father's Anger.* And *Justin* says of *Lysimachus, He suffered the Cruelty of his King as patiently, as if he had been his Father.* And in *Livy, As the harsh Temper of our Parents, so also that of our Country, is to be softened by patient Suffering.* So in *Tacitus,* [21] *The Humours of Kings must be born.* And in another Place, *Good Emperors are to be desired, but whatsoever they <108> are, they must be obeyed. Claudian* [22] commends the *Persians, who obeyed their Kings, though cruel.*

V. Neither did the Practice of the [1] primitive Christians, the best Interpreter of the Law, deviate from this Law of God. For though the *Roman* Emperors were sometimes the very worst of Men, and there wanted not those, who under the Pretence of serving the State opposed them, yet the Christians could never be persuaded to join with them. In the Constitutions of *Clement* we have βασιλεία οὐ θεμιτὸν ἐπανισταθαι, *It is not lawful to resist the King's Authority.* And *Tertullian* says in his Apology,

V. And by the Practice of the primitive Christians.

---

19. PUBL. SYRUS, *v.* 23.

20. AELIAN, *Var. Hist.* Lib. IX. Cap. XXXIII. JUSTIN. *Lib.* XV. *Cap.* III. *num.* 10. LIV. Lib. XXVII. Cap. XXXIV. *num.* 13. TERENCE makes a young Man say, *it is his Duty to bear with the ill Usage of his Mother.* Hecyr. Act. III. Scen. I. *v.* 21. CICERO lays it down as a Precept, that *Men ought not only to be silent in Regard to the Injuries received from their Parents, but also to suffer them with Patience.* Orat. pro Cluentio. St. CHRYSOSTOM has some beautiful Thoughts on this Maxim on the Epistle to *Timothy,* and in his fifth Book against the *Jews.* To the same Purpose is what EPICTETUS, and his Commentator SIMPLICIUS have said, of every Thing having two Handles. Cap. LXV.

21. *Annal.* Lib. XII. Cap. XI. *num.* 3. and *Hist.* Lib. IV. Cap. VIII. *num.* 3.

22. In EUTROP. *Lib.* II. *v.* 479, 480.

V. (1) This appears from Canon XVIII. of the Council of CHALCEDON, repeated in Canon IV. of the Council *in Trullo,* and by the IV. Council of *Toledo;* the II. *Capitulary* of CHARLES *the Bald, in Villâ Colonia;* and by the V. Canon of the Council of *Soissons.* GROTIUS. See *Note* 24. on § 7. and the *Preliminary Discourse* § 52.

² *Whence are your* Cassius's, *your* Niger's, *and your* Albinus's? *Whence those who besiege* Caesar *between the two Laurels? Whence those who* wrestle *with him only for an Opportunity of* throttling *him? Whence those who* force *the Palace* Sword in Hand, *Fellows bolder than so many* ³ Sigerius's (so the Manuscript in the Hands of those accomplished worthy Gentlemen Mess. *du Puys* expressly has it) *and* Parthenius's? *If I am not mistaken from among the* Romans, *that is, from among those who are not* Christians. What he says of the *Wrestling* relates to *Commodus's* Murder committed by a Wrestler, by the Order of *Aelius Laetus,* Captain of the Emperor's Lifeguard; but there never was a wickeder Wretch living than that Emperor. *Parthenius,* whose Fact also *Tertullian* mentions here with Horror, was he who killed that worst of Emperors *Domitian.* To these he compares *Plautian* the ⁴ Captain of the Guard, who would have slain the bloody Emperor *Septimius Severus* in his own Palace. *Piscennius Niger* ⁵ *in Syria,* and *Clodius Albinus* in *Gaul* and *Britain,* took up Arms against this *Septimius Severus,* as if out of Zeal and Affection to the Commonwealth. But their Enterprize was also disappointed by the *Christians,* as *Tertullian* glories in his Treatise to *Scapula:* ⁶ We are reproached with Treason; but never could *Christians* be found to act the *Albinians,* or *Nigrians,* or *Cassians.* Those *Cassians* were they who followed *Avidius Cassius,* a Man of great Note, who took up Arms in *Syria,* under a Pre-

---

2. *Apolog.* Cap. XXXV.

3. *The Conspirators against him* (Domitian) *were* Parthenius, *and* Sigerius (for it must be read Σιγήριος not Σιγηρός) *both Gentlemen of his Bed-Chamber.* XIPHILIN, p. 237. *Edit. Steph.* MARTIAL, addressing himself to one, who attempted to pass for a Courtier tells him, *He talks only of* Sigerius's *and* Parthenius's. *Lib.* IV. *Epigr.* LXXIX. The Name of *Sigerius* is corrupted not only in TERTULLIAN, where we find *Stephanis* in its Room; but also in SUETONIUS, *Vita Domitiani,* Cap. XVII. where we find *Saturius;* and AURELIUS VICTOR who calls that Traitor *Casperius,* Cap. XII. *Num.* 8. GROTIUS.

4. See HERODIAN, *Lib.* III. *Cap.* XI. *Edit. Boecler.*

5. But, as the learned GRONOVIUS observes on this Place, *Pescennius Niger,* and *Clodius Albinus* had been declared Emperors by the Soldiers under their Command, at the same Time that *Septimius Severus* was named by his Troops. So that it might as well be said he took Arms against the two first; who were considered under the Character of Rebels, only because they had the Misfortune to be defeated.

6. *Ad Scapulam,* Cap. II.

tence of restoring the Commonwealth, which the Negligence of *M. An-tonin* [7] was like to ruin.

Though [8] St. *Ambrose* was persuaded that *Valentinian* the second did him an Injury, and not only to himself, but to his Flock, and even to CHRIST, yet he would not take the Advantage of the People's Inclination to resist; but said, [9] <109> *Whatever Violence is offered me, I cannot*

---

7. He pretended that that Prince by a natural Excess of Clemency, and too great an Application to Philosophy, neglected the Discovery and Punishment of Offenders, and particularly the Governors of Provinces, who inriched themselves with the Spoils of the People. See *Avidius Cassius's* Letter to his Son-in-Law, in his Life, written by VULCATIUS GALLICANUS, *Cap.* XIV.

8. In the first Edition of this Work, the Author had inserted a Passage of St. CYPRIAN, before what he here says of St. AMBROSE. It is probable he retrenched it, because it is quoted, § 7. *Note* 25, where it appears with more Exactness.

9. The first of these Passages is inserted in the CANON LAW, *Caus.* XXIII. *Quaest.* VIII. *An Episcopis vel quibuslibet Clericis suâ liceat,* &c. Can. XXI. (the second appears in the same Place). *Will you hurry me to Prison? Will you lead me to Execution? I take a Pleasure in submitting. I will not defend myself by raising the People.* Epist. XXXIII. GREGORY *the Great* says something of the same Nature (which is also quoted in the Canon Law, as above, *Can.* XX.) *If I would have had a Hand in the Death of the* Lombards, *that Nation had now been without King, Dukes or Counts, and dispersed in the utmost Confusion and Disorder.* Lib. VII. Epist. I. GROTIUS.

The Authority of St. AMBROSE is so far from being to our Author's Purpose, that it may even serve to prove the contrary of what is here inferred from it, and shew how little we ought to depend on the Opinion of those old Doctors, vulgarly called the *Fathers of the Church.* The Conduct of the Person under Consideration sufficiently made it appear, that he thought Resistance allowable. Even two Passages, here quoted from him, were written on the Occasion of a signal Act of Resistance done by that great Saint. In giving the Fact, I shall borrow the very Words of Mr. BAYLE'S Narration, formed on the Circumstances, admitted by Mr. FLECHIER, and Fa. MAIMBOURG. The former, in his Life of THEODOSIUS: the latter in his *History of Arianism.* "On the Death of *Gratian,* the whole western Empire falling to *Valentinian,* his Brother, he made an Edict, at the Instance of *Justina* (his Mother) allowing the *Arians* the public Exercise of their Religion, and declaring all who should oppose the Execution of the said Order, Authors of Sedition, Disturbers of the Church's Peace, Traitors, and worthy of Death. But as all the Churches were in the Power of St. *Ambrose,* the *Arians* attempted to take one in Defiance of his Authority. The Emperor going to take Possession of the Cathedral, found St. *Ambrose* with all his People as it were barricaded in it, who were resolved to defend both the Church and Pastor, to the last Drop of their Blood." *Hist. de* THEOD. *Liv.* III. *num.* 25, &c. "He invested the Church, and summoned St. *Ambrose,* by Virtue of the late Edict, to surrender it. The Bishop answered that he would never willingly quit it. A Remonstrance was made

VI. Inferior Magistrates to make War against the Sovereign unlawful, proved by Reason and Scripture.

VI. There are some [1] Learned Men in this Age, who, suiting themselves to Times, and Places, first (as I think) persuade themselves, and then others, that what we have already said (in Relation to Non-resistance) takes Place only in Regard to private Men, but not in Regard to inferior Magistrates, who they think have Right to resist the Injuries of their Sovereign; nay, and that they fail in their Duty when they do not; which Opinion is not to be admitted. For as in Logick there is a middle Species, which with Respect to the Genus above it is still a Species, but in Respect

Genus speciale as Seneca calls it, Epist. LVIII.

of the Species below it, a Genus: So those Magistrates, in Respect to their Inferiors, are publick Persons, but in Respect to their Superiors, are but private Persons. [2] All the civil Power, that such Magistrates have, is so

Averroes, V. Metaphys. com. 6.

subject to the Sovereign, that whatever they do against his Will is done without Authority, and consequently ought to be considered only as a private Act. In a Word, according to the Maxim of Philosophers, which may be here applied, all Order necessarily relates to something that is First; and they, who think otherwise, seem to me to introduce such a State of Things as the Ancients fabled to have been in Heaven before there was a sovereign Majesty, when the lesser Gods did not submit to *Jupiter.* That Order [3] which I have spoken of, and ὑπαλληλισμὸς, *Subordination,* is not only apprehended by common Sense, as appears by the excellent [4] Sayings which we find on that Subject in Authors both

VI. (1) The Author, in a Note on this Place refers his Readers to PETER MARTYR, on *Judges* iii. PARAEUS, on *Rom.* xiii. JUNII BRUTI *Vindiciae, contra Tyrannos;* and DANAEUS, *Lib.* VI. *Politic.* &c.

2. This is true; but it may be likewise said that, supposing it lawful even for private Subjects in certain Cases to resist their Prince, as we have already shewn it is; it will follow that the Magistrates, as Persons of a public Character, who therefore must be better acquainted with State Affairs, and are capable of making an effectual Resistance, are on that Account more particularly authorized to labour for the public Good. For, in short, it is necessary that some-body should begin, and shew others the Way.

3. Thus in a Family, the Father is the first; the Mother and Children hold the next Places; after them are the ordinary Servants, and then the extraordinary Servants. See St. CHRYSOSTOM, on 1 *Cor.* xiii. 3. GROTIUS.

4. *Every Kingdom depends on a more powerful Kingdom.* SENECA, *Thyestes. v.* 612. *All Things govern and are governed in their Turns.* STATIUS, *Lib.* III. *Sylv.* III. *v.* 49, 50. St. AUGUSTIN has a remarkable Passage to this Purpose. *Consider,* says that Father, *the Degrees of Subordination in human Affairs. If an Intendant of the Police commands*

Pagan and *Christian;* but it is also supported by divine Authority; for   1 Peter ii. 13.
St. *Peter* bids us be subject to the King, otherwise than to Magistrates;
to the King as supreme, that is [5] without Exception, but only to those
Things which GOD directly commands, who approves, and not forbids,
our bearing of an Injury. But to Magistrates as deputed by the King, that   Rom. xiii. 1.
is deriving their Authority from him. And when St. *Paul* would have
every Soul be subject to the higher Powers, he also included inferior
Magistrates. Neither do we find among the *Hebrews,* where there were
so many Kings regardless of all Right both divine and human, that any
inferior Magistrates, among whom there were many pious and valiant
Persons, ever assumed the Liberty to resist their Kings by Force, unless
they had a special Commission from GOD, <111> who has a sovereign
Power over Kings themselves; on the contrary, what the Duty of great   1 Sam. xv. 30.
Men is to their King, *Samuel* instructs us, who before the Elders and
the People gave to *Saul,* though now governing wickedly, the usual
Reverence.

And so likewise the State of the publick Divine Worship always depended upon the Will of the King, and the [6] *Sanhedrim:* For whereas,
after the King, the Magistrates, together with the People, promised they
would be faithful to GOD; that ought to be understood, [7] so far as it

---

*a Thing, is it not to be done? But not, when the Proconsul orders the contrary; the same
is to be said when a Consul requires one Thing, and the Emperor another. In which Case,
you do not despise the Power, but only chuse to obey a superior Power. Nor ought the
Inferior to resent this Conduct, which gives the Preference to the Superior.* This is quoted
in the CANON LAW, *Caus.* XI. *Quaest.* III. *Can.* 97. We find almost the same in his
VI Sermon, *De Verbis Domini.* That Father elsewhere says, speaking of *Pilate,* that
GOD *gave him such an Authority, as subjected him to that of the Emperor. In Joan.*
Tom. IX. p. 369. *Edit. Basil Erasm.* GROTIUS.

5. Our Author, as the learned GRONOVIUS observes, gives these Words a different
Explanation in his Notes on the *New Testament: as Sovereign,* that is, as one, who
owns no Superior.

6. I have already observed that the Antiquity and Perpetuity of the *Sanhedrim,*
supposed by our Author, are at least uncertain.

7. That is, the Attachment, which every *Israelite* ought to have for his Religion,
obliged neither private Persons, nor inferior Magistrates, to become Iconoclasts by
their own Authority, or in any other violent Manner oppose the idolatrous Worship
introduced or tolerated by the King; because that would be an Incroachment on his
Right. But the present Question does not turn on such Cases.

should be in the Power of every one of them. Nay, the very Images of their false Gods, which were publickly set up, were never thrown down, as we read, but at the Command of the People, when the Government was Republican, or of the King, when it was monarchical. And if Force was sometimes made use of against the Kings, it is related barely as a Fact that Providence had permitted, and without any Mark of Approbation.

Those of the contrary Opinion often urge that Saying of the Emperor *Trajan,* who delivering a Sword to a Captain of the *Praetorian* Band, said, [8] *Use this for me, if I govern well; and against me, if ill.* We must know, that *Trajan* (as appears by *Pliny*'s Panegyrick) took particular Care to shew no Marks of Royalty, and [9] to act merely as Head of the State, consequently subject to the Judgment of the *Senate* and *People,* whose Decrees the Captain of the Guard was to execute, even against the Prince himself: The like we read of *M. Antoninus,* [10] who would not touch the public Treasure without consulting the Senate.

VII. *What is to be done in case of extreme and inevitable Necessity.* VII. A more difficult Question is, whether the Law of Non-resistance obliges us in the most extreme and inevitable Danger. For some of the Laws of GOD, however general they be, seem to admit of *tacit* Exceptions in Cases of extreme Necessity; for so it was determined by the *Jewish* Doctors concerning the Law of their Sabbath in the Time [1] of the

---

8. This Speech is preserved by XIPHILIN, in his Abridgment of DION CASSIUS, *Vit. Traj.* p. 248. *Ed. H. Steph.* See also ZONARAS, in the Life of the same Emperor. *Annal.* Tom. II. PLINY's *Paneg.* Cap. LXVII. *Num.* 8. *Edit. Cellar.* and CASSIODORUS, *Var.* VIII. 13.

9. *Pertinax* and *Macrinus* imitated *Trajan* in that Particular, as appears from the fine Speeches put into their Mouth by HERODIAN. GROTIUS.

But why is it not supposed that a good Emperor or modest Sovereign Prince may entertain a just Idea of the Extent of his Power? In Reality, we see but few of that Character; but such may be found; and unless their Conduct belies their Words, our Regard for their Dignity should oblige us to avoid harbouring Suspicions to their Disadvantage.

10. XIPHILIN, in that Emperor's Life, p. 281.

VII. (1) See I MACCAB. ii. 41. Since that Time the common Opinion of the *Jews* was, that *the Law allowed them to defend themselves, but not to attack the Enemy,* on the Sabbath Day. JOSEPHUS, *Antiq.* Lib. XIV. Cap. VIII. Our Author alludes to this in MARK iii. 4. as Mr. LE CLERC has very well observed.

Maccabees; whence arose the famous Saying, [2] *The Danger of Life drives away the Sabbath.* And the *Jew* in *Synesius* gives this Reason for the Breach of the Law of the Sabbath, σαφῶς ὑπὲρ ψυχῆς θέομεν, we *were in manifest Danger of our Lives,* which Exception is approved of by CHRIST himself; as also in that Law of not eating the *Shew Bread.* And the *Hebrew* Rabbins, following an old Tradition, rightly add the same Exception to their Laws concerning forbidden Meats, and some others of the like Kind. Not that GOD has not a full Right to oblige us to do or not do some Things, even though we should be thereby exposed to certain Death; but that some of his Laws are of such a Nature as cannot be easily believed to have been given in so rigid a Manner, which ought still more to be presumed as to human Laws.

I do not deny, but that some Acts of Virtue may by a human Law be commanded, though under the evident Hazard of Death. As for a Soldier not to quit [3] his Post; but it is not easily to be imagined, that such was the Intention of the <112> Legislator; and it is very probable that Men have not received so extensive a Power over themselves or others, except in Cases where extreme Necessity requires it. For all human Laws are, and ought to be so enacted, as that there should be some Allowance for human Frailty. But this Law (of which we now treat) seems to depend

---

2. This Sentence occurs in the *Babylonish Talmud.* See our Author on MATT. xii. 11. and BUXTORF, *Synag. Jud.* Cap. XVI.

3. See JOSEPHUS, where he speaks of *Saul's* Guards. We learn from POLYBIUS, that among the Romans, *he who quitted his Post was punished with Death.* GROTIUS.

The Passage of JOSEPHUS, here meant by our Author, is where *David* having found *Saul's* Guard asleep, calls out to *Abner,* who commanded it, that *this was a Crime worthy of Death, because it gave him and his Men a fair Opportunity of entering the Camp, and advancing even to the King's Tent, without being observed.* Antiq. *Lib.* VI. *Cap.* XIV. So that it is evident, the Case was not the same with that under Consideration. The Passage of POLYBIUS is here quoted, as our Author found it in SUIDAS, under the Word Πρόστμα; for the Terms are very different in the Original, *Lib.* I. *Cap.* XVII. See likewise JUSTUS LIPSIUS, *De Militia Rom.* Lib. V. p. 293, 383. And the Treatise *De Poenis militarib. Rom.* Cap. IV. written by Mr. SICHTERMAN, who in that small Piece has let the World know what might be expected from him, if his Fortune had not forced him out of the Road of Letters into that of Arms.

Margin notes: 1 Maccab. ix. 10, 43, 44. — Mat. xii. 4.

upon the Intention of those who first entered into civil Society, from whom the Power of Sovereigns is originally derived. Suppose then they had been asked, Whether they pretended to impose on all Citizens the hard Necessity of dying, rather than to take up Arms in any Case, to defend themselves against the higher Powers; I do not know, whether they would have answered in the affirmative: It may be presumed, on the contrary, they would have declared that one ought not to bear with every Thing, unless the Resistance would infallibly occasion great Disturbance in the State, or prove the Destruction of many Innocents. For what Charity recommends in such a Case to be done, may, I doubt not, be prescribed by a human Law.

Some may say, that this rigorous Obligation to suffer Death, rather than at any Time to resist an Injury offered by the Civil Powers, is not imposed by any human but the Divine Law. But we must observe, that Men did not at first unite themselves in Civil Society by any special Command from GOD, but of their own free Will, out of a Sense of the Inability of separate Families to repel Violence; whence the Civil Power is derived, which therefore St. *Peter* calls a human Ordinance, tho' elsewhere it is called a Divine Ordinance, because GOD approved of this wholesome Institution of Men. But GOD, in approving a human Law, is thought to approve of it as human, and after a human Manner. *Barclay,* the stoutest Assertor of Regal Power, does thus far allow that the People, or a considerable Part of them, have a Right to defend themselves against their King, when he becomes excessively cruel; tho' otherwise, that Author considers the King as above the whole Body of the People. I can easily apprehend that, the more considerable a Thing is which runs the Risk of perishing, the more Equity requires that the Words of the Law be restrained, to authorise the Care of preserving such a Thing. But I dare not condemn indifferently all private Persons, or a small Part of the People, who finding themselves reduced to the last Extremity, have made use of the only Remedy left them, in such a Manner as they have not neglected in the mean Time to take care, as far as they were able, of the publick Good. For *David,* who (bating some particular Facts) was so famed for living exactly according to Law, did yet entertain about him, first four hundred, and afterwards more, armed Men; and to what End

1 Pet. ii. 13.

Rom. xiii. 1.

Adversus Monarchomachos, I. 3. c. 8. & I. 6. c. 23. & 24.

1 Sam. xxii. 2.
— xxiii. 13.

did he so, unless for [4] the Defence of his own Person, in Case he should be attacked? But we must also observe, that *David* did not do this till he was assured by *Jonathan,* and many other infallible Proofs, that *Saul* really sought his Life: And moreover, he neither seized on any City, nor sought Occasions of Fighting, but lurked about, sometimes in by-Places, sometimes among foreign Nations; with this Resolution, to avoid all Occasions of injuring his own Countrymen.

The Example of the *Maccabees* might likewise be alledged here. For 'tis in vain that some pretend to justify their Enterprize, upon the Account that *Antiochus* was only an Usurper. In all History, we do not find that the *Maccabees,* and those of their Party, give *Antiochus* any other Title than that of King: And indeed they could not call him otherwise, since the *Jews* had for a long Time acknowledged the Kings of *Macedonia* for their Sovereigns, to whose Right *Antiochus* had succeeded. It is true   Deut. xvii. 15. the Law forbad a Stranger to be set over them; but that ought to be understood of a voluntary Election, and not of what the People might be forced to do through the Necessity of the Times. As to what others say, that <113> the *Maccabees* acted by Vertue of the Right which their Nation had to demand Liberty, or the Power of governing themselves, this Reason has no more Weight in it than the other. For the *Jews* having been formerly conquered by *Nebuchadnezzar,* were fallen by the same Right of War, under the Dominion of the [5] *Medes* and *Persians,* Successors of the *Chaldeans;* and the whole Empire of the *Medes* and *Persians*

4. Some Commentators on this Place say, that *David,* having been anointed King by *Samuel,* was not from that Time to be considered as a private Subject. But it has been judiciously answered by others, that *David* was not to be King during *Saul*'s Life, and that he himself, from the Time of his being anointed to the Death of *Saul,* constantly acknowledged him the lawful King of *Israel.*

5. The learned GRONOVIUS blames our Author for blindly following TACITUS, who pretends, that the *Jews* were under the Dominion of the *Medes;* which is false, unless the Assertion is understood only of *Darius* the *Mede,* or *Nabonnides,* mentioned by the Prophet *Daniel.* The *Jews* being conquered by *Nebuchadnezzar,* became subject to the *Persians* as soon as *Cyrus* took *Babylon.* I find, however, that both the Emperor *Julian,* and the Patriarch *Cyril,* tho' his Antagonist, were of Opinion, that the *Jews* had been dependent on the *Medes;* and in this they copied the Error of the common Chronology, which made the Empire of the *Medes* succeed that of the *Assyrians,* p. 210. *Edit. Spanheim.*

Ex. xxii. 28. that is, the Supreme Judges. *Thou shalt not curse the* [8] *Rulers of thy People.* In which Law special Mention being made of the supreme Powers, it plainly shews, that some special Duty is required. Wherefore *Optatus* Lib. 2. *Milevitanus,* speaking of this Fact of *David,* says, *GOD's special Command, coming fresh into his Memory, restrained him.* And makes *David* say, *I was willing to overcome mine Enemy, but I chose rather to keep the Commands of GOD.*

[9] To slander any private Person is not lawful, therefore of a King we must not speak Evil, [10] tho' it be true. Because, as the Writer of the Prob-

---

8. JOSEPHUS introduces *Joab* speaking thus to *Shimei, Shalt not thou die, who hath spoken ill of him whom GOD hath appointed to reign?* Antiq. *Lib.* VII. *Cap.* X. GROTIUS.

These are not the Words of *Joab* but of *Abishaï,* the Son of *Zeruiah,* and Brother to *Joab.* I do not know why the Author chose rather to quote JOSEPHUS on this Occasion, than the sacred Historian, 2 SAMUEL xix. 21. *Shall not Shimeï be put to Death for this, because he hath cursed the LORD's anointed?*

9. The same *Jewish* Historian observes, that when *David* had cut off a Piece of *Saul's* Garment when he surprized him in the Cave, *he immediately repented, and said it was not lawful* for a Subject *to kill his Master.* Antiq. *Lib.* VI. Cap. XIV. And a little after, that when he entered *Saul's* Tent, and found his Guards asleep, *Abishaï* would have killed him; but *David* diverted him from that Action, saying, *It was a heinous Crime to kill a King, even tho' he was wicked; and that the Person who should commit it, would be punished by him, who invested him with the Royal Dignity.* GROTIUS.

The two Passages taken from the *Jewish* Historian, are neither exactly quoted, nor justly translated. In the former our Author has forgot these Words, which immediately follow, *Master, or him whom GOD has intrusted with the Kingdom.* This determines the Maxim to something in particular, which some would make general. See Note 7. In the other, the Words κεχειροτονήμενον ὑπὸ τοῦ Θεοῦ, are not translated, which signify *ordained,* or *established by GOD.* The last Words of the same Passage ἥξειν γὰρ αὐτῷ παρὰ τοῦ δοῦλος τὴν ἀρχὴν συγκρόνῳ τὴν δίκην, ought to have been rendered thus, *For the King will in Time be punished by him who conferred the Royal Character on him.* This makes a very different, not to say a contrary Sense; and I am tempted to believe that the Author was betrayed into this Blunder, by his great Desire to find wherewithal to support his Opinion.

10. It is certain that we ought not lightly to defame Princes every Time they are guilty of Faults, or an Abuse of their Power. As I have already observed, the same Reason that obliges us to bear with their unjust Actions, to a certain Point, likewise engages us to spare their Reputation, to avoid giving Occasion of making their Authority contemptible. Those Preachers therefore, who are for bringing their Magistrates to the Scaffold, whenever they imagine them faulty, are certainly so far from being authorised to do so by the Duties of their Ministry, that they are undoubtedly

lems (fathered upon *Aristotle*) says, ὁ κακηγορῶν, &c. [11] *He that speaks Evil of the Magistrate, offends against the whole Body of the People.* But if we must not speak Evil of <115> him, much less must we use Violence against him. *David* was struck with Remorse, [12] for having cut off a Piece of *Saul*'s Garment: So much did he regard the Person of a King as sacred! And indeed, the Sovereign Power being necessarily [13] exposed to the Hatred of many, he that is invested with it, ought in a particular Manner

1 Sam. xxiv. 6.

---

very much to be condemned. But it does not thence follow, that even tho' a Prince becomes a Tyrant, it is a Crime to speak of what is notorious, and call Things by their right Names. Nor can it be proved that this is prohibited by the Law in Question. So that the Argument, or rather the Consequence which our Author undertakes to draw from it, cannot reasonably extend so far, how general soever the Terms may appear, which here, and in an Infinity of other Places, ought to be restrained, as much as the Nature of the Subject requires or allows.

11. The Philosopher, enquiring into the Reasons of the Difference of Punishments established by Law, says, *Private Persons are not punished for speaking ill one of another; but that Penalties are inflicted on those who take the same Liberty with a Magistrate.* This he calls a wise Institution, *because,* as he observes, *such a one is judged not only to offend against the Magistrate thus abused, but also against the State,* which he represents. *Probl.* Sect. XXIX. Num. 14. p. 814. Tom. II. *Edit. Paris.* The Emperor JULIAN observes that, *The Laws made in Favour of Princes are severe; so that he who commits an Outrage on a Prince, is at the same Time guilty of trampling on the Laws.* In Misopog. p. 342. *Edit. Spanheim.* GROTIUS.

The last Passage is not exactly translated by our Author. It signifies, as appears from the Terms themselves, and the Sequel of the Discourse, that *The Laws are respected for the Sake of Princes,* by whose Authority they are made; *He therefore, who commits an Outrage on a Prince, would of Course make less Difficulty of violating the Laws.* Καὶ γὰρ οἱ νόμοι φοβεροὶ διὰ τοὺς ἄρχοντας· ὥστε ὅστις ἄρχοντα ὕβριζεν. οὗτος ἐκ περιουσίας τοὺς νόμους κατεπάτησε. When it is thus understood, it is easy to perceive the Application is not just.

12. It was not because he thought he had violated the Respect due to his Enemy; but, as Mr. LE CLERC observes, tho' *David* did this to convince *Saul* how easily he might have killed him, if he had been so disposed, he felt some inward Uneasiness, (for that is the Sense of the original Expression, *David's Heart smote him,* not *he repented*) he felt, I say, some inward Uneasiness, lest *Saul,* being whimsical, should put a different Construction upon the Matter.

13. QUINTILIAN says, *Such is the Fate of all who are engaged in the Administration of the Commonwealth, that they are exposed to some Hatred and Envy, even when they are doing what is most conducive to the publick Good.* Declam. CCCXLVIII. See *Livia*'s Speech to *Augustus* on that Subject, in XIPHILIN's Abridgment of DION. p. 85, 86. *Edit. H. Steph.* GROTIUS.

to be rendered venerable, and secured from every Sort of Insult. The *Romans* even secured the Authority of the Tribunes of the People, declaring their Persons [14] *inviolable.* Among the Sayings of the *Essenes,* this was one, [15] *Kings are to be accounted sacred.* And we find that famous Passage in *Homer,*

Περὶ γὰρ δίε ποιμένι λαῶν,
Μὴ τι πάθοι.

[16] *He was afraid lest any sad Accident should happen to* [17] *the Leader of the People.* It is not without Reason, that *Those Nations, who live under a monarchical Government, reverence the Name of Kings, as if they were Gods;* as [18] *Quintus Curtius* observes. So *Artaban* the *Persian,* [19] *Among*

14. Ἄσυλοι. See Dionysius Halicarnassensis, *Antiq. Rom.* Lib. VI. Cap. LXXXIX. p. 395. *Edit. Oxon.* Livy, *Lib.* III. *Cap.* LV. Appian of *Alexandria,* Bello Civil. *p.* 628. *Edit. Toll.* and what our Author says, *B.* III. *Chap.* LXIX. § 8. *Note* 3.

15. The Author quotes no one in this Place. All I find to the Purpose in Josephus is, that according to the *Essenians, Fidelity is due to all Men, but chiefly to Princes, because they are not raised to that Dignity without the Will or Permission of GOD.* De Bello Jud. *Lib.* II. *Cap.* XII.

16. *If a Man kills a Sheep,* says St. Chrysostom, *he only makes a small Diminution in the Flock; but when the Shepherd is killed, the whole Flock is dispersed.* On 1 Tim. i. Seneca delivers himself in the following Manner, *The Subjects are on the Guard in the Night for their Prince's Security: They surround and defend him, and meet those Dangers which threaten his Person. It is not without good Reason that Nations and Cities have agreed thus to love and defend their Kings, and sacrifice their Lives and Fortunes for the Preservation of their Sovereign. Nor is it Folly, or a Neglect of one's own Life, which induces so many thousands to expose themselves to the utmost Dangers for one Person, and by the Death of great Numbers, redeem the Life of one who is, sometimes, in the Course of Nature near his End. As the whole Body is interested in the Cure of the Soul—so this immense Multitude, acting for the Defence of one Man's Life, is governed by him as their Soul, and is influenced by him in such a Manner, that the Subjects would destroy themselves by their own Strength, were they not supported by his Prudence and Wisdom: They are therefore careful of their own Safety,* &c. De Clementia, *Lib.* I. *Cap.* III. See what is said on this Subject, *B.* II. *Chap.* I. § 9. Grotius.

The Philosopher is speaking of a good Prince, as appears from the preceding Words. It is easy to discern how far the Comparison of the Shepherd and his Sheep may be carried. See Mr. Le Clerc, on 2 Sam. v. 2.

17. *Iliad.* Lib. V. ver. 566, 567.

18. *Lib.* X. *Cap.* III. *Num.* 3.

19. This Passage has been quoted in *Note* 6. on *Chap.* III. § 16.

many excellent Laws we have, this seems to be the best, which commands us
to honour and adore our Kings, as the Image of GOD, who preserves all
Things. And in *Plutarch,* of *Agis,* [20] οὐ θεμιτὸν οὐδὲ νενομεσμένον
βασιλέως, &c. *It is not permitted by the Laws of GOD or Man, to offer*
Violence to the Person of a King.

But here is a more difficult Question, Whether what was lawful for
David and the *Maccabees,* may be lawful for us *Christians,* whose Lord
and Master, CHRIST, so often bidding us [21] take up our Cross, seems
to require from us a <116> greater Measure of Patience? Indeed when
the higher Powers threaten us with Death for our Religion, CHRIST
grants Leave to flee, especially to those whom the necessary Duties of
their Calling tie to no particular Place; but [22] he allows nothing beyond

20. He says that when *Demochares,* one of the *Ephori,* was going to seize *Agis,*
King of *Lacedemonia,* the publick Officers, and others on the Spot, *declined the Task,*
thinking it unlawful to lay Hands on the King's Person. Vita Agid. & Cleom. *p.* 804.
Tom. I. *Edit. Wech.*

21. Our Saviour, at two several Times, commanded his Disciples to *carry their*
Cross, when he gave the twelve Apostles Instructions for their Behaviour in Preaching
the Gospel, MATT. x. 38. MARK viii. 34. LUKE ix. 23. and when he was going to *Cesarea*
Philippi, followed by great Crowds of People, MATT. xvi. 24. LUKE xiv. 27. By which
Words he meant no more than that *Christians* ought to be disposed to bear Perse-
cution, and all Sorts of Afflictions in general, with Patience, when they are not in a
Condition to guard themselves against them; for he no where forbids the Use of
innocent Means, when in our Power. As a sick Person, therefore, how strongly soever
he may be obliged to Patience, is allowed to take what he thinks conducive to his
Cure: So a Man, unjustly oppressed, may employ what Force he is Master of, for
delivering him from Oppression. Besides, as the learned GRONOVIUS observes on this
Place, our Lord's Precept regards all Christians in general, of all Ranks and Stations.
Now, as this Obligation to Patience does not tie up the Hands of Princes and Magistrates, or deprive them of the Power of chastising their rebellious and seditious Subjects, so neither does it deprive private Persons of a Right to resist the Rage of a Prince
or Magistrate, who behaves himself like a Tyrant to them.

22. The Passage intimated by our Author, is that of MATTHEW x. 23. *When they*
persecute you in one City, fly to another. This Advice is directed to the Apostles, and
relates to them in particular, as appears from the Words immediately following, *For*
verily I say unto you, you shall not have gone over the Cities of Israel, till the Son of Man
be come. See Dr. HAMMOND and Mr. LE CLERC on that Text. So that here is no general
Maxim, for teaching all that is allowable for *Christians,* when in any Manner oppressed or persecuted; and GRONOVIUS's Answers here are superfluous. Our Author
has confuted himself, in his Commentary on the Gospels, published since the Work

1 Ep. ii. 21, &c.   Flight. And St. *Peter* tells us, *That CHRIST in Suffering left us an Ex-ample, that we should follow* [23] *his Steps, who did no Sin, neither was Guile found in his Mouth; who being reviled, reviled not again; when he suffered,*

1 Ep. iv. 12, &c.   *he threatned not, but committed himself to him that judgeth righteously.* Nay he bids us *Christians* give Thanks to GOD, and rejoice, when we suffer Persecution for our Religion. And it was this Constancy in Suffering, that chiefly contributed to the Establishment of Christianity, as appears from History.

Wherefore, I think that the primitive Christians, who, living near the Times of the Apostles, and of apostolical Men, understood and [24] prac-

---

now before us, where he thus paraphrases the Passage under Consideration. "The Meaning is; when you shall be driven out of one City, let not this make you renounce the Functions of your Ministry: Fly then to some other Place; not to a Desart, to provide for your own Security, but to some other City, to endeavour to produce Fruit by your Instructions. Whence it appears, says he, that this Passage will by no Means afford a Proof for deciding the Question, Whether it is allowable to fly, with the sole View of avoiding *present Dangers?*"

23. The Patience to which we are obliged by our Saviour's Example, is to be un-derstood in the same Sense with his Exhortation to *carry our Cross;* of which we have already spoken in *Note* 21. on this Paragraph. Were we obliged to imitate the Conduct of JESUS CHRIST in all Particulars, every Man ought voluntarily to offer himself to Torments, and an ignominious Death; which our Author would not allow. He has himself refuted the Argument drawn from the Example of JESUS CHRIST, for the Support of the Opinion, which he himself thinks too rigid, of those who pretend we ought not to repel an Enemy so far as to take away his Life, *Chap.* II. § 8. and *Chap.* III. § 3.

24. I have already observed, and shewn by Examples, (*Note* 2. on § 52. of the *Preliminary Discourse* to this Work) that the first Christians cannot be considered as the best Expositors of the Holy Scriptures, or Models for our Conduct on all Oc-casions. We are very well assured that they entertained extravagant Notions on the Point before us, which put them on extending the Obligation of suffering Martyr-dom, far beyond its just Bounds. Our Author, who was sensible of this, retrenched the following Words in the later Editions, which in the first appeared at the End of this Paragraph, "Tho' we should grant," said he, "that this is a Counsel, and not an indispensible Precept, it would still be more safe, in the Presence of GOD, to comply with it, since the first Christians, even when they could have fled, or been silent, frequently sought so honourable a Death, in certain Hopes that such as attested their Faith in that Manner, did thereby receive a full Remission of all their Sins; that im-mediately after their Death they in some Manner enjoyed a Glory like that expected after the Resurrection; and had the Promise of a large Reward in the World to come." See Mr. DODWELL's XII. *Dissertation* on St. *Cyprian.* To this we may add, that from

tised their Precepts, bet-<117>ter than the Christians of following Ages, are very much injured by those who suppose that they rather wanted Power than Will to defend themselves, in imminent Danger of Death. Indeed *Tertullian* would have been very imprudent, nay, impudent, to have so confidently affirmed a Falshood to the Emperors, who could not be ignorant of it, writing thus, [25] *If we had a Mind to deal with you as declared Enemies, and not only as secret Enemies, could we want Forces and Troops sufficient for such an Enterprize? The* Moors, *the* Marcomanni, *the* Parthians *themselves, or such other Nations, which, however great they be, are yet confined within a certain Extent of Country, and within the Bounds*

---

some Passages of Scripture misinterpreted, they imagined the Day of Judgment very near, as is observed by the learned GRONOVIUS; and while they were full of this Persuasion, we are not to be surprized, that they had no Concern for the good Things of this World, or even for Life itself, the Preservation of which animates Men to repel the Injuries of a Tyrant. They also sometimes gave too literal a Sense to what the Gospel says concerning the good Things of this World, the Concern for which our Saviour would have us neglect, not absolutely, but only when we cannot enjoy them without Prejudice to our Conscience. Thus the Conduct of those first Votaries of Christianity ought not to be proposed as a Model for all Christians in general, who have not the same Ideas, nor are in the same Dispositions: Even tho' they had been inclined to resist their Persecutors, they would not have been in a Condition of attempting it. It is in vain to amuse the World with their great Numbers; they were a scattered Multitude, and very inconsiderable, in Comparison of their Enemies; they were for the most part Persons in mean and low Stations, without Arms, without Forces, without any other Leaders than the Ecclesiasticks, who were not Men of much Distinction; they assembled in private, and consequently could not get together in great Numbers: A single Legion would have been sufficient for defeating all their Projects. But when the Emperors had embraced Christianity, the *Christians* proceeded on very different Principles. See MILTON, *Defensio*, Cap. IV. p. 136, *&c.* As also the Speech of Dr. BURNET, late Bishop of *Salisbury*, at Dr. *Sacheverel's* Trial. In short, it was of the utmost Importance to the Establishment of the Gospel, that the Christians should not lie under the least Suspicion of being seditiously disposed. And that the more, because, as our Author himself observes on *Rom.* xiii. 1. the *Jews*, from whom the first Disciples of the Gospel came, were prejudiced by a false Notion, founded on a Passage in *Deut.* (xvii. 15.) misinterpreted, which made them look on all Authority exercised by Foreigners as unlawful, so that they did not think themselves obliged in Conscience to obey any Sovereigns but those of their own Nation. If therefore the Christians in those early Times waved their Right on so strong Considerations, no Consequence can be drawn from their Behaviour, that will affect those who have lived since Christianity is established in the World.

25. *Apol.* Cap. XXXVII. *Edit. Herald.*

of their own Dominions; Do those Nations, I say, form a more numerous Multitude than we, who are spread over the whole World? We are but of Yesterday, in a Manner, and yet we already fill all Places in your Dominions, your Cities, Islands, Provinces, Castles, Towns; your very Camps, Tribes, Wards, Palace, Senate, Courts of Judicature, publick Places; and in a Word, we only leave you the Temples of your Gods. Disposed as we are to suffer ourselves so willingly to be butchered, what Wars should we not have been in a Condition to undertake, and with what Ardour should we not have engaged in them, however inferior we might have been in Forces, had we not been taught by our Religion, that it is better to be killed than to kill? Also *Cyprian* follows his Master, and thus declares, [26] *Hence it is, that none of us, when apprehended, makes Resistance, or defends himself against your unjust Violence; tho' our People are extremely numerous. The certain Hope of a future Vengeance produces in us this Patience. Thus the Innocent yield to the Guilty.* And *Lactantius,* [27] *For we confide in the Majesty of GOD, who is able as well to revenge the Contempt of himself, as the Hardships and Injuries done to his Servants. Wherefore we suffer inexpressible Miseries, and do not repine, but refer the avenging of them to the Almighty.* St. *Augustin* had precisely in View the Case under Consideration, when he said, [28] *A good Man should take Care above all Things not to engage in War, but when he may do it lawfully; for that is not always lawful.* And again, [29] *When Princes err, they presently make Laws to defend their Errors, to the Prejudice of Truth, by which the Righteous are tried, and crowned*

---

26. *Ad Demetrian.* p. 192. *Edit. Fell. Brem.* The same Father elsewhere expresses himself in the following Manner, *The Enemy knows that the Soldiers of JESUS CHRIST are sober and vigilant, and stand armed for the Engagement; that they may die, but cannot be conquered; and are therefore invincible, because they fear not Death, nor resist those who attack them; not being allowed, tho' innocent, to kill the guilty; but thinking themselves obliged to resign their Life, and their Blood chearfully,* Lib. I. Epist. I. *Edit. Erasm.* (Ep. LX. *Edit. Fell.* p. 142.) Grotius.

27. *Instit. Div.* Lib. V. Cap. IX. Num. 9. *Edit. Cellar.*

28. *Lib.* VI. *Quaest.* X. *in Josuam.* This Passage is quoted in the *Canon Law,* Caus. XXIII. Quaest. II. Can. 11.

29. *Epist.* CLXVI. This Passage is also quoted in the *Canon Law,* Cause XI. Quaest. III. Can. 98.

(with Martyrdom). And again, [30] *So are Sovereigns to be endured by their Subjects, and Masters by their Servants, as that by suffering these* temporal *Things with* Patience *and* Resignation, *they may have just Reason to hope for Rewards that are* eternal. Which he further illustrates by the Example of the primitive Christians. [31] *Neither did the City of CHRIST, (tho' it was then wandering and vagabond upon Earth, and had vast Numbers of People to assist it against its wicked Persecutors) fight for temporal Salvation, but chose rather to make no Resistance, that it might obtain an eternal one. They were bound, imprisoned, beaten, tormented, burnt, torn in Pieces, massacred, and yet they multiplied more and more. To fight for Safety, was, in their Opinion, nothing else than to despise this Life, in order to acquire another that is more excellent.* <118>

Nor are the Observations of St. *Cyril* less admirable, upon that Passage in St. *John* of St. *Peter's* Sword. The *Thebaean Legion,* as we read in the Acts of their Martyrdom, consisted of 6666 Soldiers, and all Christians. Who, when the Emperor *Maximianus* would have compelled the whole Army to sacrifice to false Gods, at *Octodurum,* first removed to *Agaunum,* and when the Emperor had sent one thither, to command them to come and sacrifice, and they had refused to do it; he sent Officers to put every tenth Man to Death, who easily executed his Order, no Man offering to resist.

Martignac. St. *Maurice.*

Mauritius, [32] Commander of that Legion, (from whom the Town of

30. The Author doth not tell us whence he took this Passage. It is probable he quotes it on the Credit of his Memory, as well as the preceding, which is therefore somewhat differently worded than the Original.

31. *De Civit. Dei.* Lib. XXII. Cap. VI. Saint CYRIL hath some excellent Expressions on the same Subject, in his Explanation of that Passage of St. JOHN, where PETER'S Sword is mentioned, *Chap.* XVIII. *Ver. 11.* GROTIUS.

32. The *Swiss* pay a great Veneration to the Memory of that Martyr. See FRANC. GUILLIMAN, *De rebus Helvet,* Lib. I. Cap. XV. and Lib. II. Cap. VIII. The Legion commanded by *Mauritius* is also placed in the Rank of the most illustrious Martyrs, who suffered Death in the tenth Persecution, as appears from an old Relation of the Translation of St. *Justin's* Relicks, to the Monastery of new *Corbie.* ALBERT KRANTZIUS speaks of some Martyrs of the *Thebaean Legion,* whose Bodies were removed to *Brunswick. Saxonick.* VII. 16. GROTIUS.

The whole Relation of the Martyrdom of this Legion is a mere Fable. The Story itself carries several Marks of Falshood; and the small Treatise, in which it appears is

Agaunum in *Switzerland,* was afterwards called St. *Maurice*) as *Euche-rius,* Bishop of *Lyons,* records, thus spake to his Soldiers at that Time. *How did I fear, lest any of you, under the Shew of Self-Defence (as it is easy for armed Men to do) should have endeavoured by Force to prevent their blessed Martyrdom? I was preparing, in order to divert you from that Design, to set before you the Example of JESUS CHRIST, who expressly commanded the Apostle to put the Sword into the Scabbard, which he had drawn in his Master's own Defence; teaching us that all the Force of Arms is not able to shake Christian Constancy. This, I say, is what I intended to represent to you, that none of you, by employing a mortal Arm, should oppose the Glory of an immortal Action; and that, on the contrary, every one might finish with Stedfastness the Work he hath so happily begun.* When, this Execution being over, the Emperor commanded the same Thing to the Survivors, as he had before done to the others, they all unanimously answered, *In-deed,* Caesar, *we are your Soldiers, and we took up Arms in Defence of the* Roman *Empire, never has there been seen amongst us either a Deserter, or Traitor, or Coward: And we should willingly obey the Orders which you give us to Day, if the Christian Religion, in which we have been instructed, did not forbid us to worship Demons, or approach Altars always polluted with innocent Blood. We know you designed either to make Christians commit Sacrilege, or to frighten us, by the Example of those that have been decimated. But you need not search far off for People that do not conceal themselves: We are all Christians, and we declare it to you. Our Bodies are in your Power, but you cannot make yourself Master of our Souls, which are always turned towards CHRIST their Creator.*

---

not the Work of St. EUCHERIUS, Bishop of *Lyons,* whose Name it bears. We need only observe that it mentions *Sigismund,* King of *Burgundy,* as dead several Years before; whereas St. EUCHERIUS himself had been long dead, when that Prince reigned. All this is proved at large in a Dissertation, written by the late Mr. JOHN DU BOUR-DIEU, formerly Minister at *Montpellier,* and afterwards of the *French* Church in the *Savoy, London.* This *historical and critical Dissertation on the Martyrdom of the The-baean Legion,* was first published in *English,* in 1696, and then in *French,* in 1705. I say nothing of what else might be objected against our Author's Note, but for a more full Eviction of the Falseness of the Fact under Consideration, I refer the Reader to the late Mr. DODWELL's famous Dissertation, *De paucitate Martyrum,* which is the eleventh of those on St. CYPRIAN.

Then *Exuperius,* Standard-Bearer to that Legion, thus addressed them. *You see me (brave fellow Soldiers) carry the Standards of secular Wars. But it is not to that Sort of War that I now call you; you have other Battles to fight: There are other Arms you ought to make Use of, to open the Way to the Kingdom of Heaven.* And then he sent this Message to the Emperor, *It is not Despair, the most powerful Resource in Dangers, that has armed us, O* Caesar, *against you. We have Arms in our Hands,* [33] *but we do not resist, because we rather chuse to die, than overcome, and to fall Innocents, rather than to live Criminals.* And again, *We throw away our Weapons, your Executioner shall find our Hands without Defence, but our Hearts armed with the Buckler of Christian Faith.* <119>

After this followed the Slaughter of those Soldiers who suffered Death without Resistance, of which *Eucherius* gives this Account. [34] *The Greatness of their Number did not secure them from Sufferings, though innocent; whereas even Criminals come off with Impunity, when numerous.* We have the same Account of it in the old Martyrology. *They were massacred on every Side, without saying a Word. They threw down their Arms, and presented their Throats and naked Breasts to their Persecutors. They took no Advantage of their great Number, nor made Use of the Arms they held in their Hands, to defend the Justice of their Cause at the Point of the Sword; but wholly taken up with this Thought, that they confessed the Name of him, who was led dumb to the Slaughter, and as a Lamb did not open his Mouth,*

33. The *Jews* of *Alexandria* formerly expressed themselves in a like Manner to *Flaccus, We are, as you see, unarmed; and yet we are by some accused of coming hither as Enemies. We hold our Hands, which Nature has given every Man for his Defence, behind our Backs, where they can be of no Service to us; exposing our Bodies to any who are disposed to kill us.* GROTIUS.

These Words were not spoken by the *Jews* of *Alexandria,* but by those of *Judea,* to *Petronius,* Governour of *Syria,* not to *Flaccus.* We find them in PHILO, *De Legat. ad Caium,* pag. 1025. Our Author has confounded two different Stories, related in two different Pieces of that Jewish Writer.

34. *The Greatness of their Number did not secure them from Sufferings, though innocent; whereas even Criminals come off with Impunity, when numerous;* quum *inultum* (not *multum,* according to our Author's Correction) *esse soleat, quod multitudo deliquit.*

they also like the innocent Flock of CHRIST's Sheep, suffered themselves to be torn in Pieces by furious Wolves.

And when the Emperor *Valens* wickedly and cruelly [35] persecuted those Christians who according to the Holy Scriptures, and the Traditions of the Fathers professed CHRIST to be ὁμοούσιον, of the same Substance, (with GOD his Father) though they were very numerous, they never defended themselves by Arms. Certainly where Patience is recommended to us in the new Testament, there we find [36] CHRIST's own Example proposed to us (as we have just now read it was to the *Thebaean Legion*) for our Imitation; whose Patience reached even unto Death. And he himself declares, that whoever loseth his Life in that Manner truly finds it. Thus having proved, that those who are invested with the sovereign Power, cannot lawfully be resisted; we must now admonish the Reader of some Things, lest he should think those Men transgress this Law, who really do not.

1 Pet. ii. 21.

Mat. x. 39.

Luke xvii. 33.

VIII. *A free People may make War against their Prince.* VIII. *First* therefore, Those Princes who depend on the People, whether they at first were established on that Foot, or their Authority was thus rendered subordinate by a posterior Agreement, [1] as in *Sparta,* if they offend against the Laws, and the State, may not only be resisted by Force;

35. See the Fragments of JOHN of *Antioch,* published from a Manuscript, in the Hands of the late Mr. de PEIRESC, a Person worthy of immortal Reputation. p. 846. GROTIUS.

36. See my 23 *Note* on this Paragraph.

VIII. (1) PLUTARCH tells us that Lysander *being killed* (in a Battle) *the* Spartans *were so deeply affected at his Death, that they pronounced Sentence on the King.* (Pausanias.) *who fled to* Tegea, *to avoid the Execution of it.* In Lysand. p. 450. Tom. I. *Edit. Wech.* The same Author says, *that the* Lacedemonians *dethron'd some of their Kings,* whose infamous Lives had rendered them *unworthy of the Royal Dignity.* Compar. *Lysand.* and *Syllae.* p. 476. See likewise what he says of *Agis,* who was condemned to die, though unjustly. *The* Mosynecians, (or Mossynians, a People of *Pontus*) *elect their Kings, keep them under close Confinement; and oblige them to fast a whole Day, when they commit a Fault in the Execution of their Office;* says POMPON. MELA, *Lib.* I. *Cap.* XIX. *Num.* 7. See ISAAC VOSSIUS's Note on that Place. GROTIUS.

but if it be necessary, may be punished by Death, as it befel *Pausanias* [2] the *Spartan* King. Such was the Condition of the most ancient Kings of divers Countries in *Italy;* so that it is no Wonder, if *Virgil* having related the horrible Cruelties of *Mezentius,* adds,

[3] *All* Etruria, *justly incensed and rising up in Arms against that King, required him to be immediately put to death.*

IX. *Secondly,* If a King, or any other Prince, has abdicated his Government, or manifestly abandoned [1] it; after that Time, we may do the same to him, as to any private Man; but Negligence [2] in discharging the Functions of Government is not to be taken for a real Abdication. <120>

X. *Thirdly,* If a King alienates his Kingdom; or renders it dependent on any other Power, [1] he forfeits the Crown, according to *Barclay.* For my

IX. *And against a King that has abdicated his Kingdom.*

X. *Or against a King that*

2. This *Pausanias,* the *Spartan* General, was indeed of the Royal Family, but not King. He had been no more than Guardian to his Cousin *Plistarchus,* Son to King *Leonidas,* as the learned GRONOVIUS here observes. See THUCYD. *Lib.* I. *Cap.* CXXXII. *Edit. Oxon.*

3. VIRGIL, Aen. VIII. *v.* 494. *&c.*

IX. (1) As when *Henry* III. King of *Poland,* being apprised of the Death of his Brother *Charles* IX. King of *France,* left *Cracow* privately, and went for *France,* in 1574. Whereupon, the *Poles* chose another King, the following Year. See also the Debates between the two Houses of Parliament on the Abdication of *James* II. King of *England,* in the *Supplement* to Sir RICH. STEEL's *Crisis.*

2. Provided such Negligence be not very considerable; for if it be carried so far that the King lets the Affairs of the State run entirely into Disorder and Confusion, I make no Doubt that the People have a Right to consider his Conduct as a real Abdication. The Thing speaks for itself; and I find Mr. VANDER MUELEN of the same Opinion, in his Commentary on this Place.

X. (1) As when he makes the Kingdom feudatary or tributary. BOECLER pretends that the Author, here quoted, speaks only of this Case, and not of the former, or of a real, full and intire Alienation. But as BARCLAY looks on him as forfeiting the Crown, who does the least, he could not reasonably pass any other Judgment on him who does what is more. The same Commentator finds a difficulty in owning that the Case under Consideration is of such Importance and deserves so heavy a Punishment: He even endeavours to make our Author contradict himself, in Regard to what he has laid down, in the foregoing Chapter, § 21, *&c.* that a Prince, doth not cease to be a Sovereign, though he is tributary or feudatary to another. But as he who attempts to subject his Kingdom in this Manner, has no Right to do it by his own Authority, and without the Consent of the People, such an Act is sufficient for discharging the People

would alienate his Kingdom; but only to prevent the Delivery of it. Part, I dare not pronounce peremptorily in that Manner. For, when the Question is concerning a Kingdom, [2] either elective or successive, but conferred by a free Consent of the People, such an Act (of Alienation) is in itself void, and whatsoever is in itself void, can have no [3] effect of

Lib III. Ch. XVI. *Advers. Monarchomach.* a Right. Upon this Principle Civilians maintain, that an Usufructuary to whom we have compared such Princes, if he yields up [4] his Right to any other than the Proprietor himself, does an Act that is of no Force: And this Opinion seems to me best founded. For, as to what is said, [5] that the Fruits and Profits revert to the *Landlord;* it must be [6] understood

from the Obedience, which they promised him only on Condition, either express or tacit, that he should make no such Attempt. It is unnecessary to say the Good of the State sometimes requires it; for that is not the Question; and in that Case, he must always be authorized by the Consent of the Nation, either expressed, or presumed on convincing Reasons.

2. See *Cap.* III. § 10 and § 11.

3. That is, the Act of Alienation, or Subjection performed by the King, neither turns to his Prejudice, nor to the Advantage of the Person, in whose Favour he alienated or subjected the Kingdom; and consequently, he loses nothing of his Right to the Crown, by an Act like this, which is void and of no Effect. See *Book* II. *Chap.* VI. § 3, 9. But I do not see how this Doctrine agrees with the Permission granted by our Author, to resist such a Prince, when he actually undertakes to give up, or subject his Crown. He thereby only puts in Execution what was already done, as far as in him lay, by a Contract and Engagement with another Power; and if that Engagement did not make him forfeit the Sovereignty, by what Authority shall the People resist him, when he sets about the Execution of it? The Truth is, every Prince, who having no Right so to do, undertakes to alienate or subject his Kingdom, without the Consent of the People, doth thereby violate a fundamental Law of the State; and thus really forfeits the Sovereignty; as BARCLAY teaches, who is in other Respects a zealous Defender of the Sovereign's Rights. Here too Mr. VANDER MUELEN is of the same Opinion with me; and considers such an Action in a King, as a manifest Abdication of the Crown. See some Instances of this Sort in HUBER's Treatise *De Jure Civit.* Lib. I. Sect. IX. Cap. VI. § 36, 37.

4. INSTITUT. Lib. II. Tit. IV. *De Usufructu.* § 3.

5. DIGEST. Lib. XXIII. Tit. III. *De Jure Dotium.* Leg. LXVI.

6. But some maintain the contrary, and in my Opinion on better Grounds; as appears from Mr. NOODT's Treatise *De Usufructu.* Lib. II. Cap. X. where he distinguishes between the old and new Law on this Subject; and explains the Law in Question, as well as the Paragraph quoted from the INSTITUTES in the foregoing Note. So that, even though an Usufructuary might in all Respects be compared to the Sovereign of an elective or successive Kingdom, this would rather make against our Author than for him. Let Men of Judgment determine whether Mr. VAN DE WATER, has urged

after such a Time when the Use and Profits were to terminate. Yet if a King should endeavour actually to deliver up his Kingdom, or to subject it to another, I doubt not, but in such a Case, he may be resisted. For Sovereignty (as I have said) is one Thing, and the Manner of holding it another. The People may hinder any Change in the latter; the Power of making such a Change not being comprehended in the Right of Sovereignty. To which we may fitly apply that of *Seneca,* in a Case not much different [7] *Though our Father is to be obeyed in all Things, yet not in those, whereby he ceases to be a Father.*

XI. *Fourthly,* The same *Barclay* observes, that if a King shall, like an Enemy, [1] design the utter Destruction of the whole Body of his People, he loses his Kingdom; which I grant. For the Design of Governing, and the Design of destroy-<121>ing are inconsistent together. Wherefore he that declares himself an Enemy to the whole Nation, is presumed by that very Act to renounce the Government. But such an Excess of Fury [2] can hardly, in my Opinion, enter the Thoughts of a King, that is in his right Senses, and that governs only one Nation. But if he govern several, it

XI. *Or against a King that behaves himself as an Enemy to the whole Body of the People.*

---

such Reasons as are sufficient for supporting the opposite Opinion, in his *Observationes Juris,* Lib. III. Cap. XI. which appeared in 1713, soon after Mr. NOODT's Works, among which the Treatise *De Usufructu,* was first published.

7. That Author proposes an Enquiry whether this ought to be done. *Controv.* Lib. II. Cap. IX. p. 158. *Edit. Elziv.* 1672.

XI. (1) On this Principle *Gracchus* ingeniously maintained, that a Tribune of the People ceases, to be such, and is entirely divested of his Power. His Discourse on that Subject is worth reading; and may be seen in PLUT. *Vit. Tib. & C. Gracchi.* p. 831, 832. Tom. I. *Edit. Wech.* JOHN MAJOR, (or MAIR) in his Treatise on Book IV. of PETER LOMBARD's Sentences, says that a People cannot divest themselves of the Power of deposing the Prince, when he endeavours their Destruction. A Principle, which ought to be softened, and explained, as we shall here explain it. GROTIUS.

See Mr. NOODT's Discourse, *Du Pouvoir des Souverains,* p. 237, 238. and the Note in the second Edition published in 1714.

2. A Prince may be in the Case here specified, though he doth not, like *Caligula,* wish the whole People had but one Head, that he might dispatch them at one Stroke; or though he expresses no formal and direct Design of destroying his Subjects. It is sufficient that his Actions have a manifest Tendency that Way. Nor is there any Obligation of waiting till there is no Remedy for the Evil. See *Note* I. on PUFEND. *B.* VII. *Chap.* VIII. § 6.

may so happen, that in Favour to one, he should endeavour [3] to destroy another, in order to people the Lands of the former with Colonies sent from the latter.

XII. *And against a King, who breaks the Condition, upon which he was admitted.* XII. *Fifthly,* If a Kingdom be forfeited, either [1] for Felony against him of whom it is a Fief, or by vertue [2] of a Clause in the Act whereby the Sovereignty had been conferred, and which declares that if the King does such or such a Thing, his Subjects shall from that Time be absolved from all Allegiance to him, then also a King becomes a private Person.

XIII. *And against a King, who having but one Part of the Sovereign Power invades the other.* XIII. *Sixthly,* If a King should have but one Part of the sovereign Power, and the Senate or People [1] the other, if such a King shall invade that Part which is not his own, he may justly be resisted, because he is not Sovereign in that Respect. Which I believe may take Place, though in the Division [2] of the Sovereignty, the Power of making War fell to the King, for that is to be understood of a foreign War: Since whoever has a Share of the Sovereignty must have at the same Time a Right to defend it. And when the Case is so, the King may, by the Right of War, lose even his Part of the Sovereignty.

3. *Philip* II. King of *Spain* was charged with such a Design, in Regard to the Low Countries. See somewhat of the like Nature, attributed to *Philip,* King of *Macedonia,* in Liv. *Lib.* XI. *Cap.* III.

XII. (1) See the foregoing Chap. § 23.

2. See also *Chap.* III. § 16.

XIII. (1) We have an Instance of this Kind in the Republic of *Genoa* in PETER BIZAR. *Lib.* XVIII. and in *Bohemia,* under *Wenceslaus,* in DUBRAY's *Hist.* Lib. X. See AZOR, *Institut. Moral.* Lib. X. Cap. VIII. and LAMBERT of *Schaffnaburg,* in Relation to the Emperor *Henry* IV. GROTIUS.

2. The learned GROTIUS [[*sic:* GRONOVIUS]] observes that our Author in this Place gives a tacit Answer to the Heads of the Charge brought against BARNEVELD; and refers the Reader to his Defence, entitled, *Apologeticus eorum, qui* Hollandiae Westfrisiaeque, &c. *ex legibus praefuerunt ante mutationem quae evenit anno* 1618. Cap. X. But the Case is not exactly the same; as will appear on comparing what our Author says in that Piece with what he says here.

XIV. *Seventhly,* If in the conferring of the Crown, it be expressly stipulated, [1] *that in some* certain *Cases* the King may be resisted; even though that Clause does not imply any Division of the Sovereignty, yet certainly some Part of natural Liberty [2] is reserved to the People, and exempted from the Power of the King. Now every one in alienating his Rights in Favour of another may do it under what Restriction he pleases.

XIV. *And against him, who grants such a Licence in certain Cases.*

XV. We have treated of him, who has now, or has had a Right to govern; it now remains, that we say something of him that usurps the Government; not after he has either by long Possession, or Agreement obtained [1] a Right to it, but so long as [2] the Cause of his unjust Possession continues. The Acts of Sovereignty exercised by such an Usurper may have an obligatory Force, not by vertue of his Right, (for he has none) but because it is very probable that the lawful Sovereign, whether it be the People themselves, or a King, or a Senate, chuses rather that the Usurper should be obeyed during that Time, than that the Exercise of the Laws and Justice <122> should be interrupted, and the State thereby exposed to all the Disorders of Anarchy. *Cicero* condemns *Sylla*'s Laws, as cruel upon the Children of the Outlaws, making them incapable of Honours; yet he thought they ought to be observed, affirming (as *Quintilian* [3] tells

XV. *An Usurper, how far to be obeyed.*

XIV. (1) See some Examples of this Kind in Mr. De Thou's History, *Lib.* CXXXI. on the Year 1604. p. 1037, 1038. *Edit. Francof.* and *Lib.* CXXXIII. on the Year 1605. p. 1074; both relate to *Hungary.* As also in Meyer's *Annal Belgic.* on the Year 1339, in regard to *Brabant* and *Flanders;* and on the Year 1468, in Relation to the Treaty between *Lewis* XI. King of *France,* and *Charles,* Duke of *Burgundy.* See also what Chytraeus says of *Poland, Saxonic.* Lib. XXIV. and what Bonfinius relates of *Hungary,* Decad. IV. Lib. IX. Grotius.

The Instances here alledged are not to the Author's Purpose; as will appear on examining each apart.

2. Why is it not plainly and directly said that this Reservation disengages the Subject from their Obedience, whenever the Case happens; so that if the Prince is obstinately bent on doing what is prohibited by such a Clause, which has the Force of a fundamental Law, the People ought to consider him no longer as their Sovereign? It is not conceivable that the Restriction can naturally have any other End, or Effect.

XV. (1) See *B.* II. *Chap.* IV. § 14.

2. Compare all this with what Pufendorf says on the same Subject, *B.* VII. *Chap.* VIII. § 9, 10. and in his academical Dissertation *De Interregnis.* § 16.

3. Quintil. *Instit. Orat.* Lib. XI. Cap. I. *pag.* 981. *Edit. Burm.*

us) that this was so necessary, considering the Circumstances of the State at that Time, [4] that if they were abrogated it could not subsist. *Florus* also says of the Acts of the same *Sylla:* Lepidus *endeavoured to repeal the Acts of that great Man, and not without Reason, if he could have done it, without great Hurt to the Commonwealth.* And again, *It was necessary for the State, then sick and wounded, to rest at any Rate, lest her Wounds should be ripped open in going about to cure it.*

But in those Things, which are not so necessary for the public Good, and which contribute towards establishing the Usurper in his unjust Possession, if by disobeying we run no great Hazard, we must not obey. But the Question is, whether it be lawful to depose such an Usurper, or even to kill him.

XVI. *An Usurper may be killed during the War, if no Contract be made with him.*

XVI. And *First,* If he has seized on the Government in Consequence of an unjust War, and which had not all the Qualities required by the Law of Nations, and if no Treaty has been made afterwards, [1] or any Oath of Fidelity taken to him; in a word, if he has no other Title to Possession, than mere Force, the Right of War seems to continue intire, and [2] con-

---

4. Because the Children of the Outlaws would have put the whole State in Confusion. And the Persons, on whom *Sylla* had bestowed the Estates of those Outlaws, would not easily have restored them, as FLORUS observes, in the Quotation here alledged, which stands thus at large. *For* Lepidus, *full of Insolence, and fond of Innovations, attempted to annul the Acts of that great Man; and not without good Reason, if it had been practicable without great Prejudice to the Commonwealth. For when* Sylla, *the Dictator, by the Right of War, had outlawed his Enemies, who survived that Revolution,* Lepidus, *by recalling them, only called them to renew the War; and since the Estates of the proscribed Citizens, though unjustly seized, and alienated by* Sylla, *had been taken from them by some sort of Right; a Re-demand of such Estates would certainly have involved the State in fresh Troubles. It was advisable therefore on any Terms to allow the sick and wounded Commonwealth some Repose, lest its Wounds should be opened again by the very Means taken for its Cure.* Lib. III. Cap. XXIII. *Num.* 2, 3, 4.

XVI. (1) See *B.* II. *Chap.* XIII. § 15. and *B.* III. *Chap.* XIX. § 2, &c. of this Work.

2. The learned GRONOVIUS in this Place applies what a *Roman* Senator said in Regard to the *Decemvirs: As if the* Roman *People had any War, which more deserved their Attention than that which Men, . . . who, though but private Persons, assumed Marks of Magistracy, and acted in the Character of Sovereigns.* LIV. Lib. III. Cap. XXXIX. *Num.* 8.

sequently what may lawfully be done against an Enemy, may be lawfully attempted against him, whom any private Man may kill. *Against Traitors and publick Enemies every private Man* (says [3] *Tertullian*) *is a Soldier.* So against Deserters, [4] any Man is allowed by the Roman Law to take Revenge, in the Name of the Publick, for the common Safety.

XVII. I think, with [1] *Plutarch,* the same may be said of him, who has usurped the sovereign Authority in a State where there was already a Law, impowering any Person to kill him, who should do such or such a Thing, visible and manifestly designed: as for Example, if a private Man should go with a Guard about <123> him, should assault a Fort, or kill a Citizen uncondemned, or illegally condemned, or presume to create a Magistrate without being elected by legal Votes. Many such Laws were extant in the States of *Greece,* with whom it was reputed lawful to kill such

XVII. By virtue of an antecedent Law.

---

3. *Apolog.* Cap. II.

4. The *Roman* Law speaks thus: *We allow Persons in every Province full Power and Right to distress Deserters. If they shall dare to resist, we command that their Punishment be expeditious, wherever they are found. Let all Men know they are hereby invested with a Right to act in the Name of the Public against public Robbers and those who desert from the Army; and that this Right is to be employed for the Peace of the Commonwealth.* COD. *Lib.* III. *Tit.* XXVII. *Quando liceat unicuique sine Judice se vindicare, &c.* Leg. II.

XVII. (1) I shall set down PLUTARCH's Way of Reasoning, on which our Author grounds the Opinion here attributed to him. The Philosopher undertakes to prove that it cannot be said all Things are directed by *Fate,* or are so many Effects and Consequences of *Fate, Καθ' εἱμαρμένην,* though every Thing is included in Fate. He then makes Use of this Comparison. *Every Thing comprehended in the Law, is not therefore legal, or according to Law; thus Treason, Desertion, Adultery, and many other Acts of the like Nature, are comprehended in the Law; and yet no Man will venture to affirm any of them to be lawful. Nor would I say that an Action of extraordinary Bravery, killing a Tyrant, or other great Achievement, is according to Law. For only what the Law enjoins deserves that Appellation. If therefore the Law enjoins the Actions already specified, how shall a Man be cleared of Disobedience, and offending against the Law, who engages in none of the said Actions? Or if he is thereby disobedient, and offends against the Law, would it not be just to punish a Person? But if this is absurd, that only, which is prescribed by the Law, is to be termed,* legal, *and according to* Law; *and thus only what necessarily follows from, or is conformable to the divine Regulations and Determinations, can be said to be done* by Fate, *or according to Fate . . . Fate doth indeed comprehend all Things . . . but they will not fall out by Necessity; but every Thing will come to pass according to its Nature.* De Fato, p. 570. *Ed. Wech. Tom.* II. This Comparison is somewhat far fetched, and grounded on a Quibble, which is unworthy of a Philosopher.

Tyrants. Such was [2] *Solon*'s Law at *Athens,* after the Return from the *Piraeus,* against such as should abolish popular Government, or after its being abolished, should exercise any publick Office. And such was the [3] *Valerian* Law at *Rome,* if any one bore an Office without the Order of the People; and the *Consular* Law, after the *Decemviral* Government, [4] that no Man should create a Magistrate without an Appeal; and he that did it might lawfully be killed.

XVIII. *By his Commission who has a* Right *to the* Crown.

2 Chron. xxiii.

XVIII. Nor will it be less lawful to kill an Usurper if there be an express Order for it from the lawful Sovereign, whether King, People, or Senate. The Guardians of the Heir to the Crown have the same Right; and it was by Vertue of that Right, that *Jehoiada* drove *Athalia* from the Throne, which belonged to his Pupil *Joash.*

2. I find it mentioned by the Orator ANDOCIDES, who, addressing himself to *Epichares,* tells him, that *a Man who should kill him, would be deemed innocent, even according to the Law of* Solon, *viz. If any one abolishes the* Athenian *Democracy, or exercises any publick Office after such Abolition, let him be reckoned an Enemy to the* Athenians, *and be killed with Impunity to the Person who dispatches him.* Orat. I. p. 219, 220. *Edit. Hanov.*

3. DIONYSIUS of *Halicarnassus* reports this Law in the following Terms, *He* (Valerius) *made most excellent Laws, of great Advantage to the Publick; in one of which he expressly ordered, that no Man should act in a publick Office, except he received it from the Hands of the People, under Pain of Death; and declared the Person who should kill such an Intruder innocent.* Antiq. Rom. *Lib.* V. *Cap.* XIX. *p.* 281. *Edit. Oxon.* LIVY expresses himself thus, on the same Occasion, *He made Laws for appealing to the People against the Magistrates, and punishing the Man with Confiscation of his Estate, and Death, who should attempt to seize the Sovereignty.* Lib. II. Cap. VIII. Num. 2. *Edit. Cleric.* See his Note on that Place. Our Author quotes the two following Passages from PLUTARCH, in a Note, who expresses himself in Terms somewhat different, *For if any one attempts to become a Tyrant,* Solon *ordered him to be seized and punished; but* Publicola *allows such a one to be dispatched without that Formality.* Vit. Public. *p.* 110. *He made a Law which allowed any one to kill the Man, without any Trial, who should aspire at the Tyranny; and ordered, that the Person who dispatched him, should be deem'd innocent, on bringing Proofs of the Crime,* p. 103. Where it may be observed, that PLUTARCH is mistaken concerning the Law of *Solon,* as is evident from the Passage of ANDOCIDES, quoted in the foregoing Note.

4. Our Author here uses the Words of LIVY, tho' he doth not quote them. This Law was made by *Valerius,* Grandson to *Publicola,* in Conjunction with his Collegue in the Consulship, *M. Horatius,* Lib. III. Cap. LV. Num. 4, 5.

XIX. 1. Unless in one of these Cases, I do not see how it can be lawful
for any private Man, either to dethrone or kill an Usurper. Because it
may be, he that has the true Right, had rather leave the Usurper in quiet
Possession, than engage his Country in dangerous Troubles and bloody
Wars, which generally follow the expelling, or killing such Men, especially if they have a strong Faction at home, or powerful Friends abroad.
It is at least uncertain, whether the King, or Senate, or People, to whom
the sovereign Authority lawfully belongs, would be willing that Matters
should be brought to that dangerous Extremity; and whilst their Mind
on that Head is not known, all Force would be unjust. *Favonius* said [1]
χεῖρον εἶναι μοναρχίας ἀνόμου πόλεμον ἐμφύλιον, *A Civil War is worse
than the Necessity of submitting to an unlawful Government.* And *Cicero,*
[2] *Any Peace is preferable to a Civil War.* And *T. Quintius Flaminius,* [3] that
it was [4] better to leave *Nabis* Ty-<124>rant of *Lacedemon,* in Possession

XIX. *Why an
Usurper is not
to be killed, but
in these Cases.*

XIX. (1) PLUTARCH, *Vit. M. Bruti,* p. 989. *Edit. Wech.*
2. *Philippic.* II. Cap. XV. p. 445. *Edit. Graev.*
3. LIVY, *Lib.* XXXIV. *Cap.* XLIX. *Num.* 1, &c.
4. PLUTARCH expresses this in the following Manner, Titus *alledged in Defence of
his Conduct, that he had put an End to the War, because he perceived the Tyrant could
not be destroyed, without doing great Damage to the rest of the* Spartans. *Vit. T. Q.
Flamin.* p. 376. It will not be amiss to give the Reader in this Place, the Saying of a
Lacedemonian, who in reading an Epigram, the Sense of which was, *These Men fell
before the Gates of* Selinus, *in attempting to extinguish Tyranny;* said, *They deserved to
die; for they ought to have waited till the Tyranny consumed itself intirely.* Ὁ δὲ ἀναγνούς
τὸ ἐπίγραμμα τοῦτο,

Σβεννύντας ποτὲ τούς δὲ τυράννιδα χάλκεθ᾽ Ἄρης
Εἷλε. Σελινοῦντος δ᾽ ἄμφι πύλας ἔθανον.

Δικαίως, εἶπε τεθνάκαντι τοὶ ἄνδρες· ἔδει γὰρ ἀφέμεν ὅλαν αὐτὰν κατακαῆμεν.
Vit. Lycurg. p. 52. GROTIUS.
This last Passage is ill translated by the *Latin* Interpreter, who renders it, *Permit-
tendum enim fuerat, ut totum conflagraret Oppidum;* that is, *They ought to have let the
whole Town be burnt.* Nor has our Author succeeded much better in expressing the
Sense of it, tho' he perceived the Quibble in which the Point consists. The *Lacedemonian* meant, as PALMIERIUS of *Grentesmenil* observes, in his *Exercitationes in op-
timos ferè Auct. Graec.* p. 186. "These Men deserved their Fate; for they ought not to
have extinguished the Tyranny, but rather have let it burn and consume itself entirely,
instead of preserving it." So that the Criticism falls on the Word *extinguish,* which
seems to signify, that the Persons mentioned in the Epigram had maintained the
Tyranny; whereas the Poet's Meaning was, that they had destroyed it. And conse-

of the Government, than to ruin that City by endeavouring to restore its Liberty. To this Purpose was the Advice of [5] *Aristophanes, not to nourish a Lion in the City, but if he were nourished, to bear with him.*

2. It is certainly a Matter of the utmost Consequence, to determine [6] whether we ought to continue quiet, or endeavour at any Rate to recover Liberty; as *Tacitus* speaks. And *Cicero* calls it, [7] *A difficult Question in Politicks, whether when our Country is opprest with Tyranny, we may endeavour to rescue it, tho' with the extreme Hazard of the State.* Therefore private Persons must not set up for Judges in such an Affair, that concerns the whole Body of the People. So that there's great Injustice in this Expression,

[8] *Detrahimus dominos urbi servire paratae.*

We take up Arms [9] *to free the City from Tyrants, to whose Yoke it is ready to submit.* As there is also in that Answer of *Sylla,* who being asked, [10] why he came into his Country so armed; replied, to deliver it from Tyrants.

3. *Plato,* [11] and after him *Cicero,* [12] lay down a more reasonable Maxim, *Do not meddle,* say they, *in what concerns the Government, but*

---

quently, the *Lacedemonian's* Remark, rightly understood, is misapplied in this Place, being so far from making any Thing to our Author's Purpose, that it is directly against him.

5. *Ranae,* v. 1478, &c. *Edit. Kuster.*

6. TACITUS, *Hist.* Lib. IV. Cap. LXVII. Num. 5.

7. *Epist. ad Attic.* Lib. IX. Ep. IV.

8. LUCAN, *Lib.* I. *v.* 351. They are the Words of *Julius Caesar.*

9. Thus *Antiochus* the *Great,* undertaking a War against the *Romans,* did it *under Pretence of giving the* Grecians *their Liberty, who had not Need of it.* PLUTARCH, *Vit. Cat. Maj.* p. 342. GROTIUS.

10. *The Embassadors finding him on the Road, asked him why he attacked his Country in a hostile Manner? To which he replied, that he appeared in Arms in Order to free it from Tyrants.* APPIAN, *Bell. Civ.* Lib. I. p. 648. *Edit. Toll.* (384 H. Steph.)

11. Our Author here quotes that Philosopher's seventh Epistle to *Perdiccas.* I have given the Passage at Length, in my Remarks on PUFENDORF, *B.* VII. *Chap.* VIII. § 5. *Note* I. But it is more probable, that CICERO had the following Words of the Dialogue, entitled *Crito,* in View, *In the Conduct of War, in the Tribunals of Justice, and on all other Occasions, the Orders of the State, and our Country are to be obeyed; or we are to advise what is just in its own Nature. But it is not allowable to commit Violence either on a Father or a Mother, and much less on our Country.* Tom. I. p. 51. *Edit. Steph.*

12. *Lib.* I. *Epist. ad Famil.* IX. p. 50. *Edit. Maj. Graev.*

so far as you can promise yourself the Approbation of your fellow Citizens; offer no Violence either to your Father or your Country. To the same Sense is that of *Sallust:* [13] *For tho' you could govern your Country, or Parents, by Force, and correct Offences, yet it is an odious Enterprize, especially when all Changes of Government are generally attended with Slaughter, Banishments, and other Miseries of War.* Not much different is that of *Stallius* in *Plutarch,* in the Life of *Brutus,* [14] *It is not fit for a prudent and wise Man to expose himself to Dangers and Troubles for Knaves and Fools.* To which we may refer that of St. *Ambrose,* [15] *This also will gain you Reputation, to rescue the Poor out of the Hands of the Oppressor, to deliver the Condemned from Death, as far as you can do it without occasioning Troubles and Disorders, lest otherwise you should seem to have done it more out of Ostentation than Compassion, and so cause greater Wounds than those you propose to cure.* *Thomas Aquinas* said, that one becomes sometimes guilty of Sedition, by attempting to destroy even a tyrannical Government. _{Secund. Secund. Quaest. 42. Art. 11.}

4. The Fact of *Ehud,* against *Eglon* King of *Moab,* should not move us to the contrary Opinion; for the Scriptures positively tell us, that GOD raised up *Ehud* to deliver *Israel,* that is, by giving [16] him a special Commission for that Purpose. Neither is it certain, [17] that this King of *Moab* had not by Agreement any Right of Sovereignty; for GOD did execute his Judgments even against other law-<125>ful Kings, by such Instruments as he himself pleased, as by *Jehu* against *Jehoram.*

Judges iii. 15.

Neh. ix. 27.

2. Kings ix.

XX. But especially in a controverted Right, no private Person ought to determine; for then he ought to side with Possessor. Thus CHRIST commanded us to pay Tribute to *Caesar,* because the Money had his Image or Superscription; that is, because he was then in Possession of the Government; for the Power of Coining Money is a certain Sign of Possession.

XX. In a controverted Right no private Man to be Judge.

Matt. xxii. 20.

P. Bezar. Hist. Genuens. I. 18.

13. *Bell. Jugurth.* Cap. III. *Edit. Wass.*
14. *Vit. M. Bruti.* p. 989. Tom. I. *Edit. Wech.*
15. *De Offic.* Lib. II. Cap. XXI.
16. There is nothing in *Judges* iii. 15. that authorises this Explication. It is only said that GOD *raised up* Ehud *to deliver the* Israelites. See Mr. Le Clerc's Comment on Verse 20th of that Chapter.
17. Nor do we find any Thing that gives Room to suspect it.

Who may lawfully make War.

I. *The Efficient Causes of War are those who engage in it, either upon their own Account, as Principals:*

I. As in other Things, so also in moral Actions, there are wont to be three Efficient Causes, *Principals, Assistants,* and *Instruments.* The principal Efficient Cause in a War, is generally the Person interested. In a private War a private Person; in a publick, the Civil Power, especially the Supreme. Whether a War may be justly undertaken in Behalf of another, not making War, shall be treated of in ¹ another Place. In the mean Time this is most certain, that every Man has a natural Right to revenge himself; and therefore were Hands given us.

II. *Or upon the Account of others as Assistants:*

Diges. I. 18. Tit. 7. *De Servis exportand.* Leg. 7. *De furtis,* I. 7. &

II. 1. But it is not only lawful for us, as far as we are able, to be beneficial to another, but also commendable. They who write of Offices, justly say, that there is nothing so useful to one Man, as another Man. Now there are several particular Ties, which engage Men mutually to assist each other. Kinsmen assemble to help one another: Neighbours and Fellow-Citizens call for ¹ the Aid one of the other, whence comes that Saying, *Porro Quirites* and *Quiritari. Aristotle* ² said it behoved every one to take up Arms, either to defend himself upon an Injury offered him, or for his

I. (1) See *B.* II. *Chap.* XXV.
II. (1) Hence, as our Author here observes, come those Expressions among the antient *Romans, Porro, Quirites;* & *Quiritari, for complaining, and calling for Assistance.* See Gronovius on this Place.
2. *Rhetoric. Ad Alexand.* Cap. III. p. 615. *Edit. Paris.* Tom. II.

Kinsmen, or Benefactors, or Allies. And *Solon* [3] declared that a happy State, wherein every Man looked upon the Wrongs done to another, as done to himself.

2. But tho' there were no other Obligations, it is enough that we are allied by common Humanity. For every Man ought to interest himself in what regards other Men. It was well said of *Menander*, [4]

Injuriarum, si improbis, &c.

If every one would heartily engage in the Defence of those that are insulted; if Men would look on Injuries done to others, as done to themselves, and would strenuously assist one another; the Wicked would not become daily more bold and enterprising, but finding themselves watched on every Side, and suffering the just Punishment of their Crimes, few or none would run the Hazard of it. And this of *Democritus,* [5] *It is every Man's Duty to the utmost of his Power, to assist the Injured, and by no Means to neglect it; for this is just and good:* Which *Lactantius* thus expresses, [6] *GOD, who has denied Wisdom to all other Animals, has furnished them with such natural Arms, as may secure them from Insults and Dangers. But as he made Man naked and weak; chusing rather to adorn him with Wisdom, than endow him with Force;* <126> *he has given him, amongst other Things, a Sentiment of Affection, which prompts him to defend those of his own Species, to love them, to cherish them, to give to them, and receive from them Assistance against all Dangers whatsoever.*

Cod. I. 10. tit.
1. De jure fisci.
Cic. de Off. I.
11 ex Panaetio.
Bartol. ad Dig.
I. 1. tit. 1. *De Just. & jure* n. 7, 8.
Jas. ib. n. 29.
Cast. ad Leg. I. § 4. ib. *Bartol.* ad Dig. 1. 49.
Tit. 15. De Capt. &c. Leg. 24. n. 9.
Innoc. ad C. sicut De Jure jur. & in C. olim De restit.
Spol. n. 16.
Panorm. n. 18.
Sylv. in verbo Bellum, Q. 8.

---

3. *Being asked what State he thought best regulated, that, says he, where,* &c. PLUT. in *Solon,* p. 88. Tom. I. *Edit. Wech.* The following Advice of PLAUTUS may be applied here,

Stop the Course of Injustice before it reaches you.

Praetorquete injuriae prius collum, quam ad vos perveniat.
     Rudent. *Act.* III. *Scen.* II. v. 12. GROTIUS.

4. In STOBAEUM, *Tit.* XLIII. See Mr. LE CLERC's Note on that Fragment, p. 3, 4.
5. In STOB. *Serm.* XLVI. p. 310.
6. *Lib.* VI. *Cap.* X. *Numb.* 3. *Edit. Cellar.*

III. *Or are Instrumental, as Servants and Subjects.*

Cod. de Agricolis, I. II. & I. 9. *de Adulter. Sen.* I. *Con.* 4. *Arist. Eth. Ni. com.* v. 10. p. 67. *Ed. Paris.*

III. By Instruments, we mean not Arms, nor such like Things; but certain Persons who act by their own Will, but yet so as that their Will depends on another, that sets it in Motion: Such is a Son to his Father, being part of himself naturally; or a Servant, as a Part of his Master by Law. For as a Part is not only a Part of the Whole, in the same Relation as a Whole is the whole of a Part, but that very Thing which it is, because of the Whole on which it depends: ¹ So the Thing possessed makes in some Manner part of the Possessor. ² *Democritus* said, *Servants are to be used as Members of our Body, some to one Purpose, and some to another.* As a Servant is in a Family, the same is a Subject in a State, and is therefore the Instrument of the Sovereign.

IV. *By the Law of Nature none are excused from War.*

IV. Nor can we doubt, but all Subjects may *naturally* be employed in War, tho' some special Laws may exempt some; as formerly ¹ Slaves among the *Romans,* and now every where the ² *Clergy;* which Law not-

III. (1) These Ideas of the old Philosophy afford but little Satisfaction. It is sufficient that, when a Son or a Slave are considered as mere Instruments, they act, or are supposed to act, by the Orders of a Father or a Mother, so that without such Directions, they would not have determined themselves to Action. See what I have said on the Abridgment of PUFENDORF's Treatise *Of the Duties of a Man and a Citizen,* B. I. Chap. I. § 27. Note 1, 2. third and fourth Edition.

2. In STOB. *Serm.* LXII. *p.* 385.

IV. (1) See PUFENDORF, *B.* VIII. *Chap.* II. The Author, in a Note on this Place, refers us to SERVIUS, on *Aeneid.* IX. ver. 547; where we have this formal Law: Slaves are excluded from all military *Service;* if they engage in it, they are punished with *Death.* DIGEST. *Lib.* XLIX. *Tit.* XVI. *De Re Militari,* Leg. XI. See LIPSIUS, *De Militiâ Romanâ.* Lib. I. Dial. II. p. 22. *&c. Edit. Wesal.* and *Analect.* p. 444. As also the Notes of Father ABRAM, a *Jesuit,* on CICERO's *Orat. in Pisonem,* Cap. X. *& pro Rege Dejotaro,* Cap. VIII.

2. The *Levites* also were excused from bearing Arms, as JOSEPHUS observes, *Antiq. Jud.* Lib. III. Cap. XI. As to what concerns Ecclesiasticks, see NICETAS CHONIATES, *Lib.* VI. The *Capitularies of Charles* the *Bald,* in *Sparnac.* XXXVII. and the *Canon Law,* Distinct. L. Can. V. and Caus. XXIII. Quaest. VIII. Those are the Regulations made by the Canons, but we may see in the History of ANNA COMNENES, *Lib.* X. *Cap.* VIII. how much more strictly they have been observed by the *Greeks* than by the *Latins.* [Compare them with what is said in *Votum pro Pace Ecclesiasticâ,* Art. XVI.] GROTIUS.

See *Chap.* II. § 10, *Num.* 8. and Mr. BOHMER's *Jus Ecclesiasticum Protestantium,* Lib. III. Tit. I. § 62, *&c.* and *Tit.* XX. § 71, *&c.* as also Mr. THOMASIUS's Notes on

withstanding, as all others of that Nature, must be understood with the Exception of Cases of [3] extreme Necessity. Let this suffice to be spoken of Assistants and Subjects in *general.* For what Questions particularly relate to them, shall be handled [4] in their proper Places.

Thomas, Sec. Sec. 40. Art. 2. *Sylvest.* de Bell. p. 3.

The End of the first Book.

LANCELOT's *Inst. Juris Canon.* p. 154, and 350. I find nothing in NICETAS CHONIATES, quoted by our Author, concerning the Exemption granted to Ecclesiasticks; that Historian only says, in the Life of MANUEL COMNENES, *Lib.* VII. *Cap.* III. that that Emperor ordered the Monks should possess no Lands, that they might be free from such Distractions as attend the Care of temporal Affairs, and devote themselves entirely to spiritual Exercises.

3. Thus, after the Battle of *Cannae,* the *Romans,* being in great Want of Soldiers, bought 8000 young and able bodied Slaves, and listed them in the Service. LIVY, *Lib.* XXII. *Cap.* LVII. *Num.* 11, 12.

4. See our Author, *B.* II. *Chap.* XXV. XXVI.